THE EXPERIENCE OF EDUCATION IN ANGLO-SAXON LITERATURE

Anglo-Saxons valued education yet understood how precarious it could be, alternately bolstered and undermined by fear, desire, and memory. They praised their teachers in official writing, but composed and translated scenes of instruction that revealed the emotional and cognitive complexity of learning. Irina Dumitrescu explores how early medieval writers used fictional representations of education to explore the relationship between teacher and student. These texts hint at the challenges of teaching and learning: curiosity, pride, forgetfulness, inattention, and despair. Still, these difficulties are understood to be part of the dynamic process of pedagogy, not simply a sign of its failure. The book demonstrates the enduring concern of Anglo-Saxon authors with learning throughout Old English and Latin poems, hagiographies, histories, and schoolbooks.

IRINA DUMITRESCU is Professor of English Medieval Studies at the Rheinische Friedrich-Wilhelms-Universität Bonn. She is the editor of *Rumba under Fire: The Arts of Survival from West Point to Delhi* (2016). Her scholarship has been published in journals such as *PMLA, Exemplaria, The Chaucer Review, Anglia, postmedieval, Forum for Modern Language Studies*, and in various international collections. Her literary essays have appeared in the *Yale Review, Southwest Review, The Atlantic*, and *Longreads*, and have been reprinted in *Best American Essays 2016* and *Best Food Writing 2017*.

D0914528

THE EXPERIENCE OF EDUCATION IN ANGLO-SAXON LITERATURE

IRINA DUMITRESCU

Rheinische Friedrich-Wilhelms-Universität Bonn

CAMBRIDGE
UNIVERSITY PRESS

University Printing House, Cambridge CB2 8BS, United Kingdom

One Liberty Plaza, 20th Floor, New York, NY 10006, USA

477 Williamstown Road, Port Melbourne, VIC 3207, Australia

314-321, 3rd Floor, Plot 3, Splendor Forum, Jasola District Centre, New Delhi - 110025, India

79 Anson Road, #06-04/06, Singapore 079906

Cambridge University Press is part of the University of Cambridge.

It furthers the University's mission by disseminating knowledge in the pursuit of
education, learning and research at the highest international levels of excellence.

www.cambridge.org
Information on this title: www.cambridge.org/9781108416863
DOI: 10.1017/9781108242103

First published 2018

A catalogue record for this publication is available from the British Library

Library of Congress Cataloging in Publication data
Names: Dumitrescu, Irina, author.
Title: The experience of education in Anglo-Saxon literature / Irina Dumitrescu.
Description: Cambridge; New York: Cambridge University Press, 2018. |
Series: Cambridge studies in medieval literature; 102 | Includes bibliographical references.
Identifiers: LCCN 2017038710 | ISBN 9781108416863 (hardback)
Subjects: LCSH: English literature – Old English, ca. 450–1100 – History and criticism. |
Education in literature. | Teachers in literature. | Civilization, Anglo-Saxon, in literature. |
Great Britain – History – Anglo-Saxon period, 449–1066. |
BISAC: LITERARY CRITICISM / European / English, Irish, Scottish, Welsh.
Classification: LCC PR173 .D86 2018 | DDC 829/.09–dc23
LC record available at https://lccn.loc.gov/2017038710

ISBN 978-1-108-41686-3 Hardback
ISBN 978-1-108-40336-8 Paperback

for Sarah Winters and Roberta Frank,
the best of teachers

Contents

Acknowledgements

Education is a heady brew of pain and pleasure, curiosity and sloth, memory and forgetfulness, the thrill of progress and the irritation of inevitable obstacles and delays. Much the same can be said of writing a book. This project has accompanied me to six institutions and many conferences and guest lectures over the years, making me the recipient of more scholarly generosity than I can hope to acknowledge here. If wealth lies in gratitude, I am rich.

At the University of Toronto, where Milton and *Beowulf* wooed me away from the life sciences, I learned to read and, by osmosis, to teach from a stellar group of scholars. I remain grateful to Jill Levenson, Heather Jackson, Paul Downes, Thomas Pangle, and Jeffrey Metzger for showing me how to dive deep into a text and keep swimming. David Klausner introduced me to Old English, and his dramatic style informed my reading of Bata's *Colloquies*. I had the good fortune to study medieval literature and didactic charisma with Richard Toporoski, Sandy Johnston, Suzanne Akbari, and Anthony Adams. The inimitable Toni Healey became a lifelong mentor, while Andy Orchard inspired this book and taught me the right way to greet a pint of Guinness. I am thankful for the gentle guidance of Brian Corman, Kimberley Yates, Michael Ullyot, George Elliott Clarke, and the regretted Bill 'the Div' Craig. I learned just as much from my friends. At the Centre for Medieval Studies, Stacie Turner, Paige Vignola, and Damian Fleming kept the Latin light. At Trinity College I had the privilege of meeting some of the most brilliant, warm, and witty people I know: Andrew Crabtree, Eleanor Pachaud, Vanessa Scott, Matthew McCormick, Kes Smith, Leslie Atkinson, Michael Meeuwis, Emily Pawley, Dominik Hałas, Sarah Neville, and Annushka Sonek. Robert 'Beowulf' Addinall, who lent me his beer-sticky copy of Mitchell and Robinson's *Guide to Old English* so I could see what this Anglo-Saxon was all about, bears full responsibility for my subsequent questionable life choices.

I didn't meet the ultra-cool Delphine Roux at Yale, but I did have the good fortune of learning from and with individuals who approached literature with precision and passion. I am grateful to Ben LaBreche, Colin Gillis, Susannah Hollister, Gabriele Hayden, Anthony Welch, Sarah Van der Laan, Laura Miles, Sarah Novacich, Matthew Vernon, and Emily Setina not just for the support it took to get through graduate school, but for the friendship and collaboration that came after. Judith Verweijen and Laura Sacolick taught me to approach life – and New Haven – with a spirit of adventure. I thank Annabel Patterson, Claude Rawson, Matthew Giancarlo, Robert Stepto, Langdon Hammer, Carol Jacobs, and Caleb Smith for their high standards and patient tolerance of my occasional Kinbotean diversions. Howard Bloch, Bill Whobrey, Nicole Rice, Stanley Insler, Anders Winroth, and Walter Goffart made Yale a wonderful place to be a medievalist, in and outside of the classroom. Jill Campbell, the late Linda Peterson, and John Rogers brought good humour to life in the English Department and Berkeley College. Lee Patterson helped me more than he knew. Like many of his students, I drank the Joe Roach 'Kool Aid', and am still happily imbibing. He is a model of fiery teaching and visionary scholarship. Fred Robinson came back from retirement to read Old English prose with three bushy-tailed public school kids, and in the process told us enough good anecdotes for a lifetime. I miss him, as I miss María Rosa Menocal, sharp, funny, spirited, so very strong.

One could not meet a finer group of people than the English Department at Southern Methodist University. Bonnie Wheeler gave me more than I could ever adequately thank her for, both in scholarship and in life. She and Jeremy Adams combined vibrant learning with epic hospitality. Ezra and Riki Greenspan made Dallas feel like home. Willard Spiegelman spoiled me with designer clothing trips, horned helmets, and fine editing. Nina Schwartz, Dennis Foster, Rajani Sudan, Rick Bozorth, Beth Newman, and Bruce Levy mixed fine martinis and never asked me to 'assume the untenured position!' I am grateful to Steve Weisenburger, Darryl Dickson-Carr, and Tim Rosendale for their collegiality, but also for reminding me that academic parenthood is not only a women's issue. I thank my fellow younger faculty at SMU and in the Dallas area for their friendship and incisive edits: Angela Ards, Dan Moss, Lisa Siraganian, Tim Cassedy, Jayson Gonzales Sae-Saue, Charles Hatfield, Amy Freund, Sean Cotter, and Meg Cotter-Lynch. This book benefited from the insights of my 2010 graduate seminar, 'How the English Learned to Read'. I owe much to all my SMU students, but am especially grateful to Jennifer Boulanger, Megan Schott, Jessica Meeks, and Adam Jones.

I thank Tricia Dailey, Susan Crane, Susan Boynton, Hal Momma, Kathleen Davis, and Stacy Klein for welcoming me to Columbia University for a year, and to the bright intellectual community of the Anglo-Saxon Studies Colloquium for longer. Kári Driscoll, Prashant Keshavmurthi, and Dorothea von Mücke have been sources of good humour, advice, and Bollywood dance moves. At the Freie Universität Berlin, Andrew James Johnston gave me wise advice and precise feedback, and has become my Vergil in the circles of German academe. Max Hinderer, Isabel Kranz, and Kathrin Bethke made Berlin feel like an intellectual and emotional home; Tanja Schramm and Suzan Demircan made it an artistic one. The Rhenish congeniality of the University of Bonn has made finishing this book a pleasure. Nicole Meier, Imke Lichterfeld, and Mathilde Hüskes have been infinitely patient as they taught me the ropes. I thank my English department colleagues Uwe Baumann, Marion Gymnich, Klaus Schneider, Barbara Schmidt-Haberkamp, Sabine Sielke, and Uwe Küchler for their support in ways large and small. Claire Waldecker and Alice Rabeler's energy in library acquisitioning has proved a boon for my research. I am particularly grateful to the Bonn medievalists, among them Karl Reichl, Rudy Simek, Matthias Becher, and Karina Kellermann for their warm collegiality. Emma O'Loughlin Bérat read through the book at a late stage and fine-tuned many a phrase. In the ballet studio, Yvonne Hamm did her best to keep me sane. Marta Garriga, Jenny Drai, Carsten Urbach, and Katja Schiffers sometimes succeeded.

Everyone knows the downsides to being a medievalist: sparse jobs, lukewarm ale, violent stereotypes, and having to explain to early modernists that the renaissance happened in the eighth century. The upside is participating in a community of scholars characterised by boundless curiosity, instinctive generosity, and a down-to-earth sense of fun. Jorie Woods shaped much of my thinking on medieval schoolbooks. Seth Lerer, *in persona* and *in libris*, taught me to think boldly. Andy Rabin, Tom Hall, and Daniel O'Donnell encouraged me to persevere when I most needed it. Steve Justice and Eileen Fradenburg Joy showed what it means to approach the humanities with purpose and soul. For their ongoing feminist work in the academy I thank Clare Lees, Jane Chance, Karma Lochrie, Rebecca Stephenson, Robin Norris, and Renee Trilling.

For a multitude of kindnesses, too many to name here, I thank Clare Waters, Tom Hill, Bruce Gilchrist, Rita Copeland, Martin Camargo, Mae Kilker, Anna Klosowska, Drew Jones, Leslie Lockett, Sebastian Sobecki, Daniel Donoghue, Katherine O'Brien O'Keeffe, Rolf Bremmer, Emily Thornbury, Emily Butler, Niklaus Largier, Christian Leitmeir, Scott Gwara,

Aaron Hostetter, Winfried Rudolf, Johanna Kramer, Lisa Fagin Davis, Ethan Knapp, Eric Weiskott, James Simpson, Dianne Berg, Hilary Fox, Jeffrey Cohen, Monika Otter, Carin Ruff, Karl Steel, Marty Shichtman, David Perry, Frances McCormack, Robert Stanton, Stephanie Trigg, Luuk Houwen, Catherine Karkov, Carolyne Larrington, Tom Goodmann, Jesús Velasco, Mia Münster-Swendsen, Lyle Massey, Jill Mann, and Ursula Schaefer. I am particularly grateful for detailed feedback on chapters from Juliette Vuille, Ricarda Wagner, and Mary Flannery. Bruce Holsinger read this entire manuscript, and his thoughtful comments were a joy to work through. The anonymous readers for Cambridge University Press saved me from many an error. Any flaws that remain in the book have been deliberately inserted as a stimulus to the perspicacity of its readers.

For their perceptive comments and questions, I am grateful to audiences at Yale, Notre Dame, Harvard, Columbia, Ohio State, New York University, University of California, Irvine, University of California, San Diego, Heidelberg, the Sonderforschungsbereich 980 at the Freie Universität Berlin, University of North Texas, St Andrews, Poitiers, Bangor, Vanderbilt, and Kalamazoo. Research towards this book was funded by the Whiting Foundation, the Alexander-von-Humboldt Foundation, the North Rhine-Westphalian Academy of Sciences, Humanities and the Arts, as well as by Yale University, Southern Methodist University, and the University of Bonn. An earlier version of Chapter 1 originally appeared as 'Bede's Liberation Philology: Releasing the English Tongue' in *PMLA* 128.1 (2013), published by the Modern Language Association of America. Chapter 3 incorporates material from 'The Grammar of Pain in Ælfric Bata's Colloquies', which was published in *Forum for Modern Language Studies* 45.3 (2009), reprinted here with permission from Oxford University Press, as well as parts of 'Violence, Performance and Pedagogy in Ælfric Bata's *Colloquies*', *Exemplaria* 23.1 (2011), reprinted courtesy of Taylor & Francis (www.tandfonline.com).

There are a few people without whom this 'litel bok' would not have come to be. Alastair Minnis believed in the project early on, and I thank him both for his enduring support and for his sharp critique on earlier drafts. Anne Bramley gently but firmly midwifed this baby Völsung of a manuscript into existence. My student assistants Berit Andersson, Franziska Göbel, and Thomas Schmidt did heroic bibliographic work, checked every quotation and footnote (sometimes twice), and put out a multitude of fires. Denis Ferhatović, Mary Kate Hurley, and Jordan Zweck are the best Anglo-Saxonist friends one could hope for. Over the years we have shared work, checked drafts, planned events, advised each other on academic politics and self-care, ordered too much at exotic restaurants, and steadily urged each other to create beautiful scholarship and writing. The wonderful staff of my son's kindergarten, Kita Auf dem Hügel, have made combining work and family a great deal easier than it might have been. My in-laws, Rita and Peter Albrecht, have jumped to the rescue in many an emergency. My mom, grandmothers, and Sorin have balanced humour with salutary Romanian fretting. Tim and Maxi Albrecht have given me much love, adventure, and wholesome distraction.

This book is dedicated to two women who shaped the course of my life. Sarah Fiona Winters was the only reason I stayed in university past my first year. Without her encouragement, I would not have dared to follow this risky, but deeply rewarding, path. Over the years, Roberta Frank has been a tireless mentor, cheerleader, and friend. Her spry wit, scholarly generosity, and splendid writing are a model and inspiration. Her lemon chicken soup is unparalleled. These teachers have my gratitude, and my love.

Abbreviations

Old English texts are abbreviated according to the Old English Short Title in the *Dictionary of Old English*.

ACMRS	Arizona Center for Medieval and Renaissance Studies
ÆBC	Gwara and Porter, eds., *Anglo-Saxon Conversations: The Colloquies of Ælfric Bata*
ASE	*Anglo-Saxon England*
ASPR	*Anglo-Saxon Poetic Records*
BL	London, British Library
BT	Bosworth and Toller, *An Anglo-Saxon Dictionary*
CCCC	Cambridge, Corpus Christi College
CCSL	Corpus Christianorum Series Latina. Turnhout: Brepols
CSEL	Corpus Scriptorum Ecclesiasticorum Latinorum
DOE	*Dictionary of Old English: A to H online*, eds. Cameron, Amos, and Healey
EETS	Early English Text Society
	OS Original Series
	SS Supplementary Series
EH	Colgrave and Mynors, eds., *Bede's Ecclesiastical History of the English People*
GL	Gneuss and Lapidge, *Anglo-Saxon Manuscripts* (references by serial number)
JEGP	*Journal of English and Germanic Philology*
JMEMS	*Journal of Medieval and Early Modern Studies*
Ker	Ker, *Catalogue of Manuscripts Containing Anglo-Saxon* (references by serial number)
MGH	Monumenta Germaniae Historica
MLN	*Modern Language Notes*
MP	*Modern Philology*
NM	*Neuphilologische Mitteilungen*
N&Q	*Notes and Queries*
OEB	Godden and Irvine, eds., *Old English Boethius*
OEME	Magennis, ed., *The Old English Life of St Mary of Egypt*
PL	*Patrologia latina*, ed. J.-P. Migne (Paris, 1844–64)
RES	*The Review of English Studies*

Introduction

… vous convient estre saiges, pour fleurer, sentir et estimer ces beaulx
livres de haulte gresse, legiers au prochaz et hardiz à la rencontre; puis,
par curieuse leçon et meditatione frequente, rompre l'os et sugcer la
sustantificque mouelle

Rabelais, *Gargantua*[1]

The Experience of Education in Anglo-Saxon Literature offers a pedagogical
interpretation of early English prose and poetry, showing how memories of
education and theories of learning undergird much writing in the period
across a range of genres and languages. The starting point is a simple proposition: every single Old English or Anglo-Latin text we have today has
survived because someone literate wrote it down. In many cases, literate
authors, translators, and adaptors were involved as well. Every one of these
individuals learned to read and write from individual teachers who used
particular pedagogical methods. What to us are abstract concepts of 'literacy' and 'education' were for them lived experiences, and must have carried
all the joys, tensions, and traumas that going to school has always entailed.
Like us, literate Anglo-Saxons reflected on their education. However,
instead of writing campus novels as we do, they told their truth slant in
dramatic textbooks, in quirky anecdotes slipped into histories and biographies, and in tiny but important changes made as they adapted Latin
works or copied Old English ones. Trained to read closely and beneath the
surface of the text, they left clues we often miss. We have learned to read
for the subtle changes an author made in source material to promote a certain typological reading or a nationalistic agenda, but rarely do we imagine
a personal story might motivate these variations.

Scholars of the middle ages are aware of the extent to which their understanding of the period is mediated by written texts and, by extension, by
literate culture and ideology. However, the scribes, compilers, translators,
adapters, glossators, and, often, composers of medieval texts learned their

I

specialised skills in a relationship or series of relationships patterned on the roles of *magister* and *discipulus*. They generally spoke well of education and of their teachers in official writing – this much is clear to any reader of early English lives, histories, and letters. The premise underlying this book is that they recognised how emotionally and cognitively intricate the process of education is, and that they reflected on this experience by translating, adapting, and composing fictions of teaching. The study of these 'scenes of instruction' is vital, not only because of its relevance to the growing body of research into Anglo-Saxon and early medieval education, not even because of the acknowledged importance of wisdom and learning in early England, but because the processes of teaching and learning underpin the very creation of the texts that comprise much of the past's legacy to us. *The Experience of Education in Anglo-Saxon Literature* seeks to understand the emotions, tensions, and struggles inherent in the process of learning. To discover these, it investigates how Old English and Anglo-Latin texts represent encounters between teachers and students, uncovering a host of energies both dark and productive: desire, pain, fear, and failure.

Fundamental to my reading practice is New Criticism, which attends to the tensions and nuances of image and language within a literary work above their sources and historical context. While it is impossible to discuss early medieval texts without historical knowledge, the field of Anglo-Saxon studies has tended to conflate the explanation of sources or context with literary interpretation. As a result, some texts, like the Old English poem *Solomon and Saturn I*, are much studied but seldom read. Privileging the poem over its sources, and allowing that its tensions and confusions could be part of its meaning rather than failures on the part of the poet, allows us to see the drama of pedagogy enacted between the lines of *Solomon and Saturn I*. In other cases, as in the Old English *Life of St Mary of Egypt*, there are evident errors in the text as we have it, but these mistakes are also revelatory. I read the mistakes of translation and transmission in the *Life* suspiciously, as symptoms of the recognition that teachers and students establish their relationships through desire, but that desire threatens to undermine teaching itself.

I approach the works treated in this book with the assumption that a text may invite different audiences to form different interpretations.[2] Sometimes this effect is plain: the reader of *Solomon and Saturn I* is reminded by the silent runes on the manuscript page that listeners are missing part of the poem. At other points it is more subtle: the apostle at the heart of *Andreas* can be read as the model of a saint or as a failed pupil, depending on whether one focuses on the story's hagiographical affiliations or on its troubling details. What does such watchful reading mean in practice? It means taking note of authors' statements about the way their work ought to be read, as when Ælfric Bata remarks that he has slipped jokes into his *Colloquies*. It means that obvious errors of logic in the hands of a skilled author like the *Andreas* poet may be taken as clues to a hidden layer of meaning.[3] It calls for careful scrutiny of parallel passages, especially when they vary slightly from each other.[4] It requires special attention to moments when an author presents an orthodox view and later contradicts himself.[5] It means taking the speeches of rogue figures seriously, be they devils or naughty boys, as they may serve as mouthpieces for unacceptable views.[6] It also means paying attention to how citations of earlier texts are employed, especially when they are altered or taken out of context, as Ælfric Bata does with Scripture.[7] Finally, it means a close analysis of how a text's sources are adapted, especially when the changes are easy to miss.

This reading practice would have been familiar to educated Anglo-Saxons, who faced problems of interpretation when they read the Christian Bible. If the Bible is revealed text and the perfect handiwork of God, then its errors and contradictions must point to a hidden meaning. In order to examine its secrets, the reader must cultivate a mode of reading attentive to echoes, inconsistencies, telling parallels, and multivalent words. Learned Anglo-Saxons believed, after all, that Scripture must be interpreted in order to be understood.[8] The positive testament to this conviction is the work of Bede. Although the eighth-century monk and scholar is primarily remembered as an historian, the bulk of his writing was dedicated to biblical exegesis. Bede inherited a tradition that was attentive to the literal meaning of Scripture but recognised a series of figural significations beyond the literal; to the unraveling of these he devoted his considerable efforts.[9] To approach the problem of reading *ex negativo* we may turn to the tenth century and to Ælfric. In his preface to Genesis, he expresses his concern that people reading the Old Testament without the training to interpret it might be tempted to imitate the lifestyles of the patriarchs, not understanding that those patriarchs lived under the old law, one inappropriate for Christians. Ælfric is wary of translating the Bible into the vernacular and thus making it more widely available, but he is also wary of those who have learned a little Latin, for they read Scripture without understanding 'hu deop seo boc ys on gastlicum andgite' (how deep the book is in spiritual meaning).[10] In this, he anticipates Pope's maxim, 'A *little learning* is a dang'rous Thing;/ Drink deep, or taste not the *Pierian* spring.'[11]

This concern with deep reading, whether it means distinguishing between the law of the Old Testament and that of the New or uncovering a variety of meanings under the surface sense, is intimately connected to elementary grammatical education in late antiquity and the early middle ages. *Grammatica*, as Martin Irvine has shown, was not simply what we would understand as 'grammar': the structure of a language, or more broadly, its syntax, morphology, phonology, and semantics. Rather, it was an art of interpretation and of correct writing and speech, all of which aimed at 'maintaining and promoting a Christian monastic *paideia* comprising the Scriptures, Christian literature, and the liturgy'.[12] For Anglo-Saxons this was an art to be exercised, primarily, in Latin, and it is no surprise that both Bede and Ælfric wrote works of basic instruction for that language.[13] Nor was this method of interpretative reading exclusively applied to Scripture. Bede, it has been argued, intended his *Ecclesiastical History* to be read according to an allegorical scheme as well as literally.[14] Much scholarship on Old English verse from the 1960s to the 1980s took for granted that poetry, too, was meant to be read allegorically or figuratively, though critical opinions on the legitimacy of this approach are divided.[15] Riddles, which Anglo-Saxons wrote in both Latin and English, trained readers and hearers to think beyond the literal meanings of words, to perceive multiple meanings in a text, and to be attentive to incongruities within a narrative or description.[16] In short, many literate Anglo-Saxons were practised close readers as a result of their grammatical training and exposure to scriptural exegesis.[17]

A more oblique influence on my reading practice is New Formalism, represented in Middle English studies by the work of Seth Lerer, Christopher Cannon, D. Vance Smith, Maura Nolan, and Eleanor Johnson, among others.[18] Marjorie Levison has distinguished between formalist critics who aim to foreground aesthetic principles, firmly dividing artistic from historical texts, and those who understand attention to form as a corrective to and continuation of new historicism.[19] A renewed embrace of literature's aesthetic preeminence is not the goal of this book, which, after all, happily apposes history, biography, hagiography, poetry, and language textbooks. Rather, with Richard Strier, I consider that 'the results of a formalist analysis … may themselves be *data* for historical understanding'.[20] In medieval studies, formalist analysis offers a chance to perceive odd texts such as *Solomon and Saturn I* as inventive rather than egregious, and reveals the potential of form to animate practices of ethics, education, and interpretation.[21]

Although the texts discussed in this book hew to different genres, a single form quickens them: the dialogue. The dialogue had been established as a medium of education and a testing ground of wisdom and philosophy in antiquity. Anglo-Saxon literate culture was shaped, in various ways, by late antique catechetical texts and reflexes of Platonic philosophical dialogues.[22] Not only were works such as Gregory the Great's *Dialogues*, Augustine's *Soliloquies*, and Boethius' *Consolation of Philosophy* read and copied in the original Latin, but all three were rendered into the vernacular as part of the Alfredian programme of translation.[23] Even when they did not translate late antique dialogues, Anglo-Saxons often adapted them for pedagogical use or took them as models for original compositions. This is the case with Isidore's *Synonyma*, which Ælfric Bata excerpted satirically in his *Colloquies*, with the *Altercatio Hadriani Augusti et Epicteti Philosophi*, which influenced Alcuin's *Disputatio Pippini cum Albino* as well as the vernacular *Prose Solomon and Saturn* and *Adrian and Ritheus*, and with Donatus' *Ars minor*, which lent its form to Aldhelm's *De metris*. School dialogues could be used to varied ends: Alcuin used a series of dialogues to teach grammar and rhetoric, Ælfric and his pupil Ælfric Bata composed and adapted colloquies for basic Latin instruction, and someone at Æthelwold's school at Winchester wrote a biting dispute in verse between a master and a disciple, a learned counterpart to the Germanic *flyting*.[24]

Dialogues were standard tools in Anglo-Saxon schools in England and on the continent, as well as in spiritual teaching in the broader sense. This suggests something important about the nature of teaching and the place of the teacher in the early medieval period. Dialogues imply ambivalence toward authority. This is less true with catechetical works, though in the *Disputatio Pippini*, Alcuin managed to turn even a simple question-and-answer exercise into a sly and penetrating reflection on language and the world. On the whole, however, the form of the dialogue implies a dialectical process of contestation and interpretation. Late antique and early medieval dialogues that centre on education often refuse to present teachers as unassailable. Joel Relihan has argued persuasively that Philosophy fails to teach Boethius in the *Consolation*,[25] and school colloquies more often than not feature troubling masters. Classical dialogues, as Seth Lerer has noted, often explore the 'limitations of human language' rather than its unalloyed success.[26] The *agon* implicit in the educational dialogues so beloved by Anglo-Saxons permeates, by extension, the scenes of instruction studied in this book. Most of these are dialogues in their own right, and all of them are encounters between a pupil and a teacher whose assumptions, allegiances, and desires are at odds.

The subtle eristic and affective qualities of Anglo-Saxon depictions of teaching can be traced in Asser's *Life of King Alfred*, a book that features several scenes of instruction and multiple reflections on the relationship of emotions to learning. Despite the superficially celebratory, even hagio-graphic, qualities of the *Life*, Asser in fact paints an ambivalent picture of the king. He depicts Alfred as a man of many desires, longings that are laudable only when directed to the right ends. The example of Alfred shows that desire and suffering both help and hinder the processes of learn-ing and self-improvement, thus demonstrating the paradoxical qualities of pedagogically useful emotions. But there is another level to Asser's biog-raphy: while Asser is clearly the king's social inferior, he is keen to present himself as the king's intellectual superior. To do so openly would be impol-itic, but by weaving awkward references and similes into his narrative, he encourages a reading in which the balance of authority between the king and himself is reversed. And, lest readers miss his clues, he invites them to read suspiciously by denying the possibility of a suspicious reading.[27]

In chapter 76 of the *Life*, following an encomium to Alfred as a king who embodies wisdom, faith, and good governance, Asser compares him to Solomon. As Anton Scharer has demonstrated, this is an eminently suitable comparison if the *Life* is to be read as a mirror for princes in the Carolingian mould, in line with Charles the Bald's deliberate self-presentation as a second Solomon.[28] However, although his name was readily associated with wisdom, medieval writers were also conscious of Solomon's apostasy at the instigation of his wives. Bede, whose work Asser knew, treated the subject, as did Augustine, Isidore, and Rabanus Maurus.[29] Read with a measure of suspicion, the mention of Solomon underscores the notion that Asser's Alfred is a man of powerful longings both erotic and intellectual. At a young age, Alfred worries that carnal desires might keep him from doing God's will, and prays that his mind should be made 'multo robustius per aliquam infirmitatem, quam posset sustinere' (ch. 74, much stronger by some illness, which he would be able to withstand).[30] He is subsequently afflicted by *ficus*, which is thought by some scholars to refer to haemorrhoids, by others to more general skin eruptions.[31] Carnal lust is not the only kind of urge that characterises the king, however. More prom-inent in the *Life* is his enduring thirst for literacy, wisdom, and the liberal arts. Asser mentions his desire for wisdom (ch. 22, sapientiae desiderium), how he is 'enticed' (illectus) by his mother's book prize (ch. 23), his early unfulfilled desire (desiderio) for good teachers (ch. 24), how he did not leave off that same insatiable desire (insaturabili desiderio) for learning, and continues to yearn for it (inhiare) to the present day (ch. 25), the way the wisdom and learning of his four Mercian teachers both fulfilled and increased his desire (ch. 77, desiderium crescebat et impletur), the king's regal but laudable 'greed' for more teachers from abroad (ch. 78, regalis avaritia, sed tamen laudabilis), to mention but a few of the more obvious instances. While Alfred's curiosity is deeply commendable in the context of the *Life*, Asser's comparison of the king to Solomon and Alfred's own concern about sexual temptation remind us that *desiderium* is a double-valenced word, aimed rightly only when directed towards wisdom and knowledge of the faith.

In Alfred's case, as with a number of the depictions of teaching I examine in this book, desire is intimately bound up with suffering. Alfred's first illness is a result of his own attempt to control his physical urges, a self-willed punishment for his own concupiscence. His prayer to suffer some kind of manageable illness also shows that he could think of disease as a tool in his ongoing process of self-discipline and spiritual improvement, a way of making the mind 'multo robustius'. David Pratt has argued convincingly that the account of the boy's supplication for suffering is a 'retrospective rationalization' on the part of Alfred, and that the extreme piety exemplified in this story is the result, not the cause, of his illness.[32] Even if the tale is a myth, it demonstrates the conception of instrumental pain Alfred and Asser could draw on to make sense of the king's sufferings.

However, like desire, physical suffering is also a double-edged sword. Alfred's first illness proves too much for him, leading him to despair of his life, and after praying for a more manageable disease, the *ficus* is relieved. However, after his wedding, he is stricken with an even worse condition: 'subito et immenso atque omnibus medicis incognito confestim coram omni populo correptus est dolore' (ch. 74, suddenly, in front of the entire crowd, he was seized by a swift and immense pain unknown to all the doctors).[33] As Alfred will come to lament, 'crebris querelis et intimis cordis sui suspiriis' (ch. 25, with frequent complaints and sighs from the depth of his heart), when he was young enough to learn, there were no good teachers in the West Saxon kingdom. When he was older and had teachers available to him, he was distracted from study by a host of problems including pagan incursions, concerns of state, and, first of all on the list, by 'omnibus istius insulae medicis incognitis infirmitatibus' (ch. 25, diseases unknown to all the doctors of this island), apparently the illness he acquired after his nuptials.[34] Alfred's illness has been interpreted in positive terms by scholars, who have argued that his infirmity, and his resulting piety, was a mark of kingly strength, not weakness.[35] Still, as Asser's description of the king's intellectual regrets makes clear, disease had a deleterious effect on Alfred's education. The *Life of King Alfred* thus offers us two competing notions of the relationship between bodily suffering and learning. Alfred's case reveals that the role of pain in education, whether this is conceived of narrowly as a formal study of the arts or more broadly as personal spiritual progress, is a fundamentally conflicted one.

Alfred's kingly authority is thus anchored in a triangulation of desire, pain, and learning, themes which come together in Asser's curious comparison of Alfred to the fortunate thief crucified next to Christ. The context for this passage is the lengthiest instructional encounter of the *Life*, one in which Asser diplomatically guides Alfred to begin his famous *enchiridion*, or handbook. The scene is a cozy depiction of a happy exchange between a powerful student and his prudent teacher. Alfred urges Asser to copy a passage the latter has just read aloud into his book of prayers. Asser hesitates, as he tells us, 'maxime quia tam elegans regis ingenium ad maiorem divinorum testimoniorum scientiam provocare studebam' (ch. 88, because I wanted to challenge the king's fine intelligence to a greater understanding of Holy Scripture). When the king impatiently urges him to hurry, Asser delicately asks if Alfred would approve of beginning a new compendium that might be suitable for other texts as well. This done, Asser goes on to copy three more passages into the quire, to the king's delight – just as Asser had predicted (ut praedixeram). After this psychologically sensitive portrayal of a teacher who maintains his pedagogic authority while respecting his student's temporal power, Asser laments the belatedness of the king's education. He does so in a surprising way, comparing Alfred to the thief crucified next to Christ, 'qui Christianae fidei rudimenta in gabulo primitus inchoavit discere' (ch. 89, who first began to learn the rudiments of Christian faith on the gallows).

Such a comparison could be seen as a positive portrayal of Alfred. The thief is, in this simile, a student of Christ's example *par excellence*. Indeed, Asser's analogy between king and thief makes sense in the context of Alfred's many travails, and a light verbal echo underscores this point: the thief directs his physical eyes towards Christ, as his body is 'totus confixus clavis' (ch. 89, wholly transfixed with nails), and soon after Alfred is, despite his royal power, described as 'multis tribulationum clavis confossus' (ch. 91, pierced with the nails of many tribulations). Read in this light, the *passio* is a tidy interpretative capstone that places Alfred's suffering in the context of spiritual discipleship and *imitatio Christi*. On the other hand, Asser seems conscious of the potential negative implications of his simile. If the thief begins to learn on the gallows, Alfred does so 'dissimili modo, in regia potestate' (ch. 89, in a different way, in royal power). Moreover, the instructional context in which Asser uses the simile provokes another interpretation. For if Alfred, beginning his *enchiridion* on Asser's prompting, is compared to the thief who learns faith while looking towards the

Lord, the logic of the analogy proposes that Asser occupies the role of Christ.

Asser seems conscious that such an interpretation is possible; indeed, his protestations draw attention to it. In the following chapter, Asser is more explicit about his reservations:

> Sed, sicut a quodam sapiente iamdudum scriptum est, 'invigilant animi, quibus est pia cura regendi,' magnopere invigilandum mihi censeo in eo, quod ante aliquam, quamvis dissimili modo, similitudinem inter illum felicem latronem et regem composuerim: namque patibulum exosum est unicuique, ubicunque male habet. Sed quid faciat, si non possit se inde eripere aut etiam effugere, vel qualicunque arte causam suam meliorare ibidem commorando? Debet ergo, velit, nolit, cum moerore et tristitia sufferre, quod patitur. (Ch. 90)

> But, as a certain wise man wrote long ago, 'the spirits of those who have the pious office of ruling are ever watchful,' I think I have to be exceedingly watchful in the comparison I made before between the fortunate thief and the king, however dissimilar they are in degree. For the gibbet is detestable to everyone who suffers misfortune. But what should he do if he cannot rescue himself from it or even flee, or stay there and improve his situation by some art? So he must endure, with grief and sadness, what he is suffering, whether he wants to or not.

Asser's use of a hexameter from Corippus' *In laudem Iustini Augusti minoris* rewards perusal in both old and new senses of the word.[36] The hasty reader might think Asser is drawing back from any untoward implications about Alfred while recognising the cares of state, the 'cura regendi', that weigh on the king. The king's 'gibbet' is, as the next chapter will go on to outline, a combination of physical illness and the difficulties of government, woes he must endure patiently. Read slowly, however, the hexameter suggests that, since he is the one who must be watchful, it is Asser, not Alfred, who shoulders the difficulty of governing. In Chapter 88 Asser was careful to maintain Alfred's authority despite his intellectual shortcomings. However, in Chapters 89 and 90 Asser uses analogies that are awkwardly fitted to the situation and thus lead the reader to consider him superior to the king. Indeed, he invites this 'misreading' by twice denying it.

Asser's mixed presentation of Alfred – an eager pupil who sadly started too late, a man who lusts for both knowledge and bodies – demonstrates *in nuce* the two main claims of this book. The first is that scenes of instruction often involve an element of *agon* even if the depiction of education seems at first idealised. Negotiations for power and subtexts of resistance and criticism undergird the platitudes about the importance of wisdom and learning one often finds in Anglo-Saxon literature. The second claim is that education is a highly emotional process, one that often involves feelings we would now consider negative, unpleasant, or inappropriate. Anglo-Saxon writers recognise, however, that those affects that accompany and enable learning often also threaten to hinder it.

The Experience of Education offers a pedagogical reading of Anglo-Saxon literature without attempting a comprehensive history of Anglo-Saxon education. That history has yet to be written, although not for lack of effort on the part of Anglo-Saxonists, who in recent years have addressed the topic with vigour.[37] This scholarly energy is particularly evident in international collaborative projects focused on early medieval and Anglo-Saxon education. Leornungcræft: Form and Contents of Instruction in Anglo-Saxon England in the Light of Contemporary Manuscript Evidence, based in Italy, and Storehouses of Wholesome Learning: Accumulation and Dissemination of Encyclopaedic Knowledge in the Early Middle Ages, a joint Dutch–Italian project, demonstrate a growing interest in understanding the education in great part responsible for the vernacular literary works we teach, explicate, and translate.[38] But telling the story of Anglo-Saxon schooling is no simple matter, comprising as it does multiple histories with disparate sources: textbooks, pedagogic techniques, theories of education, institutions, and biographies of influential teachers. While I do not propose to write a history of Anglo-Saxon education, in what follows I describe what such a history might look like, and what its points of contact are with the chapters in this book.

The type of source that most readily recommends itself to the study of early education is any text that might be described as a schoolbook. It is sometimes asserted that the difficulty Latin posed to the Anglo-Saxons, native speakers of a Germanic tongue, spurred them to great productivity in grammar and language pedagogy.[39] Accordingly, many schoolbooks are grammars, either late antique ones passed down to the Anglo-Saxons or those written by early medieval educators such as Virgilius Maro Grammaticus, Boniface, Alcuin, or Ælfric.[40] Other works composed especially for the classroom are the colloquies devised for the acquisition and practice of Latin, such as *De raris fabulis*, Ælfric's *Colloquy*, and Ælfric Bata's *Colloquies*.[41] The evidence also includes glosses. These might be in English or Latin, as can be found in the glossed *Enigmata* of Boniface, and can of course also include Welsh or Irish glossing.[42] Lexical glosses were compiled into lists, and these glossaries could, in turn, be adapted for use in educational works such as Ælfric's *Grammar* and conversational colloquies.[43] Another area of interest is the study of texts adopted for educational purposes: this vast category contains the Psalms, the riddles of Symphosius, classical writers such as Vergil and Horace, Christian Latin poets including Prudentius, Boethius, Arator, and Prosper, and even the works of Anglo-Saxon writers like Aldhelm and Bede.[44] Finally, but by no means exhaustively, one of the more tantalising traces of the classroom is to be found in student notes, namely in the biblical commentaries associated with the school of Theodore and Hadrian at Canterbury.[45] This text hints at the lived experience of an Anglo-Saxon classroom as evocatively as the lecture notes taken by students of Saussure and Lacan have in the last century. Writing the story of Anglo-Saxon education is, in other words, an immense task, unsurprising given the various curricula and schoolbooks used in different places over the centuries.

While *The Experience of Education* cannot begin to do the material in this category justice, current research on Anglo-Saxon school texts has informed my interpretations of several scenes of instruction. Chapter 3 is an analysis of Ælfric Bata's *Colloquies*, a text that served as a schoolbook in at least one monastery and that features dialogues between teachers and students. More broadly, I am interested in the literary implications of texts used to teach the basics of reading and writing. The miraculous healing of a mute youth in Bede (Chapter 1) and the Pater Noster dialogue in *Solomon and Saturn I* (Chapter 2) both link basic reading pedagogy with pain, authority, suffering, and a powerful desire to learn. In Chapter 4, moreover, I argue that representations of teaching in *Andreas* are influenced by Boethius' *Consolation of Philosophy*. The *Consolation* was not a basic textbook *per se*, but it had close ties to education in late Anglo-Saxon England: it was widely available, glossed, and translated into Old English as part of the Alfredian educational programme, and it influenced the vernacular translation of the *Distichs of Cato*, which was a basic school text.[46]

A second approach to Anglo-Saxon schooling focuses on the institutions and individuals responsible for education. Evidence for this area of study comes mainly from documentary sources, as material culture offers less information than one might wish.[47] A typical history of Anglo-Saxon education in this sense might begin with Bede's glowing remarks about several teachers: Cuthbert as a charismatic model of eremitic monasticism, Bishop Aidan as a teacher of moderate approaches, Abbess Hild's oversight of the double monastery at Whitby, a cradle of bishops and English poetry, John of Beverley's teaching in the context of his episcopal *familia*, and, most famously, the high levels of learning brought to the island by Archbishop Theodore and Abbot Hadrian.[48] Such a story might include

Aldhelm's letters to his students on the dangers of Irish intellectual temptations and Boniface's correspondence with missionary nuns.[49] It would certainly treat Alfred's prefaces and his programme of translation, and consider the accuracy of his laments on the decline of English learning in the ninth century.[50] The history would go on to describe the Benedictine Reform and its influence on Latin and English literacy.[51]

A third way of telling the story of Anglo-Saxon schooling is to trace theories of education present in early medieval England. This can be done by examining pedagogically relevant works the Anglo-Saxons read, copied, quoted, and translated. It can also be done by tracing the influence of inherited classical and Christian writing on Anglo-Latin and vernacular compositions. I argue that close readings of scenes of instruction can also reveal what Anglo-Saxons valued in teachers, and by extension, their implicit theories of education. A number of recent studies have emphasised the importance for medieval learning of violent imagery, corporal punishment, and spectacular suffering, and indeed my own analyses of *Solomon and Saturn I* and Bata's *Colloquies* draw on the notion of pedagogically productive pain.[52] I want to emphasise, however, that there were multiple theories of teaching and learning in the Anglo-Saxon period. Bede, as I alluded earlier, shows us Aidan correcting the harsh and ineffective Irish bishop sent to King Oswald, telling him he should have offered gentle teaching to those still cutting their teeth on the faith and tough admonishment only to Christians ready for something solid to chew on.[53] In doing so, Bede implicitly propounds a flexible pedagogy he found in the writing of Gregory the Great.[54] In the *Pastoral Care*, Gregory describes at length how people of different classes and dispositions are best guided. The ideal teacher is like a harpist who plays one melody on variously tuned strings: he propounds a single doctrine, but suits the admonition to the person hearing it.[55] That Gregory's adaptable pedagogy found favour among Anglo-Saxons is evidenced by the fifteen surviving manuscripts of some or all of the Latin text of the *Pastoral Care* and by the six extant manuscripts of its Old English translation.[56]

The Anglo-Saxons inherited and built upon other theories of education as well. They found the concepts of teaching through dialectic and disputation, understanding through the interpretation of linguistic signs, and learning through recollection in Augustine and Boethius, to name but two of the most important authors. Not only were Augustine's *Soliloquies* and Boethius' *Consolation* translated into English, but their influence is traceable in vernacular poetry.[57] Accordingly, in Chapter 4 I argue for a direct influence of Boethian ideas of learning through *anamnesis* on the depiction of teaching in *Andreas*. Anglo-Saxons also found reflections on learning, affect, and the personal authority of the teacher in texts bound up with monastic culture.[58] In his *Moralia in Iob*, a standard book in Anglo-Saxon libraries, Gregory explores the roles of desire and suffering in attaining knowledge of God.[59] These emotions are essential to depictions of learning in hagiographies the Anglo-Saxons received, translated, and adapted, as in the case of the *Life of St Mary of Egypt* (Chapter 5). Monastic literature also often features tightly narrated scenes of instruction, ripe for interpretation. The *Verba Seniorum*, Gregory's *Dialogues*, Rufinus' translation of the *Historia Monachorum*, and parts of Cassian's *De institutis coenobiorum* would have accustomed Anglo-Saxons to deducing pedagogical ideas from pregnant anecdotes.[60] In a sense, my reading practice throughout this book is informed by this monastic tradition, one in which encounters between masters and disciples are frequent, and in which the lesson to be learned about spiritual edification is often allusively suggested, not made explicit.

My aim in this book is to show how much can be gleaned about educational thinking by closely reading scenes of instruction in Old English and Anglo-Latin texts. I ask a series of interrelated questions: What makes a student good or bad? What makes a teacher effective, ineffective, or dangerous? How can a student be made out of someone who has no wish to learn, or a teacher out of someone who has no wish to teach? When do teaching or learning fail? What is the importance of remembering and of forgetting? What traces does primary education leave on an individual's psyche? How do texts interpellate their audiences as educated subjects?[61] While contemporary educational theorists would no doubt offer their own answers to these questions, the Anglo-Saxon texts examined in this study approach the problem through a series of powerful emotions: fear, suffering, erotic desire, dangerous curiosity, a feeling of entrapment, terrible wonder, and cutting irony. In their various permutations and combinations, these emotions provoke, enable, and compel learning. They also occasionally serve to upset it.

The Experience of Education thus offers a fundamentally sceptical portrayal of Anglo-Saxon thinking on pedagogy, one that looks beyond idealised portraits of teachers and schools to the ruptures and paradoxes implicit in the process of learning. This reading may seem to be the result of a postmodern love of internal tension, equivocation, and self-deconstruction. No doubt it is, to some extent, but I argue that it is also consistent with Christian theories of learning that Anglo-Saxons inherited and reflected in their own works. The late antique texts that influenced Anglo-Saxon pedagogical thinking may have valued education, but they also insistently theorised its failure. Augustine reflected in several works on the limitations of human teaching as opposed to divine illumination: the linguistic signs people are forced to use to communicate can only point to something already known, and learners might not see the signs or even the teacher's pointing.[62] Boethius' insistent focus on forgetting in *The Consolation of Philosophy* casts doubt on the efficacy of teaching, and the *Consolation* itself can be read as a story of Philosophy's failure to lead her student back to his true self.[63] Even the monastic tradition, with its scrupulous attention to the place of teaching in the ascetic life, is as concerned with misreading, conflict, and spiritual danger as it is with successful lessons. Disciples are turned away, misjudge the teacher's virtues, or lie to cover up his faults.[64] Teachers avoid book learning and hordes of adoring students in the hope of staving off spiritual pride. Anglo-Saxons interested in pedagogy had recourse to several influential thinkers and traditions that threw doubt on education even while illuminating it.

The questions I pose in *The Experience of Education* are inspired by critics who have examined ideology, authority, and affect in medieval education. Studies by Elaine Tuttle Hansen, Seth Lerer, Martin Irvine, Clare Lees, Gillian Overing, and Katherine O'Brien O'Keeffe have been essential in uncovering Anglo-Saxon discourses of wisdom, literate ideologies, grammatical culture, and the relationship between gender and forms of knowing.[65] Equally valuable has been research into late medieval education, often with a focus on its relationship to literature in Latin or English. In particular, the work of Mary Carruthers, Rita Copeland, Marjorie Curry Woods, Jody Enders, Edward Wheatley, Bruce Holsinger, Jill Mann, and Peter Travis has informed my approach.[66] In their explorations of the multi-faceted interactions of violence and authority in late medieval teaching, by establishing the formative role of grammar and grammatical education in the lives and works of literate persons, and by imagining the psychological dimension of pedagogical texts and methods, these critics have provided a road map for further work on Anglo-Saxon education.

The Experience of Education begins with a miraculous scene of healing in Bede's *Ecclesiastical History of the English People*. A prolific scholar, Bede wrote with admiration and acumen about charismatic teachers and the liberation provided by Christian faith and education. Reared in a monastery from an early age, his narrative of the English peoples' entry into Roman Christianity was seminal for English historiography and national identity. In his depiction of a mute boy who is taught to speak by John of Beverley, Bede reveals his understanding of the Latin alphabet as key to the emancipatory potential of Christian literacy. Surprisingly, and unlike

Cædmon and other learners in the *History*, the youth explicitly refuses to enter a Christian institution after having been taught to speak. In depicting the youth's refusal, Bede presents a new phase in the relationship of the English peoples to Latinity, one that recognises the English vernacular as the grammatical and salvific equal of Latin.

While Chapter 1 argues for the liberating power of the alphabet, Chapter 2 shows its deadly side. It focuses on the depiction of pedagogy in *Solomon and Saturn I*, a meditation on the bizarre, awesome powers of the Lord's Prayer that ends in a battle between the prayer's letters and the devil. I argue that *Solomon and Saturn I* plays out a drama of knowing and unknowing, provoking the reader to recall his own education. The Lord's Prayer recalls the first steps of learning to read in the middle ages, and the silent runes inserted into the verse make the poem's reader aware of himself as a reader, not a listener. By encouraging the reader to identify with Saturn's desire for a well-known text, the poem addresses one of the central problems of monastic prayer and a major issue around the Pater Noster for lay and religious alike: how to worship attentively even when the words of the prayer have become rote.

If the importance of violence for learning is implicit in *Solomon and Saturn I*, it is patent in Chapter 3. The eleventh-century Latin *Colloquies* of Ælfric Bata have drawn attention for the violence and other irregularities depicted in the daily scenes of the dialogues. I argue that Bata is aware of the nuances of authority in second-language teaching, its implications for the student, and the ways that a language of power can be manipulated and subverted. His *Colloquies* encourage pupils to learn discipline through vicious and disturbing language, but eventually also reveal the uncontrollable nature of violence introduced into the classroom. The deliberately ambiguous textbook thus functions as a workshop in which young students might play with potential monastic identities, learning to speak Latin while questioning the very authority that demands this skill.

The *Colloquies'* approach to memory is in line with classical and medieval mnemonic theories in which shocking and brutal images are used to improve recollection. In Chapter 4 I argue that *Andreas* is informed at every level by a different classical theory of memory, one in which learning is defined as the process of recollecting what one already knows. The poet of *Andreas* borrowed heavily from *Beowulf* and the works of Cynewulf, and his attempt to translate a well-known apostolic story into Old English heroic vocabulary resulted in ironic or nonsensical plot details and locutions, ungrammatical lines, and lapses of translation. However, these errors and oddities are part of the work's poetic and pedagogical programme.

Andreas is filled with repurposed remnants of the past, wandering revenants, discussions of origins, and cannibals or 'self-eaters'. The reader is invited to wonder at the strangeness of leftover objects and poetic lines, at materials recycled and regurgitated, and to ponder their sources. The aesthetic experience of the poem is anchored in a pedagogy of recollection, one the poet found in his sources and in the description of Platonic *anamnesis* in Boethius' *Consolation of Philosophy*.

In the final chapter, I turn to Mary of Egypt, one of the girls gone wild of late antique hagiography. Like Mary Magdalene and Thaïs, Mary of Egypt is a sinful woman who converts to Christianity and becomes a model of ascetic, self-punishing virtue and evidence for God's willingness to forgive even the most dissolute wretches. Indeed, the Old English *Life*, a close prose translation of a Latin *vita*, depicts her as holier than the observant monk Zosimus, more perfect in her imperfection. Yet the tale is, like many narratives originating in the tradition of desert saints, about a teacher's oblique lessons and a student's eagerness and pride. While Mary has renounced her past sexual voraciousness, teaching Zosimus threatens to tempt her once again. Through deliberate word choice and errors of translation and copying, the Old English version of the *Life* insists that teaching redemption is dangerous to teacher and student alike.

It is perhaps no surprise to find that educated Anglo-Saxons were interested in reflecting on the nature of education, the acquisition of wisdom, and the path to spiritual improvement. What I hope to show in this book is how knotty their perspective on learning was, and how cryptic – and witty – they could be when communicating their thoughts. The enigmatic quality of their expression does not indicate a lack of seriousness, however. Learned Anglo-Saxons knew that a lesson could be *altus* in both senses of the word: at once high and low, lofty and profound. The literature around education in Anglo-Saxon England is woven through with dark passions and coded resistance, sly allusions and boisterous jokes, but its core is earnest: a dedication to learning, with its stumbles and setbacks, and to teachers, fallible though they sometimes are.

CHAPTER I

Letters
Bede's Ecclesiastical History of the English People

The first step I say awed me and pleased me so much,
I have hardly gone and hardly wish'd to go any farther,
But stop and loiter all the time to sing it in ecstatic songs.

Walt Whitman, 'Beginning My Studies'[1]

Fictions of learning often concentrate on beginnings. The educated individual reflects on his or her entry into a world of literacy, knowledge, or wisdom. This requires imagining the time before: the experience of lacking language, of being ignorant, sceptical, or proud. It also means recalling the emotions woven around that prior state, the fear, frustration, and curiosity involved in lacking something precious without wholly understanding what it is. Stories of beginnings reflect on the importance of community by imagining its absence. Accordingly, a number of the learners I discuss in this book are lonely figures, unable to speak with or recognise others, incapable of fitting into institutions, wandering in search of sublime experiences and spiritual teachers. In his *Ecclesiastical History of the English People*, Bede describes the education of one such isolated man, a youth who had never been able to communicate with the people around him. Bishop John of Beverley heals him miraculously with the ABCs, the fundamentals of literacy and, in Bede's view, of language. In relating the young man's first words, Bede tells another story of beginnings, one of nascent English participation in literate culture and the Roman church.

Although Bede dedicated most of his intellectual energy to biblical commentary, he is now better known as the historian of the beginnings and growth of Christianity among the Germanic inhabitants of Britain. Bede was deeply committed to the project of incorporating the English church and its story into an international Christian Latin culture centred on Rome; indeed, he wrote his *History* in Latin to reach a wider European audience.[2] He was intensely aware of Britain's place on the geographic periphery of Europe, of inhabiting an island that had already been a province of the Roman Empire before his Germanic ancestors even reached it, and that was spiritually recolonised by Rome through the Gregorian mission begun in AD 597.[3] English was a marginal language at the time, rarely written and without the formal structure articulated in grammars of Latin. However, despite being a monk and writing in the Latin patristic tradition of Augustine and Jerome,[4] Bede could envision a role for the English vernacular in the service of Christian education and pastoral work: he was a poet in Latin and English, translated the Creed and Lord's Prayer for the benefit of the unlettered, and apparently translated the Gospel of John.[5] Bede's narration of the healing miracle at the centre of this chapter offers a vision of Latin learning and Christian authority that liberates English speech without necessarily redirecting it to the uses of faith. In this miracle story, the scene of pedagogy occasions a creative linguistic fusion, one that forces the dominant language to make space for the sounds and vocabulary of marginal tongues.

Despite his confident stance as a monk, priest, and Latin author, Bede occupied a double position with respect to his native culture. Having entered the monastery at Wearmouth as an oblate at age seven, he spent most of his life immersed in the written and sung texts of Christian Latinity, yet he understood the peripheral position of the English and had an active interest in the spiritual reform of clergy and laity. While he would never have understood himself as a 'hapless Caliban who dutifully learns the language of the colonial master',[6] he was deeply interested in the symbolic qualities of speech deficiencies. This may be connected to what he describes as a miraculous healing of the tongue he experienced while composing poetry, suggesting that he may have also suffered a linguistic or physical impairment.[7] The scenes I discuss in this chapter reveal his meditation on problems of linguistic alienation in the vernacular through figures who are deficient speakers of their own tongue. Bede, I will show, understood linguistic disability not simply as a deformity of the body, but as a symbol of political and spiritual enslavement.

In the final book of his *History*, Bede relates a miracle that yokes together his interest in miraculous healing and his enduring engagement with the liberating potential of Christian grammar. It is the beginning of Lent, and Bishop John of Inderauuda (now Beverley) seeks out a pauper to receive his ministrations. John is brought a youth who has been speechless since birth and whose head is so scabrous that no hair can grow on it. After enclosing him in a hut for a week, John orders him to put out his tongue, and, seizing his chin, makes the sign of the cross over the unspeaking organ. He then teaches the young man to speak:

> 'Dicito' inquiens 'aliquod uerbum; dicito *gae,*' quod est lingua Anglorum uerbum adfirmandi et consentiendi, id est 'etiam'. Dixit ille statim, soluto uinculo linguae, quod iussus erat. Addidit episcopus nomina litterarum: 'Dicito A'; dixit ille 'A'. 'Dicito B'; dixit ille et hoc. Cumque singula litterarum nomina dicente episcopo responderet, addidit et syllabas ac uerba dicenda illi proponere. Et cum in omnibus consequenter responderet, praecepit eum sententias longiores dicere, et fecit.

> 'Say some word', he said, 'say *gæ*', which in English is the word of assent and agreement, that is, yes. He said at once what the bishop told him to say, the bonds of his tongue being unloosed. The bishop then added the names of the letters: 'Say A', and he said it. 'Say B', and he said that too. When he had repeated the names of the letters after the bishop, the latter added syllables and words for the youth to repeat after him. When he had repeated them all, one after the other, the bishop taught him to say longer sentences, which he did.

His speech therapy concluded, the young man unleashes a torrent of language, speaking to other people as long as he can stay awake, expressing his secret thoughts and wishes for the first time in his life. John subsequently refers the young man to a physician, who cures his scalp, leaving the formerly mute and hideous boy with both eloquence and a full head of curly hair (458–59).[8]

Compared with Bede's other miracles, this event has received little attention.[9] As a healing of the body, it is anticlimactic: the youth's scalp is healed by a medic, with Bishop John's prayers and blessing as secondary help. Although the young man's disability is reflected in his bodily disease, it is internal and cured apart from the body. As a story about the miraculous acquisition of a particular kind of language, it seems to pale beside the canonised – and canonically important – angelic inspiration of the poet Cædmon, the simple cowherd credited with composing the first Christian poetry in the Anglo-Saxon vernacular. While Cædmon ruminates the very notion of English religious poetry into existence, the nameless youth healed by John of Beverley undertakes a journey of private significance. Instead of leaving the secular world for the confines of the monastery in order to embody the origin of a poetic tradition,[10] the mute boy escapes the prison of his mind and returns home an attractive, but fundamentally ordinary, person. And yet the healing of the mute youth occasions one of Bede's meditations on how language is to be taught and what its powers are once acquired. Bede rigorously constructs his narration of this miracle in a way that resists categorisation according to linguistic genre or use, literacy or orality, English or Latin. Instead, he uses the details of the mute adolescent's healing to reflect on the very possibility of signification, on the nature of language itself.

The story also brings together the themes of liberation, baptism, and divinely inspired speech woven throughout the *History*. It functions as an interpretative capstone to the better-known stories of Cædmon; of Imma, a warrior who is liberated by masses instead of pagan magic; and of the beautiful but heathen slave boys who awaken Gregory the Great's desire to convert the English (and to pun memorably on the name of their people). Cædmon's poetic inspiration and the young man's cure are both stories of linguistic outsiders who gain the power of their own vernacular through miraculous Christian teaching. The unnamed youth's acquired speech, however, is unbound, beholden neither to monastic objectives nor to Bede's attempt to translate English experience into Latin. Seth Lerer's rich reading of the Imma episode has shown how it substitutes the emancipatory potential of Christian liturgy for the pagan, Germanic belief that written charms can unlock chains.[11] The healing of the youth supplements and surpasses this story by teaching that the very letters of the alphabet are signs with power to liberate, whether or not put to liturgical use. In a move remarkable for a monk so manifestly oriented towards an ecclesiastical audience, the healing of the mute youth extends the power of Latinate signification beyond the church and its monastery. The story of Gregory the Great's marketplace punning, by contrast, has been interpreted as Bede's recognition of 'own racial identity as a Christian Angle'[12] or, more broadly, as Bede's organisation of the disparate Germanic settlers into an intelligible entity.[13] It is also a story about grammar, about a sophisticated manipulation of words that is assumed to uncover a truth unavailable to unskilled readers.[14] Bede adapted his version of the anecdote in small but subtle ways, opening the possibility for the healing of the mute youth in book 5 to answer Gregory's colonial gaze. Bede presents the heathen Angles as enslaved and mute, but by the end of his *History* he shows how an English youth can use Latin grammar to acquire the emancipatory power of his own vernacular. In book 5, chapter 2, of the *History*, Bede stages a scene of healing in which language pedagogy is figured as poetic liberation. Most basically, he portrays the tongue's loosening as escape from the impediments of physical disability and figurative deliverance from the bonds of pagan sin. It is also liberation from the desolation of being entrapped in one's own consciousness, the freeing of a youth who had been a lifelong outsider into communion with other people.

Bede on Language

In examining this early medieval wild child, separated from society by his inability to communicate and disgusting appearance, Bede anticipates the Enlightenment use of feral children as sites of linguistic speculation. The mute adolescent bears closer resemblance, however, to what James Berger calls 'post-modern wild children', for he embodies not the ultimate origins of language but redemption from a traumatised language.[15] For Bede, as for other medieval commentators, the trauma would have been the division of tongues at Babel. Isidore of Seville begins the ninth book of his *Etymologies* by reflecting on the linguistic diversity that resulted from the pride displayed at Babel, and after discussing a variety of languages, he remarks that, despite the difficulty of learning languages, no person can be so lazy as not to know the language of his or her own people. One who did not know it would be inferior to stupid animals, which at least make noises in their own voices.[16] In his commentary on the Pentecost miracle in Acts, Bede claims that the humility of the church gathers together the languages sundered by Babylonian pride,[17] though he is also remarkable in his generosity towards linguistic diversity, adding that the variety of languages signifies gifts of various graces.[18] In his *History*, Bede figures grammatical teaching as a means of redemption both for the original trauma of linguistic fragmentation and for the personal suffering of a youth who is, in Isidore's words, 'animalium brutorum deterior'.

The unlocking of the youth's tongue reveals Bede's fundamentally literate understanding of language: here the learner acquires spoken language not as Augustine described, by imitating the speech of nurses and other adults, but according to the methodical progression used in the antique and medieval pedagogy of reading and writing and reflected in Bede's own pedagogical treatises.[19] As a young boy at Wearmouth, Bede likely acquired oral Latin proficiency by learning to perform the liturgy, but he probably learned to read and write the language by studying individual letters, syllables, and then words, writing them on wax tablets to memorise them.[20] Correspondingly, in his *De arte metrica* Bede discusses the qualities of letters and syllables before proceeding to feet and metrical forms, and the spelling guidelines in *De orthographia* are arranged alphabetically.[21] Bede would have had a model in Donatus' *Ars maior*, which begins with a division of sound into meaningful and meaningless, proceeds to a discussion of letters and their qualities, and covers syllables, metrical feet, and word accent before arriving at the parts of speech.[22]

This language lesson is preceded by a releasing of the tongue's chain (soluto uinculo linguae) that directly recalls Jesus' healing of the mute and deaf man in Mark 7:32–36, 'solutum est vinculum linguae eius' (the chain on his tongue was loosed), a miracle which Bede explicitly connects to teaching in his commentary on Mark.[23] Miracles of healed or restored speech are frequent in medieval texts, and, indeed, Bede includes another earlier in the *History*, in which Torhtgyth, a nun at Barking, loses the use of her limbs and tongue; she regains enough speech for a conversation with the spirit of her departed abbess, Æthelburh, and dies a day later (362–63; bk 4, ch. 9). Torhtgyth's impairment, a result of an advanced illness, is what Roman Jakobson called 'true apraxia', an inability to carry out the physical movements required for the production of sounds of language. I propose that the mute youth, whose physical deformity is neither cause nor related symptom of his speechlessness, suffers instead from something closer to 'sound-dumbness' – that is, 'an apraxia for conventional linguistic signs'[24] – and that the textual aspects of his therapy represent Bede's solution to the youth's lack of ability to signify.

That a medieval writer can distinguish between muteness due to physical inability to speak and a complete lack of linguistic signs is demonstrated by a speech miracle associated with the cult of John of Beverley. In his *Miracula Sancti Johannes*, William Ketell, a clerk of Beverley writing in the twelfth century and long after John's canonisation, relates the story of an educated boy from York who suddenly loses the power of speech. On pilgrimage in the church at Beverley, his father addresses him and expects him to reply, as usual, in signs. To the father's surprise, the boy speaks.[25] This later medieval story is rigorously concerned with the physical ability to utter words rather than with the ability to make and share meaning. The fact that the boy has studied implies that he has attained some level of literacy, and he can communicate with his father in sign language. Although deprived of the power of speech, he lives a linguistic existence before the miracle.[26] In Ketell's narrative speech is carefully differentiated from other forms of signifying, while in Bede's miracle, speech is blended with literacy and made to represent every possibility of language. The real miracle for Bede's mute young man is the ability to express his interiority at all – hence the lack of any mention of sign language or writing. Bede emphasises the psychological relief of signification by telling us at the start of the miracle that the youth had never been able to speak a single word and by describing the frantic, nearly manic torrent of speech he emits when released from his oppressive interiority.

The interest of Bede's miracle is not, however, limited to the fact that an individual acquires language but also resides in the structured way in which he learns to speak. Bede's description of the linear progression from the alphabet to syllables to words and sentences recalls the method for teaching reading famously described by Quintilian in the *Institutio oratoria*,[27] although Quintilian explicitly opposed teaching the alphabet in order, stressing that children should learn to recognise the shapes of letters independently of their sequence:

> For this reason teachers, even when they consider that they have sufficiently impressed upon children the letters in the order they are usually first written, then go backwards and mix up the letters in various kinds of disorder, until the children know the letters they are learning by shape, not by order. For this reason it will be best for pupils to be taught the appearance and names of letters together, as one does with people.[28]

Bede's decision is for a fixed order, and the Beverley miracle implies that the progression beginning with A, B, and C leads not only to a facility in reading Latin but also to linguistic capability in general, including in speaking English. Bede's strategy of linking universal linguistic structures as he understood them to the learning of speech and to the language of aphasics anticipates aspects of Roman Jakobson's discussion of child language and phonological universals.

According to Jakobson, a standard progression of phonemic oppositions determines the order in which children learn the phonological systems proper to their language. These structural laws also determine the sequence in which sound aphasics lose their ability to discern phonemic oppositions: they begin by losing the latest ones developed and proceed backward, 'unlearning' the system.[29] In Bede's and Jakobson's narratives, linguistic disability is figured as being on the same spectrum as primary-language learning and indeed helps to define the structure they share.[30] Bede also posits a logical series of sounds and sound combinations independent of any individual language: he introduces English into the text with the youth's first word, *gae*, and we can assume that English is what the young man learns to speak, but after the word of assent the ordering of the letters and subsequent progression to syllables and words recapitulate elementary education in Latin and in Latin literacy.[31] Bede thus implies that spoken English has a discernible structure and can be acquired through the same pedagogical processes as written Latin, perhaps even suggesting that Latin is an ideal paradigm for English.[32] The young man, who was a foreigner in his own language, becomes a model for the adaptability of sacred Christian signs to quotidian English life.[33]

Muteness and Liberation in the *Ecclesiastical History*

John of Beverley's healing of the mute youth near the end of Bede's *History* reveals Bede's understanding of language structure, acquisition, and their relation to disabled speakers. Moreover, the miracle's connections to several key scenes in the *History* inscribe the release of one physical English tongue into a larger rhetoric of lingustic healing and vernacular liberation. My reading of the *Ecclesiastical History* assumes that Bede understood historical events to function as signs, amenable to exegetical interpretation by trained readers and carrying hidden, symbolic truths.[34] However, as Sharon Rowley and Allen Frantzen have argued, despite Bede's careful narration of the triumphant participation of the English in Christian history, major historical facts and everyday practices occasionally elude his exegetical scheme.[35] My approach seeks to account not only for Bede's adaptation of his sources but also for his treatment of details in the John of Beverley miracle that do not readily suit his narrative, presuming that they have a basis in the story as it came down to Bede. Bede weaves liberation imagery with reflections on language and teaching throughout his narration of historical events, knotting together these conceptual threads in the healing of the mute youth.

The miracle of the mute boy should be read against the background of the fourth book of the *Ecclesiastical History*, which testifies to a revival of Christian faith and ascetic life.[36] This section of the *History* is bookended by examples of consummate Christian teaching and extraordinary ability in language. It begins with the arrival of Theodore of Tarsus in AD 669 and his foundation with Abbot Hadrian of a school at Canterbury famous for its learning. Bede seems particularly impressed by the linguistic achievements of some of their surviving English students, 'qui Latinam Graecamque linguam aeque ut propriam in qua nati sunt norunt' (who knew Latin and Greek just as well as their native tongue; 334–35, ch. 2). The book's final chapters relate the latter part of the career of the monk and bishop Cuthbert, also a great teacher because of his exemplary life and rhetorical prowess. Cuthbert, we learn, was so eloquent that all present for his speeches were moved to confess their sins fully (432–33; ch. 27). The beginning and end of book 4 thus demonstrate Bede's capacious understanding of language's role in teaching, tracing an arc from Theodore and Hadrian's scholarly instruction in the liberal arts, including metrical composition (metricae artis) and pagan classics alongside sacred works (litteris sacris simul et saecularibus; 332–33; ch. 2), to Cuthbert's charismatic orations, which call forth an outpouring of penitential speech from his listeners.

Bede himself was not immune to Cuthbert's spiritual appeal, having written a prose and a verse life of the saint. Cuthbert is particularly interesting for this discussion of linguistic disability because, in the epistolary dedication to the verse *Life*, Bede describes having personally experienced Cuthbert's miraculous power 'per linguae curationem, dum miracula ejus canerem' (through a healing of my tongue, while I was singing his miracles).[37] Later readers have, predictably, disagreed on the precise nature of this miracle. Reginald of Durham's twelfth-century interpretation was that Bede suffered from a speech impediment, while modern scholars' theories range from a canker or sore tongue to lack of poetic inspiration.[38] What is interesting for my purposes is that Bede's ambiguous language leaves open the possibilities of physical defect, speech disorder, and writer's block, all impairments of the 'tongue' that he explores in his *History* as part of his interest in linguistic outsiders. I have mentioned Torhtgyth's loss of the use of her tongue on her deathbed in book 4, chapter 9; John of Beverley's speech therapy is more closely linked to Cædmon's dream vision, another redemption of a man whose linguistic deficiencies made him unable to participate in society.

Bede crafts John's healing of the mute adolescent and Cædmon's poetic miracle along the same lines to underscore the powerful role of Christian teaching in the empowerment of the English vernacular. Cædmon's status as the first named Christian poet in English has made him the object of literary interest and scholarly controversy. Considered primarily an oral-formulaic poet by some scholars, Cædmon is noted by others for the grammatical and monastic learning revealed by the hymn and for his subsequent career in the monastery at Whitby.[39] While his achievement is generally understood as the adaptation of Germanic poetic vocabulary to Christian praise, some critics consider his nine-line hymn unremarkable in its diction or even 'rather tedious', and still others think the Old English text as we have it is a back translation of Bede's Latin.[40] Although the precise nature of his miracle is disputed, the cowherd who famously left feasts because he could not take his turn at the harp clearly received the gift of song from an angel and, like John of Beverley's mute boy, serves as a model for linguistic insufficiency.[41] While I shall emphasise the close textual and thematic parallels between the two miracles, there is a close historical tie as well: after his divine inspiration, Cædmon was educated as a monk under

Hild's direction at Whitby, where John of Beverley also received his early training.[42] Cædmon and John thus participate in the same genealogy of teaching, one symbolically extended to the mute adolescent John heals.[43]

Scholars have found analogues to Cædmon's tale of divine poetic inspiration in a broad range of texts, linking him to Muḥammad, Aeschylus, Ntsikana, Prudentius, the *Rāmāyaṇa*, and dream songs of Australian aborigines and Native Americans, as well as to closer, northern European stories of Aldhelm, Hallbjörn hali, the *Heliand* poet, and Godric of Finchale, to name but a few.[44] While this work sheds light on the way Cædmon's story rehearses a theme common among world literatures, C. Grant Loomis has traced Bede's more immediate source, the angelic visitation of Equitius in Gregory the Great's *Dialogues*,[45] a text that, I argue, also hovers behind the John of Beverley miracle. In the Gregorian story, a man named Felix notices that Equitius has been preaching without having been ordained. When asked how he dares to do this, Equitius says that:

> nocte quadam speciosus mihi per uisionem iuuenis adstitit, atque in lingua mea medicinale ferramentum, id est flebotomum, posuit, dicens: 'Ecce posui uerba mea in ore tuo. Egredere ad praedicandum'. Atque ex illo die, etiam cum uoluero, de Deo tacere non possum.

> On a certain night a splendid young man stood by me in a vision, and placed a medicinal iron, that is, a lancet on my tongue, saying: 'Look! I have placed my words in your mouth. Go out and preach.' And since that day, even if I want to, I cannot be silent about God.[46]

Bede uses the motif of the nocturnal, angelic visitor in the Cædmon story, and Cædmon, like Equitius, is a person who rises above his earthly station to serve God through language. John of Beverley's miracle remains closer to the biblical source it shares with Equitius but takes from it the motif of a 'healed' person who is unable to be silent after a miraculous treatment.

Bede reinforces this connection by composing the two teaching scenes with similar didactic imperatives. John of Beverley and the angel are forceful in their commands to their students, and both call for sound making and signification. 'Caedmon,' says the angel, 'canta mihi aliquid' (sing something). After protests from Cædmon, the angel commands him to begin with the beginning: 'Canta … principium creaturarum' (416–17, Sing me the beginning of created beings). The hymn Cædmon composes on the Creation recalls the beginning of Augustine's catechetical *narratio*, the outline of Creation and biblical history Augustine recommends for the instruction of beginners in faith; Cædmon's subsequent course of study and poetic composition in the monastery continues along this curriculum, spanning the Old and New Testaments as well as the Last Judgement and the joys of heaven.[47] Beverley follows the model of Cædmon's angel, also starting with a vague instruction that he then makes specific: 'Dicito aliquid uerbum; dicito *gae*' (Say some word … say *gae*), he says, before spelling out the ABCs. While one student acquires a sophisticated literary skill based in thorough Christian education and the other learns only the basics of communication, both follow an organised course of study: A, B, and C as the stepping stones of language, the Creation as the baseline of Christian knowledge and the mythologised origin of Christian Anglo-Saxon poetics.

Bede's parallel construction of these two teaching miracles highlights their achievement in English. While the Cædmon story is most commonly associated with Bede's thoughts on the vernacular, it is the John of Beverley miracle that quotes English, albeit the single word *gae*.[48] Moreover, just as John's therapy fuses speech and written letters to heal the adolescent's linguistic faculty, Cædmon's poetic achievement is not simply one of oral composition. The descriptions of his rumination and his eventual poetic corpus correspond to monastic textual practices, and while it is generally assumed that Cædmon remained illiterate, Donald Fritz has argued persuasively that he learned to read Latin once he entered the monastery.[49] More important, the opposition the story seems to set up between English orality and Latin literacy is false: the monastic practices of liturgy and oral reading made Latin a language to be spoken and sung as well as written, and Old English poetry shows the influences of both oral Germanic poetics and Latin verse.[50] Bede uses his miracles of language to explore exactly this creative fusion, poetic in one case, linguistic in the other, but with a small difference. He renders Cædmon's hymn in Latin, and while he acknowledges the difficulty of translating verse and uses hexameter cadences to convey some of the poetry of the Old English original,[51] no word of the English survives. Cædmon and his poetic oeuvre are fully assimilated to the monastic mission, while the mute boy speaks English into the text that is translated but not effaced.

Language and Liberation

John of Beverley's precisely described speech lesson, with its careful naming of the first letters of the Roman alphabet, also echoes and completes the story of Imma (400–5; bk 4, ch. 22). The noble retainer Imma, left for dead at the Battle of the Trent, in 678, is taken captive by a follower of King Æthelred. Fearing for his safety, he hides his identity and class, pretending to be a poor peasant. Meanwhile, his brother, Tunna, a priest and abbot, offers masses in his name, generally around nine in the morning; at the same time each day, Imma's chains come unfastened. Imma's frustrated captor asks him if he carries releasing spells, or 'litteras solutorias' (loosing letters), which scholars have generally understood to indicate runes or other pagan magical charms.[52] Imma's answers betray that he is thane and not peasant, and he is sold to a Frisian slave dealer in London from whom he eventually ransoms himself.[53] Common imagery of imprisonment and release, along with a few light verbal and thematic echoes, binds the two miracle stories in their parallel movements of liberation. This is an emancipation at once physical, spiritual, linguistic, and social. Imma lies unconscious on the battlefield a full day and night (die illo et nocte sequenti), and then he stands and walks (leuauit se et coepit abire), his chains are loosed (eius sunt uincula soluta), his speech reveals his real identity, and he is finally freed and allowed to go home (patriam reuersus). The mute youth is confined in a hut for a week before the miracle, the chain on his tongue is loosed (soluto uinculo linguae), his newfound speech allows him to reveal his interiority all day and the following night (tota die illa et nocte sequente), he is compared with a lame man who miraculously stood and walked (stetit et ambulabat), and he ultimately chooses to go home (domum reuersus est). The youth's escape from his interior solitude thus echoes the scene of Imma lying, as if dead, among the corpses near the Trent, emphasising the horror and the inaccessibility of his previous silence. Moreover, while Imma pretends to be a poor peasant (rusticum … pauperem) but is restored to his true station by Christian miracle and by his mode of speech, the youth really is a pauper, who after John of Beverley's intervention is no longer 'ugly, destitute, and dumb' (deformis pauper et mutus).

Seth Lerer has argued that Bede's telling of the Imma miracle effects a reorientation from pagan superstition towards a symbolic understanding of religious rites, thus 'acculturating early legend into the literate and literary structures of a Christian knowledge, be they those of a saint's life, institutionalized prayer, or written history'.[54] The story of the mute youth's healing by John of Beverley not only supports this movement to a Christian literate mentality, but in its interplay with the Imma episode, it also shows the systematic, grammatical comprehension of language to be a decisive part of this shift. The miracle of Imma replaces the suspected *litteras solutorias*, written charms with the virtue of releasing chains, with the power of the mass. While Imma's physical chains are loosed by the masses his brother offers for the absolution of his soul, the metaphoric chain on the mute youth's tongue is released by the sign of the cross. Lerer points out that Bede is vague about what the wording of a releasing charm might be, but I propose that Bede's painstaking detail in his description of John of Beverley's teaching miracle encourages us to understand the ABCs as another set of *litterae solutoriae*. The unbinding of Imma, a release he himself understands to be connected to spiritual delivery (the *solutio*, or loosing, in *absolution*), is also parallel to the escape of a person without language from his or her internal prison. The ABCs are releasing letters, allowing, through systematic teaching and not pagan magic, the integration of a youth into his community and into a hybrid textual world, shaped by Latin literate culture but expressed in the speaking of English.

While Imma is freed by masses, John of Beverley's miracle echoes the performance of baptism, a sacrament that is both deliverance from evil and entrance into the community of the faithful. John's gesture, recalling as it does the healing at Mark 7.32–36, would have reminded Bede and his audience of the *effeta* or *ephphetha* rite, a touching of baptismal candidates' ears and nose (with spittle or oil) based on the scriptural model.[55] Indeed, in his homily on Holy Saturday, Bede states that the baptismal *effeta* rite originates in Mark.[56] Just as baptism was thought of from its earliest days as a release from the bonds of the devil, the *effeta* ritual was imagined, at least in the Roman rite, to have a distinctly exorcistic character.[57] Although Bede uses a vocabulary of liberation (often variations on *solvere* [to loosen, release] or *vinculum solvere* [to loosen the chain]) for a variety of experiences in the *History*, I contend that this kind of formulaic diction does not therefore lose the power to signify. Instead, his incremental repetition of the image has a cumulative effect, a subtle cadence playing in the background of the *History*'s temporal events.[58] Its relation to political enslavement is foregrounded when King Æthelwealh gives Bishop Wilfrid the land at Selsey, along with its livestock and tenants, among them 250 slaves. Wilfrid instructs all of them in the faith, baptises them, and liberates them spiritually and legally: 'quos omnes ut baptizando a seruitute daemonica saluauit, etiam libertate donando humanae iugo seruitutis absoluit' (375–77, all of whom he released from the slavery of the devil, at the same time releasing them from the yoke of human slavery by granting them their liberty). By imbuing his speech miracle with baptismal imagery, Bede suggests that the entry into language is also an entry into Christian community.

The liberating potential of the Christian linguistic understanding of the world and its relation to the English language and peoples, two strands of thought prominent in the cases of Imma and Cædmon, are woven into the well-known story surrounding Gregory the Great's decision to convert the

English (132–35). As Bede relates it at the start of the *History*'s second book, Gregory is captivated by the sight of several beautiful, pale slave boys on sale in the Roman marketplace. He asks their race and, told they are Angles, is inspired to say that the boys' angelic faces should make them fellow heirs with angels. Gregory continues to pun, twisting their political designation, *Deiri*, into *de ira*, the wrath of God, from which they should be snatched, and the name of their king, Ælle, into *Alleluia*. Scholars have debated whether Bede believed the story, to what extent it represents a conception of an English race or only the Anglian people, the erotic implications of Gregory's gaze and the boys' beauty, and Bede's position as a postcolonial subject.[59] Moreover, Gregory's repeated play on English names, deceptively intelligible to the modern reader as a groan-inducing predilection for paronomasia, is really the expression of a grammatical mentality, one in which etymology is a key to truth.[60] As David Townsend points out, Gregory's puns can also be interpreted as 'wrenching the vernacular language away from its autonomous use by the English themselves, as imposing Latin upon it as the bearer of all spiritually authentic meaning', though they can also be read as signs of a 'hybrid culture' born in the interplay between English and Latin.[61] However we read the colonial dynamics of the scene, it remains the case that Gregory speaks and the slave boys are silent.

Bede found the anecdote in the early eighth-century Whitby *Life of Gregory the Great*, and his changes to the source material serve the larger rhetoric of the *History*.[62] The Whitby *Life* contains surprising variations on the story: the Angles are described not as slaves but simply as people who have arrived in Rome, and they answer Gregory's questions themselves instead of remaining speechless.[63] Bede, on the other hand, enslaves his Angles and takes away their power of speaking. In the context of book 2, Bede's version of the tale makes the Angles into 'simple objects of scrutiny',[64] but this is only the beginning of an English colonial relation to Rome, not the entire story. Bede's Angles are heathen, mute, and enslaved, passively explained by the grammar of a powerful and prestigious foreign language. They are located at the imagined origin of the English church, when English salvation is still a twinkle in Gregory's eye. By book 5 of the *History*, a Northumbrian bishop can free an English youth from the captivity of his muteness using the gestural vocabulary of baptism and the grammatical structure of Latin.

The subtle link between slave boys and mute youth, bookends to the story of English Christianity, is supported by a curious textual variance between the Whitby and Bedan versions of the marketplace anecdote. The appearance and age of the Angles are ambiguous in the Whitby *Life*. It first describes the boys as being 'forma et crinibus candidati albis' (fair-skinned and light-haired), and a little later it acknowledges different accounts in the oral tradition on which it claims to draw: 'Quos quidam pulchros fuisse pueros dicunt et quidam vero crispos iuvenes et decoros' (Now some say they were beautiful boys, while others say they were curly-haired, handsome youths).[65] Bede compresses and generally clarifies the account, describing the Angles as 'pueros uenales positos candidi corporis ac uenusti uultus, capillorum quoque forma egregia' (132–33, some boys put up for sale, with fair complexions, handsome faces, and lovely hair). He maintains the idea that the boys are white, *candidi*, with that word's rich connotations of angelic purity, not to mention the possible suggestion that the boys should be candidates – that is, religious novices.[66] While the Whitby *Life* offers an ambiguous account of the Angles' age, Bede represents them clearly as boys, *pueros*, even if his Gregory later expands the importance of his missionary comments to all the Angles by calling the boys *homines*.[67] In one detail, however, Bede is more vague than the Whitby monk: instead of the precision of 'curly-haired', Bede describes the boys as having a 'capillorum forma egregia', which Colgrave translates as 'lovely hair' but Stephen Harris reads as an unusual tribal hairstyle.[68] Finally, Bede uses a form of *venustus* instead of the Whitby *Life*'s *pulcher* to describe the boys' beauty, a decision Harris considers slightly feminising and indicative of physical loveliness; *pulcher*, used by Bede elsewhere in the *History* to describe angelic messengers, indicates a perfected, idealised beauty.[69]

These small differences between the narratives can be and have been explained as the result of competing oral traditions on which Bede and the Whitby monk draw. And yet the curly-haired, good-looking youth, the *pulcher crispus iuvenis* who is at least a potential in the Whitby *Life* and who in that text is free and capable of speaking, does appear in Bede's *History*. He simply appears much later. John of Beverley's patient is first called an *adulescens mutus* and *pauperem*; after John and the physician have treated him, he is made 'iuuenis limpidus uultu et loquella promtus, capillis pulcherrime crispis' (458–59, a young man with 'clear complexion, ready speech, and beautiful curly hair'). By presenting a more vulnerable vision of the Angles than the Whitby *Life* does, one in which they are very young, enslaved, and incapable of speaking for themselves, Bede seems to reinforce their inferior position as potential colonial subjects. And, in a sense, he does, but only for that point in English history (AD 574–78). In narrating events of the late seventh century, Bede offers his readers a miracle that dramatises the powerful change in English subjecthood: an English adolescent learns to speak his own language, becoming figuratively liberated. His appearance changes too, making him look like the curly-haired youths of the Whitby *Life*. But while the Whitby monk recognises a potential English – or at least Angle – autonomy even before conversion, Bede understands that autonomy to be the result of a longer historical and spiritual process, achieved by individual acts of teaching and baptism and gained through Christian learning, not despite it.

Bede's description of the John of Beverley miracle presents two surprises for the reader expecting a story with clear biblical allusions and incorporation of the magically healed speaker into the fold of the church. As one might expect of an exegetical scholar, Bede compares the youth's healing with a biblical precedent, but not, surprisingly, with Mark 7:32–37.[70] Instead, he compares the boy with the lame man healed in Acts 3:2–10, 'qui curatus ab apostolis Petro et Iohanne exiliens stetit et ambulabat, et intrauit cum illis in Templum' (458–59, who, when healed by the Apostles Peter and John, stood up, leapt and walked, entering the Temple with them). Furthermore, at the end of the chapter, after tongue and scalp are healed, Bede mentions that the youth returned home, refusing John of Beverley's offer of a place in his episcopal *familia*, or household. John seems to have been responsible for the education of a number of young men, including clergy members and lay nobles,[71] and the offer may have implied further tutelage. Despite the speech miracle's powerful imagery of integration into a sacred Christian community and into a teaching relationship permeated by Latin learning, the young man returns to secular society and is, apparently, content with his acquisition of spoken language. His decision contrasts with Cædmon's progression from the hall to the monastery. Indeed, if, as Lerer has argued, the stories of Imma and Cædmon 'argue for the institutional authority of the Roman Church and its rites',[72] the formerly mute youth's refusal to enter John's household both belies the baptismal connotations of his miraculous healing and reverses a trend evident elsewhere in the *History*.

I suggest that Bede cites Acts precisely because he must account for a historical fact that does not fit the general trend of his history. In his commentary on Acts, Bede interprets the formerly lame man's entry into the temple as a step through the gate of the heavenly kingdom, 'regni ianuam'.[73] By comparing the mute adolescent's outburst of language with this passage, Bede can allusively inscribe the young man into the structure of the church despite his unwillingness to join it formally. Indeed, the reference does double duty: by directing Bede's reader to a passage immediately following the description of Pentecost in Acts 2, it recalls the healing of the linguistic rupture at Babel. Moreover, in his commentary on Acts

2:2 Bede is careful to note that the sensible aspects of Pentecost, the fire and sound, are only exterior signs of the Lord's internal process of teaching.[74] This is appropriate, according to Bede, because the Holy Spirit first gave human beings the gift of language, through which wisdom is taught and learned.[75] In this reading, the pan-linguistic, grammatical aspects of John of Beverley's miracle reflect the Pentecostal unity of all tongues and are linked to the evangelising agenda of Acts.

Still, it is notable that Bede chooses to relate the young man's refusal in the first place, that he finishes the chapter with the words 'magis domum reuersus est' (he preferred to go home; my trans.). His inclusion of this detail underscores the idea, already present in the miracle of Imma, that the rhetoric of Christian liberation can even include a return to secular society. Read as a figure complementing the heathen Angles on sale in a foreign land, the young man embodies a more general return 'home': the products of pedagogy are brought back to an English village, while the practices of Latinate literacy are opened up to the spoken vernacular. This homecoming enacts the potential implicit in his speech therapy and in the young man's powerful expression of his interior thoughts and desires. This formerly mute youth, who learns his native tongue like a second language, demonstrates the way linguistic ability differs from Christian rite: once acquired, it can be put to any use. By stretching the structure of Latin grammatical learning to encompass the English tongue, he offers a fresh model for English participation in the Roman church, one that exploits its intellectual resources to conceive a spiritual emancipation that is both singularly English and deeply individual. While the youth's healing begins with a yes – that is, with assent to the authority of Christian teaching – by the end of his story he has also learned to say no.

CHAPTER 2

Prayer
Solomon and Saturn I

Regard his hellish fall,
Whose fiendful fortune may exhort the wise
Only to wonder at unlawful things,
Whose deepness doth entice such forward wits,
To practice more than heavenly power permits.

Christopher Marlowe, *Doctor Faustus*[1]

Although we might expect most Anglo-Saxon scenes of instruction to be focused on the teaching of children, the opposite is the case. Aside from the Latin colloquies discussed in the next chapter, most depictions of education centre on older figures. They portray the frustration, yearning, and relative powerlessness that characterise being a student, even when that student happens to be a king, apostle, or venerable monk. Anglo-Saxon texts reveal learning to be a lifelong discipline, one in which the struggle to learn is suffused with the tumultuous emotions of youth. One literary strategy some texts use to bring to mind a feeling of childlike insufficiency is to describe the process of acquiring a particular competence as being like learning to read. The ABCs remind the reader of a text – if not necessarily potential listeners – of what it was like to attain this specialised skill, either as children or as adults. They serve as imaginative shorthand for the struggle of learning in all its affective fullness.

The Old English poem *Solomon and Saturn I* uses the building blocks of literacy to draw its reader into a drama of knowing and unknowing. The poem transforms one of the fundamental texts of the Christian faith, the Lord's Prayer, into a ciphered alphabet with accompanying runic charm. For a literate Anglo-Saxon reading *Solomon and Saturn I*, both the Pater Noster and the play on its individual letters would have recalled elementary grammatical education, the thrilling first steps of learning how to read and how to be a Christian. However, this prayer – memorised, recited daily, sometimes automatically – would also have presented the problem of overfamiliarity. How can the Christian pray with feeling and concentration if the words have become rote? *Solomon and Saturn I* uses mimetic desire to solve this problem. It invites its reader to identify with Saturn, a curious prince who desperately wants to learn the Pater Noster but cannot. In doing so, the poem teaches its reader to desire a prayer he already knows. *Solomon and Saturn I* thus stages a deliberately incomplete and unsuccessful scene of instruction because its real lesson is one of absence and longing. Quotidian prayer is made magical and out of reach; old knowledge feels fresh again.

I argue in this chapter that *Solomon and Saturn I* teaches its reader how to desire the Pater Noster through graphic and violent defamiliarisation of the prayer. My choice of the word 'reader' is deliberate throughout. Katherine O'Brien O'Keeffe has argued that the poem represents a 'synthesis of oral and literate understanding', one in which the prayer's powers are inherent in its written letters, but released by the person who speaks it.[2] However, when recited, the text of the poem as it survives in one of its manuscripts quietly distinguishes between orality and literacy. The individual facing the open pages of CCCC 422 and reading aloud for an audience or for private edification or enjoyment would have been reminded by the silent runes in that version of the poem that something before him eluded speech. *Solomon and Saturn I* as it appears in CCCC 422 evokes a readerly consciousness, it affirms the privileged position of a literate person, and it does so at the precise instant when the text of the Lord's Prayer appears. *Solomon and Saturn I* not only constructs its own reader as a reader, but it implies the existence of multiple audiences with varying levels of access to the veiled message of the poem. Indeed, despite my insistence here and throughout this chapter that the poem is intensely concerned with literacy, education, and the Pater Noster's relationship to both, it is more accurate to say that *Solomon and Saturn I* is most interested in tracing different ways of knowing and of being ignorant.

Solomon and Saturn I exploits the polyvalent associations of the Lord's Prayer to reflect on the problem of knowledge. The Pater Noster was often bound up with issues of ignorance and lay superstition, and indeed, the last section of the poem depicts the Lord's Prayer as a protective charm or chant, efficacious against the demons who hurt cattle and paralyse the arms of warriors in battle.[3] Still, knowing the prayer too well could be just as troubling as not knowing it at all. For an educated reader, it would have been a text so familiar as to become rote. The Pater Noster thus raises the problem of attention and distraction, the difficulty of praying with full affective engagement, the task of finding overwhelming power in an ordinary text. This is why *Solomon and Saturn I*'s attention to multiple audiences and to the privileged position of a reader is key to its interpretation: the reader's awareness of what he has gained through education can lead him to what he has lost. The reader must imagine what it would mean not to know this most basic prayer in order to truly possess it again. To achieve this end, the poem exploits the Pater Noster's associations with primary learning to remind the reader of his or her own first encounter with the prayer, with the feeling of being a child in pedagogical terms.

Solomon and Saturn I creates desire by encouraging its reader to identify with Saturn, a pagan who has travelled far to understand the prayer's power. Saturn's eagerness for the prayer is emotionally vivid and painful, but the poem suggests that he, like the devil, would be destroyed by the Pater Noster if he were to encounter it. His desperate longing is for an untouchable text, one that could prove deadly to him. To tear an observation by Slavoj Žižek from its psychoanalytic context, 'knowledge is marked by a lethal dimension: the subject must pay for the approach to it with his own being'.[4] This danger to his being, the implication that Saturn will not only be the active possessor or learner of the Pater Noster but also the passive victim of its brutal power, echoes the lethal nature of knowledge and learning in many scenes of instruction discussed in this book, taking place as they do on the raw edges of death or destruction. They suggest an ambiguity in the Anglo-Saxon perspective on wisdom, at once valuing it and recognising its perils. In what follows, I trace the tense steps of Saturn's, and the reader's, education.

Solomon and Saturn I

Solomon and Saturn I begins with Saturn's complaint. This wandering scholar has studied – or in his words, 'onbyrged' (2, tasted) – the books of India, Libya, and Greece, but has not learned the truth about the powers of the Pater Noster.[5] He offers Solomon thirty pounds and his twelve sons if Solomon can satisfy his desire for knowledge. Rather bitingly, given that Saturn is such a willing student, Solomon replies that anyone who does not know the prayer is like dumb, wandering cattle, and vile in the eyes of the Lord. He then catalogues its many powers, including the ability to heat the devil's blood. Saturn, in turn, describes how his curiosity makes him suffer, like a burning rising near his heart. Solomon goes on to explain how the prayer fights evil when someone sings it. Each letter of the Pater Noster enters a duel with the devil, inflicting varying amounts of brutality: Τ, for example, 'hine teswað ond hine on ða tungan sticað,/ wræsteð

him ðæt woddor ond him ða wongan brieceð' (94–95, injures him and
stabs his tongue, twists his throat, and smashes his cheeks). S, in an action
inspired by Prudentius' *Psychomachia*, inflicts even more cinematic injury:[6]

> wraðne gegripeð
> feond be ðam fotum,   læteð foreweard hleor
> on strangne stan,   stregdað toðas
> geond helle heap   (112b–15)

> … grasps the angry fiend by the feet, dashes his cheek forward onto
> a strong stone, and strews his teeth throughout the host of hell.

Not only is the Pater Noster split up into individual letters, but the text
of the prayer in CCCC 422 is encoded, albeit with errors. The principle
behind the code is that no single letter is given twice, so after the letters of
the prayer's first word in Latin, *pater*, only *N*, *O*, and *S* from *noster* should
appear, *Q*, *U*, *I*, from *qui*, *C*, *L* from *es in caelis*, and so on. (In practice, the
letters *O*, *I*, and *B*, are missing, while the pairs *L* and *C*, *G* and *D*, appear in
the wrong order.) There is also a graphic component to the battle. CCCC
41 only features the first three letters of the prayer, in which the Roman
letters stand alone. In CCCC 422, however, most of the Roman letters
are preceded by their runic equivalents. These runes are extraneous to the
verse, which describes the shapes of *C* and *G* as *geap* or 'curved' (a description not suited to their accompanying runes), and which sometimes relies
on the pronunciation of Roman letters for its alliteration.

The song thus blends, as O'Brien O'Keeffe notes, orality and literacy.
To harness its power, one must sing it truly (85a, *singan soðlice*), but the
Roman letters are arranged according to a graphic word game and the
silent runes can only be appreciated by a reader of the manuscript page.
At the same time, the individual letters are anthropomorphised just like
the Pater Noster itself. Unlike the 'dead letter' usually opposed to 'living'
oral literature, these written letters come alive in the act of speaking, since
the act of speaking and the act of writing the Pater Noster are fused in the
poem. And still, despite Solomon's detailed treatment of the Lord's Prayer,
both in the description of its powers and the characterisation of its component letters, there is no indication that Saturn is satisfied, nor, indeed, that
he even knows how to recite the text.

As this description of the poem suggests, *Solomon and Saturn I* embodies
the most marginal, esoteric qualities of Old English literature. Its first
ninety-five lines do so literally, scribbled as they are in the margins of
Bede's *Ecclesiastical History* in CCCC 41.[7] A nearly full copy of the poem is
found at the beginning of CCCC 422, in which the first page, about thirty

lines' worth, was pasted to the cover and later treated with gall, and is now unreadable.[8] Just as its manuscript transmission reflects the fragmentary and ephemeral nature of the Old English corpus, the text of the poem presents, in a nutshell, many of the interpretative problems that bedevil scholars of Anglo-Saxon literature. Faced with this unusual dialogue about the powers of the Lord's Prayer between Solomon and Saturn, the poem's early critics were dismissive, referring to its 'fantastic superstition and childish literalism', calling it 'rather insipid', and claiming that its treatment of the prayer 'would seem to require wisdom even greater than Solomon's to understand'.[9] More recently, O'Brien O'Keeffe, Charles D. Wright, Patrick O'Neill, and Daniel Anlezark, among others, have worked to translate the poem into a new register, raising it from its former place among the superstitious charm-lore of folk Anglo-Saxons into a network of rarified allusions to Latin patristic, apocryphal, and philosophic writing, as well as to Irish liturgical and paraliturgical texts.[10] Still, critics have tended to shy away from a reading of the poem as a work of literature. Just as *Solomon and Saturn I* dramatises the violent dismemberment of the Lord's Prayer, its own enigmatic content and indeterminate structure invite erudite readers to put it, as it were, out of joint. And yet, as with the Pater Noster itself, the meaning is in the text as a whole, not in its individual letters.

The Pater Noster and Knowledge

A particular metaphor in *Solomon and Saturn I* hints at how the Pater Noster could embody both basic and advanced Christian wisdom. In one of his more subdued moments, Solomon calls the Lord's Prayer 'sefan snytera and sawle hunig/ and modes mealc' (CCCC 41, 66–67a, the mind's wisdom and the soul's honey, and the spirit's milk), evoking both the prayer's spiritual nourishment and its intellectual centrality for Christians. Milk and honey suggest the abundance of the Promised Land in Exodus 3:8 and repeatedly throughout the Bible. It is an apt allusion for a prayer that comforts but is rich in meaning. Milk also recalls Paul's description of easier teaching, 'lac vobis potum dedi non escam' (I gave you milk to drink, not solid food) in 1 Corinthians 3:2, a figure for palatable doctrine taken up by Bede in his own writings. This easier learning is the 'lac doctrinae mollioris', the 'milk of simpler teaching' Bishop Aidan recommends for those new to the faith and unready for solid spiritual food in Bede's *Ecclesiastical History*.[11] In his commentary on the Song of Songs, Bede repeatedly returns to the idea of graded pedagogy, comparing the teachers of the church to the breasts of the bride, which provide spiritual infants with milk.¹² Honey, in turn, signifies 'the fecundity of the holy scriptures'.¹³ Glossing Proverbs 25:27, 'sicut qui mel multum comedit non est ei bonum sic qui scrutator est maiestatis opprimitur gloria' (as it is not good for a man to eat much honey, so he that is a searcher of majesty shall be overwhelmed by glory), Bede explains that the line does not prohibit seeking God's majesty, but warns against probing into matters that exceed our understanding. The bride of Christ thus 'has honey and milk under her tongue when she knows rightly how to discern what things must be said to beginners, what things to those making progress, and what things to those who are perfect in the knowledge and love of [God]'.¹⁴ Solomon's characterisation of the Pater Noster as intellectual soul food is in line with its position as a key text of Christian education for both children and adults, for those who are infants in the faith and those who have grown into the heady taste of honey.

The Pater Noster appears twice in the Bible, in Luke 11:2–4 and Matthew 6:9–13. It is the only prayer Jesus taught to his disciples, and early on it became essential knowledge for a Christian. One of its most important uses was in the instruction of adult converts to Christianity. Those who sought baptism were taught the Creed and the Lord's Prayer, which they later had to recite from memory. In antiquity, these prayers were treated as secrets or mysteries of the faith: taught late in the process of candidacy, their full recitation was avoided in the presence of unbaptised persons. As Josef Jungmann stresses, 'The sacred words of both of these set texts were not permitted to be written out. The candidate should only write them on the tablets of the heart. They should rest in his memory as a secure, precious treasure.'¹⁵ Heretics, unbelievers, or other catechumens were to be kept from learning the cherished prayers.¹⁶ It is possible that from the time of Paul, the first prayer to be spoken by the newly baptised in communion with the congregation of their fellow Christians was the Pater Noster.¹⁷ This ancient sense of the Pater Noster as a gateway to the faith, one too precious for Saturn's eyes, has reverberations in *Solomon and Saturn I*.

In contrast to the secrecy surrounding the Pater Noster and Credo in early practice, as Christianity spread and child baptism became common the greater problem became ignorance among Christians of the faith's basic tenets. Repeated insistence that these two prayers had to be known is a sign that, in fact, many early medieval Christians did not know them. For example, Charlemagne once questioned a few prospective godparents on their knowledge of the Creed and Lord's Prayer; when he found they were ignorant of the texts he prevented them from becoming godparents until they had learned the prayers. Charlemagne's bishop Gerbald responded to this by calling upon his priests to be more diligent in their teaching of the prayers.[18] The concern was just as pressing in England. In his letter to Ecgbert, Bede writes of the need to teach the faith first through the Creed and Lord's Prayer, and in the vernacular when priests and laymen are ignorant of Latin.[19] More than two centuries later, Ælfric and Wulfstan underscore the importance of these prayers in their sermons, and each translates the Pater Noster into Old English prose.[20] For Wulfstan, it and the Creed are prayers 'þæt ælc cristen man huru cunnan sceal' (that each Christian man certainly should know), adding that 'Crist sylf sang pater noster ærest 7 þæt gebedd his leorningcnihtum tæhte' (Christ himself first sang the Pater Noster, and taught that prayer to his disciples), thus highlighting its pedagogic function.[21]

The Lord's Prayer is also closely linked to a specific area of education: learning to read. Examples abound of primers from the medieval period up to the nineteenth century using the Creed and Pater Noster as the very first texts to be learned by a beginning reader.[22] After learning the alphabet, and often syllables in a variety of combinations, the student would learn to read the Pater Noster. Although no such abecedaries survive from the Anglo-Saxon period, there are copies of alphabets in tenth- and eleventh-century books; one, written in the margins of Alcuin's *Letters*, has the alphabet from *a* to *z*, followed by signs for 'and' in Latin and English, the Anglo-Saxon letters *wynn, thorn, aesc, eth*, and the words 'pater noster qui es in celis sanctificetur nomen tuum adveniat reg'.[23] The text of the Lord's Prayer contained, for many a student, the first meaningful words he or she would read, and in this sense the *written* Pater Noster can be considered to stand at the beginning of literacy, along with the alphabet, the Creed, and the Psalms.[24]

Solomon recognises this special relationship of the Pater Noster to literacy when he describes it as 'deafra duru, dumbra tunge' (CCCC 422, 78, door of the deaf, tongue of the dumb). This seems at first to be a simple description of the Pater Noster's charm-like healing power; in the previous line, the prayer was described in similarly medicinal terms: 'lamena he is læce, leoht wincendra' (CCCC 422, 77, leech of the lame and the light of the blinking). Taken out of this miraculous context, however, line 78 also functions as a laconic riddle, the answer to which is writing. The Lord's Prayer teaches reading and writing, which enables the mute and the deaf to communicate in language. The line echoes a list of God's virtues in Vercelli Homily IV, 'Þu eart … dumra gesprec 7 deafra gehyrnes' (You are … the speech of the dumb, and the hearing of the deaf),[25] but Solomon's presentation of the Pater Noster as a kind of door or gate reinforces the liminal importance of the prayer, standing as it does at the entry to both Christianity and literacy. This brief enigma inserted in *Solomon and Saturn I* reminds us of the prayer's role as one of the first, most basic steps of learning to read.

Due to its status as an elementary text of the faith, the Pater Noster is also intimately bound up with the problem of ignorance, and this ignorance takes many forms. There is the problem of not knowing or forgetting the text, in Latin or in the vernacular; there is the problem of not knowing the meaning of the words, in Latin or in the vernacular; and there is the problem of not knowing the importance of praying with the right mindset, which leads to absent-mindedness and distraction. Pater Noster literature in Middle and Early Modern English responds to or parodically replicates concerns about ignorance, forgetfulness, and mental absence.[26] In the late fifteenth-century poem 'How the Plowman Learned his Paternoster', an ignorant farmer is tricked by a priest into memorising the prayer as he gives his bushels of corn to poor folk, each of whom is named after a word or section of the prayer.[27] In the mid-sixteenth-century poem 'The Proude Wyve's Pater Noster', a woman sitting in church is constantly distracted from her recitation of the Lord's Prayer by her desire for clothing as lovely as other women's:

> Adueniat regnu*m* tuu*m*, thy kingdom come to us
> After this lyfe when we hens shall wende
> But whyle we be here now swete Jesus
> As other woman haue suche grace in me sende   (49–52)[28]

Both of these poems 'teach' the text of the prayer just as they comically dramatise the problem of forgetting it, or of not understanding its true meaning.

The fact that the Pater Noster was used daily, in contexts sacred and otherwise, generated a wide variety of parodic treatments in European literature of the middle ages. These generally operate by dismembering the text of the prayer and emptying its component elements of their usual meaning, or even by using the very name 'paternoster' as a stand-in for an opposing idea. Examples of these include the macaronic Old French poems on wine, women, and usury collected by Jean Subrenat, in which the prayer's phrases and words are decontextualised and surrounded by vernacular 'commentary', and even, as Jan Ziolkowski has argued, the use of Pater Noster or the idea of praying it as a synonym for sexual intercourse.[29] While *Solomon and Saturn I*'s treatment of the Lord's Prayer is hardly humorous, it does participate in a long tradition of texts that capitalise on the prayer's familiarity by taking it apart and scrambling it to the point of incomprehensibility. The poem's dismantling of the text, like the Pater Noster itself, is polyvalent: it stands for ignorance, insofar as it indicates misunderstanding of the Latin or wandering of the mind, and it stands for learning, since it can also be used for a process of translation or memorisation. *Solomon and Saturn I* encompasses both of these extremes.

Absent-mindedness during prayer, a problem of both intellect and affect, is recurrently addressed in devotional writing of the early middle ages. The ideal practice of prayer is succinctly described by Augustine in his *Rule*: 'Psalmis et hymnis cum oratis Deum, hoc uersetur in corde quod profertur in voce' (When you pray to God with psalms and hymns, ponder in the heart what you speak with the voice).[30] Indeed, *Solomon and Saturn I*'s description of the Lord's Prayer as 'sawle hunig' (CCCC 41, 66b, honey of the soul) supports a connection to the practice of attentive prayer. Charles Wright compares the honeyed metaphor to Sedulius Scottus' praise of the Pater Noster: 'Fauus est mellis et est odor suauitatis coram Altissimo, si pura conscientia atque sollerti intensione decantetur' (It is a honeycomb of honey and it is the odour of sweetness in the presence of the Highest, if it is chanted with pure conscience and skilled attention).[31] Sedulius implicitly acknowledges that the Lord's Prayer is sometimes sung inattentively, and he insists that its sacred, sensuous qualities are available only to those who pray properly. Wright translates 'sollerti intensione' as 'careful attention', but the primary denotation of *sollers* as 'skilful, clever, expert' indicates that concentration is not a matter of the will alone: it is the result of practised meditative techniques.[32] Some of these, as I will argue later, are evident in *Solomon and Saturn I*, a poem simultaneously interested in the most basic and most advanced approaches to the Pater Noster.

Saturn's Desire

Solomon and Saturn I teaches the Pater Noster in a dialogue that is eristic, but quietly so. In contrast to *Solomon and Saturn II*, which begins by describing the encounter of these two figures as a battle of wits between roughly equal 'modgleawe men' (2, men wise in spirit), antagonism is threaded subtly through Solomon and Saturn's exchange in the first dialogue. It is the result of several factors: the complicated, sometimes dark, associations introduced by calling the interlocutors 'Saturn' and 'Solomon', an implicit recognition that Solomon's possession of knowledge deeply desired by Saturn constitutes an advantage in power, and the characters' own words. Robert Menner argues that the character of Saturn, along with his replacement in other medieval Solomonic dialogues, Marcolf/Morolf, maintains some traits reminiscent of the Hebrew, Arabic, and Greek legends of Solomon in which the king subdues various demons.[33] While it is difficult to find direct influence of this legacy on *Solomon and Saturn I*, Saturn himself introduces an element of pagan danger into the proceedings when he offers Solomon his twelve sons, reminding us uncomfortably of the ease with which the classical Saturn disposed of his own children. As Ælfric puts it in his euhemeristic work *De falsis diis*, Saturn was a Cretan man who bit his sons to pieces 'and unfæderlice macode heora flæsc him to mete' (in an unfatherly way made a meal out of their flesh).[34] Moreover, this pedagogical encounter between Solomon and Saturn is reminiscent of the meetings between eremites and demons in late antique writings. One of the disguises favoured by demons was the figure of a pagan god, and aside from beating or sexually tantalising their victim monks, demons also tempted them by discussing theological questions.[35] Although Solomon does not seem susceptible to temptation in this poem, the character of Solomon was ambiguous throughout the middle ages. As Mishtooni Bose has shown, he was at once a figure of wisdom, the author of Ecclesiastes, Proverbs, and the Song of Songs, and infamously uxorious, a friend of the Queen of Sheba, worshipping pagan gods under the influence of his wives. Bede and Rabanus Maurus thought that Solomon had not, indeed, been pardoned by God for his idolatry. It was precisely this dubious and enigmatic stature, according to Bose, that made Solomon such a suggestive literary figure,[36] standing at once for wisdom and unbridled desire.

In other words, while the dialogue is, on the surface, a teaching moment between two wise men, its undercurrents are pagan idolatry, temptation, aggression, devilish curiosity, and demonic desire. Katherine O'Brien O'Keeffe reads the poem as 'the verbal encoding of struggle, even violence'.[37] At the poem's start, Saturn offers his sons to Solomon 'gif þu mec gebringest þæt ic si gebrydded/ ðurh þæs cantices cwyde' (16–17a, if you cause me to be terrified through the saying of this canticle). While the *hapax legomenon gebrydded* has been variously glossed as 'terrified', 'overawed', or 'inspired', O'Brien O'Keeffe supports a more violent gloss of the verb, maintaining that Saturn's desire is to experience the fierce power of the Pater Noster.[38] Her Saturn is 'a learned man', a 'Chaldean prince'[39] who is nevertheless kept at arm's length from the text of the prayer throughout the poem.

The suggestion of fear in *gebrydded* is appropriate in several respects. It fits a reading of *Solomon and Saturn I* as a poem of sophisticated teaching that recalls the emotional environment of the basic classroom. The topos of fear as a teaching device also appears in the question and answer dialogue *Adrian and Ritheus*, a cousin text of *Solomon and Saturn I*. This work belongs to the *Joca monachorum* genre of intellectual trivia, and its material overlaps with the *Collectanea Pseudo-Bedae* and the *Prose Solomon and Saturn*. One exchange reads:

> Saga me feower stafas dumbe.
> Ic þe secge, an is mod, oðer geþanc, þridde is stef, feorðe is ægesa.[40]

> Tell me what are four mute letters.
> I tell you, one is spirit, the second is thought, the third is writing,
>   the fourth is fear.

In their note to this passage, James Cross and Thomas Hill claim that this is an 'incoherent' and 'corrupt' version of a maxim like the following, found in the *Collectanea Pseudo-Bedae*:

> Quae sunt tria muta, quae docent sapientiam in corde hominis?
> Est mens, oculus et littera.[41]

> What are three mute things that teach wisdom in the heart of man?
> They are the mind, eye, and letter.

The Latin version is focused on the process by which written knowledge enters and is processed in the mind, while the Old English version of the aphorism adds the affective component of fear into the process of teaching. The idea that spirit, thought, and fear are to be thought of as 'letters' implies that cognition itself, with its emotional and intellectual processes, is textual. In this light, Saturn's desire to be 'terrified' by the Pater Noster is consistent with a theory of learning in which fear, reading, and teaching are intimately knotted.

Gebrydded is fitting for another reason as well. If Saturn maintains some of his demonic associations, his desire to know and to experience the devil-whipping Pater Noster could result in a truly terrifying experience. In short, Saturn's curiosity is for a prayer which could destroy him. Curiosity will recur in chapter 5, and there too it is ambivalent. Insofar as curiosity represents attentive and careful striving toward religious knowledge, what comes to be known in later medieval writing as *sollicitudo* or *religiosa curiositate*, it is positive.[42] However, it is also a force that militates against devotion: it either distracts the mind or draws it to reach beyond its proper sphere of knowledge. Cassian recognises the role curiosity plays in distracting from prayer in particular when he describes the monk's mind moving associatively from one text to another:

Cum enim capitulum cuiuslibet psalmi mens nostra conceperit, insensibi-
liter eo subtracto ad alterius scripturae textum nesciens stupensque *deuolui-*
tur. cumque illud in semet ipsa coeperit uolutare, necdum illo ad integrum
uentilato oborta alterius testimonii memoria meditationem materiae prioris
excludit. de hac quoque ad alteram subintrante alia meditatione *transfertur,*
et ita animus semper de psalmo *rotatus* ad psalmum, de euangelii textu
ad apostoli transiliens lectionem, de hac quoque ad prophetica *deuolutus*
eloquia et exinde ad quasdam spiritales *delatus* historias per omne scriptur-
arum corpus instabilis uagusque *iactatur,* nihil pro arbitrio suo praeualens
uel abicere uel tenere nec pleno quicquam iudicio et examinatione finire,
palpator tantummodo spiritalium sensuum ac degustator, non generator
nec possessor *effectus.*[43]

When our mind has understood a passage in any psalm, this imperceptibly
escapes it, and the mind, ignorant and confused, spins off to another text of
Scripture. And when it has begun to mull over that one within itself, before
it has tossed it around thoroughly, the memory of another witness springs
up and prevents the contemplation of the previous matter. Again it moves
from this thought to another when another contemplation comes to mind,
and so the soul ever rolls from psalm to psalm, skips from the Gospels to the
Epistles, tumbles from these too to the prophets, and after that it is carried
away to certain spiritual stories, and tossed, roving and unstable, throughout the entire body of Scripture. It is not able either to abandon or hold on
to anything by its own choice, nor can it finish anything by judging and
examining it fully. It becomes a mere toucher and taster of spiritual meaning, not its producer or possessor.

The curious mind's aimless trip through Scripture is not so different from
the associative reminiscence and composition typical of monastic culture,
in which a word or image recalls a similar but unconnected passage of the
well-digested scriptural text.[44] The difference is one of control: this wayward mind does not move by its own choice, 'pro arbitrio suo', and the
high proportion of passive verb forms (italicised above) indicates the extent
to which it is led about by curiosity. Finally, in a detail that will seem felici-
tous to any intellectual working on a long project, Cassian specifies that
the over-curious mind cannot bring its meditative process to completion.

This endless openness and hunger of curiosity typifies Saturn as well.
He seems to have wandered in the physical sense, and certainly has erred
through ancient Libyan, Greek, and Indian wisdom. He claims to have
tasted their books, 'boca onbyrged' (3), a locution whose monastic implications are often ignored. I will argue later that it is meant to recall the process of rumination, but wish to note here its additional echo of Cassian's
superficial 'tasting' mind. Patrick O'Neill has noted that curiosity characterises Saturn in both of the poetic dialogues, and that his Chaldean

background reinforces this association.[45] The Chaldeans were associated with philosophy and science.[46] An interpolation in the Old English translation of Boethius has the Chaldeans building the tower of Babel because 'hi woldon witon hu heah hit wære to þam hefone and hu þicke se hefon wære and hu fæst, oððe hwæt þær ofer wære' (they wanted to know how high it was to heaven and how thick heaven was and how firm, or what was over it).[47] In this passage, the Chaldeans represent an overweening, self-destructive desire to understand heavenly mysteries, making them an appropriate people for the dangerously curious Saturn.

It may seem odd to describe Saturn as curious for a terrifying or hazardous prayer, but an essential attribute of curiosity is that it need not be directed toward pleasant objects. In his *Confessions*, Augustine holds that curiosity, the 'concupiscentia oculorum' (lust of the eyes), is what leads men to the theatre, excessive scrutiny of nature's secrets, magical arts, and the search for signs and prodigies. But curiosity differs from pleasure:

> voluptas pulchra, canora, suavia, sapida, lenia sectatur, curiositas autem etiam his contraria temptandi causa, non ad subeundam molestiam, sed experiendi noscendique libidine.[48]

> Pleasure pursues things that are beautiful, melodious, sweet, savory, easy. Curiosity, however, seeks even the opposites of these just to try them, not to undergo discomfort, but from the desire to experience and know.

It is one of the small ironies of *Solomon and Saturn I* that Saturn longs for an object that is beautiful, melodious, and sweet, and, at the same time, potentially dangerous to him. A suggestion of the prayer's violence can be found in the rhyming description of the Pater Noster at lines 50b–52 (CCCC 422):

> he gewritu læreð
> stefnum steoreð   ond him stede healdeð
> heofona rices,   heregeatewa wigeð.

> It teaches scripture, guides people and holds a place for them in the kingdom of heaven, carries war gear.

Here, the Pater Noster's role as a teacher of Scripture is joined to a more martial function; it not only opens the holy doors of heaven to people, but warrior-like guards a place for them in it. There is a faintly Mosaic tone to this passage, an impression supported by the resemblance of the *gyrde lange* (90, long rod) of the first letter, P, to Moses' *gyrdwite* (15, punishment inflicted by rod) that binds the Egyptians in the Old English *Exodus*.[49]

Solomon's description of the Lord's Prayer associates the idea of teaching with imperial imagery that is reassuring or frightening, depending on one's affiliation. It also hints at Solomon's own position as a formidable and terrifying teacher and at the fraught pedagogic relation that obtains throughout the poem.

Underneath Solomon's exposition of the Pater Noster is a dark hint that Saturn is not only the student but also part of the lesson. While Solomon's first response to Saturn seems to be no more than a description of the Pater Noster, and thus a tacit acquiescence to Saturn's desperate desire to know its powers, his speech contains subtle and antagonistic references to Saturn's lines.[50] Saturn's description of the books he has 'tasted' is followed by Solomon's observation that not knowing the Pater Noster is like being a field animal, a suggestion, perhaps, that Saturn has been masticating the wrong books. To Saturn's claim of having unlocked the sciences of Libya, Greece, and India, Solomon replies that he who cannot use the canticle to praise Christ is 'unlæde … on eorþan, unit lifes' (21, wretched on earth, useless in life). This slightly formulaic line nevertheless serves as a counterpoint to Saturn's claim of worldly and worldwide learning: Solomon expands the reach of the Pater Noster to the entire earth, and to all of life. When Saturn offers to pay tuition of '.xxx. punda/ smætes goldes' (14b–15a, thirty pounds of pure gold) besides his twelve sons, Solomon replies pointedly that,

> Þonne him bið leofre   ðonne eall þeos leohte gesceaft
> gegoten fram ðam grunde   goldes and silofres,
>
> feðerscette full   fyrngestreona,
> gif he æfre ðæs organes   owiht cuðe. (CCCC 41, 30–33)

> Therefore it would be dearer to him than all this bright creation, of gold and silver, poured out from the earth, the four cornered [world] full of ancient treasures, if he ever knew something of this song.

Finally, there is a sinister undertone in Solomon's response to the end of Saturn's first speech, in which Saturn promises to go, after his lesson, over the river Chebar to seek his people the Chaldeans. Solomon transforms Saturn's presentation of himself as a travelling scholar into a vision of a wanderer deprived of divine community:

> Fracað he bið þonne and fremde   frean almihtigum,
> englum *ungesibb*   ana *hwarfað*. (CCCC 41, 34–35)

> He is vile then and foreign to the almighty Lord, no kin to the angels, he wanders alone.

Stanley Greenfield identifies four components of conventional exilic imagery: status, deprivation, state of mind, and movement in or into exile. In this passage, the person who does not know the Pater Noster has his status described in terms of deprivation (i.e. he is a person defined by his separation from God and angels), and he moves alone in his exile, *hweorfan* being the typical word for this kind of wandering.[51] Solomon not only figures the person ignorant of the Pater Noster, by implication Saturn, as a typical exile, but as the most hopeless of exiles, a devil. In *Christ and Satan*, Satan insists on his own wide wandering (hweorfan ðy widor) and his separation from the angels (120–25, nænigne dream agan/ uppe mid englum).[52] Indeed, an even closer verbal parallel occurs in *Christ and Satan* when Satan commands the devils to go to earth:

> Sume sceolon *hweorfan*   geond hæleða land
> and *unsibbe*   oft onstyrian
> monna mægðum   geond middaneard.   (270–72)

> Some must wander through the land of men, and continually incite discord throughout the world among the tribes of men.

This passage suggests a reinterpretation of the lines in *Solomon and Saturn I* in which the person who cannot praise Christ through the Pater Noster is not only unrelated to the angels, but hostile to them, as another denotation of *ungesib* suggests.[53] Solomon's dark hints regarding the torments facing one who does not know the prayer may seem odd considering that Saturn has just offered a pretty penny to learn it. The demonic allusions in Solomon's speech, however, suggest he does so because Saturn is an exchange student with a devilish background.

There is a painful quality to Saturn's curiosity. He describes the urge to know and experience the Pater Noster in terms of physical suffering:

>   Mec ðæs on worolde full oft
> fyrwit frineð,   fus gewiteð,
> mod gemengeð.   Nænig manna wat,
> hæleða under hefenum,   hu min hige dreoseð
> bysig æfter bocum.   Hwilum me bryne *stigeð*,
> hige heortan neah   hædre *wealleð*.   (CCCC 422, 57b–62)

> Very often in the world curiosity asks me about this, eagerly reproaches, disturbs my mind. No man knows, none of the warriors under heaven, how my mind becomes weak, busy in the pursuit of books. Sometimes a burning rises in me, surges oppressively near my heart.

Saturn emphasises that his inquisitiveness acts upon him and muddles his mind (tropes already seen in Cassian), notes the way it separates him from men, and describes the experience of curiosity as a burning sensation near his heart and mind. His cardiocentric heat is typical of Anglo-Saxon vernacular descriptions of intense emotions. As Leslie Lockett explains, 'heat generates or is generated by distress (most often anger and grief) and sometimes by the experience of strong positive yearnings (intense love, longing for God, desire for wisdom or learning)'.[54] Lockett also notes here that the diversity of emotions felt as a seething, boiling heat in the chest cavity meant that Old English poets had to specify the precise nature of the emotion felt. Saturn's longing here is morally ambivalent, potentially demonic, but aimed towards the divine. *Fyrwit*, the word Saturn uses for his inquisitiveness, is primarily used in Old English for curiosity, and carries connotations both sacred and profane.[55] It is used in the sense of sexual lust in *Juliana*, in which Heliseus' passion for the saintly virgin is described as 'hine fyrwet bræc' (27b, desire tormented him).[56] But it also appears twice in the Durham Hymnal glossing Latin *ardor*, a spiritual passion or desire.[57] Durham, Cathedral Library, B. III. 32, also known as the Durham Hymnal, is an eleventh-century manuscript probably produced in Canterbury.[58] The manuscript contains a Latin hymnal and monastic canticles with Old English interlinear glosses as well as proverbs in Old English and Latin. It was bound with a copy of Ælfric's *Grammar* early after its production. As Inge Milfull has pointed out, the glosses, proverbs, and grammar suggest that the manuscript was used as a schoolbook.[59] In 'Ymnus ad tertiam', *ardor* is glossed as 'ferwyt' and 'bryne',[60] suggesting that Saturn's hot curiosity could also recall devotional poetry, and further, that the vocabulary of such longing was imprinted on novices early on in their education.

What is startling is that Saturn's lament also systematically echoes the imagery and wording of an earlier speech in which Solomon describes the Pater Noster's effect on the devil:

> Swylce ðu miht mid ðy beorhtan gebede   blod onhætan,
> ðæs deofles dros,   ðæt him dropan *stigað*
> swate geswiðed   seofan intigum,
> egesfullicran   ðonne seo ærene gripu,
> þonne heo for.xii. fira   tydernessum
> ofer gleda gripe   gifrust *wealleð*.   (CCCC 422, 43–48)

> In such manner you can, by means of the clear-sounding prayer, heat the blood, the devil's dross, so that the drops, strengthened with the

> blood, rise up in him near to the heart, more terribly than that brazen
> cauldron, when it most greedily surges over the grip of glowing coals for
> twelve generations of men.

This is a difficult passage to visualise, but it does seem that the Pater
Noster's power is to heat the devil's blood, so that it rises up close to the
sefa, that is, the mind, spirit, or heart. The parallel between this image of
hot blood rising up in the devil's heart (him dropan stigað) and Saturn's
burning sensation rising up near his heart (me bryne stigeð) is startling.[61]
Although it is not clear what the source or meaning of the bronze caul-
dron is,[62] the surging of its contents (gifrust wealleð), to which the devil's
blood is compared, echoes the surging of Saturn's burning curiosity (hædre
wealleð) both in lexical choice and in syntax. Saturn describes his desire
for the Pater Noster using the same images and words he has just heard
Solomon use to describe the devil's experience of the prayer. For a monastic reader, his longing would very likely have recalled spiritual passion,
as the liturgical glosses of the Durham Hymnal indicate, but in Saturn's
mouth this curiosity or desire is a dangerous one. He distinctly connects
his own pain with the devil's torment upon hearing the Lord's Prayer, a text
he might never truly know. Read in this light, the Pater Noster 'lesson' of
the fighting letters is a warning to Saturn about what the apotropaic text
might do to him if he should happen to be a demon. This idea is supported
by Solomon's description of the devil's retreat after being violently shaken
by the letter R:

> Huru him bið   æt heartan wa
> ðonne he hangiende   helle wisceð
> ðæs engestan   eðelrices. (104b–106)

> Surely he will have woe in his heart when, hanging, he longs for hell,
> the cruellest of homelands.

Here, Solomon bitingly revisits images linking Saturn to the devil, namely
the exile motif and the pain near the heart. This is the only moment in the
Pater Noster battle scene in which the devil's emotions are described, and
Solomon tellingly introduces them in order to mock Saturn's desire. 'If
your heart hurts now with longing,' he seems to be saying, 'when the Pater
Noster is sung, your only wish will be to go home.'

Saturn's desperate desire to know how to open the gates of heaven and
be cleansed of sorrows and crimes (55b–56a) may indeed be hopeless.
However, surprisingly enough, the text invites its reader to identify with
Saturn – and the devil's condition. I have noted a number of the themes

that characterise the devil, and often Saturn, in the poem: wandering, overvaluing worldly riches, undergoing physical punishment, and most notably, the powerful image of a strong passion described as cardiocentric heat. We have also seen how the devils are attacked in ways that deprive them of speech: the letter T stabs a devil's tongue, twists his throat, and shatters his jaw, while the letter S's breaking of a demon's cheek results in the laconic result: 'sceaða bið gebisigod,/ Satanes ðegn swiðe gestilled' (116b–17, the devil is overcome, Satan's thane is violently silenced). These images are also clustered in Psalm 38 (in the Septuagint numbering), in which the speaker describes his own silence in the face of the impious, expresses his passion as a warming of his heart and a burning inside him ('incaluit cor meum', 'my heart has grown hot', a phrase frequently quoted to describe a variety of passions), reflects on man's vain gathering of riches, describes the way God has scourged and overcome him, and ends by characterising himself as a *peregrinus*, a foreigner, an alien.

Psalm 38 need not be a direct source for *Solomon and Saturn I*, but it is possible that the poem's author had internalised the vocabulary of the Psalms and recombined these motifs in his composition. As Jean Leclercq's work has shown, this is typical monastic use of Scripture.[63] In her study of the Psalms' use in Anglo-Saxon poetry and liturgy, Patricia Hollahan notes the wide-ranging practice of memorising the psalter, and confirms the Psalms' flexible use in poetry: a poet could cite a psalm verse explicitly, make a clear allusion to a particular psalm, compose with an image occurring in multiple psalms, or even employ a psalm-like image without a direct source in the psalter.[64] I propose that the reader of *Solomon and Saturn* would have recognised the topoi used to describe demonic suffering as typical of the Psalms. And, just as any sinful man might identify with the speaker of Psalm 38,[65] so does the Old English poem suggest, albeit subtly, that its audience might take part in its drama of ignorance, desire, and learning.

A literate Christian of the Anglo-Saxon period would have recalled his own early education when reading or hearing the poem. He might have reflected on the difficulty of truly understanding and living a prayer so essential to his faith. He might also have wished to be newly overwhelmed by words which had grown commonplace. The desire depicted in *Solomon and Saturn I*, a desire intended for the reader to emulate, has a distinct monastic flavour, reflecting the fervour with which desire for God is often described in monastic writings.[66] Scott DeGregorio has described an early form of affective spirituality in Bede's work, a meditative focus on the passion to the deliberate exclusion of 'uagationem cogitationum superfluarum' (the wandering of superfluous thoughts).[67] In explaining Bede's move toward a 'love-based devotion', DeGregorio notes the typical 'burning heart' vocabulary of the following passage:

> *What manner of one is thy beloved of the beloved, O thou most beautiful among women? what manner of one is thy beloved of the beloved, that thou hast so adjured us?* This means, that a brother should say openly to a brother, or a faithful person to another, 'Because I find that you are burning with love for the Redeemer, I beg you to say some words about him to me too, to strengthen me with a beneficial exhortation, until that same love grows in my heart too, by hearing of his kindnesses and gifts'.[68]

Bede's commentary here not only emphasises loving devotion, but the idea that this burning love can be taught, transmitted from one monastic to another. Indeed, this is reiterated in 'Ymnus ad tertiam': the line glossed by 'fyrwyt l bryne' reads 'accendat ardor proximos', or, 'let ardor enflame those near us'.[69] Saturn's longing is for an unreachable, divinely given object; his striving inflames readers of the poem with desire for the same prayer.

Learning to Read

While *Solomon and Saturn I* presents the character of a curious, wandering scholar who desires a close encounter with the Lord's Prayer in order to spur a similar burning within its readers, it also offers a method of meditative reading to help them to that end. The first indication that the poem is concerned with ways of reading occurs at the very start, with Saturn's complaint that he has tasted the books (2, boca onbyrged) of all the islands and is still unsatisfied. Jonathan Wilcox and Kathryn Powell consider this expression to be proof that Saturn does not know that books are to be read, not chewed. Indeed, Powell connects this to a larger fetishisation of the book as object in both *Solomon and Saturn* poems.[70] I propose that, at least in the context of *Solomon and Saturn I*, we are intended to think of rumination. In his reply to Saturn's opening speech, Solomon compares the man who does not know the canticle to wandering cattle, livestock without understanding (22b, 23b, weallað swa nieten … feoh butan gewitte). This allusion to cattle functions much as the cow chewing the cud in Bede's story of Cædmon does, an earthy reminder of a sophisticated intellectual process. *Solomon and Saturn I*'s reading programme has two components, both contained within the fantastical letter battle that makes the poem so remarkable. The first is linked to the Pater Noster's status as a text bound up with early literacy and, in many cases, childhood: namely, recollecting the process of learning to read in order to recover a sense of effort, intensity, and childlike innocence. The second practice draws on the prayer's close relationship with questions of memory and inattention, and consists in taking the text apart and encoding it in order to make it memorable and intriguing.

The method used to teach reading in the middle ages was based on the ancient Greek and Roman system, a pedagogical method of such longevity that we continue to see its principles put to use in reading primers of the early modern period. As described in Chapter 1, students were first taught the individual letters of the alphabet backwards and forwards, and then made to combine and recombine them into various nonsensical syllables. The focus was less on meaning or on recognition of the phonetic building blocks of the language in question, and more on building a familiarity with the letters as such, and a facility at manipulating them.[71] The lessons then progressed to words of increasing length, and subsequently to full sentences. As Mary Carruthers points out, this was a system of teaching that encouraged a playful attitude towards written language, and the kind of mindset that delights in anagrams, ciphers, and rebuses. She adds that this pedagogy resulted more generally in a 'tendency to view knowledge less as a language, in our sense of that word, whose primary units are semantically whole and entirely referential, and more as involving a recombinant set of design-elements, whose units are sub-semantic "signs" of all sorts that make meanings (rather than necessarily having them) in constantly varying combinations with other "signs"'.[72]

This way of approaching texts is typified by the Pater Noster battle of *Solomon and Saturn I*. As fantastical as this section of the poem is, it also calls up an image of the elementary classroom, where seriousness of purpose in learning that fundamental text, the Pater Noster, is combined with playfulness in encoding it. Within the poem, Solomon's 'lesson' seems partly to be that even if Saturn has read many books and talked with scholars of the Eastern world, in terms of Christian, Western knowledge, he is a child. On the other hand, to be a child in this sense is no mean thing, since it means undertaking a course of study that will result in ability to interact with texts by taking them apart, recombining them, and using them as the basis of poetic composition. The hints of disciplinary violence present in the letter battle, the Pater Noster's link to early learning, and the pedagogic method evidenced by the scrambling of the letters combine to create a fiction of early learning for the poem's readers as well. In his discussion of school material in the *Nun's Priest's Tale*, Peter Travis argues that 'Chaucer takes his readers back to basics in order that they might reexperience, now at a more sophisticated level, both the profundities and the baffling complexities of literature.'[73] The version of *Solomon and Saturn I* in CCCC 422 reminds its reader of the privileged knowledge his education has given him, but also takes him 'back to the basics' of his own reading pedagogy.

The letter combat in *Solomon and Saturn I* embodies and exemplifies more advanced arts of the mind too. At one point in the poem, Saturn asks, 'Ac hulic is se organ ingemyndum/ to begonganne' (CCCC 422, 53–54a, but how is the song to be cultivated in the memory?). Since Solomon does not answer this question directly in the following speech, it seems at first glance to be a throwaway line in what is only nominally a dialogue, an opportunity for Solomon to continue his lengthy description of the Pater Noster's powers. However, Saturn's question does recall a multiplicity of issues surrounding the Pater Noster. The verb *began* can mean 'to cultivate', but can also mean to carry out, perform, engage in, cherish, or worship. *Ingemyndum*, a dative plural noun meaning 'memory, mind, remembrance', could be either locative or instrumental.[74] Saturn's question might variously be rendered, then, as 'how is the song to be remembered?', 'how is the song to be kept in the mind with the correct devotional attitude?', and 'how is the song to be practised by the mind?' However we interpret it, the question is important, and Solomon does indeed answer it in the dialogue.

In the first place, Solomon's treatment of the Pater Noster in the battle passage responds directly to the issue of memorisation. This section of the poem, as fantastical and mythological it may be on the surface, exhibits many of the memory techniques described by Carruthers.[75] First, the Pater Noster prayer is taken apart into its constituent units, a reference, as I argued earlier, to its role in elementary education, but also an initial step in the work of memorising it. It was the advice of writers on memory from Quintilian to Hugh of St Victor that difficult texts be broken up into smaller pieces for easier memorisation; the Pater Noster has frequently undergone this procedure, not only due to the pressing need to commit it to memory, but also because the need to understand it has resulted in a tradition of commenting on the individual clauses.[76] The second remarkable quality of these letters is their accompaniment on the pages of CCCC 422 by their runic equivalents. The way a reader interprets Anglo-Saxon runes tends to betray her broader assumptions about Anglo-Saxon literature, and in the case of *Solomon and Saturn I* it is easy to read the runes as a sign of popular, perhaps even pagan, magic. To be fair, this is, after all, the primary reading prompted by the poem and its manuscript context. In CCCC 41, where a fragment of the poem appears in the margin, it is joined by *loricae*, Old English and Latin charms, and the SATOR AREPO formula, suggesting, according to Don Skemer, a common theme of supernatural protection.[77] (However, it is worth noting that this fragment, which includes the beginning of the letter battle, does not feature runes.) Still, just as the Lord's Prayer can call up both an atmosphere of bookish learning and connotations of superstitious folk magic, *Solomon and Saturn I* also leaves open the possibility of readings in different registers. While Thomas Hill has suggested that the poem might be 'a poetic gloss on a Pater Noster amulet, an inscription in runes or insular script which some Anglo-Saxon carried on his or her person',[78] the magical implications previously ascribed to runes have increasingly been questioned in recent scholarship.[79] Carruthers has suggested that the tables of foreign and imaginary alphabets found in many medieval manuscripts might have served as sets of loci to be used in mnemonic work.[80] The poem can thus be read as a gloss on a runic table, an elaborate mnemonic use of two alphabets the better to learn and remember a text.

Indeed, *Solomon and Saturn I* could serve as a textbook example on how a strange alphabet might be used for memorisation. The letters are anthropomorphised and described in terms of their new, assumed human bodies of warriors (90, guðmæcga) and chiefs (99, 111, brego, geræswa), though retaining their nature as letters. The urge to connect the letters of the alphabet to human figures seems to be as old as non-hieroglyphic alphabets themselves. Marrou recounts the story of Herodes Atticus who, frustrated at his son's inability to remember the names of the Greek letters, considered raising twenty-four young slaves with him, named Alpha, Beta, Gamma, and so on.[81] In a much later period, Peter of Ravenna used alphabets to memorise law extracts, and gave human shape to the letters to make them more living and vivid. For Peter, the anthropomorphic figures most stimulating to his memory were enticing women.[82] For the author of *Solomon and Saturn I*, the stimulation comes from warrior letters which make themselves even more memorable by fighting the devil (later devils) in a series of brutally violent attacks.

Carruthers' argument that the *Psychomachia* of Prudentius demonstrates the relationship between memory and '*enargeia*, the ornament that paints pictures in the mind', is also particularly apt for a consideration of *Solomon and Saturn I*, which itself shows the influence of the *Psychomachia* in both conception and direct borrowing.[83] The warrior letters are vigorous, and many of the attacks are rich in vivid, frightening detail that can be easily visualised, such as the setting on fire of a devil's hair (129b–30a). The scourging of a demon 'oððæt him ban blicað' (144a, until his bones shine) demonstrates, if not a sense for colour as hue, a sensitivity to the contrasts in texture and luminosity that enable the reader to create an image in her mind.[84] But if the violent, personified warrior letters are useful for mnemonic techniques in and of themselves, they also reinforce memory in another way. Jody Enders has argued that scourging scenes in medieval drama would have prompted their audiences to recall their own experience of pedagogical violence, making the drama more memorable by reinforcing it with the recollection of painful lived experience.[85] The battle sequence's repeated mentions of whipping add another dimension of teaching and memory, again gesturing both to elementary classroom and advanced mental practice. Daniel Anlezark, building on the gloss 'flagella: tuig', has even proposed that the 'palm-twigged' Pater Noster could itself be a whip,[86] thus figuring the prayer as the disciplinary means of its own painful remembrance.

Returning to Saturn's question about the proper worship or practice of the prayer allows a third reading, one in which the letter battle deliberately encodes the Pater Noster to combat the problem of inattentive prayer described earlier in this chapter. One technique for focusing the mind, described by John Cassian in *De institutis coenobiorum*, closely echoes *Solomon and Saturn I*'s treatment of the Lord's Prayer. Cassian describes the very heat of prayer as a particular incitement to the devil, who 'rushes to seduce our mind away from its intention to pray by stirring up our humours, and thus striving to make it tepid when it had begun to burn'. He recommends short and frequent prayers as performed by the Egyptians, and, to avoid the tedium of lengthy psalms, advises breaking them up into smaller sections especially during solitary prayer. Cassian thus outlines the strategic use of snippets of prayer as defences in a metaphorical battle with the devil, whose *iacula*, or darts, come in the form of distractions.[87] This kind of psychomachia is revisited with a twist in *Solomon and Saturn I*, in which it is the most elemental components of prayer that take the offensive, attacking the hostile devil with a rod (90, gierde), whips (109, 121, sweopan), spears (120, 128, speru), arrows or darts (130, flana), as well as in hand-to-hand combat.

The projectile weapons used by the warrior letters recall the devil's darts, but the whips and the rod add another layer to the poem's imagery, suggesting disciplinary violence as well as spiritual warfare. A passage in Gregory's *Dialogues* illustrates how these two kinds of pain are fused in the monastic imaginary. A monk who has trouble concentrating during prayers, wandering away in both body and mind, is sent to Benedict for intervention. Benedict sees a little black boy leading the wayward monk away from prayer, an allusion to one of the tempter devil's disguises in

Athanasius' *Life of St Antony*. Mary Carruthers describes this scene as one of *curiositas*, the ceaseless drifting of the mind that so plagues monastic meditation and prayer, and explains how Benedict turns the case into a teaching moment:

> He finds the monk standing as usual outside the place of prayer and hits him with a stick, *virga* – a stick that also should send vibrations through an audience's textured memory stores. In Gregory's culture, the physical gesture made by Benedict was basic to sound education, placing the monk in the position of a lazy schoolboy, with Benedict as his *grammaticus*.[88]

Carruthers' compelling reading of this scene in Gregory's *Dialogues*, a text present in multiple extant Anglo-Saxon manuscripts and in an Old English translation by Bishop Werferth, teases out the multivalent associations of violent imagery in medieval texts. The blow against a demon, and the temptation he embodies and represents, is also a disciplinary strike, one that recalls the trope of pedagogical beating. While the scene gains its force from its textual allusion to Athanasius, Benedict's gesture also shows the use of kinesthetic imagination.[89] Benedict's blow, in other words, reminds readers of the *Dialogues* of their own schoolboy errancy and discipline, and reinvents the corrective wallop in the context of ascetic spiritual practice. This doubleness is subtly reflected in Werferth's translation of the scene. Werferth renders *virga* as 'gyrde', and closely translates the conclusion of Gregory's chapter thus:

> Ond þa swa se ealda feond ne dorste ofer þæt gehrinan þæs muneces geþohte, efne swylce he selfa wære geslægen ond beswungcen mid Benedictus swinglan.[90]

> And then the old enemy did not dare to touch the monk's thought any further, just as if he himself had been struck and scourged with Benedict's stroke.

Werferth expands Gregory's *percussus* to 'geslægen ond beswungcen'. While alliterative doubling is not unusual for an Anglo-Saxon translator, Werferth uses it here to introduce the pedagogical associations of *beswingan*, a verb used in Ælfric's *Grammar* to refer to the whipping of boys. Distraction at prayer can be resolved through advanced learned spiritual techniques, by structuring the practice to hold attention and meditating on the spiritual power of the individual words, but it can also be achieved by a renewed spiritual infancy. This might be sweet, as it recalls the 'milk' of first lessons to which the Pater Noster is compared, or it can be harsh, in the recollected and renewed pain of a disciplinary rod.

The Pater Noster's encoding in *Solomon and Saturn I* not only reflects monastic techniques of skilled prayer, but serves to stimulate interest and intellect in a simple-seeming text. The process of scrambling letters, syllables, and words was termed *scinderatio fonorum* by the seventh-century, probably Irish grammarian Virgilius Maro Grammaticus.[91] He was neither alpha nor omega of the practice, widespread as it is in medieval writing, but his succinct explanation of it sheds light on its use in *Solomon and Saturn I*:

> Sounds are split apart for three reasons. The first is to test our students' shrewdness at inquiring and learning all those things that are obscure. The second is to beautify and construct eloquence. The third is so that things that are mystical and should only be revealed to experts not be learned easily and indiscriminately by inferior and stupid people, lest swine step on gems, as the ancient proverb has it.[92]

All three uses of *scinderatio fonorum* described by Virgilius obtain in *Solomon and Saturn I*: the scrambling of the letters encodes the prayer and hides it from Saturn, it 'decorates' the poetic composition, and it is a stimulus to keen minds. Lucie Doležalová has argued that *scinderatio* served as a mnemonic technique, and connects it, along with the widespread vogue for riddles in the middle ages, to elite readers' interest in secret knowledge.[93] But it was also a way of combating the pride and boredom of intellectuals. In *De doctrina christiana*, Augustine thus explains the enigmatic nature of Scripture itself:

> But casual readers are misled by problems and ambiguities of many kinds, mistaking one thing for another. In some passages they find no meaning at all that they can grasp at, even falsely, so thick is the fog created by some obscure phrases. I have no doubt that this is all divinely predetermined, so that pride may be subdued by hard work and intellects which tend to despise things that are easily discovered may be rescued from boredom and reinvigorated.[94]

While difficult passages can be a way of testing or training students to read carefully, they are, despite Virgilius' insistence, also for the experienced. Accordingly, in *Solomon and Saturn I*, the humbling of the intellectually proud Saturn serves to invigorate the poem's bored reader. These readings of the letter battle as technology of prayer and stimulus to lethargic intellectuals do not exclude my earlier interpretations of it as classroom recollection and mnemonic device. For the purposes of analysis I have artificially divided these functions, but the point is that the scene contains a multiplicity of meanings already present in the Pater Noster, a prayer of lucid simplicity and infinite significance. Augustine seems to anticipate both audiences of Solomon's final, violent depiction of the Pater Noster when he adds, 'those who fail to discover what they are looking for suffer from hunger, whereas those who do not look, because they have it in front of them, often die of boredom. In both situations the danger is lethargy'.[95] Saturn's desperate desire, his hunger to taste the Pater Noster, prompts the experienced reader to look once more at the prayer at hand.

The reader or listener of *Solomon and Saturn I* is invited to occupy two positions at once. The first is one of vulnerability. The techniques of basic reading pedagogy incorporated into the fabric of the poem recall the state of being a child, at least with respect to learning. The reader's identification with the potentially demonic and lamenting Saturn allows him to experience the painful desire for this mighty prayer, as well as to fear that knowledge of the Pater Noster may be withheld. And yet, the reader is also offered a second, privileged perspective. The poem's use of vivid mnemonic and meditative techniques emphasises the potential power of learning, its cognitive efficacy, and even its playfulness. Although the text of the Pater Noster is never available to Saturn, it *is* to the Anglo-Saxon reader. This is the ultimate lesson of the Old English *Solomon and Saturn*: by identifying with Saturn's impossible desire for the Pater Noster, by recreating his physical longing, the reader learns to treasure the quotidian, familiar prayer already available to him.

CHAPTER 3

Violence
Ælfric Bata's Colloquies

L'homme est un apprenti, la douleur est son maître

Alfred de Musset, 'La nuit d'octobre'[1]

The popular image of the medieval period is of a brutal age in which violence was dealt out liberally and unthinkingly.[2] This stereotype extends to education, and was propagated by a series of earlier scholars. A. F. Leach discussed flogging in Ælfric's *Colloquy* and concluded that 'education and corporal chastisement' were inseparable.[3] Pierre Riché insisted on the harsh treatment of children in the seventh and eighth centuries,[4] while Walter Ong claimed that the violence common to late antique schools 'grew more intense and evident' in the middle ages.[5] A newer generation of critics have explored violence in late medieval education with greater nuance, recognising, as Jody Enders does, the 'self-contradictions' inherent in 'coercive, spectacular' uses of corporal punishment.[6] However, while late medieval schooling has been shown to be more reflective and complex in its treatment of corporal punishment than previously thought, the early middle ages remain metaphorically 'dark' and cruel. Ben Parsons represents a typical view when he argues that 'the early Middle Ages … bear witness to a deeper entrenchment of physical castigation into schooling. In the monasteries corporal punishment moves beyond having a fluid and debatable relationship to education into something firmly anchored therein.'[7] Surface readings of early medieval literature certainly support this impression: descriptions of and allusions to schoolroom violence are frequent, so that the use of corporal punishment comes to seem self-evident.

Corporal punishment certainly played its part in early medieval pedagogy, even if educators were not as uncritical in its use as they are sometimes represented to have been by modern scholars. It is, however, a mistake to assume neat equivalence or a straightforward historical connection between allusions to physical discipline in texts and its use in everyday life. When whipping appears in historical, literary, or classroom texts, it is

part of a consideration of the uses of violent punishment and imagery –
and of their limits. As *Solomon and Saturn I* and Werferth's translation of
Gregory's *Dialogues* show, violence was a rhetorically useful topos. Anglo-
Saxon writers used the motif of pain in education as a tool to think with,
an aid to comprehension and memory, and a stimulant to curiosity and
attention. In his *Colloquies*, Ælfric Bata presents readers with deceptively
realistic depictions of pedagogical violence while systematically undercut-
ting the unthinking acceptance of discipline. The *Colloquies* do show how
effective fearful and violent language can be for teaching Latin and incul-
cating monastic identity. At the same time, they dramatise how violence
can disrupt the monastic projects of building community, an ethical self,
and reflective textual practice.

Near the end of Ælfric Bata's *Colloquies*, the master asks his students
who stole the monastery's apples the previous day.[8] The oblates accuse two
of their group of stealing the fruit as well as a variety of other items such
as books, cheeses, and fish. One of the suspects eventually capitulates, and
the master orders two boys to fetch rods and beat the young thief: 'Sumite
uirgas duas et stet unus in dextera parte culi illius et alter in sinistra, et sic
inuicem percutite super culum eius et dorsum, et flagellate eum bene prius,
et ego uolo postea' (166, Take up two rods. One boy should stand on the
right side of his arse and the other on the left. Hit him on his arse and back
by turns. Flog him well first, and I'll do it after). When the pupil being
disciplined cries that he is about to die, the master coldly replies: 'non es
mortuus adhuc, sed uiuis' (166, You're not dead yet, you're alive). The boy
then launches into a vivid complaint composed of borrowings from Isidore
of Seville's *Synonyma*,[9] and the scene ends with the boy's apology and the
master's warning not to sin again, lest something worse happen to him.

This dramatisation of a young monk's punishment can be seen as the
violent catastrophe of Bata's *Colloquies*, the fulfilment of expectations that
have been built up throughout the work. The boys of the dialogues cower
under the threat of corporal punishment, they bully each other, and the
older monks overstep the bounds of propriety. The scene also encapsulates the overarching contradiction of the *Colloquies*: by having his pupils
memorise this dialogue, Bata indoctrinates them into a system of self- and
mutual discipline meant to maintain monastic order and moral purity; in
the same colloquy, however, he shows the system slipping to an extreme
where both master and students are implicated in brutality. The fact that
aggressive scenes in the *Colloquies* are also funny complicates our reading
of Bata's tone and message, but does not reduce their significance to his
disciplinary programme.

The *Colloquies* have been studied as a source of information about Latin teaching in England at the turn of the millennium, and as a promising but ambiguous window into Anglo-Saxon monastic life and practices.[10] I propose a strategy for reading the *Colloquies* that focuses on how and to what purpose they were created. An examination of Bata's presentation of grammar, as well as of the passages he adapts from his sources, shows that his *modus operandi* is to introduce conflict into situations depicted. This technique has the immediate pedagogic function of making his Latin textbook more interesting and memorable for his students, but has the secondary effect of creating a challenging and troubled text for its modern readers. What the *Colloquies* lose in moral clarity, however, they gain in fruitful ambiguity: like some works of drama or dialogue, they allow opposing points of view to be played out and worked through in such a way as to make a tidy summation of the work's meaning impossible. While the *Colloquies* are not drama in the Greco-Roman tradition, their use in the classroom would have constituted a performance. This is essential to understanding the repeated mentions of corporal punishment in the *Colloquies* and what psychological and behavioural effects they might have had on boys memorising and reciting them as part of classroom practice. The lack of a simple answer to the problem of violence is due partly to ambiguity intrinsic to the dialogue form, and partly to the uncertainty evinced in the *Colloquies* regarding the ultimate usefulness of corporal punishment.

Reading Bata in Context

Around the turn of the eleventh century, at a Canterbury community thought by some scholars to be Christ Church priory,[11] Ælfric Bata composed two sets of colloquies to help his students with their Latin, now preserved only in Oxford, St John's College 154.[12] The second set, now referred to as the *Colloquia difficiliora*, contains thirteen short speeches, only two of which are real dialogues, which make ample use of the type of difficult, learned vocabulary associated with the hermeneutic style.[13] The first set, my focus here, divided by the most recent editor into twenty-nine separate colloquies or scenes, is a series of dialogues between individuals in different parts of a monastery; the events depicted in them roughly follow the proceedings of the monastic day,[14] and portray the masters and oblates engaging in everyday activities. The manuscript gives limited indication of how the dialogues might be used, however. The *Colloquies* are written in running text, divided into scenes by larger, rubricated capital letters, while individual lines of dialogue are sometimes set apart by regular capital letters and semicolons or *punctus interrogativus*. There are no clear speech divisions, nor any markings to indicate speakers, so a number of passages could be given to one speaker or split among multiple figures.

Bata writes at the beginning of this collection that he composed the dialogues so that 'students might be able to resume an introduction to speaking Latin' (80, qualiter scolastici ualeant resumere fandi aliquod initium latinitatis sibi) and the texts are carefully constructed to build flexible oral fluency. As David Porter has shown, the *Colloquies* are comparable in design to modern communicative language teaching methods, in which functional speaking ability in day-to-day situations is prized above abstract grammatical knowledge.[15] Porter rightly stresses the flexibility of the language as it is taught to the students. Bata often provides functional equivalents for similar statements and a 'menu' of comparable vocabulary items, offering students a variety of words and phrases with which to construct their own dialogues.[16]

Bata had several models for this pedagogical method.[17] The best known is his own teacher Ælfric of Eynsham's *Colloquy*, in which characters from various walks of life, including the monastic, answer questions about their daily work. One of the surviving versions of this text is found in the same manuscript as Bata's *Colloquies*, and indeed, Porter has argued that Bata is responsible for additions to all three extant versions of his teacher's *Colloquy*.[18] The senior teacher's work poses similar problems of interpretation: the fictional and performative nature of the *Colloquy* has repeatedly escaped critics, and lines in which monastic oblates claim they would rather be whipped than be ignorant call for a careful reading.[19] A second, more immediate, model is a set of Latin dialogues known as the *Colloquia e libro De raris fabulis retractata* (henceforth: *Retractata*), a shortened version of the earlier *De raris fabulis*, composed in Wales or Cornwall before c. 900.[20] The *Retractata* can also be found in Oxford, St John's College 154, and Bata borrowed and adapted at length from a version much like it.[21] A third set of texts related to the *Colloquies* is a series of Greek–Latin manuals with their roots in Roman antiquity, surviving in nine redactions, found mainly in Carolingian manuscripts, and known because of a former misattribution to Dositheus Magister as the *Hermeneumata Pseudodositheana*.[22] Besides alphabetical glossaries of words, lists of everyday nouns organised by topic, and occasional texts for reading, many also contain practice colloquies, and Gwara has argued for a connection between Ælfric Bata's *Colloquies* and a London recension of the *Hermeneumata*.[23] In short, Bata was influenced by a long tradition of colloquies that taught language by staging everyday conversations. These dialogues were probably used in conjunction with formal grammars of Latin like that of Ælfric, a version of which is also included in Oxford, St John's College 154. Beyond this, Bata was in line with the wider medieval practice of teaching knowledge through colloquies, whether related to language, as with Alcuin's dialogues on grammar, orthography, and rhetoric, or on other subjects such as music, biblical trivia, and astronomy.[24]

The problem of how to read Bata's unorthodoxy has vexed critics for some time. Beyond scenes of cruelty, the *Colloquies* are filled with other worrying activities: the oblates own and deal in personal property, hurl filthy Latin insults at each other, and are frequently left alone to their own, often nefarious devices. They are also beset on all sides by dubious older monks who force them to eat and drink to excess, ask them to accompany them to the bathroom alone, and request kisses and embraces. W. M. Lindsay, appalled by Bata's Latin as well as by his morals, concludes: 'No plea can save a man capable' of composing the argument full of scatological vocabulary and beating of the apple thief discussed above.[25] Porter recognises that Bata 'may in fact have been a rascal', alluding to a legendary incident in which St Dunstan prevents Bata from disinheriting Christ Church.[26] He prefers, however, to think of Bata as a monastic *bon vivant*, good-humoured and eccentric if lacking in moral rectitude.[27] Christopher Jones, who examines the deviation of the *Colloquies* from the typical regulations of the tenth-century Benedictine Reform, is careful to acknowledge the limitations of the *Colloquies* as a representation of Bata's monastery, but he wonders why Bata would write or recycle such troubling educational texts, and why his superiors would allow him to continue in his position as master. He suggests that Bata's monastery may not have been wholeheartedly dedicated to monastic reform, or that the monks in it may have been willing to admit to lapses in discipline if they saw themselves as part of an older monastic tradition.[28]

Readers of the *Colloquies* have often accepted the events depicted as historical fact, and sometimes conflated the *magister* with Bata himself. The text of the *Colloquies* invites this confusion. The daily scenes seem too ordinary and realistic to be fictional, and indeed, they can be a profitable source of information about monastic life.[29] In addition, the passage in Colloquy 29 in which the master says that he has written the colloquies invites us to identify this fictional figure with the *Colloquies'* author, as Garmonsway did when writing that Bata 'frequently talks too much and interrupts the flow of conversation, sometimes browbeating his pupils unmercifully'.[30] However, the *Colloquies* bear too much evidence of their

textual construction to be trusted uncritically as an historical source for
practice at Canterbury in the early eleventh century. Michael Lapidge has
argued against the implication in Colloquy 3 that each student possessed
his own book, pointing out that too few student copies of manuscripts survive to believe that students owned personal copies of school texts.[31] With
respect to violent or provocative passages, we should consider the possibility that Bata intended to make the *Colloquies* disturbing and unorthodox,
that he was not only well aware that certain activities were infractions of
either the Benedictine Rule itself or of reformed practices, but that he
intended them to be so.

One reason to think that Bata deliberately intended the dialogue to be
troubling is the fictional master's claim in Colloquy 29 that he wrote the
Colloquies in the spirit of play so as to make them more attractive to young
boys who could not attend to more sober instruction:

> Ergo, sicut in hac sententia didicistis, pueri mei, et legistis in multis locis,
> iocus cum sapientiae loquelis et uerbis inmixtus est et sepe coniunctus. Ideo
> autem hoc constitui et meatim disposui sermonem hunc uobis iuuenibus,
> sciens scilicet quosque pueros iugiter suatim loquentes adinuicem ludicra
> uerba sepius quam honorabilia et sapientiae apta, quia aetas talium semper
> trahit ad inrationabilem sermonem et ad frequens iocum et ad garrulitatem
> indecentem illorum. (170)

> So, as you learned in this speech, my boys, and as you've read in many
> places, joking is often mingled and joined with language and words of wis-
> dom. This is why I arranged and ordered this speech in my own way for
> you boys. I know, of course, that boys frequently say playful words to one
> another rather than words that are honourable or wise. For their age always
> draws them to their unreasonable talk and frequent joking and improper
> chattering.

This is a hint that the reader should *not* take the events depicted seriously,
to view Bata's fictional monastery as a fantasy world where much that can
go wrong does go wrong, often outrageously. The trouble enters with the
phrase 'iocus cum sapientiae loquelis et uerbis inmixtus'; it is difficult to
determine which parts of the *Colloquies* are intended to be foolish and
which wise. Indeed, although we should pay attention to Bata when he
warns us not to read all of the *Colloquies* in the same spirit, we also cannot
assume that his statement of purpose here accurately describes his entire
project. Many of the possible infractions Bata depicts in his *Colloquies*
seem much too serious to be adequately described as jokes. This is especially true of the passages describing the oblates' terror at being beaten and

their attempts to ward off abuse by an elder monk. It is hard to tell whether Bata's real students laughed wholeheartedly or with a nervous titter when asked to memorise and recite these dialogues. Another way of treating this problem of tone is to say that joking words are also deeply serious. Indeed, humorous and violent speeches in the *Colloquies* function in analogous ways, allowing boys both to learn Latin and to manipulate and undercut authoritative Latin texts.[32] Bata adopts the early medieval view that there is a productive relationship between pain and pedagogy, a notion he found explicitly articulated or implied in Ælfric's schoolbooks, but he does so in a way that allows his students to question both the morality and the disciplinary usefulness of the practice.

Grammar, Suffering, and Ælfric's *Colloquy*

The iconography of grammar, especially in the later middle ages, supports the idea that the beginnings of language are inevitably painful. In manuscripts from the twelfth century to the eighteenth, a personified Grammatica is pictured carrying a scourge to strike the students seated around her. Although Grammatica also has milder incarnations, sometimes portrayed as mother or gardener, the frequency with which she appears bearing a flagellum betrays the extent to which the ideas of grammar teacher, young boys, and harsh correction were clustered together.[33] The grammarian, by virtue of teaching the most elementary of arts, generally found himself guiding children, who most needed to be kept in line; because of the youth of his charges, his lessons were as much moral and disciplinary as technical, thus increasing the need for punitive action. He was typically depicted holding a rod or bundle of branches to remind his pupils of his corrective power.[34] Nevertheless, the importance of this association between grammar and violence extends beyond early childhood: *grammatica*, as Martin Irvine has shown, extended from the basic ABCs of Latin to a comprehensive, structured way of reading texts.[35] For monks, learning Latin meant more than picking up a second tongue: it was the entrance into the enclosed society to which they owed subjection and which would define their identities, and, at the same time, it was a gate that opened out to a wider world of texts, unbound by time or place.

Bata's teacher, Ælfric, also conjoins the ideas of language and pain. In his *Colloquy*, Ælfric offers a conventional, if rather wishful, treatment of corporal punishment.[36] His boys complain that they are stupid and speak Latin incorrectly, and when the master asks them if they wish to be whipped while learning, they reply that they would rather be whipped than to be ignorant (although they coyly add that they know their master is too merciful to whip them unless they force him to do so). The implied logic of learning goes like this: if boys make mistakes when speaking Latin, they must be whipped; the whipping helps them learn Latin correctly, thus reaching a point when their Latin is so perfect that their kind teacher no longer needs to whip them. It may seem redundant to spell this out, since this is the rough logic of all pedagogical punishment. Still, in contrast to the simplicity of the social model in the *Colloquy*, Ælfric's *Grammar* offers us a linguistic model with a radically different relationship between violence and language.[37] Influenced by the violent examples and terminology of Isidore and the grammarians, Ælfric presents the grammar of Latin, and by implication, that of English, as defined by imagined violence.[38] Verbs especially are to be understood as violent, and understanding comes by imagining one's own pain when learning them. Moreover, rather than suggesting that the teacher's love will keep him from hurting his students, as he does in the *Colloquy*, Ælfric's choices in the *Grammar* imply that hurting is parallel to, and bound up with, teacherly love.

While variations on the verb *flagellare* (to flog or whip) appear throughout the *Grammar*, it could be argued that they are there because this is a first-conjugation verb guaranteed to catch children's attention. Even if that were the entire explanation, the choice to use it repeatedly would not be without implications, but it is in Ælfric's definition of 'verb' in the 'Praefatio de partibus orationis' that we see how profoundly violence enters into Ælfric's grammatical thinking:

> VERBVM is word, and word getacnað weorc oððe ðrowunge oððe geþafunge. weorc byð, þonne ðu cwest: *aro* ic erige; *uerbero* ic swinge. þrowung byð, þonne ðu cwyst: *uerberor* ic eom beswungen; *ligor* ic eom gebunden. geðafung byþ, ðonne ðu cwyst: *amor* ic eom gelufod; *doceor* ic eom gelæred.[39]

> VERBVM is verb, and verb means an action or suffering or consent. An action is when you say, *aro* I plough; *uerbero* I flog. Suffering is when you say: *uerberor* I am flogged; *ligor* I am bound. Consent is when you say, *amor* I am loved; *doceor* I am taught.

Ælfric first translates Latin *verbum* with Old English *word*, thus maintaining the ambiguity of the Latin lemma, which means primarily 'any word' and only in a secondary, grammatical sense, 'verb'.[40] Of course, Ælfric needs to explain what *word* means in this case, so he expands it with three other ideas. The first one, *weorc*, is used here as a grammatical term meaning 'action'; it has, however, the equally common meaning of 'labour', as well as the often poetic meaning of 'pain, travail, grief'.[41]

The second, *prowing*, can mean 'suffering as opposed to doing'. Bosworth-Toller also gives us 'suffering which is painful', 'suffering that is undergone for the sake of religion', and 'suffering which ends in death, passion, martyrdom'.[42] Although its grammatical use is Ælfric's invention, it is a neat rendering of Latin *patior*, which means 'to suffer, bear, undergo' and 'to have a passive sense' when used of verbs. Both *weorc* and *prowing*, given their grammatical denotations by Ælfric, bring with them a powerful connotation of physical suffering. It is only the third, *gepafung*, 'permission, consent, submission', which provides some respite, although in the miniature narrative encapsulated in this definition, it seems to follow that extreme pain should be followed by submission or passivity.

It is, of course, hard to judge the efforts of a scholar searching to express concepts which do not exist in his language, difficult to determine how many options Ælfric had that would have accurately conveyed his grammatical meaning. I have had trouble finding a synonym for *prowing* which is unambiguously passive and maintains a distinction from *gepafung*; here, indeed, the violence implied by *prowing* seems necessary to keep the sense that the subject of the verb is unwillingly acted upon, and is warranted given the affliction implicit in the Latin *patior*. On the other hand, Ælfric might have used either *dæd* (deed, action) or *wyrht* (doing, work) instead of *weorc* and avoided the connotation of laborious suffering. The effect of choosing *weorc*, for example, to describe the active function of verbs is to colour our imagination of what can be said with those verbs. Such a definition is unlikely to be followed by the active verb 'I play'.

In order to explain the verb, Ælfric chooses words with implications of suffering to translate the grammatical term, and then uses verbs involving piercing, binding, or striking to illustrate the first two uses of the verb as he has defined it. These examples render the concept vividly clear to the reader, and by their nature are likelier to remain in his memory than more benign verbs. In Chapter 2 I discussed the creative use of shocking and gruesome images in classical and medieval mnemonic work, and Ælfric's strategy of using emotionally charged verbs to explain his lemma would certainly have helped his students to fix the definition in their memories.[43] However, there is also a sense in which the violence of the verbs Ælfric chooses is necessary to understanding what verbs (as opposed to nouns) do. His most vivid example, *verbero*, is not original. Isidore explains the difference between active and passive verbs using the same contrast: 'Ipsa autem activa dicuntur, quia agunt, ut "verbero", et passiva, quia patiuntur, ut "verberor"' (Those [verbs] are called active, because they perform, like I flog; and passive, because they undergo, like I am flogged).[44] The reader is asked to imagine flogging someone else in order to comprehend what it means to be acting on an object; he must call up the feelings of helplessness and suffering suggested by being bound and whipped to understand what it means to be a passive subject of action. Ælfric supplements the active meaning with the piercing image of plowing in *aro* (with a possible implication of agricultural and pedagogic cultivation) and reinforces the passive sense with *ligor*. Ælfric's Latin learner must open himself to the possibility of filling both active and passive roles in an act of violence at the same time that he is loved and taught, as the two examples for 'consent' indicate. While *amor* and *doceor* are intended to contrast with the previous verbs, they become at the same time conceptually linked to them: being loved and taught may feel quite different from being flogged or bound, but they are tied to them in this knot of cultivation and domination.

Bata's *Colloquies* and the Pedagogy of Pain

A copy of the *Grammar* appears in the same manuscript as Bata's *Colloquies*, and it is against this backdrop that we should read Ælfric Bata's innovations in the dynamic relationship between imagined pain and language. A close look at the mechanics of how Bata constructs his schoolbook reveals that darker elements in the *Colloquies* are present by design. One of the peculiarities of Bata's pedagogical strategy is that he often places what might be dull lists of vocabulary and phrases into a negative grammatical framework. A basic example is the list of verbs and verb forms presented in negated forms in Colloquy 14: 'Nihil mali facio, nihil feci, nihil habeo factum, nihil facere uolo, quod malum sit, si Deus uult. Nullum malum facit iste, nec fecit, nec factum habet ullum malum, nec facere uult' (110, I'm not doing anything wrong, I didn't do anything, I haven't done anything, I don't want to do anything that might be wrong, God willing. He's not doing anything wrong, nor did he do anything, nor has he done any wrong, nor does he want to). This strategy is repeated even when the verbs are varied, as in the short list of verbs in Colloquy 14, 'Bene scio, quod non canto, nec lego, neque scribo, nec disco, neque doceo' (112, I know well that I don't sing, nor do I read, nor do I write, nor do I learn, nor do I teach) and a similar list in Colloquy 15, 'Nescimus, domne, bene scribere nec nihil pingere neque sculpare' (116, Sir, we don't know how to write well, nor how to paint anything, nor how to carve).

Bata uses this technique with lists of nouns as well, frequently having the boys declare that they lack the vocabulary items to be learned rather than saying that they own or use them. At one point in the *Colloquies* this strategy gives the impression that the boys in the monastery are not only incompetent, but tragically impoverished as well. In the classroom, we hear the complaint '[n]on habeo librum ad cantandum in eo neque ad legendum' (112, I don't have a book to sing or to read in). At bath time, the boys whine 'non habemus forficem … [n]on habemus smigma … [n]on habemus nouacula<s>, non calidam aquam' (126, we don't have scissors … we don't have soap … we don't have razors, or warm water). The clothing situation is even more dire; as one boy puts it, '[f]emoralia … non habeo, nisi cruentata cum uirgis nuper uapulata' (160, I don't have breeches, except for the ones bloodied when I was recently beaten with rods). This last instance in particular reveals how Bata elaborates a negative, emotionally charged situation out of simple vocabulary exercises. It is an example *in nuce* of the close relationship between linguistic pedagogy and dramatic action in the *Colloquies*. While Bata does not use this technique everywhere, he does employ it often enough for it to become a recognisable pattern.

Noting this pattern gives us an indication as to how Bata composes, and how we might read him accordingly. He attempts to make his dialogues more interesting, and the presentation of long lists of words more engaging, by introducing some variation in the sentences. This is easily done by having the boys claim they are unable to do things, or that they lack certain items. The resulting dialogues are tense and dramatic, and it makes sense to elaborate the scenes with even more vivid images, as in the case of the boy who owns only blood-stained trousers. At the same time, this technique poses certain difficulties for the modern scholar looking for historical information in the *Colloquies*: one may not assume the boys were missing basic supplies if that passage was simply a consequence of Bata's desire to introduce variation. Indeed, if we take Bata's use of glossaries into consideration, we cannot even assume all objects mentioned were present in his monastery.[45] This particular mistake is not one scholars often make, though Colin Spencer does uncritically base his description of the medieval monastic diet on the lengthy glossarial lists of food, herbs, and kitchen tools in the *Colloquies*, even concluding that the monastery allowed 'a large amount of drinking'.[46] Still, it demonstrates on a smaller scale the reason that modern readers of the *Colloquies* might confuse their events with those of the monastery in which they were written. The *Colloquies* are seductively realistic, inviting us to think of them as a transparent window into the daily life of an eleventh-century Anglo-Saxon monastery. However, the extent to which the scenes are determined by Ælfric Bata's desire to lend variety and interest to his educational text should warn us that the glass is stained. I argue that the more violent and morally questionable parts of the *Colloquies* are also due to Bata's desire to explore the workings and fallibilities of monastic discipline rather than to historical lapses in behaviour.

In his consideration of non-reformed customs in the *Colloquies*, Jones considers it 'striking … that some of Bata's episodes flouting silence and *custodia* in zones of particular anxiety to the reformers – the refectory, dormitory, bathing-house, and latrines – ultimately bear, via the *Retractata*, the impress of the pre-reformed *De raris fabulis*'.[47] The flouting of silence should not concern us too much, since it would be quite impossible to write an effective language manual in which all of the characters kept rigorous vows of silence. What is striking, however, is not only that some of Bata's questionable scenes have their roots in the *Retractata*, but that he sometimes rewrites them in such a way as to draw attention to their inappropriateness, and that he prefers to raise objections using the voices of the oblates. This practice is observable in the way he recycles material from this oddly affectionate scene in the *Retractata*:

> Audi, pistor uel coce. Da mihi cibum meum ex cella tua, et ueni; sede cito iuxta me, ut simul manducemus et bibamus.
> O frater, ueni huc statim, et osculare me, et pone manus tuas circa collum meum, et da mihi osculum, et dic ad me 'Dominus tecum, et tu secum!' (32)

> Listen, baker or cook! give me my food from your storeroom, and come, sit quickly beside me, so that we can eat and drink together.
> O brother! come here right away, kiss me and put your hands around my neck and give me a kiss, and say to me, 'The Lord be with you, and you with him!'

The first part of the passage might have provided the idea behind a similar invitation to sit and dine in the *Colloquies*, but in Bata's version, the boy addressed declines out of politeness:

> Sta hic, et manduca super hanc mensam coram me, aut sede hic mecum uel nobiscum interim dum manducas. Bene sit tibi.
> Non audeo sedere tecum, nec mea humanitas est, sed uolo stare hic ante te et manducare et bibere humiliter et sobrie, et tibi et sociis tuis et fratribus et hospitibus propinare libenter, si mihi precipis. (96)

> Stay here, and eat on this table in my presence, or sit here with me or with us while you eat. May it go well with you.
> I don't dare to eat with you, nor is it according to my manners, but I do want to stand here before you and eat and drink humbly and soberly. I'll serve you and your companions and brothers and guests gladly, if you order me to.

The boy is, in this case, the one who is keen to preserve a proper distance. Bata subsequently exacerbates the conflict of wills in this scene by having the over-friendly older monk bully the polite youngster into eating and drinking to excess, until the boy has to beg for respite, claiming his stomach is weak and will not take any more. Bata gives the second, and more outrageous, part of this selection from the *Retractata*, the request for a kiss, to an older monk, and has him ask it of a younger monk or oblate:

> Osculare me antequam exeam, et ora pro me, et memoriam habe meam in tuis sanctis orationibus, et ego uolo memor esse tui, per Deum.
>   Non audeo osculari te, frater. (122)

> Kiss me before I go, and pray for me, and remember me in your holy prayers, and I will remember you, by God.
>   I don't dare to kiss you, brother.

We are now well in the realm of sexually inappropriate behaviour, at least in light of reformed monastic customs. The *Regularis concordia* (c. 972) carefully limits inappropriate expressions of affection between older and younger monks: 'Neither brothers nor abbots should embrace youths or little boys or thoughtlessly kiss them. Instead let them love with charitable affection in their hearts, without flattering words, reverently and with great caution.'[48] The fictional boy of the colloquy seems aware of this injunction, even as the elder monk infringes it.

Jones has discussed the possibility that Bata's monastery was unreformed, ultimately arguing that 'Bata's context was one of transition, even surly or spiteful resistance, to new strictures being imposed' by the tenth-century reform movement.[49] The above passage would likely strike a reformer as troubling, but Bata may also be deliberately, and playfully, engaging with the *Regularis concordia*'s strict directives by having an adult flout them and a boy maintain them.[50] Once again, it is the boy who protests the monk's immoderate affection. In this case, the older monk accepts the boy's refusal without qualm, and gives him a blessing.

In the following example of a reworking from the *Retractata*, the boy is not spared. In Colloquy 7 of the *Retractata*, a monk asks another to accompany him:

> O frater, ueni, et perge mecum ad meam necessitatem.
> Non ibo, frater, hac uice, quoniam aliud opus occupat me.
> Audi, amice, noli stare inter me et lucem, sed sta superius.
> Faciam libenter.   (32)

> O brother! come and go along with me for my needs.
> I won't go, brother, in that office, because I'm busy with some other work.

Listen, friend, don't stand between me and the light, but stand
    further away.
I'll do it gladly.

The first monk's request is most likely a request for company at the
latrine.[51] The monks address each other as equals, there is no indication
that one is younger than the other, and the refusing monk uses his work,
not the impropriety of the request, as an excuse. The passage follows
a series of disparate lines which do not make sense read together, and
indeed, the second interchange I quote here seems to be separate from
the first.[52]

In his Colloquy 9, Ælfric Bata begins with a similar phrase as the passage
in the *Retractata*, but constructs out of it a strikingly different scenario:

Tu, fratercule mi, perge mecum ad latrinam.
Domne, non audeo uadere sine licentia magistri mei tecum.
Mentiris certe!
Non mentior, crede mihi.
Ego rogare eum uolo modo. Domne frater, licet huic puero pergere
    mecum ad necessitatem meam?
Licet bene, karissime amice.   (98)

You, my little brother, come with me to the privy.
Sir, I don't dare to go with you without my teacher's permission.
You're lying for sure!
I'm not lying, believe me.
I'll ask him now. Brother, sir, is this boy allowed to go with me to my
    necessity?
He may indeed, dearest friend.

In the first line, Bata has made several subtle alterations that nevertheless
change the atmosphere and implications of the dialogue. The first is that
the monk addressed is now, instead of *frater*, 'brother', a *fraterculus*, 'little
brother'. The man asking for help makes his request a little more intimate
with the possessive adjective, calling him 'fratercule mi' (my little brother),
perhaps with hint of risqué double entendre for the more advanced Latin
learners.[53] The boy addresses him respectfully as 'domne' (sir). This is no
longer just a scene in which a brother asks his equal for a favour. It is now
an inappropriate request by an older man to a young monk to help him
at the toilet. Although all members of a monastic monastery were typically under supervision,[54] special care was taken to preserve the purity of
children from the dangers of masturbation, sexual relations, or abuse by
elders. They were supervised by their master during the times specified for
group visits to the latrine, and some customaries also specify that children

needing to use the bathroom at night be accompanied by the master *and* another boy.[55] The *Regularis concordia* is unambiguous in its injunction against any private meeting between youth and older monks, even if the elder is the master himself:

> A monk should not presume to lead away any of the boys or youths for a private indulgence, not even on the pretense of a spiritual matter. But as the Rule instructs, each boy should remain under the constant supervision of his teacher. Nor should the teacher himself have the liberty to go away with any single boy without a third nearby as a witness.[56]

We see here an awareness that even teachers are not completely to be trusted alone with the children, whether in the latrine or elsewhere. Although Bata's dialogue suggests that a boy might serve an older monk at the latrine and remain within the bounds of propriety, this violates the strictures of the *Regularis concordia*.[57] Again, we note that it is the boy who worries about correctness, refusing not because he is busy, but because he feels this is something it would be inappropriate to do without his master's permission. In the next Colloquy, perhaps since permission was already granted, another request for bathroom help is more readily attended to:

> O puer bone, ueni, et perge mecum in latrinam propter
>   necessitatem meam.
> Eo, domine.
> Audi, amice; noli stare sic inter me et lucem, sed sta superius paululum
>   … Deo gratias, non sum cecus nec ebrius nimis.   (108)
>
> O, good boy, come, and go with me to the privy for my need.
> I'm coming, sir.
> Listen, friend; don't stand between me and the light, but stand a little
>   further away … Thank God I'm not blind or too drunk.

Here, as in the last section quoted, Bata indicates the young age of the monk whose help is requested by having the first speaker address him as 'puer'. Just in case the imagery implied is not sufficiently vivid, Bata has incorporated the material following the original exchange in the *Retractata* into the scene at the latrine itself. The man urinating asks another (perhaps the boy himself) to leave him more light, and then thanks God for not being too blind or drunk to manage the task.

These examples should make it clear that, whatever questionable material may have already been present in the *Retractata*, Bata purposefully recycles into something profoundly disquieting. Nor does he do this out of ignorance of proper monastic behaviour: he regularly inserts a voice that draws attention to inappropriate requests and comments, and this refusing, protesting voice is that of a boy. Indeed, the master in Colloquy 9 quite happily agrees to let the boy attend to the older monk in the latrine, and in instructing him in detail how to serve him, commands an even greater degree of contact between the boy and the older monk (98–99). The picture that emerges is of a situation in which the older monks, who ought to maintain the purity of the oblates, sometimes undermine it. One implication is that it is the boys themselves who are ultimately responsible for monitoring their own behaviour and avoiding immoral activity, perhaps having learned to do so through proper discipline and education. On the other hand, the fact that they are only moderately successful at doing so suggests the limited effectiveness of discipline and upbringing, especially when the masters of the *Colloquies* regularly neglect to watch over their charges.

What Bata is investigating is the question of the proper balance between monastic custody (*custodia*) and discipline (*disciplina*) in enforcing behaviour and maintaining the purity of child oblates. As Jones has remarked, custody is almost completely absent in the *Colloquies*, while discipline is unceasing.[58] Although the *Rule of St Benedict* describes a variety of forms discipline could take, the *Colloquies* are exclusively concerned with the physical variety. The whip was indeed a pedagogical reality in the monastery: the *Rule* suggested whipping as an appropriate punishment for boys too young to understand the meaning of psychological measures such as excommunication (in the sense of being temporarily barred from the community), and monastic customaries affirm that Benedict's advice was followed. While the abbot was responsible for the discipline of the community, it was the *magister* who generally fulfilled this disciplinary role for the oblates. Although whipping was a given, many monastic histories and lives feature boys who are excessively punished, suggesting that its disproportionate use was also a source of concern.[59] Indeed, Hildemar of Corbie, in his commentary on the *Rule*, argues for unceasing *custodia* in the raising of oblates, and the use of *disciplina* (of any kind) only when supervision has failed.[60]

Monastic educators dealt in varying ways with what was probably a constant pedagogical paradox over the centuries, a tension between the perceived need for punishment and its frequent ineffectiveness and negative behavioural results. Although Bata in no place argues explicitly against corporal punishment in either his own voice or that of a representative master, his treatment of it embodies this paradox: he embraces the disciplinary prospect of violence, but also recognises its negative psychological effects on the child. What makes Bata's treatment of this issue at once more powerful and more unsettling is the fact that his prose is not expository, but performative: his intended audience does not engage intellectually with ideas about discipline simply by reading and thinking about them, but is meant to experience its workings by performing the roles of punisher and punished.

Classroom Performance

Anglo-Saxonists interested in performance often resemble Jorge Luis Borges in his attempt to describe Averroes contemplating the words 'tragedy' and 'comedy' in Aristotle's *Rhetoric*. Not only is performance notoriously ephemeral, but it often remains difficult to imagine its existence in a period with no recognisable theatre. The Anglo-Saxon contribution to European drama has, in the eyes of scholars, generally been confined to tenth-century English liturgical practice, particularly to the *Visitatio Sepulchri* (or *Quem quaeritis*) of the *Regularis concordia*.[61] Judged according to Roman theatrical conventions on the one hand, and in comparison to later medieval plays on the other, even the liturgical instructions of the *Visitatio Sepulchri* seem rudimentary. Old English poetry has occasionally been considered 'dramatic', either because the heightened emotions and possible multiple speakers of lyrics such as *The Wanderer* suggested a certain theatricality, or with the contention that an Anglo-Saxon *scop* presenting poetic dialogue would have used voice and gesture to impersonate characters.[62] Recent work on the later middle ages has, however, expanded our understanding of performance, often in ways relevant to the early medieval period. Carol Symes notes the twentieth-century scholarly obsession with distinguishing between 'liturgy and theater' and ascertaining what counts as 'true performance', a distinction often made on the basis of documented stage directions, costumes, and other forms of scripting that readers of modern plays expect.[63] Working with French plays dating pre-1300, Symes shows that early theatrical texts were recorded in manuscripts in various ways, depending on the conventions of individual scriptoria or using layouts from other genres, such as fabliaux and narrative in verse. The fact that we have more information about fifteenth-century performance practices, for example, reflects that period's fuller documentary practices, not necessarily its greater interest in drama.[64] Scholars such as Joyce Coleman and Evelyn Vitz have argued for the importance of public reading practices and recitation as performance in the later middle ages, a line of research that complicates the orality–literacy divide so important to Anglo-Saxon scholars in the twentieth century.[65] Equally troubling to that dichotomy is the scholarship of Susan Boynton and Bruce Holsinger, which recentres liturgy (beyond the *Visitatio Sepulchri*) as a vital performance practice in and around early medieval monasteries, one intimately related to pedagogy.[66] Early medieval performance forms may be hard to trace, lacking as they do the expected generic markers of later drama, but there is enough evidence to suggest that they existed and are to some extent recoverable.

Because they are educational texts, and deceptively realistic ones at that, school colloquies have contributed little to written histories of drama. They are, however, 'deeply performative',[67] and likely the closest thing to theatre in Anglo-Saxon England. Bata's *Colloquies* are scripts requiring memorisation and imply, by their very function as tools for oral language teaching, some measure of enactment and personification. The *Colloquies* are also, as I have demonstrated, fictional, and the real monastic oblates who learned and recited these dialogues acted out the roles of students (and perhaps teachers) just as Ælfric's students performed the voices of hunter, cook, or merchant. The *Colloquies* combine imagined scenarios with the kind of scripted everyday practices described by Ervin Goffman. Goffman, much like the late twentieth-century performance art movements that have shaped contemporary performance theory, eliminated the stage and with it the clear demarcation between performer and audience.[68] Early medieval performances are easiest to trace when they occur in rituals, whether in the scripted confession of penitentials, or in the *Regula magistri*'s instructions for the would-be novice to throw himself at the feet of the abbot and beg for admission in front of the entire community.[69] Pedagogic colloquies imply a more flexible scripting of behaviour, and when they treat dangerous or taboo themes, allow students a way to imagine positions of agency and powerlessness.[70] Indeed, classroom role play, I would argue with Marjorie Curry Woods, is dual in nature: it is at once a performance in its own right for an audience of teachers, tutors, other students, and one's self, and it is a workshop or pre-formance in which behaviours can be tried on in preparation for future, adult performances.[71] Drawing on Richard Schechner's description of the playful and improvisational nature of performance, whether in theatre workshop games or in official productions, we might think of classroom performance as 'subjunctive, full of alternatives and potentiality'.[72]

In Bata's *Colloquies*, as we have seen, the roles to be acted are vividly close to home, but the text maintains a double orientation towards present and future. A boy memorising and repeating his lines would not have been representing a wholly fictional character, nor would he have, strictly speaking, been performing his own identity. Rather, he would have been taking on the role of someone like him, or, if he learned the master's lines, of someone he might become. The scenes of the *Colloquies* are imagined, but the boys acting them out would have performed real possibilities of themselves. In an inversion of the modern idea of the theatre as a space where people can be educated in taste, morals, or comportment,[73] Bata's classroom itself becomes a theatre, a space where performance can be used to inculcate discipline, but also a workshop in which the effects of discipline on young psyches might be explored in a spirit of play. Hence the deliberate ambiguity of 'iocus cum sapientiae loquelis et uerbis inmixtus est' (170, joking is often mingled and joined with language and words of wisdom): the *Colloquies* are at once mischievous and deadly serious, a slippery interplay of inculcation and subversion.

While the notion of performance in the medieval classroom is still taking hold, the use of drama in modern pedagogy is widespread. Although there are important differences between the educational use of drama in the medieval period and today, contemporary research into the didactic power of performance can give us some indications of why and how it may have worked a thousand years ago. To begin with, a number of scholars have noted that drama and enactment aid the memories of spectators and performers. Joe Winston notes that young spectators best remember 'elements that shock, disrupt or surprise' in the theatre,[74] reminding us of Bata's own use of startling scenes and exchanges in his *Colloquies*. More helpful for understanding what Bata's real life students might have learned as they acted out the *Colloquies* is the ongoing research of Helga and Tony Noice. Beginning with the question of how actors memorise lengthy texts verbatim, the Noices have carried out a series of memory studies and experiments with professional actors, college students, senior citizens, and with the mnemonist Harry Lorrayne. They have found that a trained actor will focus on reading the text carefully and involve herself emotionally with a character, and that perfect memorisation of the lines occurs as a side effect of this deep interaction with playtext and character. According to the Noices, actors employ:

> devices such as extensive elaboration (imaginative embellishment), perspective taking (adopting the perspective of one character in a narrative), self-referencing (relating material personally to oneself), self-generation (remembering one's own ideas better than ideas of others), mood congruency (matching one's mood to the emotional valence of the material), and distinctiveness (considering details that render an item unique).[75]

Although professional actors are most adept at these techniques, the Noices also found that untrained college students could remember more dialogue verbatim by engaging in what they call 'active experiencing' than those simply attempting to memorise the text, and that this kind of dramatic emotional engagement in senior citizens resulted in better memory overall.[76] We have seen how Bata uses emotionally charged language to create tense and immediate situations. The oblates' enactment of and identification with the characters in the *Colloquies* would, it seems, have helped them to remember the Latin words and phrases all the better.

Another study on the role of acting in memory has shown that people who learn a monologue and then improvise on it remember more of it than subjects who write about it or discuss it with a group, concluding that 'active learning strategies in the classroom might help students to remember the material later'.[77] This study is particularly rigorous in that it isolates the practice of enactment from the mnemonic properties of discussion and reflection or analysis. As I have already noted, Porter has argued convincingly that the *Colloquies* are a matrix out of which students could shape their own conversations.[78] This improvisational activity would have further improved their recollection of Latin. Finally, a study of the effect of post-traumatic stress on the memories of Danes who lived through World War II has shown that, despite 'disintegration theories' that consider traumatic events to lead to fragmented memories, 'participants scoring higher on posttraumatic stress reactions had WWII memories that were more subjectively clear, more consequential and more often rehearsed'.[79] These individuals had better recollection of both positive and negative events from the period, and their traumatic memories were central to their life story and identity.[80] Chapter 2 explored medieval uses of violent imagery in memory work, showing how *Solomon and Saturn I*'s staging of a brutal teaching encounter would have recalled the pain and fear associated with basic pedagogy. Both modern psychological research and medieval mnemonic practice suggest that the traumatic or stressful events enacted by Bata's students could have helped them to learn passages from the *Colloquies*.

The studies discussed above, engaged as they are in tracing the ways the human mind works, can reasonably be used to illuminate Bata's *Colloquies*. There is, in addition, a rich body of research on 'educational drama' or 'drama in education', as it is called in the United Kingdom, or 'process drama', the Australian and North American term.[81] Research into educational drama has the benefit of extensive classroom observation, but it is difficult to apply its conclusions directly to early medieval texts. First, students who participate in drama activities in a twenty-first-century classroom not only understand the concept of theatrical make-believe, but also live in a society saturated with dramatic representation. Their experience of educational drama must be qualitatively different than that of Bata's students. Second, modern educators generally prize, and use drama to inculcate, a different set of values than those of medieval monastic teachers (for example, independence instead of obedience). A related issue is the discomfort today's educators often have with violent or sexual matters, one not necessarily shared by their medieval counterparts. Some, like Brian Edmiston, do argue that play-acting unethical scenes can benefit children, but researchers of early childhood education tend to focus on uncontroversial themes.[82] Despite these limitations, however, contemporary discussions of drama in education do resonate with the putative conditions and goals of Bata's *Colloquies*.

A few studies treat Bata's exact area of teaching: language pedagogy. Studies of the use of drama in language instruction stress that the teacher should start the improvisational drama with a 'pre-text', and that a debriefing session follow in which the lessons of the activity, linguistic or otherwise, are reviewed.[83] This closing reflection is structurally not unlike the teacher's 'sermon' at the end of Bata's *Colloquies* (discussed below). They also note the broader pedagogical implications of drama used to teach language. Patricia Dickson remarks that 'learning to use a second language is, in many ways, like learning to become a different person', adding that language teachers need to coach their students in culture-appropriate behaviour as well, and that the 'holistic experience' of drama can 'integrate language and culture'.[84] My own approach to Bata incorporates the idea that language education incorporates psychological, ethical, and social formation.

A number of analyses take up the ethical implications of pedagogical drama in general. Jonathan Levy scans the past four centuries for theorisations of how theatre forms a child's morality. Besides the potent dialogue, repetition, and memorisation bound up with drama, the thinkers surveyed by Levy also held that drama held up virtue to be emulated, ridiculed vice, and influenced the inner person through his outer actions.[85] One argument for the way theatre shapes the moral person, a favourite, as Levy notes, of the Jesuits and Brecht, is the presentation of a difficult moral choice to be made on the stage. This characteristic of theatre as an area where moral problems are posed, without necessarily being resolved, is a focus shared by a number of scholars today. Winston in particular argues that 'the teacher can use the drama to scaffold moral learning by offering the children opportunities to try out appropriate virtuous actions within the security of the make-believe', and that through drama, 'young people can learn to know pity, admiration, indignation, repulsion by feeling them in particular contexts'.[86] Winston, Edmiston, and Mallika Henry all note the 'perspectival' nature of drama: it allows children to adopt the positions of others imaginatively, to understand and judge their actions, and, through this process, to come to a better understanding of their own ethical identities.[87] While their analyses are grounded in contemporary classrooms, these scholars' discussions of the ethical uses of drama can prompt us to ask certain questions of Bata's textbook. What set of morals did Bata's students enact as they learned his *Colloquies*? Which perspectives did the dialogue form open for them? And what role did ethical ambiguity play in the boys' experience of the *Colloquies*?

The Violent Logic of Discipline

A reader encountering the *Colloquies* for the first time is likely to get the impression that violence is omnipresent in this fictional monastery, but in fact, only Colloquy 28 stages a disciplinary action, the beating of the oblate I discussed at the beginning of this chapter. What gives the impression of pervasive violence is the fact that the boys in the dialogues repeatedly discuss the threat of being punished by their teachers. Bata's *Colloquies* are more concerned with speaking about discipline than with discipline itself. This process begins early on in Colloquy 3, which starts with a threat from the master, who enjoins his students to save their hides by memorising what they have learned the previous day. The teacher then seems to leave the room. One student asks another to borrow a book, since he has lost his own and cannot search for it in fear of his stern master, adding: 'Et si aliquem ex nobis exire uiderit, statim uult eum flagellare bene' (82, And if he sees any of us go outside, he immediately wants to flog him well). The implication is that the master is just outside, ready to whip anyone who dares to leave the room. This sentence is the model for a trope which will appear again in the *Colloquies*: the prospect of punishment makes the boys imagine the master's desires and reactions even in his absence. This effect is further elaborated in Colloquy 5, which begins with the children on their own. One deputises another to warn the *schola* of their master's coming: 'Tu, puer, perge, et curre *cito* foras, et uide caute ubi magister noster sit *modo*, et si huc adpropinquauerit, tunc *citius* caue nos' (88, You, boy, go and run *quickly* outside, and check carefully where our master is *now*. If he should come near, then warn us *right away*). The boy runs out and reports that he has seen the master coming out of the church, and adds breathlessly:

> *Statim nunc* perueniet ad nos. Cauete uos, et cauti estote, et accipite *cito* libros uestros, et legite et cantate antequam perueniat huc, ne nos otiosos aut iocantes, cum uenerit, inueniat. Caueo uos. Ecce, post hostium stat *modo*, et auscultat si legentes aut cantantes aliquid erimus, et ecce *modo* adest. (88. My italics.)

> *Now* he'll reach us *at once*. Beware, and be careful, and grab your books *quickly*, and read and sing before he comes here, lest he find us idle or kidding around when comes. I'm warning you. There! He's standing behind the gate *now*, and he's listening to whether we're reading or singing anything. And look, he's here right *now*!

The effect is tense, gradual, cinematic, and climactic, building up to an almost physical sense of apprehension even in the silent reader. The use of the adverbs *cito*, *modo*, *statim*, *nunc* in both passages adds to the sense of immediacy. The young boys who learn this text are being taught to be self-policing, to imagine an authority figure who, like God, is always potentially watching, always standing right behind the door, always just about to open it and discover their slothfulness. The potential presence of an angry *magister* causes the boys to take an inventory of their own activities, to take on the role of the disciplinarian in his absence. Of course, the use of adverbs meaning 'now' and 'right away' obscures the fact that master is still only potentially present. That is, although the dynamic of imagined punishment and subsequent self-correction I am describing here seems self-evident to the modern reader schooled in panopticons and their power to turn prisoners into the agents of their own subjugation,[88] in the monastic context the prescribed custody has to have been neglected in order for this disciplinary mechanism to be activated. The potential discipline in this case not only corrects the boys' misdemeanours, but also hides the negligence of their teacher.

This repeated process of imagining punishment has a psycholinguistic effect as well as a behavioural one. The boys learning the rudiments of Latin through this dialogue literally learn how to express fear in their new language. Moreover, not only do they learn the proper vocabulary words (such as the forms of *caveo*) to use when warning and worrying, but they learn to bind the other common parts of speech used in this exchange to a feeling of apprehension. The student memorising Colloquy 5 remembers adverbs such as *cito* and *statim* all the better for having associated them with the powerful emotions induced by a frightening authority figure, and at some level, the language itself takes on a residue of these feelings. The fear which fixes Latin in the memory of the young learner is imprinted on his memory, quietly but indelibly bound up with the nature of Latin itself. While I would argue for the special affective power of any text used in the early stages of teaching a foreign language, Bata's *Colloquies* promise to be all the more powerful due to their added dimension of performance. His students would have gone beyond the already active processes of analysis and memorisation of texts we associate with medieval grammatical study: they would have embodied the roles set out by these texts. This kind of role-playing has a parallel in the medieval recitation or chanting of the Psalter, itself one of the central texts of early Latin pedagogy in the middle ages.[89] While the structure of the psalms invites identification with a biblical persona, the colloquies invite identification with a potential self. The boy's classroom performance consists not only in representing a role by reproducing the appropriate phrases, but also in incorporating the qualities and language of that role into himself.[90]

Or, to be more precise, roles. While the boys learning these colloquies practise being the frightened objects of an ever-present disciplinary gaze, they also begin to learn a language with which to police one another. In Colloquy 3, the boy who asks to borrow a book is met with an unfriendly response. His classmate refuses to lend him the book, and ascribes to him a catalogue of boyish misbehaviours:

> Quare uoluisti sic perdere tuum librum? Tota die huc et illuc discurris uagando, nihil boni faciens, nec uis nobiscum legere, nec sponte discere, nec uoluntarie cantare, nec scribere in tabula, nec in scedula nec in ullo pergameno nec in nulla quaternione. (82–4)

> Why did you want to lose your book like this? You run about all day, wandering here and there, doing nothing good. You don't want to read with us, nor learn of your own accord, nor sing voluntarily, nor write on your tablet, nor on your sheet nor on any parchment or quire.

As language pedagogy, this passage is masterful. Bata manages to work in the verbs for classroom activities (*legere, discere, cantare, scribere*) and the nouns for writing tools (*tabula, scedula, pergamenum, quaternio*), and he keeps the speech exciting by putting them all in negative grammatical structures. The effect is that the boys practising this speech are not only acting as students, but already taking on the role of the masters they may some day become. They are learning from the very beginning to criticise and influence each other's behaviour.

The sense of discipline becomes more powerful as the speech continues: 'Et nullus ex nobis scit ubi eris, nisi quando manducare uel bibere debemus uel ludere, et tamdiu hoc facis quamdiu magister noster foris remanet' (84, and none of us knows where you'll be, except when we should eat or drink or play, and you do this as long as our teacher stays outside). Here, as before, we have the suggestion that it is the master's absence which requires the boys to discipline each other. The wording of the accusing boy's complaint that his ne'er-do-well classmate only comes to eat and play, with its emphasis on *nullus ex nobis scit*, implies that the group of oblates has a right to know the whereabouts of each of its members. In other words, the boys themselves have a custodial function in the absence of the teacher. This authority, as implied by the boy's rhetoric, comes from his own pain. He later complains, 'pene omni die propter stultitiam tuam flagellis ac uirgis dirissimis cedimur a nostro papate' (84, nearly every day we're beaten with the most terrible whips and rods by our tutors because of your stupidity). The practice and prospect of punishment sanctions the boys to serve as each other's masters. Not surprisingly, the first boy later objects to this: 'quis constituit te super me uel super meos alios socios in magistrum, seu ad docendum nos siue ad regendum?' (84, Who set you up as master over me or my fellows, either to teach us or to control us?).

While monastic oblates often did have a responsibility to observe each other's behaviour as well as their own and to report accordingly in children's chapter, the practice of mutual discipline is brought to the foreground in colloquies where the master is absent.[91] In Colloquy 4, a (possibly older) student exhorts his fellow classmates to be studious in the teacher's absence:

> petite libros uestros cito, et in scamnis uestris sedentes legite, et firmate acceptos uestros, ut properanter reddere ualeatis cras in primo mane, et deinde plus discere a nostro instructore, ut quando senes eritis, tunc memoriter in cunctis libris latinis legere possitis et aliquid intellegere in illis, ut alios rursum queatis et docere et morigerari. (84–6)

> Reach for your books quickly. Sit in your seats and read. Study your assignments, so that you'll be able to recite them speedily early tomorrow morning and then learn more from our instructor, so that when you're old, you will be able to read from memory in all the Latin books and understand something in them, so you'll be able to teach others in return, and be of good character.

In this passage, the ultimate object of study is described as the ability to teach future students in turn. Indeed, much later in the *Colloquies*, one of the characters argues that the very process of teaching another is also one of learning, or rather, of teaching oneself: 'qui alium recte et bene docet uel ammonet, animum proprium ad doctrinam instigat' (146, he who teaches and admonishes another well rouses his own soul to learning). However, the equivalence established between *docet* and *ammonet* suggests that the material to be learned is not confined to the skills of reading and writing, or even to standards of proper behaviour and belief. (These, after all, were also the *magister*'s purview.) The boys are not only being taught what to teach, but to wield power and authority over their future students, in other words, how to be a teacher.

In this light, it may be worth thinking a little further about the use of the *Colloquies* in the classroom, especially considering the difference in structure between them and other medieval master–student dialogues. The structure of a typical dialogue of alternating questions and answers between two interlocutors, one clearly given the status of teacher and the other that of student, suggests that if the dialogue was ever performed in a classroom, teacher and student acted out the roles appropriate to them. This may not have even been the case, and even a typical school dialogue could play with notions of authority and power. Alcuin's dialogue on rhetoric features Charlemagne in the role of eager student and himself as teacher.[92] However, on the surface at least, the roles of dominant teacher and dominated student are clearly defined. Bata's *Colloquies* rupture any neat relationship of authority between master and student. They are multivocal, and many conversations take place between boys alone. There are also intermediary figures, such as students who seem older than their peers but still refer to other 'teachers' as authority figures. I write 'seem' because the manuscript gives no indication of who should deliver which line, and only the lines themselves hint at the identity of their speakers. While we cannot know how Bata apportioned roles to his students, the freeform structure of the dialogues suggests that boys may have taken on the roles of masters or older boys, or even that the master may have chosen at some point to speak in the voice of a student. Although the repeated theme of harsh discipline evokes a rigid power structure, the dialogues embody a dynamic process of gaining and practising authority over oneself and others.

Thus examined, the *Colloquies* seem to offer a neat and logical prescription for the education of oblate boys into monks and teachers. Even the focus on corporal punishment as opposed to other, non-violent forms of discipline makes sense when the application of pain is considered as a technique of socialisation into a group. Like the pain which characterises many initiation practices around the world, the physical anguish inflicted on these fictional boys can be seen as a way of introducing them into the society of the monastery. Alan Morinis argues that the pain inflicted during initiatory rites marks on the body of the young man the limitations he will have to accept to participate in the group.[93] For the real students learning Latin through these dialogues (who may or may not have suffered physical punishment on their own bodies), the act of repeatedly speaking about discipline constitutes a parallel form of integration into a society defined by self and mutual control.[94]

At the same time, the passages I quoted above imply that accepting the strictures of the classroom and the grammar of Latin will allow a boy to be a member of the monastic group, and to see himself as part of its history. He will have a relationship to the past through the books he has learned to read and committed to memory, and a relationship to the future through the students he will come to teach. In Colloquy 24, one monk asks another to identify the scribe of a certain book: 'Quis scripsit hoc? Aut quis scripsit scripturam hanc? … Aut quis scripsit paginam hanc aut lineam istam aut alphabetum hoc, aut uerba haec aut litteras has?' (134, Who wrote this? Or, who wrote this writing? Or, who wrote this page, or this line, or this alphabet, or these words, or these letters?). The other replies that the scribe in question is now old and can no longer write because of his old age and failed vision. A third monk adds:

> Dignus est certe, ut bene uiuat. Multum bonum sue manus habent factum. Multos iuuenes, ut nostri fratres dicunt, pueros et adholescentulos, quando fortis in corpore suo fuit, instruendo docuit ad scribendum, et aliqui ex ipsis boni scriptores adhuc uiuunt, aliqui mortui sunt, et monasterii istius scriptores sunt modo, et sepe multos scribunt libros, et uendunt eos, et multum sibi lucrum inde adipiscuntur. (134)

> He certainly deserves to live well. His hands have done much good. When his body was stronger, he taught many youths, boys, and young men to write, as our brothers tell it. Some of those good writers are still living, some are dead. They are now the scribes of this monastery, and they often write many books, sell them, and gain much profit from it.

This old scribe has not only become a figure of consequence because of the books he has created, books which will cause others to speak of him even after his death, but by teaching his craft to others he has become the scribal grandfather of many other manuscripts. He is, we may take it, a model for the young boys to emulate, and his legacy a reason to submit to and embody the constant discipline of the classroom.

In a further move at the end of the *Colloquies*, Bata suggests that acting out the roles of a punished, tormented man and of an admonishing teacher prepares the boys for the most important performance, a life modelled after Christ. The final Colloquy of the collection takes the form of a sermon from the master, the one place where the speaking teacher invites us to identify him with Bata. Near the end of his speech, he tells the boys that 'Christum, qui caput nostrum est, sequi debemus, qui cunctis bona docet et ammonet' (174, we should follow Christ, who is our guide, who teaches good things and admonishes all). He is presenting Christ in one of his traditional roles of teacher, but he is a teacher to be obeyed precisely because of his suffering:

> Audite ipsum Christum. Timete; facite quod precipit, ne contempnatis mandata ipsius, quia pro omnibus incarnatus, pannis circumdatus est, esuriuit, sitiuit, lassus ad puteum sedit, fatigatus in naue dormiuit, contumelias et obprobria a Iudeis audiuit, et sputa eorum non abegit, alapas in faciem accepit, in ligno sancte crucis pependit, animam effudit. (174)

> Hear Christ himself. Fear him. Do what he instructs, do not disdain his commands, for he was made into flesh for all, he was enveloped with rags, he hungered, he thirsted, he sat weary at the well, he slept tired in the ship, he listened to the insults and abuses of the Jews, and he did not remove their spit, he received blows on his face, he hung on the wood of the holy cross, he poured out his soul.

The physical hardships suffered by Christ remind the audience of the *Colloquies* of the children's complaints about their own penurious living conditions, and the insults and blows echo both the infighting and corporal punishment the fictional oblates repeatedly undergo. Christ, the teacher who must be obeyed, has withstood these stoically; the oblates are invited to do the same, and to enjoy the corresponding heavenly rewards.

This kind of catalogue of Christ's sufferings is found frequently in medieval writing, but Bata's use of it in a pedagogical context suggests a connection to 1 Corinthians 4:11–12. There, Paul describes the sufferings of the apostles: 'et esurimus et sitimus/ et nudi sumus/ et colaphis caedimur … maledicimur et benedicimus/ persecutionem patimur et sustinemus' (we are both hungry and thirsty, and we are naked, and buffeted by blows … we are cursed and we bless, we suffer persecution and we endure).[95] The apostles' travails are, of course, an imitation of Christ, and Paul later enjoins the Corinthians to imitate him: 'rogo ergo vos/ imitatores mei estote' (1 Corinthians 4:16, I ask you therefore, be my imitators), and, later, 'imitatores mei estote sicut et ego Christi' (1 Corinthians 11:1, be my imitators, just as I imitate Christ). David Capes reads the Gospels in the context of ancient laudatory biography, which offered up the lives of good men as patterns to be imitated. He notes especially the way Paul locates authority, and by implication, exemplarity, in the cross, in weakness, and in human suffering.[96] In the final sermon of the *Colloquies*, Bata incorporates both kinds of exemplarity, beginning with the master's injunction to the students, 'quos bonos uidetis et iustos et pios et misericordes imitamini' (174, imitate those men you see as good and just and pious and merciful), and culminating with the model of a suffering Christ discussed above. Both types of imitation can be said to further the master's disciplinary programme.

This cannot be the whole story, however. If the threat of corporal punishment is justified by the bright academic career it opens to oblates and by the opportunity it provides to engage in an *imitatio Christi*, it is nevertheless a powerful, potentially explosive force to introduce into the monastic community. In teaching them how violent language can be used to modify their own behaviour and to influence the behaviour of others for positive ends, the *magister* who whips is also teaching his students that violence *should* be used. I would argue that Bata recognises this at some level, and in Colloquy 25 he shows how the system of punishment and mutual correction falls apart. The colloquy begins with one monk of indeterminate age (perhaps an older student) upbraiding a young boy for a variety of bad behaviours: arriving late for reading or work, being lazy, and always thinking evil. His attack seems to follow the model of earlier arguments in which boys took on the disciplinary roles of absent teachers. However, in this case, his anger spirals out of control. 'Vnus stercus es' he exclaims, 'Vnus diabulus es' (136, You're a piece of shit! You're a devil!). When the accused defends himself, the argument degenerates into an impressively creative and varied list of vile insults, most of them faecally themed.

These are undoubtedly some of the 'joking words' Bata's pedagogic sensibility has led him to introduce into the dialogue, and it is fair to assume that these speeches made Latin more engaging and memorable for the students memorising them. On the other hand, the scene also shows how readily the practice of mutual discipline can become aggressive and hateful. Later, in Colloquy 28, when the *magister* does have a boy beaten, his encouragements to the students doing the beating to 'hit harder' and his curt, cold replies to the boy's pleading for sympathy show that his desire to hurt the child is as great as his desire to correct. As much as Bata's *Colloquies* condone the use of punishment to keep the society of children in order, they also recognise that once violence is introduced into child rearing, it is itself very difficult to restrain. This paradox is related to another dilemma implied by the sermon on Christ quoted above: in order for Christ to suffer spits, insults, and blows, there have to be persecutors to deliver them. The boy submitting to punishment may learn to glorify his suffering by comparing it to Christ's, but this act also turns the well-meaning disciplinarian into a hateful – and hating – figure.

In Colloquy 25, the angry monk complains, 'Ego uero saepe te corrigo uerbis et correptione et flagellis duris et minis nimiis, sed nihil mihi prodest' (142, I often correct you with words and reproofs and harsh whips and excessive threats, but it doesn't do me a bit of good). In staging this brief moment of frustration, Bata explicitly recognises the pedagogical limitations of corporal punishment. While the monk speaking the line means to harry and accuse the oblate, the multiplicity of interpretations called forth by classroom performance suggests another reading, one in which the monk reveals himself to be misguided in his use of threats and whips. The ability of a single phrase to support conflicting pedagogical ideologies is true more generally for the *Colloquies*, and it is what makes them so challenging and provocative: Bata, like Chaucer's gods, speaks in amphibologies. By constructing his Latin textbook to be at once threatening and funny, serious and ludic, he offers his students the opportunity to perform both discipline and dissent.

CHAPTER 4

Recollection
Andreas

Our birth is but a sleep and a forgetting

William Wordsworth, 'Ode'[1]

Anglo-Saxon fictions of teaching foreground memory as an essential component of education. This is, at first glance, not surprising. After all, what else is learning if not building up a store of memories? The texts treated in this book use memory in different ways and to different ends, however. In *Solomon and Saturn I*, the mnemonic quality of the runic letters of the Pater Noster reminds the poem's reader of his early education. The letters' goal is not to help him remember the familiar prayer, but the excitement and attentiveness bound up with learning to read it. Ælfric Bata crafts a set of dialogues that teach Latin through emotionally charged or violent speeches. These are intended to fix vocabulary in the pupils' memories, and by extension, to incorporate the young monks into the institutional memory of the monastery. Memory is also central to the Old English poem *Andreas*, but in a significantly different form than in the other two texts. *Andreas* understands learning as a dynamic process of recollection, forgetting, and remembering again. Like *Solomon and Saturn I* and Bata's *Colloquies*, it shows how memory is bound up with emotion. In the case of *Andreas*, this emotion is a sense of terrifying wonder that prompts the learner to reflect on what he already knows.

Andreas does not rank among the greatest hits of Anglo-Saxon literature. A hagiographic adventure story told in the heroic vocabulary of Old English verse, it features a protagonist who is neither hero nor saint. Its landscape is littered with curious, unlikely creatures, including a stone angel that speaks and walks and an ancient column that releases a deadly flood. Although it is a poem deeply concerned with teaching and conversion, most of the pedagogy it depicts fails, and the ultimate conversion of heathens is performed not through teaching but by an act of genocide. Worse, it is a deeply anti-Judaic work, repeatedly depicting Jews as blind unbelievers, little better than savage cannibals. Finally, *Andreas* is notorious for its awkward, even ungrammatical, appropriation of phrases and images from other Old English poems. If anything can be said for *Andreas*, it is that it rewards typological and allegorical criticism, an approach that succeeds in making a nice Christian poem out of this wayward text.

In this chapter I argue that *Andreas*, despite its quirkiness and errors and unruly hero, makes sense. In fact, the sense of *Andreas* is to be found precisely in what does not fit, from the shape of the larger story right down to individual half lines and single words. *Andreas* uses a scene of teaching between Christ and the apostle Andrew to model its relationship to its readers, whom it educates through wonder, recollection, and reflection. The product of a literary culture shaped by *aenigma* and dialogue, *Andreas* uses embedded riddles to spur its readers to think about objects and words from the past, to meditate on what they already know, and to consider whether they truly understand it or not. In shaping the apocryphal life of Andrew into a poem, the poet drew on a theory of learning as recollection found in Cynewulf's *Elene* and in Boethius' *Consolation of Philosophy*. As a result, *Andreas* is filled with wondrous things that prompt contemplation, but it offers no pleasant, purely aesthetic wonder; rather, it is a wonder that discomfits, frightens, and instructs.

Introduction

The apocryphal adventures of Andrew and Matthew are transmitted in a number of Greek and Latin recensions as well as in two Old English prose versions.[2] While we do not have the direct source of *Andreas*, it is closest to an extant Greek text found in ninth-century manuscripts, the Πράξεις Ἀνδρέου καὶ Ματθεία εἰς τὴν χώραν τῶν ἀνθρωφάγων (Acts of Andrew and Mathias in the City of the Cannibals), here called the *Praxeis*. Most scholars, however, assume *Andreas* is based on a now-lost Latin translation. Other surviving Latin versions relevant for comparison to *Andreas* include an eleventh-century fragment discovered by Maximilien Bonnet ('The Bonnet Fragment') and a complete version from the twelfth-century manuscript Rome, Codex Casanatensis, Nr 1104 (*Casanatensis*).[3] The Old English homiletic prose account is found in two versions: the full text is in CCCC 198, and a shortened version counts among the Blickling Homilies.[4] *Andreas* itself is in the Vercelli Book; it is of unknown authorship, and datable roughly from the middle to the end of the ninth century.[5]

The story begins with Matthew, who has had the terrible misfortune of landing in Mermedonia, a legendary place probably near the Black Sea. Its locals have the unpleasant habit of capturing strangers, putting out their eyes, giving them a poisonous drink that will damage their wits and render them beastlike, and after letting them marinate for a while, making them into dinner. When Christ commands Andrew to travel to Mermedonia and save Matthew from the cannibals, Andrew refuses, claiming the task is impossible. Christ rebukes him, and the next day a mysterious boat appears on the seashore ready to convey the apostle and his men to Mermedonia. Little does Andrew know that the young, very intelligent-looking helmsman is Christ in disguise, though the poem's readers do. When a storm breaks and terrifies Andrew's companions, the sailor advises Andrew to comfort his men by describing the miracles Jesus performed when he was living.

The helmsman teaches Andrew by having him teach his disciples in turn. In the most unusual miracle Andrew recalls, Jesus addresses an angel carved into the wall of the Jewish temple in the presence of recalcitrant rabbis, commanding it to leave its place and announce his divine lineage to everyone present. The stone proclaims Jesus to be the son of God, and despite the Jews' accusations of magic, it carries on with its task. It heads to a grave in Mambre where Abraham, Isaac, and Jacob are buried, awakens them from their deathly sleep, and charges them to proclaim the glory of god to the people. The people are, naturally, terrified.

Over the course of their pedagogic dialogue, the helmsman repeatedly asks Andrew why the Jews did not believe in Jesus' divinity, if, perhaps, he did not perform enough wonders that would serve as signs of his true nature. Andrew paints the Jews as sinful, poor students of Jesus' teaching, but he in fact has also faltered in his faith. As a direct witness of the wonders Jesus performed in his lifetime, he should have understood that Christ could bring him to Mermedonia in time to save Matthew. Scholars have noted how ironic it is that Andrew lectures Christ without recognising him,[6] but one might excuse him for being fooled by a god in disguise. The problem, rather, is that the faith he learned as a disciple of Christ is weak.

While the first part of *Andreas* is concerned with confusion and mistaken identities, the second part promises recognition and clarity. After a saintly catnap, Andrew and his men awake on the Mermedonian shore, where he realises shamefully that he had been ferried by Christ himself. Christ appears in the form of a boy and instructs Andrew to go into the city and suffer in imitation of him. He tells the apostle that he will convert the Mermedonians by following his own example of heroic endurance. Once in the city, Andrew liberates Matthew and the other prisoners, but the Mermedonians, under the influence of the devil, capture Andrew and torture him. Despite Christ's promise that Andrew's tolerance of unbearable pain will teach the heathens, it does not, in fact, convert anyone. Instead, Andrew is put back in prison, where he commands a column to let forth a flood that drowns most of the Mermedonians. This finally seems to impress the cannibals, and they acknowledge the might of God. Andrew brings a number of young people back to life, baptises the Mermedonians, and sets a bishop named Platan over them. Still, Andrew remains an unwilling teacher, and is about to set sail when Christ appears to him again, warning him that he cannot simply abandon the new converts without properly teaching them the faith.

'The *Andreas* poet's cannibalizing of other Old English verse has seemed tasteless, overdone, and, above all, botched,' writes Roberta Frank, summarising a body of work often dismissive of the poem. 'His composition serves up a gallimaufry of previously loved formulae, sound bites chewed on, flaunted, but not always fully digested.'[7] Indeed, much early criticism of *Andreas* explored the tension between the poem's narrative source, that is, the story of Andrew's adventures as the poet probably found it in a Latin text, and its poetic sources, those Old English poems that the *Andreas* poet plundered for phrases. Already in the nineteenth century, scholars noticed the overlap between *Andreas*, *Beowulf*, and the poems of Cynewulf, and attempted to establish whether the cause was common authorship or borrowing.[8] Faced with the counterargument that phrases or formulas common to *Andreas* and other poems might simply be part of the inherited stock of early English heroic poetry, those who supported the theory of direct borrowing pointed to the ungainly, even ungrammatical, ways these elements appeared in *Andreas*. If it seemed logical and natural for the *Beowulf* poet to say he had never heard of a boat more splendidly laden with treasure when describing the lushly outfitted burial ship of Scyld Scefing, it was obviously nonsensical for the *Andreas* poet to make nearly the same hyperbolic statement about the boat steered by Christ: his passenger, Andrew, had, after all, just explained that he had no money for the fare.[9] It was appropriate for Hygelac to offer his men 'hund þusenda/ landes ond locenra beaga' (2994b–95a, a hundred thousand's worth of land and linked rings),[10] but it was surprising when Andrew complained to the ship's helmsman:

> Næbbe ic fæted gold   ne feohgestreon,
> welan ne wiste,   ne wira gespann,
> landes ne locenra beaga. (301–303a)

> I do not have plated gold or rich treasure, neither riches nor food nor wrought wires, neither of land nor of linked rings.

As Krapp and Schaar note, the line 'landes ne locenra beaga' is modified from *Beowulf* but remains ungrammatical in its new context. In the epic, the nouns are in the genitive because they are governed by 'þusenda', while in *Andreas*, they follow a list of nouns in the accusative.[11] This type of apparently negligent borrowing led scholars such as Satyendar Das to declare the composer of *Andreas* 'a poet of a very low order, who … introduced fine situations and descriptions after the manner of the previous poetry for the mere love of a fine phrase'.[12]

Despite Leonard Peters' 1951 argument that any similarities between *Andreas* and *Beowulf* can be traced back either to the *Praxeis* or to conventional Anglo-Saxon poetic formulas,[13] recent scholarship has reinforced the view that *Andreas* features deliberate borrowings from both *Beowulf* and the Cynewulfian poems. In several articles, Anita Riedinger strengthens our understanding of the *Andreas–Beowulf* connection by comparing their shared formulas and formulaic sets to the corpus of Old English poetry. She argues that the poems share many formulas that do not appear elsewhere in the poetic corpus, that *Andreas* borrowed from *Beowulf*, and that the pattern of borrowing – adapting heavily from certain sections of *Beowulf* while ignoring others – suggests a poet working with a written version of the earlier epic.[14] Most thorough and conclusive is Alison Powell's 2002 unpublished Cambridge dissertation. Using concordance software to isolate significant parallels between the poems, that is, unique parallels between poems and within *Andreas* featuring verbatim repetition, Powell comes to several conclusions.[15] She demonstrates that the *Andreas* poet has a 'tendency to recall phrases, collocations and passages' from earlier in the poem, that the poet clearly borrows from *Beowulf*, often in clusters of echoes, and that he borrows heavily from the signed works of Cynewulf too.[16] More interestingly, Powell shows that *Andreas* borrows in different ways: its parallels with *Beowulf* tend to attract attention, or in her words, 'demonstrate a concern with contrast, perspective and irony', while borrowings from Cynewulf tend to be free of irony, worked more smoothly into the texture of the poetry.[17] The nature of the relationships between *Andreas* and its poetic sources now seems relatively clear. The question remaining is how to interpret them.

Readers more generous to *Andreas* than its early critics have seen in the poet's method a creative reworking of traditional formulas, whether due to a narrative strategy of increasing the drama and tension of certain episodes, as a mode of adapting the so-called Germanic heroic vocabulary to the tenets of Christian faith, or even as a nudge to allegorical interpretation.[18] Likewise, one of the major ways of recovering *Andreas* from its difficult critical past has been to read its incongruities of plot and diction, the quirky elements it inherited from its apocryphal source along with puzzling alterations that seem to be original to the poem, as elements in a carefully constructed typological narrative. Inspired by Thomas D. Hill's article on figural narrative in *Andreas* in 1969, a host of scholars have dug up scriptural and patristic sources, echoes, and explications for *cruces* large and small in *Andreas*.[19] At its best, typological criticism illuminates how the poetic craft of *Andreas* serves its theological message, as in Lisa Kiser's sensitive reading of how paths and roads depicted in the poem literalise the Christian motif of the *via*, or 'way', of Christ. But such studies also tend to smooth over *Andreas*' quirks and interpretative problems in their attempts to recover an orthodox message of devout Christianity.[20] They bring *Andreas* into line with the conventions of other hagiographic and religious writing, portraying the often-maladroit Andrew as an effective saint and imitator of Christ.

Teaching in *Andreas*

As we might expect from a hagiography, *Andreas* is deeply interested in the teaching of Christian faith. It is rife with scenes of pedagogy: Christ teaches the Jews, Andrew teaches his men, Christ teaches Andrew, Andrew's men teach him, the devil teaches the Mermedonians, and finally Andrew teaches them too. What we might not expect is how frequently teaching fails. Critics have recognised Andrew's less-than-heroic behaviour in the narrative: David Hamilton notes the irony of Andrew talking about how Christ revealed himself through miracles without recognising that he is speaking to Christ himself, Ivan Herbison describes Andrew's 'moments of weakness and vulnerability' but maintains that the saint remains a model, and Edward Irving, Jr remarks on the comic effect of Andrew's complaints after his torture.[21] Andrew's repeated stumbles speak to a nuanced view of baptism and conversion, as Amity Reading has argued, one in which 'turning' to Christian faith is an ongoing process rather than a single, completed event.[22] Reading's article convincingly explains much of the poem's interest in failure: Jews, Mermedonians, and Andrew himself represent varieties of incompletely converted Christian subjects.[23] But *Andreas* is not only interested in the ends of education; it is also deeply attentive to its methods. Over the course of its many pedagogical moments, the poem introduces several teaching techniques, only to show them founder.

When Andrew first appears, he is presented as a holy teacher; in Achaia he 'leode lærde on lifes weg' (170, taught the people the path of life). When

God commands him to travel to Mermedonia, Andrew becomes stun-ningly ignorant, claiming that an angel might know the way to that land, but he does not. He does not know any friends in the strange land (198b, ne synt me winas cuðe), nor does he know the minds of men there (199b–200a, ne þær æniges wat/ hæleða gehygdo), and anyway, he does not even know how to get there the way an angel would. Despite being a teacher who shows others 'the way', when asked to save Matthew he claims ignor-ance and impotence and attempts, quite transparently, to pass the buck.

After establishing that Andrew is ignorant despite being a teacher, the early part of the poem explores the process of teaching through miracles. Christ is depicted as a pedagogue who convinces and comforts by per-forming wonders; his students continue his teaching by relating the mira-cles in turn. When a storm breaks out at sea, the helmsman suggests to Andrew that he relate those mysteries (419a, rece þa gerynu) that Christ had performed on earth in order to comfort his men. Andrew relates Jesus' calming of the storm, and in doing so teaches his retainers (462b, þegnas lærde). Duly soothed, they fall asleep. The helmsman then presses the point, asking Andrew why the Jews did not recognise that Christ was God despite the wonders he performed in their presence. Andrew insists that Jesus performed many miracles, and lists the typical ones: wine out of water, the multiplication of loaves and fish, healing of the dumb, deaf, and sick of limb (573–94). This is how 'he drew people through teaching to the joyous faith' (597b–98a, þurh lare speon/ to þam fægeran gefean). Still, despite Andrew's insistence that Jesus adequately taught through the performance of wonders, the Jews refused to learn:

> ... haliges lare
> synnige ne swulgon,   þeah he soðra swa feala
> tacna gecyðde   þær hie to segon.   (709b–11)

The sinners did not swallow the holy one's teaching, although he performed so many true signs where they observed them.

The apostle seems amazed at this inability to learn on the part of the Jews, describing them as having a 'tweogende mod' (771b, a doubting mind). Andrew Scheil has argued that this representation of Jews is typically 'anti-Judaic rhetoric of spiritual and mental deficiency'.[24] While this is true, at this point in the narrative, Andrew has also doubted Christ's power. His narration of the miracles Jesus performed while alive suggests that he observed them firsthand. Despite having witnessed these wonders, and having seen in them a sign 'that the living God never abandons a champion on the earth, if his courage avails' (459–60, þæt næfre forlæteð lifgende God/ eorl on eorðan, gif his ellen deah), when Andrew was asked to obey God's command, he did not believe in the lord's omnipotence or support. The poem is anti-Judaic to be sure, but it is more than that, since Christ fails to teach *anyone* with his miracles, including his own apostle.[25] Despite seeming to excoriate the 'blindness' of the Jews,[26] *Andreas* throws doubt on the very idea that faith can be taught through miracles.

When Andrew awakens outside Mermedonia, he recognises his error. He prays, describing his failure as a lack of knowledge, perception, and recognition, all concepts denoted by the verb *ongietan*, a key term in the poem. The word is repeated, emphasising the point that Andrew has suffered from spiritual and intellectual blindness. 'Nu ic ... ongiten hæbbe' (897, now I ... have understood) he states, although when he stepped on the ship he 'ongitan ne cuðe' (901b, could not recognise) Christ. Most of all, he claims that he now grasps Christ's ability to comfort and help his followers. Christ then appears to him, and Andrew once again chastises himself for talking too much and understanding too little, for not being able to recognise the good man on the sea voyage (922–23a, þæt ic þe swa godne ongitan ne meahte/ on wægfære). Andrew's dramatic recognition of his mistake is interesting in two respects. First, in the poem's analogues, Jesus comforts Andrew by telling him that he did not sin.[27] In *Andreas*, Jesus claims instead that he did not sin *as much as* when he refused his original request to travel to Mermedonia. That is, in the Old English poem, Andrew sins *twice*, first by doubting Christ's power to help him, then by misrecognising the Lord himself. The second point is that Andrew's language continues the vocabulary of perception and knowledge so central to the poem as a whole. He was stubborn and ignorant before the sea journey, dense while being catechised on the boat, but now he claims to have learned his lesson. Christ confirms that the miracle of the sea passage has now taught Andrew the extent of divine power. He is now ready to be a teacher to the heathen Mermedonians.

In order to help him do so, Christ introduces a second type of pedagogy: instruction by example. He informs Andrew that he will be tortured and admonishes Andrew to bear his pain by remembering Christ's travails, in short, to accomplish his mission through *imitatio Christi*.[28] Christ explicitly calls his own suffering a model lesson or *bysen* for his disciples, promising Andrew that in following his example, he will convert the Mermedonians:

> Ic adreah feala
> yrmþa ofer eorðan;   wolde ic eow on ðon
> þurh bliðne hige   bysne onstellan,
> swa on ellþeode   ywed wyrðeð.

Manige syndon   in þysse mæran byrig,
þara þe ðu gehweorfest   to heofonleohte
þurh minne naman,   þeah hie morðres feala
in fyrndagum   gefremed habban.   (969b–76)

I suffered many hardships on earth; through that I wanted to set you an
example with a happy mind, as it will be revealed among this foreign
people. There are many in this splendid city whom you will turn to the
heavenly light through my name, although they have perpetrated many
a murder in times past.

When he comes to be tortured by the Mermedonians, Andrew succeeds in
his mission, at least for a while. On the first day of his persecution, Andrew
still has faith: 'Hæfde him on innan/ ellen untweonde' (1241b–42a, he had
inside him courage undoubting). The second day, despite weeping loudly,
Andrew delivers a model oration, affirming his belief that Christ will not
abandon him as long as he stays true to the lord's teachings. Even the
devil, when he inevitably appears, understands Andrew to be claiming the
land by imitating Christ's passion on the cross, highlighting the pedagogic
aspect of *imitatio Christi* by remarking that Andrew behaves 'swa dyde
lareow þin' (1321b, as did your teacher).

On the third day, Andrew's attempt to imitate Christ fails. Torture gets
the better of him, and he begins to call to God sad-hearted, or 'geomormod' (1398a). His complaint is in one sense evocative, firmly in the tradition of the Anglo-Saxon lament, often the lyric outpourings of speakers
who are *geomor*. Read another way, however, Andrew is petulant, shock-
ingly associating his despair with Christ's weakness:

Hwæt, ðu sigora weard,
dryhten hælend,   on dæges tide
mid Iudeum   geomor wurde,
ða ðu of gealgan,   God lifigende,
fyrnweorca frea,   to fæder cleopodest,
cininga wuldor,   ond cwæde ðus:
'Ic ðe, fæder engla,   frignan wille,
lifes leohtfruma;   hwæt forlætest ðu me?'
Ond ic nu þry dagas   þolian sceolde
wælgrim witu!   (1406b–15a)

Lo, ruler of victories, Lord saviour, you became troubled on that
daytime among the Jews, when you, living God, lord of creation, called
to the father from the gallows, and spoke thus: 'I wish to ask you, father
of angels, life's beginning of light; why have you forsaken me?' And now
for three days I have had to suffer violent tortures!

The penultimate line of this passage, with its alliteration on 'þ' emphasising 'þry' (three) and 'þolian' (suffering), reveals how Andrew perceives the magnitude of his pain: Christ suffered on the cross for only one day, after all, while Andrew is being put through three days of torture. To put this in context, Tertullian encouraged martyrs to demonstrate both their faith and God's power by suffering stoically.[29] An Anglo-Saxon reader or hearer of *Andreas* might have thought of Vincent, described by Prudentius in his *Peristephanon* as 'tanto laetior/ omni vacantem nubilo/ frontem serenam luminat' (125–27, all the more cheerful, his serene face beaming without a trace of gloom) even as his torturers became exhausted, or of Bede's St Alban, who bore his beatings 'patienter … immo gaudenter' (patiently … indeed joyfully).[30] Not only is Andrew not impassible like most saints, but he goes on to remind Christ that he had promised his disciples that their bodies would not be harmed 'if we would follow your teaching' (1424, gif we þine lare læstan woldon). He describes his fallen hair, slit sinews, and spent blood, implying that Christ has not made good on his word. He even twice wishes for death. Unlike other saints, however, he does not ask to die in order to enjoy the crown of martyrdom or to be joined with God in heaven. In Andrew's case, the pain is simply too much to bear: 'Is me feorhgedal/ leofre mycle þonne þeos lifcearo!' (1427b–28, death is dearer to me than this wretched life) he finally exclaims.

This would-be exemplary passion follows a similar strategy to the earlier teaching of faith through miracles. Here, again, is a carefully constructed scene of pedagogy, but one that allows the close reader to see fissure lines. Frederick Biggs sees in Andrew's passion a perfect imitation of Christ's. His 'geomormod' echoes the dying Jesus' 'geomor', and he even expresses his dejection with the words Christ spoke on the cross.[31] It is true that, as on his sea voyage, Andrew remembers a scene from the life of Christ, but it remains questionable what he understands from it. For this quote from Matthew 27:46 and Mark 15:34, 'My God, my God, why hast thou forsaken me', is itself a quotation of the first line of Psalm 22, or Psalm 21 in the Septuagint numbering. It has long been debated whether Christ adopts David's lament to express despair, or if he is citing the beginning of a psalm because it ends with confidence in God: 'he hath not slighted nor despised the supplication of the poor man. Neither hath he turned away his face from me: and when I cried to him he heard me.'[32] Late antique and medieval commentators on the Gospels and Psalms offered a variety of interpretations: in his commentary on Matthew, Jerome notes that the psalm refers to the Saviour rather than to David or Esther, and argues that the 'verborum humilitatem et querimonias derelicti' (the humility of the words and the complaints of the abandoned one) are not to be wondered at, because they demonstrate the sin or 'scandalum' of the crucifixion of God.[33] Elsewhere, he claims that Christ recited the entire psalm while on the cross (animaduertimus totum psalmum a Domino in cruce posito decantari).[34] Augustine points out that God had not forsaken Christ, since he himself was God (non enim dereliquerat illum Deus, cum ipse esset Deus). Instead, Christ spoke to draw the attention of Christians to the fact that the prophetic psalm was written about him.[35] Cassiodorus writes that the lament is meant to express Christ's humanity, but also suggests that Christ was confused or agitated by his impending death.[36] Bede echoes Jerome, adding that Christ showed the fragility of his body, while maintaining the strength and wisdom of God.[37] What seems clear is that Andrew ignores the psalm's promise of divine aid, as well as the fact that Jesus' call makes good on the messianic prophecy Christians read into the Psalms.

While Christ does heal Andrew's body and transform his blood into flowers, Andrew's passion remains a scene of failed learning. When Andrew awoke on the beach and realised that he had misrecognised and underestimated Christ, we seemed to have witnessed the successful education of an apostle, one who would then use what he had learned to teach the heathens. Unfortunately, Andrew's not-quite-brave suffering has no effect on the Mermedonians. In a typical passion, members of the audience – be they individuals or multitudes – are moved by the saint's miraculous endurance to convert to Christianity. In *Andreas*, precisely none of the Mermedonians convert. Healed from his wounds, Andrew releases a devastating flood that kills most of them, and the remaining few are terrorised into accepting baptism. Even then, Andrew seems an inadequate teacher, eager to leave his new flock: Christ must appear to him one last time to convince him to spend a week with the former cannibals, teaching them the faith and establishing a bishop to lead them.

Andreas carefully dismantles not only the conventions of hagiography, but also pedagogical commonplaces. The demonstration of miracles fails to convince not only the Jews, which we might expect, but also one of Christ's disciples and a saint in his own right. Andrew's careful emulation of Christ's passion reveals his lack of understanding of Christ's words. Despite Christ's prediction that this suffering will teach, it converts no one. Indeed, the only typically medieval pedagogic notion *Andreas* seems to uphold is the effectiveness of violence and fear. The point, however, is not that teaching is impossible. Rather, *Andreas* presents education as a dynamic process of forgetting and recollection, doubt and faith. Andrew does not simply know what he has learned, but repeatedly forgets, makes mistakes, misunderstands. Christ appears several times to teach him, and he does so not by presenting new information, but by reminding Andrew of what he has already seen and comprehended.

There is, however, a pedagogical method that accounts for the falters and stumbles we find in *Andreas*. This is the theory that we learn by recollecting, by answering questions and drawing on knowledge already present. It would be convenient to claim it as the only effective, or at least the most effective, form of teaching in the poem, but that is not so. According to the logic of my reading it fails, just as do miracles and *imitatio Christi*; only a stunning act of violence succeeds in thoroughly teaching and converting. And yet this is the most important kind of pedagogy represented, at once closely linked to the other forms of teaching in the narrative, a clue to the interpretation of some of the stranger scenes in the poem, and a key to the poetics of *Andreas* as a whole. Moreover, as a set of ideas about how the human mind works, it accounts for the very failure of teaching and belief.

Learning by Remembering

The doctrine of recollection, or *anamnesis*, was developed by Plato in three of his dialogues, the *Meno*, the *Phaedo*, and the *Phaedrus*. Dominic Scott explains it succinctly:

> The soul pre-exists the body, and was consciously in possession of knowledge in its earlier state. Upon entering the body the soul forgets its knowledge, but retains it latently in the form of a memory. What makes discovery possible, therefore, is our ability to recollect and revive these forms within us.[38]

In his dialogue *De magistro*, 'On the teacher', Augustine adapts Platonic *anamnesis* to a theory of Christian teaching. Rather than imagining the student as a blank slate on which the teacher inscribes material to be learned, or as a vessel to be filled up with knowledge – both metaphors for teaching passed down through the ages – Augustine argues that human teachers only draw out knowledge that is already present within the learner. His claim is based on an argument that it is impossible to teach the unknown using language, or more broadly, signs; signs can only point to what is already known. When human teachers use linguistic signs to 'teach', they are really only directing the student through a process of introspection.[39] The true teacher, the one who placed the wisdom there in the first place, is Christ.

De magistro was not a popular work in Anglo-Saxon England. It appears in a tenth-century manuscript from Canterbury, and the title is cited by Aldhelm.[40] More likely conduits for the idea were Augustine's *Soliloquies* and Boethius' *Consolation of Philosophy*, both attested in multiple Anglo-Saxon manuscripts, and both rendered into Old English as part of King

Alfred's translation programme.[41] The Latin originals of these texts are similar in a number of ways; both are dialogues interested in the power of philosophy to heal and illuminate. Boethius knew the work of Augustine well, and it has been proposed that he wrote the *Consolation* as a kind of sequel to Augustine's dialogues *Contra academicos*, *De beata vita*, and *De ordine*, using the form of the *Soliloquies*.[42] The Old English translations are even closer. As Thomas Carnicelli and Nicole Discenza have shown, the Old English *Consolation* shows the influence of the Latin *Soliloquies*, while the Old English *Soliloquies* show the influence of both Latin and Old English *Consolations*. So similar are the two translations in phrasing and translation strategy that most scholars believe them to be the work of a single author.[43]

Augustine's ideas about recollection versus divine illumination change throughout his life, but in the *Soliloquies* at least, he claims that good students of the liberal arts 'illas … in se oblivione obrutas eruunt discendo' (in the process of learning, dig up the knowledge buried in oblivion within them).[44] The Alfredian translation of the *Soliloquies* is loose – the translator adds a third book to finish the job Augustine left incomplete – but it retains the concept of *anamnesis*. Reason asks Augustine why he will not believe in the immortality of the soul despite the fact that Christ and his apostles repeatedly taught the doctrine in many words and 'myd manegum bysnum and tacnum' (89, with many examples and signs). This pedagogical failure recalls the similar problem in *Andreas* of teaching by example, or of Augustine's treatment of teaching in *De magistro*. Augustinus claims to believe after all, adding 'æall þis ic wiste þeah ær, ac ic hyt forgeat, swa ic ondrede æac þæt ic ðis do' (89, yet I knew all of this before, but I forgot it, just as I fear that I will forget this). A few lines later, he repeats a similar idea: 'eala, ic eom myd earmlicre ofergiotolnesse ofseten, þæt ic hyt ne myhte gemunan swa cuð swa hyt me ær wæs' (90, alas, I am oppressed by a pitiable forgetfulness, that I cannot remember it, however known it was to me before). Reason's advice is a turn inward: 'sec nu on ðe selfum ða bysena and þa tacnu, and þonne gearu witan þe ðu ær woldest witan, þæt ic ðe rehte be ðam uttran bysinum' (90, seek now those examples and those signs in yourself, and then readily know what you wanted to know before, which I explained to you with external examples).

The doctrine of recollection is also transmitted in Boethius' *Consolation*, most notably in Book 3 metrum 11, where it is explicitly ascribed to Plato, and in Book 5 metrum 3.[45] In 5m3, Boethius describes the incomplete forgetfulness of the embodied soul: 'nunc membrorum condita nube/ non in totum est oblita sui' (22–23, now the mind is shrouded in the clouds of the body, but it has not wholly forgotten itself).[46] In 3m11, the person who searches for the truth with a deep mind (1, Quisquis profunda mente vestigat verum) is advised to turn the light of inner vision on himself (3, in se revolvat intimi lucem visus). The seed of truth within him can be awakened by learning and, as Plato's Muse reminds, 'quisque discit immemor recordatur' (16, whatever is learned is a recollection of something forgotten).

The Boethian metres were first translated into prose Old English, and then partially re-versified; 3m11 is translated into both prose and verse, while 5m3 is left out of both.[47] In the prose version, Wisdom teaches that truth must be found 'mid inneweardan mode' (1.330, with inner mind) comparing intellectual illumination to observing the sun: 'Þonne mæg he swiðe raþe ongitan ealle þæt yfel and þæt unnet þæt he ær on his mode hæfde, swa sweotole swa ðu miht þa sunnan geseon' (1.330, then he can very quickly perceive all the evil and vanity that he had in his mind before, as clearly as you can see the sun). Like Augustine, Boethius, and even more so the Old English Boethius, understands the process of introspection to be aided by catechism and teaching:

> And þeah bið simle corn soðfæstnesse sædes on þære sawle wunigende, þa hwile þe sio sawl and se lichoma gegaderode bioð. Þæt corn sceal bion aweht mid ascunga and mid lare gif hit growan sceal. (1.330)

> And yet there will always be a grain of the seed of truth dwelling in the soul, so long as the soul and the body are gathered together. The grain must be aroused with questioning and teaching if it is to grow.

Through Boethius and Augustine, Anglo-Saxons had access to a theory of pedagogy that assumed truth, wisdom, or knowledge was already within the learner, and could be brought out of him or her through questioning. Of course, this was also widespread practical knowledge among Christians. The tradition of dialogues, especially of those composed of questions and answers, attests to this. The *Prose Solomon and Saturn* and *Adrian and Ritheus* are good examples of this catechetical instruction, as is Alcuin's *Disputatio Pippini cum Albino*.[48] Indeed, in the *Disputatio de rhetorica et de uirtutibus*, Alcuin has Charlemagne declare that 'interrogare sapienter est docere: et si alter sit qui interrogat, alter qui docet, ex uno tamen, hoc est sapientiae fonte, utrisque sensus procedit' (to ask questions wisely is to teach. And if one person asks, and the other teaches, still the ideas of both come from the same place, that is, from the font of wisdom).[49] Even the Anglo-Latin *enigmata* and Old English *Riddles* attest to the pedagogical utility of veiling what is known and then encouraging the learner to uncover it.

The idea of teaching by asking and learning by remembering was, in other words, a common one in Anglo-Saxon England. The *Andreas* poet could have discovered it in many places; as a literate Christian he probably was educated to some extent in this fashion. In the following section I intend to argue that he found it articulated in the specific form of *anamnesis* in Cynewulf's *Elene*, a known source for the poem, and in the Latin text of Boethius' *Consolation of Philosophy*, which has not to my knowledge been discussed together with *Andreas*.[50] He then used his understanding of *anamnesis* to emphasise the process of learning through recollection also contained in his narrative source, sometimes changing it only slightly, sometimes inserting significant Boethian material. Finally, as further evidence for the Boethianism of recollection in *Elene* and *Andreas*, I will suggest that the versifier of the *Metres of Boethius* drew on their precise phraseology to explain the process of *anamnesis*.

Cynewulf's *Elene*

The *Andreas* poet borrowed heavily from *Elene*, a narrative poem about the search for the True Cross.[51] *Elene* also survives only in the Vercelli Book, and it is ascribed to one of the few named Old English poets, Cynewulf, considered to have been active anywhere from the first half of the ninth century to the tenth century.[52] Cynewulf's legendary, and sometimes epic, poem about Helen's quest for the True Cross is structured around the inquisitive saint's search for knowledge of a particular sort, namely, the burial place of the Cross. However, the poem is not only concerned with the answer to this question: it also explores the ways individuals seek, gain, and are occasionally kept from knowledge. It is, in other words, a poem about the desire for and process of learning.[53]

The poem begins with Constantine, who is rescued in the midst of a losing battle by a vision of the Cross. He gathers an assembly of wise men to explain the symbol to him. Their book smarts are of little avail, but those few who had been taught by baptism enlighten the curious king as to the meaning of the sign. Converted to Christianity, he sends his mother, Helen, to search for the relic. Helen, once in Jerusalem, calls together the three thousand Jews who best know the law and the mysteries of the Lord (280–81), then narrows this group to a thousand, then to five hundred, until she finally reaches a man named Judas. Judas really does know something about the Cross, having been told by his father the meaning of Jesus' crucifixion. Helen threatens the Jews with burning, and, in increasing frustration, imprisons Judas in a well and starves him there until he relents. When God answers his prayer for help in finding the Rood with a well-placed wisp of smoke, he is also converted to the Christian faith. In these stories of three converts eager for Christian truth, Cynewulf repeatedly examines the linked processes of learning and conversion. At the end of *Elene*, the aged poet-speaker reflects on his own sorrows, on the divine illumination granted to him, and his meditation on the story of the Cross.

The poem is, as many scholars have already remarked, about searching and finding. It is not, however, about looking for something new. Rather, *Elene* is structured around a quest to find a precious object which had previously been available and now is lost. This much is obvious, but what is less obvious is that the three major scenes of conversion and education in the poem, those of Constantine, Judas, and the poet-speaker, are shaped along similar lines. Each is portrayed as learning the power of the true Cross twice: first through signs, then through experience. It is only through experience that they come to believe or understand what was already in their minds. And although *Elene* is filled with wise men and teachers, including, in some sense, Helen herself, their role tends to be limited either to intellectual midwifery – they help bring forth what is already within the student – simple ignorance, or outright violence.

The first scene of pedagogy is Constantine's conversion. The Cross is revealed to him in a dream and described by an angelic messenger; he recognises its efficacy on the battlefield; it is upon returning home that he seeks to learn from wise men what god the Cross symbolises. In one sense, he seeks teachers because of his ignorance; looked at in another way, however, he has earthly instructors explain for him a sign he has already seen, one introduced directly into his mind by divine means.[54] This much is to be found in Cynewulf's source text, the *Acta Cyriaci*.[55] Helen's interrogation of Judas is in it too, but Cynewulf elaborates his source at this point a great deal. When Helen threatens Judas with death if he does not reveal where the precious Cross was buried, the Latin version of his response reads:

> Quemadmodum habetur in gestis qui sunt anni ducenti plus minus et nos cum sumus iuniores quomodo hoc possumus nosse[56]
>
> (Holder, p. 7, ll. 200–203)

> Insofar as this was carried out more or less two hundred years ago, and since we are younger than that, how should we know it?

Judas' response in the Old English is more loquacious:

> Hu mæg ic þæt findan   þæt swa fyrn gewearð?
> Wintra gangum   is nu worn sceacen,

tu hund oððe ma   geteled rime;
ic ne mæg areccan   nu ic þæt rim ne can;
is nu feala siðþan   forð gewitenra,
frodra 7 godra   þe us fore wæron
gleawra gumena;   ic on geogoðe wearð
on siðdagum   syððan acenned
cnihtgeong hæleð;   ic ne can þæt ic nat,
findan on fyrhðe   þæt swa fyrn gewearð.   (632–41)

How can I find that which happened so long ago? A great many winters
have hastened by, two hundred or more all told. I cannot declare it,
since I don't know the number. There are many wise men, now passed,
sage and good, who lived before us. I was young, was born in later days,
a boy-young man. I can't know what I don't know, I cannot find in my
mind something that happened so long ago.

Whereas the Latin Judas makes a communal excuse for his people, claiming they cannot know past events, the Old English Judas takes the question
personally. He reflects on his age with respect to the historical event of the
Crucifixion and burial of the Cross, his own inability even to figure out
how long ago it was, and most importantly, on his inability to recall something that is not there. Here we see how Cynewulf takes a theme already
present in his source and psychologises it. This is emphatically no longer
about the Jewish people hiding the True Cross, but about Judas as an individual – he uses the word *ic*, or 'I', six times in ten lines – and his inner
mental process.[57]

If anything, Judas' elaborate counting and repeated emphasis that he
cannot know the distant past only serve to highlight the irony of the situation: he is lying. He already knows from his father the meaning of the
Cross, and seems to have a sense of where it was hidden. Despite claiming
his youth as an excuse, it was in fact when he was a boy that his father told
him of the Crucifixion. Indeed, Judas' grandfather and father were both
baptised, and in a chronological impossibility, his uncle was the martyr
Stephen.[58] Earlier in the poem, Judas has related this story to his fellow
Jews, concluding:

Đus mec fæder min   on fyrndagum
unweaxenne   wordum lærde,
septe soðcwidum   (528–30a)

Thus my father taught me with words, in the old days when I was not
yet grown, he instructed me with true sayings.

In both the Latin and Old English texts, Helen replies by asking how the
Jews know about the exploits of the Trojans, since their war also happened

long ago, and in both Judas replies that they read about it in books. But Cynewulf wants us to pay attention to the way Judas learns, which is decidedly not through books. He is taught the truth by his father and for some reason he does not follow through on it: perhaps he forgets, or perhaps hearing the truth is simply not enough to believe it. He will, indeed, have to find the truth in his own mind, as the phrase 'findan on fyrhðe' (641a) indicates, and he will do so through a direct experience of the Cross.

I propose that Cynewulf recognised that the theme of discovery present in the *Acta Cyriaci* was echoed in the ways Constantine and Judas learn, rediscovering the Cross they have already been told about, and that he decided to expand the poem to underscore this as part of a personal process of education.[59] He does so even more obviously in his epilogue, which is a wholly original addition to the text.[60] Near the end of the poem, the speaker, an old man, reflects on his own sorrow before receiving divine wisdom.

>   nysse ic gearwe,
> be ðære rode riht   ær me rumran geþeaht,
> þurh ða mæran miht   on modes þeaht,
> wisdom onwreah;   ic wæs weorcum fah,
> synnum asæled,   sorgum gewæled,
> bitrum gebunden,   bisgum beþrungen,
> ær me lare onlag   þurh leohtne had,
> gamelum to geoce,   gife unscynde
> mægencyning amæt   7 on gemynd begeat,
> torht ontynde,   tidum gerymde,
> bancofan onband,   breostlocan onwand,
> leoðucræft onleac   þæs ic lustum breac,
> willum in worlde;   ic þæs wuldres treowes
> oft nales æne   hæfde ingemynd
> ær ic þæt wundor   onwrigen hæfde,
> ymb þone beorhtan beam   swa ic on bocum fand,
> wyrda gangum,   on gewritum cyðan
> be ðam sigebeacne.   (1239b–56a)

I did not know the full truth of that cross before wisdom disclosed a more capacious thought to me, through that glorious power, in the thought of the mind. I was stained in deeds, confined by sins, vexed with sorrows, bitterly bound, pressed in by afflictions, before the mighty king bestowed teaching on me through a bright form, help for an old man; the king meted out and got in the memory a noble gift, brightly disclosed it, at times extended it, unbound the body, opened the spirit, unlocked the power of song, which I have used with pleasure in the world. I often, not just once, had the tree of glory in my memory before

> I discovered that wonder, about the bright tree, as I found it in books,
> the course of events of the victory tree explained in writing.

This epilogue has – justly – proven difficult to interpret. The speaker
describes, first, not having known the truth clearly until wisdom was
opened in his mind 'Þurh ða mæran miht' (1241a, through the glorious
power). His first illumination involves no books or conversations with
other people: it is a wholly internal intellectual process enabled by divine power. A few lines later, he refers to God as bestowing instruction
upon him through a lucid or bright form, thus releasing him from his
sinful state.

The next part of the process is the recognition of the Cross in books, but
the passage describing it is difficult to make sense of without the idea of
learning through recollection we have already seen in the poem. Antonina
Harbus explains that 'his own memory of the Cross was revealed through
books which comprised the literary tradition of the Cross'.[61] This begs the
questions of how the speaker might have a memory of a Cross he never
saw, and what it might mean for books to 'reveal' it if he already has it in
his memory. The narrator's ambiguous statement can be explained in two
ways: first, he may be saying that he had the Cross in mind because of its
role in the Passion, and later read of the miracle surrounding its *inventio*;
the other option, and one not necessarily incompatible with the first, is
that he remembers the Cross because of the direct instruction he received
from the Lord – the signs in books remind him of wisdom he has already
been granted.[62] What Cynewulf adds to the story of the search for the
True Cross is another scene of layered, multiple teaching, one in which the
individual rediscovers the divinely granted wisdom already present in their
memory.[63] The signs people use to communicate, in this case in books, do
not so much teach wisdom as provoke the learner to search for it.[64]

Anamnesis and Boethius' *Consolation of Philosophy*

The *Andreas* poet, who borrowed extensively from the works of Cynewulf,
would have been familiar with the idea of learning through recollection
as it is presented in *Elene*. Indeed, a number of echoes of the Christian-
Platonic versions of *anamnesis* are at play in *Andreas*, namely: the difficulty of teaching through visible signs, the idea of Christ as the ultimate
or first teacher, the problem of forgetting, and the focus on teaching by
asking questions that prompt the learner to turn into his mind. We begin
to see these themes on the sea voyage to Mermedonia. When a storm
arises, the men are frightened, and although the helmsman offers to take

them ashore, they refuse to leave their 'leofne lareow' (404a, dear teacher). Scholars often discuss this scene in terms of loyalty to one's lord, but it is also explicitly one of teaching.[65] The helmsman suggests Andrew comfort his disciples by recollecting how Christ taught:

> Gif ðu þegn sie   þrymsittendes,
> wuldorcyninges,   swa ðu worde becwist,
> rece þa gerynu,   hu he reordberend
> lærde under lyfte.   (417–20a)

> If you are a follower of the glorious king who sits in majesty, as you say in words, relate those mysteries, how he, bearing language, taught under the sky.

This pedagogical *mise en abyme* plays out in a few ways. Andrew comforts his men by reminding them of an act of teaching that has already taken place, relating to them the miracle in which Jesus calms the storm.[66] In doing so, he is also guided to teach himself by remembering the miracle he witnessed. However, this is not really the ultimate teacher of Augustine's *De magistro*, nor, obviously, is it a case of the forgotten memory of the soul's existence before the body. Rather, the Christ of Andrew's memory is a mortal *under lyfte*, 'under the sky', and if we read *reordberend* as applying to him, one who is consigned to teaching through verbal signs.[67]

This passage is found in the *Praxeis* and *Casanatensis* in very similar terms. While it might have reminded the poet of the doctrine of *anamnesis*, its inclusion does not prove influence. A slight alteration in another passage, however, does show the poet's continued interest in pedagogy through catechesis and recollection. When the helmsman keeps on questioning Andrew about Christ's teaching, Andrew begins to get annoyed:

> Hwæt frinest ðu me,   frea leofesta,
> wordum wrætlicum,   ond þeh wyrda gehwæs
> þurh snyttra cræft   soð oncnawest?   (629–31)

> Why do you question me, dearest lord, with curious words, although you know the truth of all events through wise skill?

This passage is present in the other versions of the story, but with a slight difference. In the Greek *Praxeis*, Andrew asks, 'O man, I see you have a great spirit of wisdom. How long will you tempt me?'[68] In the Latin *Casanatensis* manuscript, Andrew asks, 'O homo video te habere spiritum magnum sapientie, quam diu temptas me?'[69] (O man, I see that you have a great spirit of wisdom, how long will you test me?). The focus in both of these versions is on Andrew's feeling that he is being tested. The Old

English strikes a slightly different note: Andrew is not annoyed at being tried, but at being asked questions by someone who already knows the answers. He resembles a student who has begun to suspect he is the object of a subtle pedagogic method. By calling the helmsman's words *wrætlic*, a word that appears twenty-one times in the Old English *Riddles*, he may also be drawing on the tradition of Latin and Old English *enigmata*, with the pedagogical associations it carried in Anglo-Saxon England.

Scholars have noted the irony and sophisticated narrative technique of this passage as well as of the entire exchange between Andrew and Christ.[70] Andrew has spent much of the sea voyage being amazed that the helmsman has never heard of Christ's miracles, but now he is starting to suspect that the helmsman is not as ignorant as he had seemed. The poet's change also shows that he understands the story to be fundamentally about recollection of what is already known. The scene plays wittily on the notion of Christ as teacher. Disguised as a regular person, Christ teaches Andrew in the ways that mortals can, prompting him to search his own memory. The lesson his pupil remembers was one performed by Christ, the ultimate teacher, during his time incarnate.

This evidence suggests that the poet recognised the pedagogical use of asking and answering, but this alone need not be specifically Boethian. The *Andreas* poet did, however, respond to Boethius in direct ways, using the natural imagery of the *Consolation* to reinforce his argument about the vicissitudes of human cognition in the face of divine power. A distinctly Boethian moment occurs about halfway through the poem, when Andrew and his men fall asleep on the boat and Christ deposits them on the Mermedonian shore. In the analogues closest to *Andreas*, the transition from sleeping and waking happens quickly: in the *Praxeis* and the Old English homily there is a brief suggestion that Andrew and his men slept at night, in *Casanatensis* there is no sense of the time of day whatsoever.[71] The *Andreas* poet inserts a description of the sunrise:

> leton þone halgan   be herestræte
> swefan on sybbe   under swegles hleo,
> bliðne bidan   burhwealle neh,
> his niðhetum,   nihtlangne fyrst,
> oðþæt dryhten forlet   dægcandelle
> scire scinan.   Sceadu sweðerodon
> wonn under wolcnum;   þa com wederes blæst,
> hador heofonleoma,   ofer hofu blican.   (831–38)

They left the saint sleeping in peace by the highway, under the sky's covering, to await joyful close to the city wall and his deadly enemies, for the space of a night, until the Lord allowed the day-candle to shine brightly. The shades withdrew, dark under the clouds. Then came the sky's flame, bright heavenly light, shining over the dwellings.

Immediately after waking, Andrew recognises that he is near Mermedonia, sees his men sleeping on the shore, awakens them, and tells them who had transported them. The word *oncneow* is used twice: Andrew 'oncneow' (perceived) the heathen city, and as he tells his men, he 'oncneow' (recognised) the lord's words on the boat. It is, in other words, a scene of physical and intellectual awakening.

The choice to describe a sunrise at greater length might be considered a poetic flight of fancy. But the details of the description are odd. This is a sunrise that looks like the calming of a storm, with shadows withdrawing, dark under the clouds. Nighttime darkness is not caused by clouds, of course, but the gloom of a storm is. The half-lines describing the clouds are themselves enigmatic, recalling the *Dream of the Rood*'s moody description of the death of Christ: 'sceadu forðeode,/ wann under wolcnum' (54b–55a, the darkness went forth, dark under the clouds), albeit with the contrary meaning.[72] The phrase 'wederes blæst' is most obviously apposed to 'hador heofonleoma' and best translated as 'the sky's flame'. However, *blæst* can also mean a 'gust of wind', suggesting at a secondary level the breeze that blows clouds away to reveal the sun.

The poet introduces the imagery of sunshine after a storm at this point to highlight Andrew's sudden lucidity after his spiritual turbulence. Throughout the *Consolation of Philosophy*, he would have found storm clouds and sunshine employed as metaphors for mental states. In 1p2, Philosophy draws on cloud imagery to describe Boethius' inability to recognise her or know himself: 'Sui paulisper oblitus est. Recordabitur facile, si quidem nos ante cognoverit; quod ut possit, paulisper lumina eius mortalium rerum nube caligantia tergamus' (12–13, He has forgotten himself a little. He will quickly be himself again when he recognises me. To bring him to his senses, I shall quickly wipe the dark cloud of mortal things from his eyes). In the subsequent metrum, 1m3, Boethius lyrically develops the metaphor:

> Tunc me discussa liquerunt nocte tenebrae
> luminibusque prior rediit vigor,
> ut cum praecipiti glomerantur sidera Coro
> nimbosisque polus stetit imbribus
> sol latet ac nondum caelo venientibus astris
> desuper in terram nox funditur;
> hanc si Threicio Boreas emissus ab antro

verberet et clausum reseret diem,
emicat et subito vibratus lumine Phoebus
      mirantes oculos radiis ferit.   (1–10)

> Then, when the night was over, darkness left me and my eyes regained
> their former strength; just as when the stars are covered by swift Corus,
> and the sky is darkened by storm clouds, the sun hides and the stars
> do not shine; night comes down to envelop the earth. But if Boreas,
> blowing from his Thracian cave, beats and lays open the hiding day,
> then Phoebus shines forth, glittering with sudden light, and strikes our
> astonished eyes with his rays.

Here we have darkness of night and storm, as in the *Andreas* passage, a violent, lashing wind that parallels the ambiguous *blæst*, followed by dazzling sunshine. The poem over, Boethius emphasises in 1p3 that this is a figure of recognition, and as in *Andreas*, this is recognition of who his teacher is: 'Haud aliter tristitiae nebulis dissolutis hausi caelum et ad cognoscendam medicantis faciem mentem recepi' (1–3, In a similar way, I too was able to see the heavens again when the clouds of my sorrow were swept away; I recovered my judgement and recognised the face of my physician).

These are the closest parallels to the sunrise in *Andreas*, but the metaphor cluster of storm and sunshine occurs frequently enough in the *Consolation* that the poet may simply be drawing on a remembered motif rather than gesturing to a particular passage. At 1p6, Philosophy notes that men who have lost the truth suffer under 'perturbationum caligo' (56, cloud of anxiety), but will use gentle remedies 'ut dimotis fallacium affectionum tenebris splendorem verae lucis possis agnoscere' (58–59, so that when the darkness of deceptive feeling is removed you may recognise the splendour of true light). In 3m9, Boethius prays to God that his mind may find light: 'Dissice terrenae nebulas et pondera molis/ atque tuo splendore mica' (25–26, Burn off the fogs and clouds of earth and shine through in thy splendour). In one of the metres describing *anamnesis*, 3m11, the process of recollection is described in similar terms: 'dudum quod atra texit erroris nubes/ lucebit ipso perspicacius Phoebo' (7–8, then all that was hidden by the dark cloud of error will shine more clearly than Phoebus). Other examples feature clouds as metaphors for the forgetfulness of the body, as in the passage from 5m3 cited above that begins, 'nunc membrorum condita nube' (22, now the mind is shrouded in the clouds of the body). Boethius' natural imagery is a fitting choice for the *Andreas* poet: it echoes the earlier sea storm but in a way that incorporates the themes of recognition, recollection, and perception. However, it is also appropriate because illumination in the *Consolation* is, as in *Andreas*, a temporary condition, like the rising and setting of the sun, like stormclouds that darken the sky and then are blown away. The individual trapped in a mortal body will forget again, will need to be taught and guided back to himself once more, just as Christ must keep reminding Andrew of his mission even at the end of the poem.

The *Andreas* poet inserts Boethian imagery at another place in the narrative, although in this case it is not directly linked to a cognitive process. Early in the ship voyage, Andrew asks the helmsman to explain how he steers the boat so smoothly. In the analogues, Jesus replies succinctly that their smooth sailing is due to God's favouring Andrew, as in the *Praxeis*: 'Even we often sail the sea and take a risk; but since you are a disciple of this Jesus, the sea has detected that you are righteous, and it is calm and it did not stir up its waves against the boat.'[73] *Casanatensis* is similar in content, though adding that Andrew is 'discipulus summe potestatis' (the disciple of the greatest power).[74] In *Andreas*, Christ begins and ends his response to Andrew with the same remarks, but between them he inserts a distinctively Boethian praise-poem to the lord:

> Oft þæt gesæleð,   þæt we on sælade,
> scipum under scealcum,   þonne sceor cymeð,
> brecað ofer bæðweg,   brimhengestum;
> hwilum us on yðum   earfoðlice
> gesæleð on sæwe,   þeh we sið nesan,
> frecne geferan.   Flodwylm ne mæg
> manna ænigne   ofer meotudes est
> lungre gelettan;   ah him lifes geweald,
> se ðe brimu bindeð,   brune yða
> ðyð ond þreatað.   He þeodum sceal
> racian mid rihte,   se ðe rodor ahof
> ond gefæstnode   folmum sinum,
> worhte ond wreðede,   wuldras fylde
> beorhtne boldwelan,   swa gebledsod wearð
> engla eðel   þurh his anes miht.   (511–25)

It often happens when we are on a sea voyage, in ships manned by crews, that a shower comes and we break through the ocean-way with surf-horses. Sometimes things go hard for us on the waves, on the sea, though we survive the journey, pass through the danger. The surging flood cannot quickly hinder any man over the Ruler's will. He has power over life who binds the seas, restrains and controls the dark waves. He is sure to rule over the nations with justice, he who with his hands raised and secured the firmament, created and maintained it, filled the bright glorious dwelling with glory. Thus the homeland of angels became blessed through solitary might.

Whereas the analogues have Christ tell Andrew that the sea will not harm a disciple of Jesus, the *Andreas* poet also has him explain why. In the *Consolation* he would have found frequent celebration of God as creator of heavens, governor of oceans, and judge of men. Metre 1m4 of the *Consolation* even offers a model for the kind of virtuous man who cannot be affected by stormy seas: 'non illum rabies minaeque ponti/ versum funditus exagitantis aestum … movebit' (5–10, The threatening and raging ocean storms which churn the waves cannot shake him). In 1m5, Boethius prays to God, 'stelliferi conditor orbis' (1, creator of the star-filled universe), describing how he assigns paths for the stars, moon, and son, controls the seasons, and governs all, 'Omnia certo fine gubernans' (25, You govern all things, each according to its destined purpose). At this point, God's control of the natural world is connected to his government of men, but negatively; Boethius complains that men are left to fortune, and prays:

> Rapidos, rector, comprime fluctus
> et quo caelum regis immensum
> firma stabiles foedere terras!   (46–48)
>
> Ruler of all things, calm the roiling waves and, as You rule the immense heavens, rule also the earth in stable concord.

Philosophy, however, argues at various points for God's justice over sky, water, and the earth, that is, over human affairs. In 2m8, divine love rules over all three: 'hanc rerum seriem ligat/ terras ac pelagus regens/ et caelo imperitans amor' (13–15, all this harmonious order of things is achieved by love which rules the earth and the seas, and commands the heavens) while the *Consolation*'s best-known metre, 3m9, begins 'O qui perpetua mundum ratione gubernas/ terrarum caelique sator' (1–2, O God, Maker of heaven and earth, Who govern the world with eternal reason). Finally, in 4p6, Philosophy argues for divine judgement, an argument which she then expresses lyrically in 4m6:

> Sedet interea conditor altus
> rerumque regens flectit habenas,
> rex et dominus, fons et origo,
> lex et sapiens arbiter aequi   (34–37)
>
> Meanwhile the Creator sits on high, governing and guiding the course of things. King and lord, source and origin, law and wise judge of right

What makes the Boethianisms of *Andreas* difficult to spot is the organic way they are incorporated into the story. The source narrative already contains sea storms and divine protective power, but the poet adds details like the creation of the sky and governance over men to flesh out Christ's speech, thus locating Andrew's survival of the storm in God's larger binding of creation. Christ's declaration of divine omnipotence sounds most like Philosophy's, appropriate since he, too, teaches a forgetful, fearful disciple.

The influence of the *Consolation of Philosophy* on *Andreas* suggests that an often-overlooked detail may be more significant than previously thought. After Andrew converts the Mermedonians, he establishes 'Platan' as their bishop, 'ond þriste bebead/ þæt hie his lare læston georne' (1652b–53, and earnestly commanded them to follow his teaching eagerly). Brooks proposes that the bishop's name is derived from the stem 'Platon-', but I have found no suggestions in *Andreas* scholarship that the poet could have had the philosopher in mind.[75] After all, a bishop named Plato appears in a rhythmical retelling of the story found in the Italian manuscript Rome, Biblioteca Apostolica Vaticana, Vat. lat. 1274 (*Vaticanus*), and is also featured in Greek and Latin recensions of the *Martyrium Matthaei*, another apocryphal adventure about an apostolic mission to a cannibal land.[76] But if Plato is not original to *Andreas*, he may still be there as the result of a choice on the poet's part. His name appears in none of the poem's close analogues: not in the *Praxeis* or *Casanetensis*, and not in the Old English homilies. Moreover, the *Vaticanus* is an eleventh-century manuscript, its narrative quite different from *Andreas*. Certainly, a bishop named Plato seems to have been part of the wider tradition of apostolic apocrypha, but *Andreas'* use of it still stands out in its immediate context. I propose that the *Andreas* poet includes the bishop's name knowing that Boethius ascribed the theory of *anamnesis* to Plato in 3m11 and in 3p12. He also explicitly makes his Plato an authority to be learned from, which is not the case in *Vaticanus*. In this, too, he follows the *Consolation*, where Philosophy tells Boethius that he has learned with Plato as a confirming authority: 'cum Platone sanciente didiceris' (96). As with his treatment of the storm imagery, the poet takes material already part of the Andrew tradition and adds a small twist. His change reveals the greater philosophical and didactic relevance of what seems, at first, a banal detail.

The *Andreas* poet found in Boethius (and possibly also in Augustine) an explanation for Andrew's stumbles in faith. He found a theory of learning as dynamic process that spans forgetting, remembering, erring, and once again being prodded to learn and recollect. He understood learning as self-examination, a process of analysing one's own perception and memory that echoed Andrew's repeated moments of enlightenment. Even the structuring metaphor of the 'way' or 'path' in *Andreas* may have been influenced by the *Consolation*'s rich use of *uia* and *semita* as figures for philosophical method and moral path.[77] He did not, however, simply add light Boethian touches to the story. Rather, he created a poem that enacts the very pedagogy Andrew undergoes, one that prompts its readers and listeners to ask: Where is this from? Do I recognise it? Do I understand it?

After Andrew undergoes three days of torture and is healed by Christ, the narrator's voice breaks into the poem. This is the only authorial interruption in the Old English poetic corpus, and is based on nothing in the source material. It is an enigmatic passage, but one that, I argue, connects the notion of *anamnesis* to the poetics of *Andreas*.

> Hwæt, ic hwile nu   haliges lare
> leoðgiddinga,   lof þæs þe worhte,
> wordum wemde,   wyrd undyrne.
> Ofer min gemet   mycel is to secganne,
> langsum leornung,   þæt he in life adreag,
> eall æfter orde;   þæt scell æglæwra
> mann on moldan   þonne ic me tælige
> findan on ferðe,   þæt fram fruman cunne
> eall þa earfeðo   þe he mid elne adreah
> grimra guða.   Hwæðre git sceolon
> lytlum sticcum   leoðworda dæl
> furður reccan;   þæt is fyrnsægen,
> hu he weorna feala   wita geðolode,
> heardra hilda,   in þære hæðenan byrig.   (1478–91)

> Lo, for a while now I have sounded in words, in songs, praise of the holy one's teaching, of what he worked, a well-known event. There is much to say, over my metre, enduring learning, about what he suffered in life, all according to the source. A man more learned in the law on earth than I consider myself must find that in his mind, who knows from the source all the hardship of grim battles that he endured with courage. Nevertheless we will relate more, a portion of poetic words in little pieces. It is an old story, how he suffered a great number of torments, of hard battles, in that heathen city.

In this address, the poet reflects on his poetic craft; I read the 'lytlum sticcum' as referring to lines or half-lines of poetry, perhaps the ones he borrowed from other works. If we are right about how he wrote *Andreas*, the narrator here reflects on the piecemeal nature of his composition, and in doing so, draws the audience's attention to it. He emphasises his interest in sources, origins, and the retelling of old and well-known stories such as Andrew's. He also offers a typical modesty topos, but it contains a telling

detail. The wiser man may know the story of Andrew from the source used by the *Andreas* poet, or even from his poem, but in order to tell it he will have to find it in his mind, 'findan on ferðe'.

The cognitive process the poet describes is much like the one Andrew undergoes on the ship: recollecting what was already learned, then retelling it to continue a narrative tradition. Appropriately, the half-line that encapsulates this, 'findan on ferðe', is recollected from *Elene*. Judas used it in a modesty topos of his own, when he deceptively claimed he could not find in his mind knowledge that was not there. If we accept the suggestion that the *Andreas* poet's discussion of little bits of poetry is a meta-reflection on his practice of textual recycling, what we have in this passage is a model for literary invention that parallels the process of teaching depicted in the poem.

'Findan on ferðe' sounds like it should be a common Anglo-Saxon poetic formula. From the perspective of modern English, it also sounds as if it should be an idiom for having an impression or opinion, as in 'I found it good', rather than a description of recollection. The Corpus of Old English reveals that it appears in only two texts other than *Andreas*, and in a third with a different form. It is identical in *Andreas* and *Elene*, which are both in the Vercelli Book; the poem *Soul and Body I* in the same manuscript has a version of the line 'funden on ferhðe', which in that context does seem to indicate an emotional reaction. It also appears twice in the Boethian *Metre* corresponding to 3m11, which describes Platonic *anamensis*:[78]

> Nis þeah ænig man   þætte ealles swa
> þæs geradscipes   swa bereafod sie
> þæt he andsware   ænige ne cunne
> *findan on ferhðe*,   gif he frugnen bið.
> Forðæm hit is riht spell   þæt us reahte gio
> ald uðwita,   ure Platon.
> He cwæð þætte æghwilc   ungemyndig
> rihtwisnesse   hine hræðe sceolde
> eft gewendan   into sinum
> modes gemynde;   he mæg siððan
> on his runcofan   rihtwisnesse
> *findan on ferhte* fæste gehydde   (1.484, ll. 49–60)

There is no man, however, that is so entirely bereft of discretion that he cannot find any answer in his mind if he is asked. For it is a just speech that the ancient philosopher, our Plato, formerly told us: he said that anyone unmindful of wisdom should turn himself back quickly to the inward thoughts of his mind. Then he can find wisdom in his inner heart, his spirit, deeply hidden.

When the poet of *Metre 22* sought to express the idea of Platonic recollection in English verse, he used a line perfect for the concept, one that described finding in the mind.[79] It is not unlikely that he found it in either *Elene* or *Andreas* – though the dates make it unlikely that he found it in the Vercelli Book itself – and he recognised in the use of the phrase that it did not refer simply to an impression, but to active searching within one's self for a forgotten truth.

A Rhetoric of Riddling

The *Andreas* poet found in his narrative source a story replete with scenes of pedagogy and recollection, which he interpreted in light of Platonic Christian *anamnesis*. He was not necessarily interested in the doctrine, for when he tells it, he tells it slant, but in the cognitive processes it implies. By extension, *Andreas* is a poem filled with traces of the past in the present, prompting the reader to recognise and decipher them. This obsession with survivals, relics, and leavings manifests itself in several thematic strands; I propose that each one trains the reader or listener to interpret the poetry of *Andreas* in a mode consistent with the pedagogy of recollection. The first issue is that of Christ's origin, the key to his identity as the son of God. The emphasis on provenance is new to *Andreas*, the result of alterations and additions to the source material, and it would have primed the poem's audience to reflect on the sources and origins of its poetic images and formulas. Closely related to Christ's divine identity is cannibalism, a major theme in *Andreas* and a source for delicious puns.[80] Besides its Eucharistic echoes and suggestions of heathen barbarism and Jewish error, cannibalism serves as a figure for the poem's textual practice of cannibalising and regurgitating the tradition.

Andreas' use of objects also models a relationship to the past. As Denis Ferhatović has shown, the landscape of *Andreas* is dotted with *spolia*, historical objects incorporated into new physical contexts in a way that preserves their charged difference.[81] Not only are there things in the story that come from the past to act in the present – a stone angel, revivified corpses, an inscribed marble column – but the very language used to describe them is often spoliated from *Beowulf*. Finally, light use of scriptural citation and heavy use of Cynewulfian and Beowulfian borrowings spur the reader to identify and interpret textual echoes. The reader is thus aware of the poem's multiple origins: the apocryphal source narrative, the Bible, and Old English poetic tradition. One might describe these objects, processes, and textual citations as enigmas, and indeed, both Nathan Breen and Ferhatović have noted the poet's use of cognitive gaps and riddles inviting confusion, rumination, and wonder.[82] It is most accurate to say that the poet found a source narrative already replete with miniature riddles, and he made them even more puzzling and thought-provoking when he rendered them into verse. *Andreas* is not a poem to be absorbed passively. Even enjoying its clever wordplay or typological patterning is not enough. *Andreas* is a poem that calls upon its audience to reflect, question, and ruminate. It teaches its audience through dynamic recollection, just as Philosophy teaches Boethius.

One way *Andreas*' interest in remembering and decoding presents itself is as an obsession with sources, beginnings, and origins. This fascination is discernible in a number of scenes, often cued by the word *hwanon*, or 'whence'. For example, when Andrew describes the Jews' disbelief in Christ's divine descent, one rabbi points out that they have already asked whence this man comes, and his parents are the quite earthly Maria and Joseph: 'Þæt is duguðum cuð,/ *hwanon* þam ordfruman æðelu onwocon' (682b–83, that is known to the warriors, whence the lineage of that leader sprang). The *Andreas* poet cannot resist a pun, not when it allows him to make his point even more emphatically. The word denoting Christ here, *ordfruma*, can mean 'chief, head, prince' when applied to persons, but can also mean 'source' or 'origin'. In fact, both *ord* and *fruma* can be translated as 'beginning' or 'origin' depending on context, making Christ a 'beginning-origin' as well as a prince, and giving the lie to the rabbi's argument.[83] Just a little later, Christ commands the stone angel to speak the truth about his descent, 'hwæt min æðelo sien' (734b, what my lineage is). In the *Praxeis* and *Casanatensis*, Christ requests the stone to declare whether he is God or man; in *Andreas*, he asks it to say where he comes from.[84]

The innovations in *Andreas* emphasise not only Christ's parentage, but also his geographic origins. One of the *Andreas* poet's strangest alterations to his source material can be found in the first seaside encounter between Andrew and the mysterious helmsman. In the *Praxeis*, *Casanatensis*, and Old English homily, Andrew asks the disguised Christ where the ship is going, and the answer is conveniently Mermedonia.[85] The phrasing of the Old English homily makes the direction explicit, with Andrew asking, 'hwider wille ge faran' (where do you intend to travel?). In *Andreas*, the direction is also clear, but surprising:

> Hwanon comon ge   ceolum liðan,
> macræftige menn,   on mereþissan,
> ane ægflotan?   Hwanon eagorstream
> ofer yða gewealc   eowic brohte? (256–59)

> Where do you come from, sailing in a ship, you mighty men, on this seaboat, this single vessel? Whence did the ocean bring you, over the rolling of waves?

The repetition of *hwanon* reveals that this is no mistranslation:[86] the poet asks us to think about sources and origins of movement rather than their goals. Christ's answer is even more surprising: 'We of Marmedonia mægðe syndon/ feorran geferede' (264–65a, we have travelled from afar, of/from the tribe of the Mermedonians). As Robert Boenig has pointed out, this is a momentary suggestion that Christ is, himself, a Mermedonian and even a cannibal.[87] Boenig reads this as an inversion of the normal Eucharistic relationship between Christ and his follower: Andrew might have the chance to imitate Christ by being consumed by him.[88] We might, however, intepret it another way. The horror of the Mermedonians is that they are *sylfætan* (175b), 'self-eaters'.[89] They consume their own species and, when pressed, even their own countrymen and relatives. But the poem *Andreas* is also a *sylfæta*, having borrowed extensively from *Beowulf* and from Cynewulf's *The Fates of the Apostles*, *Christ II*, *Elene*, and *Juliana*. We can call this mode of versification a *cento*, but I argue – with Aaron Hostetter – the poet is also playing with the notion of a cannibal poetics, one that regurgitates the tradition.[90] If Christ is a cannibal, even for a flickering moment, it may be because the Jesus of the Gospels is also an inveterate citer, a *sylfæta* of the Old Testament.[91] The theme of consumption in *Andreas* is not only a joke, a comment on the Eucharist, or a way of establishing the Mermedonians' monstrosity, but also the flip side of the poem's interest in origins, memory, riddling, and the ruins of the past.

Andreas is filled with ruins and revenants. Its ancient objects and bodies texture the poem's landscapes and take part in its actions. Whether speaking or quiet, agential or passive, these figures prompt reflection on the past and its uses. Both objects and bodies might be described as *spolia*, a sixteenth-century art historical term for 'reused antiquities', 'borrowed … from the semantic field of war'.[92] *Spolia* were originally the spoils of battle, plundered weaponry and art, but the word is now also used to describe recycled building materials and ornamentation. Ferhatović has argued that *Andreas* uses these manmade artifacts to reflect on divine and poetic creation. According to him, the poet deliberately leaves narratives open-ended, even confusing, to challenge readers to 'play the game, to fill out "the blank spaces in the map"'[93] of Andrew's travels and Christ's miracles. Building on Ferhatović's analysis, I argue that the poet uses *spolia* in its broader sense not just as a locus of reflection on the process of crafting, but also as a prompt to recollection.

Andrew's movement towards Mermedonia is paralleled by his mental move backwards in time, into his own memory. Appropriately, the heathen city is inscribed with pastness. Lori Ann Garner has suggested that the tesselated buildings of Mermedonia, 'tigelfagan trafu' (842a), may have recalled Roman stone temples.[94] Even Andrew's torture is partly carried out against the backdrop of ancient buildings, as he is dragged through Mermedonia along the 'enta ærgeweorc … stræte stanfage' (1235a, 1236a, old work of giants … streets paved with stones). These objects have occasionally confounded critics and editors. Without a trace of irony, Brooks points out that the roads in lines 1235–36 seem to be 'Roman tesselated pavements, examples of which might have still been seen in the England of his time', but adds that 'the idea is foreign to the context here; the poet is perhaps using a formula inappropriately, if not consciously echoing *Beowulf*'.[95] Aside from the fact that an ancient city on the Black Sea is at least as good a place to find Roman roads as legendary Denmark, Brooks, I think, misses the point. The ancient objects that capture our attention in *Andreas*, either because they act in fantastic ways or because they ring at once familiar and foreign, are among the poem's visual leftovers, cueing us to their sources both in the story of Andrew and in Old English verse.

The poet has chosen a narrative source that features various scenes in which the past intrudes into the present, and he uses them to explore the workings of imagination and memory. Take the stone angel, a 'frod fyrngeweorc' (737a, wise ancient work) that rips itself from the temple wall, speaks and walks and calls dead things to life. It can serve as a figure for the way memory works: once bidden, what was at rest becomes active, travels along various paths, and pulls even more out of the past, just as the stone angel enlivens the dead patriarchs. The revenant patriarchs are even more interesting. On the one hand, they can serve as a figure for the Jewish past of Christianity, dead but lying in wait for a command to rise again and serve a new narrative. This is one reason why figural analyses of *Andreas*, dated as they are methodologically, make so much sense: the poem itself imagines the text of the Old Testament as a dead letter waiting to be filled with spirit, a long-closed mouth ready to talk again upon command. This much is in the source narrative, but the *Andreas* poet troubles such an easy allegorisation. As Ferhatović points out, in the *Praxeis*, which features both the talking statue (in this case, a sphinx) and the vivified Patriarchs, Christ commands all these monstrous figures to return to their places, and they explicitly do. But in *Andreas* the Patriarchs are only commanded to seek heaven, and it is not clear where they or the stone angel wind up.[96] *Andreas* offers us a version of the past that is useable, but not easily solveable. Like the Old English *Riddles*, which open up multiple possible interpretations without settling on one, the *spolia* of *Andreas* are unbiddable, things to think with, but not to explain away.

The stone column that releases the genocidal flood is also a riddle with multiple solutions. As Ferhatović has noted, the fact that the prison columns seem to be *inside* the building but are 'storme bedrifene' (1494b, battered by the storm) has posed a problem for commentators. But it need not be a crux if we think of them as Roman *spolia* that were once outdoors, but were reused by the Mermedonians when they built their prison.[97] These columns are described as 'eald enta geweorc' (1495a, old work of giants), language used in Anglo-Saxon poetry to denote found objects and ruined structures. But one of the columns also bears language. Andrew addresses it and reminds it that God wrote upon it, and apparently what he inscribed was the ten-fold law he gave to Moses:

> on ðe sylf cyning
> wrat, wuldres God,   wordum cyðde
> recene geryno,   ond ryhte æ
> getacnode   on tyn wordum,
> meotud mihtum swið,   Moyse sealde,
> swa hit soðfæste   syðþan heoldon,
> modige magoþegnas,   magas sine,
> godfyrhte guman,   Iosua ond Tobias.   (1509b–16)

> On you yourself the king, the God of glory, wrote, revealed in words marvellous mysteries, and signified the right law in ten sentences. The Lord, mighty in power, gave it to Moses, just as the righteous, brave retainers held it afterwards, his kinsmen, the god-fearing men Joshua and Tobias.

He asks the column to show whether it has understanding of any of the words God inscribed on it (1521, gif ðu his ondgitan ænige hæbbe). This pedagogical touch is original to *Andreas*, as is the inscription of the column itself; in the *Praxeis*, we are meant to understand that stone was inscribed with Moses' laws, not the particular column in Andrew's prison.[98] Andrew, who earlier recollected how Christ taught a carved stone to teach, uses the same method now in Mermedonia. Moreover, he imitates Christ's pedagogy even further, asking the column whether it can understand or perceive what was already written on it by God. The word he uses for 'understanding' is 'ondgite', echoing the verb *ongitan* used earlier to describe both Andrew's and the Jews' inability to recognise Christ.

The marble column thus becomes another model for learning by recollection: like the *Consolation of Philosophy*'s Boethius, *Elene*'s Judas, and Andrew, it has forgotten itself. There are two important differences, however. What God wrote on the marble were 'recene geryno' (1511a, marvellous mysteries). Andrew is not simply asking the column to recall something it used to know but has forgotten, but to interpret what is inscribed on itself. This is an Anglo-Saxon twist on the pedagogy of *anamnesis*, suggesting that the self is a riddle to be decoded. The other innovation is the violent result of this education: a deluge that drowns many Mermedonians and terrifies the rest: 'duguð wearð afyrhted/ þurh þæs flodes fær' (1529b–30a, the people became frightened through the fear of the flood).

Indeed, if *spolia* in a broader sense represent a relationship to the past that draws things from it and sets them free in the present, they also represent a return that is frightening even as it is fascinating. When the stone angel leaps from the side of the temple and speaks, it seems wondrous, or *wrætlic* (740b), to the stubborn rabbis. The angel tries to use this moment of wonder to teach them the way Christ does: 'Septe sacerdas sweotolum tacnum' (742, it taught the priests with clear signs). But their first response after listening to the angel's speech is silence: 'swigodon ealle' (762b, they were all silent). Perhaps they are overwhelmed by the stone's argumentation, but given that they do not agree with it, this might be rather an excess of wonder, a paralysing stupor in the face of what cannot be comprehended. The Jews' reaction to the zombie Patriarchs is even stronger. When they leave their grave:

> Þa þæt folc gewearð
> egesan geaclod,   þær þa æðelingas
> wordum weorðodon   wuldres aldor.   (804b–806)

> Then the people became frightened with horror, where the noble men praised the prince of glory with words.

The poet of *Andreas* shows us how teaching is performed by entering the memory and excavating things from the past, by asking things petrified to move and speak. But he also models possible audience reactions to these living recollections, and those reactions can be stupor and terror.

The *Andreas* poet's fascination with old things that speak, or simply stand out because they are intricately crafted and a touch out of place, offers a new way of understanding his 'cannibalising' of Old English verse. Indeed, *Andreas* uses various themes – origins, cannibalism, spoliation, citation – to train its audience to reflect on the sources and meanings of things. It teaches its readers and listeners to 'answer' its verse the way they would an enigma, decoding but also remaining open to multiple interpretations. One might think of it as a poem composed of small riddles, metaphorically speaking, but in fact some passages function as riddles in a more concrete fashion. Alison Powell has identified multiple passages in *Andreas* that feature clusters of borrowings and echoes from *Beowulf*.[99] I propose that such clusters are deliberately composed puzzles, provocations to readers and listeners of *Andreas* to insert Beowulfian scenes and characters into the hagiographic narrative.

The most prominent such 'source' riddle occurs, appropriately enough, just as the narrator reflects on his own compositional method and then segues back into the narrative:

> grimra guða. Hwæðre git sceolon
> lytlum sticcum   leoðworda dæl
> furður reccan;   þæt is fyrnsægen,
> hu he *weorna feala*   wita geðolode,
> heardra hilda,   in þære hæðenan byrig.
> He *be wealle geseah*   wundrum *fæste*
> under sælwage   sweras unlytle,
> *stapulas standan*   storme bedrifene,
> eald *enta geweorc*   (1487–95a)

… cruel battles. Nevertheless we will relate more, a portion of poetic words in little pieces. It is an old story, how he suffered a great number of torments, of hard battles, in that heathen city. He saw great columns by the wall, wondrously fixed below the hall wall, pillars standing beaten by storm, old work of giants.

In the passage above, the words emphasised echo one or more formulations in *Beowulf* identified by Powell.[100] Most interesting are the multiple borrowings from the end of the epic, first, from Beowulf's entrance into the dragon's hall:

> Geseah ða *be wealle*   se ðe *worna fela*
> gumcystum god   *guða* gedigde   (2542–43)

He saw then by the wall, he who had endured a great many battles, good in manly virtues.

Second, from the passage describing how the dying hero gazes at the dragon's hall:

> Ða se æðeling giong,
> þæt he *bi wealle*   wishycgende
> gesæt on sesse;   *seah* on *enta geweorc*,
> hu ða stanbogan   *stapulum fæste*
> ece eorðreced   innan healde.   (2715b–19)

Then the prince went so that he sat on a seat by the wall, thinking wisely. He looked at the work of giants, how the arches and columns held the eternal earth-hall fast from the inside.

I suggested earlier that 'lytlum sticcum leoðworda dæl' (*And.* 1488) may refer not simply to verse in general, but to formulas and half-lines borrowed from other poems; the thick references to *Beowulf* in the passage immediately following the authorial interruption are evidence for this. But more is happening here. The narrator introduces the notion of finding a story within one's mind, and then describes his own cento-like mode of composition. Then he begins to tell an old story, or *fyrnsægen*, about a hero who underwent battles in a heathen city before looking upon ancient and majestic columns in a hall. Until Andrew begins to speak to one of the columns, the description of this hero and his adventures remains vague. It is an embedded riddle with two solutions. The hero may be Beowulf, who fought grim battles in a heathen city in Denmark and then gazed at the ancient ruins inside the dragon's hall, or, of course, Andrew.

Like some of the Old English *Riddles* of the Exeter Book, this riddle in *Andreas* calls for its solution and gives hints as to how to find it. The narrator's exclamation, 'þæt scell æglæwra/ mann on moldan þonne ic me tælige/ findan on ferðe' (1483b–85a, a man more learned in the law on earth than I consider myself must find that in his mind), has generally been read as a modesty topos. It is, rather, an oblique challenge to the reader wise enough to solve the riddle that follows by identifying its elements and going back to the source. It loosely resembles the beginning of Exeter *Riddle 1*, 'Hwylc is hæleþa þæs horsc ond þæs hygecræftig/ þæt þæt mæge asecgan' (1–2a, which of the men is so sharp and so sage, that he may proclaim that), the ending of *Riddle 28*, 'Micel is to hycganne/ wisfæstum menn, hwæt seo wiht sy' (12b–13, much there is to meditate on for wise men, what that creature might be), and similar phrases in *Riddles* 31, 32, 35, 41, 43, and 67.[101] Furthermore, while the implication of the narrator's interruption seems to be that the wiser man should tell the story given the author's inability, in fact the wiser man has only one task: to find the story in his mind, that is, to recollect it. Likewise, the narrator's meta-reflection on the composition of *Andreas* echoes those riddles that provide clues to their own decoding, such as *Riddle 23*'s 'Agof is min noma eft onhwyrfed' (1, 'Agof' is my name, turned around backwards), as well as *Riddles* 24 and 58. The complex literary effects intended by *Andreas'* many allusions to *Beowulf* have yet to be substantially analysed. The riddling structure of the interruption reveals, however, that the audience was expected to recognise *Beowulf* as a hypotext for *Andreas*, and that *Andreas'* echoes of the epic are part and parcel of its broader pedagogical programme.

The cognitive process behind this pedagogy is, as I have argued, recollection. There is an emotional component to it too, however, one shared by Anglo-Saxon riddles and Boethian philosophy: wonder. This is a slightly different kind of 'wonder' than what is usually meant today. The modern English noun 'wonder' has a congenial meaning, denoting curiosity, amazement, marvelling, awe, surprise. Even the verb 'wonder' is primarily positive, except when it means 'to doubt', which means discounting the truth of the thing perceived, not necessarily having a negative reaction to it. Caroline Walker Bynum has described the varieties of medieval wonder, noting that 'the wonder-reaction ranges from terror and disgust to solemn astonishment and playful delight', later adding 'dread' to the list.[102] Dennis Quinn describes this richer notion of wonder in more detail in his essay on the role of wonder in the *Consolation of Philosophy*. He notes that one of the most prominent Greek words for wonder, *thambos*, derives from the idea of being struck by something ... there is an exact Latin equivalent in *stupor*, which also has in its root the idea of being struck. The *thambos–stupor* words tend to stress the mental and physical manifestations of wonder – bewilderment, confusion, stupor, paralysis, silence, trembling. In this sense wonder may be associated with other emotions, especially fear, joy, love, and even shame.[103] Quinn shows that wonder, especially in the *Consolation*, serves as a stimulus to meditation and the search for truth. Patricia Dailey has also explored this pedagogical use of wonder in the Old English riddles, which 'exemplify an approach to knowledge and wisdom characteristic of Anglo-Saxon England that invokes wonder to effect a salutary ordering of the relation of a person (and this person's mind) to the surrounding world, as is the case in the Old English Boethius'.[104] This older sense of 'wonder', one that includes awe and fear in the emotional response to something surprising and amazing, is implied by the word *wrætlic*.

Bosworth-Toller glosses *wrætlic* as 'wondrous, curious', 'of wondrous excellence, beautiful, noble, excellent, elegant'.[105] In other words, it defines it as a wholly positive aesthetic term, and this is, indeed, the way the word tends to be translated. Joshua Davies has argued that the word connotes 'impressive workmanship or scale, audacious technical skill or great age', stressing its aesthetic qualities.[106] To see *wrætlic* as a wholly positive term, however, is both to modernise the medieval and to ignore the nuances of its use in Old English poetry. In *Andreas*, *wrætlic* or a form of it appears five times: first, to describe God's voice addressing Matthew from the heavens, 'wrætlic under wolcnum' (93a, 'wrætlic' under the clouds), then by Andrew when he complains about Christ's 'wordum wrætlicum' (630a, 'wrætlic' words) in questioning him. It is used twice to describe the stone angel that Christ addresses: first, both of the angels are 'wrætlice' (712a), then, after one of them has detached itself from the wall of the temple and begun to speak, we learn that 'wrætlic þuhte/ stiðhy-cgendum stanes ongin' (740b–41, the stone's action seemed 'wrætlic' to the stubborn ones). Finally, in an ironic echo of language earlier used to describe God's speech, the devil denigrates Andrew in the eyes of the Mermedonians by saying that Andrew argues in 'wordum wrætlicum' (1200a). These uses of the word are simply not adequately glossed by Bosworth-Toller's definition, nor can their effects be explained as aesthetic in an approving sense. The Jews are stunned by the stone angel, and although it is a crafted, aesthetic object, it is also something they consider deceitful and likely terrifying. The devil means to characterise Andrew as a trickster or deceiver when he calls his speech *wrætlic*. Even Andrew's use of 'wordum wrætlicum' occurs when he is frustrated with Christ's questions; yes, he admires the mysterious helmsman's intelligence, but he also feels uncertain, caught in a situation he no longer understands.

Anglo-Saxons understood teaching to be a positive process that often happened through negative or difficult emotions. We miss this, because our ideal pedagogies do not frighten or traumatise students; we prefer to inspire, nourish, and comfort them. Anglo-Saxons understood negative emotions as tools that could be used in teaching, or in mental work more broadly, but not uncritically: like the *wrætlic* stone angel, wondrous, terrifying things were liable to go their own way once you had called them to do your bidding. We understand *wrætlic* to be a positive aesthetic term, when it can, and often should, bear negative emotional charge. A good example for this misreading can be found in the way the first few lines of *The Ruin* are translated. Here is the Old English:

> Wrætlic is þes wealstan,   wyrde gebræcon;
> burgstede burston,   brosnað enta geweorc.
> Hrofas sind gehrorene,   hreorge torras,
> hrungeat berofen,   hrim on lime,
> scearde scurbeorge   scorene, gedrorene,
> ældo undereotone.   (1–6a)[107]

Here is Roy Liuzza's translation:

> Wondrous is this foundation – *wyrd* has broken
> and shattered this city; the work of giants crumbles.
> The roofs are ruined, the towers toppled,
> frost in the mortar has broken the gate,
> torn and worn and shorn by the storm,
> eaten through with age.[108]

Burton Raffel's rendition also maintains a sense of positive aesthetic response to a grippingly awful scene:

> Fate has smashed these wonderful walls,
> This broken city, has crumbled the work
> Of giants. The roofs are gutted, the towers
> Fallen, the gates ripped off, frost
> In the mortar, everything molded, gaping,
> Collapsed.[109]

These are both beautiful translations, but they make a pleasant aesthetic experience out of what should, in this context, be awe tinged with horror. Joshua Davies argues that this *wealstan* is *wrætlic* 'despite being broken'.[110] I argue it is *wrætlic* because it is broken. The speaker not only admires the skill with which the old work was crafted and its massive scale, but is also astounded at the level of destruction in view. We may not have a perfect word to gloss it, but 'astonishing', 'striking', 'staggering', or 'stupefying' would all be closer to the emotion evoked here by *wrætlic*. Perhaps best of all would be 'awful', like Grendel's head or the dragon Sigemund kills in *Beowulf*, both of which are *wrætlic*.[111] *Wrætlic* represents a mixture of horror and admiration that provokes reflection. It is also a word that occurs twenty times among the riddles of the Exeter Book, suggesting that it denotes not only passive amazement, but wonder that leads to active thinking. Moreover, salutary wonder is not a thoughtless reaction but a trained intellectual skill. In Quinn's description of the role of wonder in premodern thinking, wonder is not 'an instinctive response that could be taken for granted but … an appetite hard to keep, easily dulled, and sometimes altogether lost, even by the wisest of men'.[112] Riddles awaken wonder, as do the many embedded enigmas of *Andreas*.

Andreas draws on the tradition of teaching through riddles as well as on Boethius' explorations of forgetfulness, wonder, and recollection to craft a pedagogic programme for its audience. Just as *wrætlic* combines admiration with disquiet, the teaching in *Andreas* can be troubling, frightening, challenging to the senses and imagination. (It can also, like the riddles, be funny.) Put differently, the teaching dialogue that takes place between Christ and Andrew on their sea voyage serves as a model for the poem's dialogue with its readers and listeners. Like Andrew, they find themselves presented with things and characters they know, but veiled, and invited to identify them. Like Andrew, they are provoked to amazement, terror, and confusion. Like Andrew, they are guided to wonder, remember, and ruminate. The poem's many discomforts – awkward borrowings from *Beowulf*, strange adjustments to the source narrative, a disappointing hero – are *wrætlicu word*, with all the startling wondrousness that implies.

CHAPTER 5

Desire
The Life of St Mary of Egypt

I view my crime, but kindle at the view, Repent old pleasures, and
sollicit new

Alexander Pope, 'Eloisa to Abelard'[1]

As the texts examined in this book demonstrate, Anglo-Saxons understood
suffering and danger to be useful for learning, but only within limits. King
Alfred, who wishes for a physical ailment to curb his desires and allow
him to study, finds that the disease ultimately hinders his concentration.
Bede uses the case of a linguistically disabled, scrofulous youth to show the
liberatory potential of grammar, but that freedom is symbolised by a complete cure from bodily illness. *Solomon and Saturn I* draws on the mnemonic power of imagined violence to teach the Lord's Prayer, although the
true student of its lesson, the reader, only needs to imagine it happening
to a demonic figure. Ælfric Bata fills his Latin textbook with dangerous
situations and negatively charged vocabulary; at the end of the *Colloquies*,
however, he also shows how classroom violence can interfere with discipline and authority. *Andreas* uses terrible wonder to spur moments of
recollection and learning, but leaves the lesson open-ended. Desire is inter-
twined with suffering in a number of these examples, although the precise
nature of the relationship changes. In Alfred's case, bodily pain is intended
to extinguish lust, while in Bata's *Colloquies*, carnal desire is a disruptive
force in the monastery. On the other hand, *Solomon and Saturn I* and
Andreas use their student figures to model productive curiosity for their
readers, to inflame them with longing for prayer and knowledge.

The Old English *Life of St Mary of Egypt* presents a new relationship
between pain, desire, and learning. Saintly passions are usually violent
proof of a holy person's exemplary virtue, heroic scenes in which Christian
truth is asserted and taught. Mary suffers a different kind of passion, one
that combines old and new meanings of the word. Her 'passion' is not
one of pincers or hot coals but of relentless temptation. Erotic desire is

her torture; it comprises the martyrdom that gives her the authority to teach Zosimus, an elderly monk who begs her for spiritual enlightenment. There is a quandary at the centre of their instructional encounter, however. The displacement of a saint's torture from body to conscience renders it less visible. In order for Mary to teach Zosimus the lesson of God's grace, she must reveal the nature of her suffering. Unfortunately, describing her sexual longings threatens to renew them and to imperil Zosimus' spiritual purity. Mary thus turns out to be an ambivalent mentor, at once drawing Zosimus away from his dangerous spiritual pride and pulling him into her sordid sensuality.

The *Life*'s synthesis of pain and desire is illustrated by a telling translation in a passage where the aged holy woman describes her hesitation about being a teacher.[2] Zosimus, an elderly monk perfected in ascetic practices, has chased Mary through the desert and compelled her to tell him the story of her sanctity. She accepts her didactic role with apprehension: coerced into relating her youthful escapades, in this case her decision to buy passage by sea to Jerusalem with sexual favours, she nevertheless fears its seductive potential:

> Miltsa me, abbud, forðon ic gewilnode mid him to farenne, þæt ic þe ma emwyrhtena on þære þrowunge mines wynlustas hæfde. Ic cwæð ær to þe, 'Ðu halga wer, miltsa me, þæt þu me ne genyde to areccenne mine gescyndnysse.' God wat þæt ic heora forhtige, for þam þe ic wat þæt þas mine word ægðer gewemmað ge þe ge þas lyfte. (OE 401–407)

> Take pity on me, abbot, because I wanted to travel with them so that I would have more associates in the passion of my sensual pleasures. I said to you earlier, 'You holy man, take pity on me, so that you do not compel me to recount my confusions.' God knows that I fear them, for I know that my words corrupt both you and this air.

Here, Mary recognises the continuing danger of her past sins. Her words can defile, pollute, or injure Zosimus and the very air around them, as the verb 'gewemmað', translating 'maculant' (420), indicates. The Old English translator's choice of *gewemman* echoes the verb *geweman*, 'to turn, incline, seduce', a verb that could be used for the positive guidance offered by a teacher, but also to denote tempting or devilish seduction.[3] In the Old English translation, Mary recognises even more profoundly the dual nature of her teaching of Zosimus: the words she uses to explain God's grace and lead him to truth can also injure and seduce him.

Mary's brief, emotional speech condenses the subtle tensions that characterise her pedagogical encounter with Zosimus. It also contains a linguistic expansion. The translator renders the Latin 'libidinis passionem' (417, the passion of wantonness) as 'þære þrowunge mines wynlustas'. In contrast to the Latin *passio*, which ranges in meaning from suffering, pain, and martyrdom to strong emotion, affection, desire, and lust,[4] Old English *þrowung* has the more restricted sense of passive or painful suffering of an action.[5] *Þrowung* is the lexeme of choice for translating the crucifixion of Christ and martyrdoms of the saints into Old English.[6] Whether by choice or revealing error, the translator of the *Life* presses *þrowung* into service as 'lust' or 'desire'. Mary, a saint who will die of natural causes after years of penitential abstinence in the desert, thus describes herself as enduring an unlikely martyrdom in the very heat of her fleshly desires. By placing Mary's suffering at a point in her life when she is most emphatically following the flesh, the translator suggests a notion of penitence and learning intimately bound up with moral frailty. In contrast to Christian martyrs whose charismatic authority is crystallised as they deny the needs of their bodies and passively suffer tortures imposed by temporal authorities, Mary's *þrowung* occurs when she pursues her bodily lusts.[7]

The *Life's* adaptation of *þrowung* gestures to the unexpected locus of Mary's authority, and it also marks a turn inward.[8] In an echo of Ælfric's description of the Virgin Mary's suffering, Mary of Egypt's *passio* is primarily of the emotions, less so of the body. In his homily on the Assumption of the Virgin, Ælfric writes that the Virgin Mary was even greater than the martyrs, because 'heo þrowade þone martyrdom on hire sawle þe oþre martyras þrowodon on heora lichaman' (she suffered that martyrdom in her soul that other martyrs suffer in their bodies).[9] Just as Ælfric claims that Mary is entitled to the greatness of a *passio* despite not having died a martyr, so does the *Life of St Mary of Egypt* posit a saint whose inner anguish gives her spiritual authority.[10] However, while the tortures most martyrs undergo are visible to the eye, a fact reflected in the trope of the witnessing multitude in medieval *passiones*, the martyrdom of the soul must be described, argued for, and imagined. While the audience of a physical passion can, at least within the narrative frame, watch and passively learn, the student of an internal martyrdom must actively picture the saint's suffering in order to understand the magnitude of her sacrifice.[11] Accordingly, the instructional relationship in the *Life of St Mary of Egypt* centres around the need for acts of narration and imagination. As the slippage of *þrowung* suggests, for Zosimus to comprehend Mary of Egypt's salvation and subsequent sanctity, he must first understand her sinfulness.

The Latin and Old English lives of Saint Mary of Egypt present passion as an essential component of the most successful mode of pedagogy. In its examination of model teachers, the *Life* traces an arc from the textbook perfection of Zosimus to the radical imperfection of Mary, and it does so because only Mary's sinfulness can demonstrate the capaciousness of divine grace. Mary's pedagogic effectiveness depends on her frailty and desire, on saintly *passio* experienced in the midst of sensual lusts rather than undertaken to avoid them, and on the communication of longing that, like much monastic expression, draws its affective force from intimate and erotic language. The result is two instructional encounters between Zosimus and Mary characterised by oscillation between sanctity and temptation, curiosity and coercion, holy desire for learning and lust for the teacher's body. This wavering is intensified in the Old English version, which emphasises Mary's corporeality, her seductive force, the presence of temptation in her encounter with Zosimus, and the relationship of these elements to Zosimus' vigorous curiosity.[12] Through a systematic series of translation choices, the Old English *Life of St Mary of Egypt* makes unstable desire a key element of spiritual discipleship.

The *Life*'s intensified focus on desire leads to an acknowledgement of the danger inherent in the teaching encounter, a recognition of the perilous agency of student, teacher, and the very lesson being imparted. First, the student must desire to learn, and yet curiosity itself has negative connotations in medieval writing. Moreover, if what the student wants to learn is the nature of the ascetic teacher's former sinfulness and the extent of her penitence, he threatens to force her to revisit her sin once again. Indeed, the *Life* at various points depicts both student and teacher as potential rapists so as to convey the violence of their desires and their willingness to coerce. The teacher, on her part, must draw the student to her by alternately concealing and revealing the truth he seeks. The *Life* recognises the same structure of desire we saw at play in *Solomon and Saturn I*, repeatedly showing that only that which is just out of reach, out of grasp, can awaken longing. And yet, Mary cannot teach this particular lesson of God's grace without completely revealing her sordid past, thus threatening Zosimus' purity and her own hard-won peace of mind.

In this chapter I argue for both the centrality and the danger of pedagogic desire in the *Life of St Mary of Egypt*, a reading I believe holds true for its Latin source but is emphasised in the Old English variants. If the *Life* reflects an ascetic strain in insular spirituality, one influenced by figures such as Antony and Paul the Hermit and reflected in Cuthbert and Guthlac, it also demonstrates Anglo-Saxons' interest in and attention to the workings of desire and its intellectual facet, curiosity, in the process of teaching. It offers a salutary contrast to the rhetoric of ascetic perfection by showing the failings of Zosimus, a monk whose flawless observance of monastic rules has seduced him into pride. Despite the fact that it is not typically part of the story told about the Benedictine Reform or Ælfric's teaching programme, the *Life* should appeal to us precisely because it hints at an alternative tradition in tenth-century Anglo-Saxon hagiography and intellectual life.[13]

Ideas of Teaching in the *Life of St Mary of Egypt*

Saints' lives have a way of multiplying themselves, as though the barren bodies of holy people must be compensated for with an excess of textual reproduction.[14] The tale of Mary of Egypt originated in an anecdote in Cyril of Scythopolis' sixth-century Greek *Life of St Cyriacus*, and was elaborated into a fuller narrative later in the sixth century or early in the seventh, questionably attributed to Sophronius of Jerusalem.[15] The story entered the Western tradition when Paul, a deacon of Naples, translated it into Latin. There were other Latin versions as well, but Paul's proved to be particularly influential, found in over a hundred medieval manuscripts. This version served as the source of the tenth-century Old English translation.[16] The earliest mentions of Mary of Egypt in Anglo-Saxon England occur in late ninth- and tenth-century calendars, and her *Life* in the version of Paul of Naples was present in England in the tenth and eleventh centuries, though Hugh Magennis considers it likely that Theodore of Tarsus introduced Mary of Egypt to England in the seventh century.[17] Paul's version of the *Life* can be found in the Cotton-Corpus Legendary, a multivolume collection of saints' lives compiled on the continent but known from English manuscripts. This collection, or something similar to it, served as Ælfric's main source for his *Lives of the Saints* in the late tenth century.[18] The Old English *Life* is closer to the texts of the *Vita Sanctae Mariae Egyptiacae* found in the Cotton-Corpus Legendary manuscripts BL Cotton Nero E.i, Part 1 and Salisbury, Cathedral Library 221, than to other versions.[19] However, in some cases the Old English deviates from the Cotton-Corpus text but preserves readings original to the Greek *Life* attributed to Sophronius. For this reason, Magennis argues that the Old English translation must have been based on a Latin text much like those found in the Cotton-Corpus manuscripts, but older and better.[20] For the purposes of this chapter, I compare the Old English translation and its variants to Magennis' text of Paul's *Vita*,[21] based on BL Cotton Nero E.i, Part 1, with the understanding that this is the closest text we have to the English translator's source and not the direct source.

The primary testimony to the Old English *Life of St Mary of Egypt* is BL Cotton Julius E.vii (early eleventh century).[22] Here, the life of this penitent desert hermit has been inserted into a manuscript of Ælfric's *Lives of Saints*. That this was a late addition is suggested by the fact that it is out of place in the calendar sequence, and by its absence from the table of contents.[23] It is one of four non-Ælfrician additions to the *sanctorale*, along with the *Legend of the Seven Sleepers*, the *Life of St Eustace*, and the *Life of St Euphrosyne*. Its translator followed the Latin original very closely, keeping so many participles that the English rendering can sometimes read more like a gloss on the Latin rather than a true translation.[24] Fragments of the Old English translation are also preserved in BL Cotton Otho B.x (first half of eleventh century) and in Gloucester, Cathedral Library 35 (mideleventh century).[25] Despite the dismissiveness the Old English *Life of St Mary of Egypt* has occasionally drawn from critics – in his earlier work, Magennis characterised it as 'much inferior to the lives by Ælfric' and 'not the work of an experienced translator'[26] – the fact that pieces from three copies survive testifies to its contemporary appeal.

The *Life* begins with Zosimus, a monk so perfect that, at the age of fifty-three, he begins to suspect that he has nothing left to learn. He travels to join a community of monks even more desolate, even more devout, and even more self-denying. Every year at Lent, the men go out into the desert to fast and humble themselves. After days of wandering in the wilderness, Zosimus spies a phantom-like woman, her body blackened by the sun, her hair white as wool. The aged Zosimus is filled with desire, begins to chase her, and ultimately compels Mary to tell him her life story. After leaving her family at the age of twelve for the sinful city of Alexandria, she abandoned herself to vices and lusts, so driven by her libido that she took no money for her favours.[27] Her conversion is propitiated when she joins a group of pilgrims taking sail for Jerusalem, offering the free use of her body as payment. Once in Jerusalem, Mary attempts to enter the temple to see the Holy Cross, but is repulsed by an invisible force. She prays to an image of the Virgin Mary, repents her sins, and is subsequently baptised and flees into the desert. After the encounter in which she recalls her conversion, Mary and Zosimus meet two more times: a year later, Zosimus administers the Eucharist to her, and a year after that, he finds her dead body and buries it with the help of a lioness.

Critical approaches to the Old English *Life* have addressed its quality and features as a translation,[28] its treatment of Mary's sanctity from allegorical and generic perspectives,[29] and its depiction of gender relations between Mary and Zosimus,[30] often with open-ended results. Indeed, analyses of the *Life* typically find the text ambiguous and opaque. In Colin Chase's reading, for example, the answer to the *Life*'s central question of how to become perfect 'remains unexpressed in words in the text, residing in thirty years of desert silence which she barely mentions and cannot describe'.[31] Andrew Scheil focuses on the indeterminacy of Mary's body and Mary's *vita*, showing how Mary appears to us – and to Zosimus – as woman, animal, spirit, and body in rapid succession.[32] Clare Lees and Gillian Overing see this ambiguity in Mary's form and meaning as a sign of Zosimus' inability to read and see spiritually, and an impetus to his subsequent education.[33] In Lees' later return to the text, she and Diane Watt argue that Mary's transcendence of her 'womanliness and physicality' render her 'transgendered or genderqueer'.[34] Patricia Cox Miller, writing about the Latin version of the *Life*, argues that 'the figure of the harlot-saint is a grotesquerie – a not-quite-coherent construct – and as such brings to its most acute expression the problematic quality of early Christian attempts to construct a representation of female holiness'.[35] The difficulty of placing Mary may lie as much in certain modern perspectives on sanctity. After all, in her sexual availability, Mary resembles other reformed harlot saints such as Mary Magdalene, the prosperous actress Pelagia, and the prostitute Thaïs, each with her own long textual tradition.[36] Virginia Burrus has noted that interpreters of these holy harlots tend to consider 'sinfulness and sanctity' as necessarily opposing terms. Instead, Burrus argues for recognising that the power these women hold to turn their viewers to Christian faith is closely allied to their erotic seductiveness. Burrus stresses – in a way that is even more true for the Old English *Life of St Mary of Egypt* than for the Latin – 'the *continuity* of her seductive seducibility, the *enviability* of her convertibility, the *lure* of her capacity to desire'.[37] The fact that so many literary analyses of Mary of Egypt's narrative end in equivocality might mirror the ambivalent nature of Mary's holiness, but it might also reflect the complex notion of sanctity and didactic authority at work in her *Life*.

While the *Life*'s most important instructional relationship is that of Mary and Zosimus, it is introduced by reflections on the kinds of teaching that take place in Zosimus' two monasteries. Indeed, the *Life*'s close attention to modes of monastic education prepares the reader to understand how Mary's pedagogy works. These monasteries represent two different ways of learning, namely by imitation of charismatic example and through introspection and solitary ascetic experience. These didactic methods are presented as successful, but only to a certain extent. As I will show, Mary's teaching incorporates aspects of each, but the transformative power of her pedagogy is founded in its astute use of pure and impure desire to spiritually edifying ends.

The story begins with what seems to be a terrifically successful model of teaching. Zosimus' life is unsullied, his practices steady and fruitful, even though his textbook asceticism leaves him unsatisfied and proud. He is constant and spiritual in psalmody and meditation on Scripture, and his dedication is often rewarded with divine enlightenment, 'godcundan onlihtnysse' (OE 40–48). Indeed, knowledge of his apparent perfection has made him the ancient monastic equivalent of a star professor:

> Swa soðlice he wæs fulfremod on eallum munuclicum þeawum, þæt wel oft munecas of feorrum stowum and of mynstrum to him comon, þæt hi to his bysne and to his larum hi gewriðon and to þære onhyringe his forhæfednysse hi underðeoddon. (35–39)

> He was indeed so perfected in all monastic practices, that very often monks came to him from distant places and monasteries, so that they bound themselves to his example and to his teachings, and subjected themselves to the imitation of his self-restraint.

Zosimus serves as a *bysen*, or example, to the monks who come to imitate him, in the tradition of education, or *paideia*, through charismatic pedagogy. Ancient *paideia* was an intimate process, a close relationship between teacher and pupil in which the student perfected himself by modelling his words and manners on the example of his master. The masculine pronouns are deliberate: Peter Brown has stressed the importance of male bonding at the heart of this relation. In antiquity, writes Brown, 'a literary tradition existed for the sole purpose of "making [persons] into classics": exposure to the classics of Greek and Latin literature was intended to produce exemplary beings, their raw humanity molded and filed away by a double discipline, at once ethical and aesthetic'.[38] Christian thinkers took up the idea of a teacher whose very life and body are example and text to be imitated, only with God as the ultimate exemplar. Exemplary teaching was a common feature of ascetic life as it is represented in the *Sayings of the Desert Fathers* and in other early eremitic lives, and it is no surprise to find it in the *Life of St Mary of Egypt*.[39] The draw of an exceptional master or model could also be attributed to charisma, a gift or grace of God diffused to laymen through saints and holy persons. Stephen Jaeger, who has studied the continuation of this form of pedagogy in the cathedral schools of the tenth to twelfth centuries, stresses that 'charisma stimulates imitation'. And so it is that, despite the intense focus in charismatic pedagogy on the presence, the body, the immediate sight of the teacher, this same teacher also functions the way a text does, a classic that moulds its readers, or in Jaeger's terms, 'a learnable discourse', 'a living textbook'.[40] This is the relationship Zosimus evidently had with the men who came to emulate his ascetic habits, and it is the relation he seeks with another master as he begins to journey away from the monastery he inhabited since childhood.[41]

The widespread admiration Zosimus enjoys for his seemingly flawless life tempts him to pride. Troubled by the idea that he might not be able to find any more teachers, he laments:

> Hwæðer ænig munuc on eorðan sy þæt me mage aht niwes getæcan oððe me on ænigum þingum gefultumian þæs þe ic sylf nyte oððe þæt ic on þam munuclicum weorcum sylf ne gefylde, oþþe hweðer ænig þæra sy þe westen lufiað þe me on his dædum beforan sy. (62–67)

> Is there any monk on earth who could teach me anything new or support me in any matters that I did not myself know, or that I had not accomplished in monastic works, or is there any among those who love the desert who is better than me in his deeds?

Zosimus' role as an idealised, exemplary teacher thus results in his own spiritual stagnation, and impedes him from further learning. The *Life* does not explicitly state that his pupils' adoration has resulted in Zosimus' perception of himself as unequalled throughout the world, but the language used to describe both his perfection and his pride supports the idea. While students come to him because he is 'fulfremod' to emulate his 'bysne' and 'larum' (35–39), these words reoccur when he is 'gecnyssed fram sumum geþancum swa swa he wære on eallum þingum *fulfremed* and he nanre maran *lare* ne *bysene* ne beþorfte on his mode' (59–61, troubled by the thought that he might be perfected in all things and might not need any more teaching or example in his mind). The angel who appears to Zosimus succinctly presents the *Life*'s critique of exemplary pedagogy when he points out that 'nis nan man þe hine *fulfremedne* æteowe' (70–71, no one can reveal himself to be perfect). The first sense of this somewhat convoluted advice is that perfection is impossible for mere mortals, especially for someone like Zosimus, who has yet to know real spiritual struggle. The angel's phrasing also hints at the problem of representing perfection to others.

Consciously presenting oneself as perfect can lead to pride, itself a decline from perfection. An illustrative example from the *Verba Seniorum* demonstrates the tendency of truly 'perfected' hermits to conceal their strict practices in order to avoid fame and the adulation of the multitude Zosimus seems to enjoy.[42] When travelling brothers decide to test Agathon's famed humility by accusing him of pride, fornication, and other faults, the saintly man admits every one of the sins and throws himself on the ground to beg for forgiveness. He affirms every false accusation, with the exception of heresy, which is a separation from God. He later explains: 'I maintained the previous faults and sins for humility's sake, so that you may believe me a sinner. For we know that if the strength of humility is guarded, great is the health of the soul.'[43] As Agathon demonstrates, among Christian ascetics the only convincing performance of perfection is a rigorous show of fallibility. The *Life* will introduce a similar notion that true humility resides in acknowledging one's sinfulness when Mary recounts her past exploits, with the important difference that Mary's faults are real.

The practices of Zosimus' second monastery embody another theory of learning: there, solitary ascetic experience is key to spiritual improvement, and the fruit of this process of discovery is closely guarded. In contrast to the first monastery, which was evidently porous enough for Zosimus' discipline to become famous beyond its walls, here the most profound lessons are kept hidden, as is, indeed, the monastery itself. Upon arriving, Zosimus presents himself as a potential student, telling the abbot: 'ic for lare intigan eow her gesohte' (87–88, I sought you here for reasons of learning). The discerning abbot replies by ignoring Zosimus' claim that he wants to learn, and implicitly addresses the famous monk's understanding of himself as a model and teacher: 'Ne mæg ænig mann oþerne getimbrian buton he hine sylfne gelomlice behealde and he mid sylfrum andgyte þæt beo sylf wyrcende, God to gewitan hæbbende' (94–97, Nor can any man teach another unless he observe himself frequently, and unless he works on that himself with sober perception, with God as a witness). In an instructional moment with mildly antagonistic subtext, the abbot implicitly questions the extent to which Zosimus could have been an excellent teacher in the first place. He calls into question the simple exemplary model of pedagogy, in which externally sensible practices such as prayer, work, and stability are admired and emulated. Instead, he bases didactic authority on a move inward, on wrestling with one's sinfulness in the face of God, not before an audience of disciples. However, while the new monks' practices give every indication of being spiritually salutary, their insistence on secrecy and silence keeps them from teaching the grace of God.

The *Life*'s introduction first announces its concern with secrecy and revelation, with stories that must be told and those better left unsaid. Its narrator begins by citing Raphael's injunction in the Book of Tobit not to keep the works of God secret: 'Soðlice hit is swiðe derigendlic þæt man cynnes digle geopenige, and eft þære sawle is micel genyðrung þæt mon þa wuldorfæstan Godes weorc bediglige' (11–14, Truly it is very harmful to reveal the secrets of one's kin, and again it greatly debases the soul to hide the works of glorious God). While he subsequently uses this as justification to relate the story of Mary despite its implausibility, his (altered) citation of Tobit reveals an awareness of the problem posed by secrets. The divine must be discerned from the human, the danger of telling weighed against the consequences of silence. The theme of secrecy occurs again in the description of Zosimus' second monastery, located in a place 'swa westen and swa digle þæt næs na þæt an þæt heo wæs ungewunelic ac eac swilce uncuð þam landleodum him sylfum' (130–32, so isolated and so secret that not only was it unfrequented but also unknown to the very people of that country). While Zosimus is accustomed to being famous for his severe practices, in the new monastery monks are required to remain quiet about the ascetic wandering they undertake in the desert during the first week of Lent. Not only do they not boast of their abstinence, they are forbidden to ask one another about what practices they undertook: 'heora nan oþerne ne axode on hwilce wisan he þæs geswinces gewin gefylde' (177–78, none of them asked each other how he accomplished the struggle of that exercise).

The monastery's rule is intended to preserve the monks' humility, a quality Zosimus has notably lacked. Since the abbot explains to Zosimus that sober introspection is necessary for anyone who might become a teacher to others, the monastery's practice of secrecy at Lent also seems to support the kind of inward focus that will result in learning. During their most profound ascetic experience, the monks are to concern themselves only with their own souls, not with the achievements of others. And yet, the consequence of this policy is that any divine experience occurring in the desert may not be taught. The monastery's fine practices during the rest of the year serve as a model for imitation: 'Þas weorc Zosimus behealdende hine sylfne geornlice to fulfremednysse aþenede' (117–19, when Zosimus beheld these works he eagerly extended himself to perfection). However, when the monks exit their monastery doors entrusting themselves to divine providence, the results of that providence remain concealed. Contra Raphael's command, whatever God works in the desert is kept hidden. Mary's teaching ultimately strikes a balance between the prideful visibility of Zosimus' instruction of other monks and the unproductive secrecy of his second monastery's ascetic practice, vacillating between the desire to hide the secrets of her personal sins and the need to reveal God's interventon in her life. Strictly speaking, neither her solitary reflection nor her ascetic feats in the desert teach Zosimus. Rather, he learns because she chooses to tell him about them, the revelation of her own sordid past being necessary to demonstrate the extent of divine grace.

Mary of Egypt's Pedagogy

But what, and how, does Mary teach? Education in the *Life's* first monastery consists of exemplarity with inadequate reflection, while the second monastery privileges intense personal reflection but neglects to transform its lessons into exemplary teaching. Mary, on the other hand, models introspection and the resulting compunction for Zosimus, showing him how she faced her sinfulness so that he may come to terms with his own. The central moment in her own education occurs at the church in Jerusalem, when, exhausted by repeated attempts to enter, she reflects on her sinfulness:

> Þus ic þrywa oþþe feower siþum þrowode minne willan to geseonne and eac to fremanne, and þa ða ic naht ne gefremode þa ongan ic ofer þæt georne wenan, and min lichama wæs swiðe geswenced for þam nyde þæs geþringes. Ða gewat ic witodlice þanone, and me ana gestod on sumum hwomme þæs cafertunes and on minum mode geornlice þohte and smeade for hwilcum intigum me wære forwyrned þæs liffæstan treowes ansyn. Þa onhran soðlice min mod and þa eagan minre heortan hælo andgit, mid me sylfre þencende þæt me þone ingang belucen þa unfeormeganda minra misdæda. Ða ongan ic biterlice wepan and swiðe gedrefed mine breost cnyssan and of inneweardre heortan heofende forðbringan þa geomorlican siccetunga. (476–89)

> Thus I suffered my will to see and to do, and since I did not accomplish anything I began then to think about that eagerly. And my body was very tired because of the force of that pushing. Then, truly, I went from there, and stood alone in a corner of the courtyard, and in my mind I thought and considered carefully for what reason the sight of the living tree was denied me. Then the understanding of salvation touched my mind and the eyes of my heart, with me thinking that my inexpiable transgressions had locked the entrance to me. Then I began to weep bitterly, exceedingly troubled I beat my breast, and, lamenting from my inward heart, I began to bring forth sorrowful sighs.

This passage is noteworthy for several reasons. To begin with, the first line contains another unusual use of 'suffering', all the more remarkable because it seems not to be a translation. In the Latin, Mary describes herself as 'conans et nihil proficiens' (483–84, attempting and not accomplishing anything), and there is no mention of suffering or will. Magennis translates this as 'I attempted to see and also attain what I wished', thus loosely following Skeat, who renders the line 'I endeavoured to behold and also to fulfil my will.'⁴⁴ Both Skeat and Magennis thus translate *prowian*, a word meaning 'to suffer', with an active sense it does not possess.⁴⁵ Indeed, this confusing passage in the Old English contains another mini-passion for the future Saint Mary, one combining physical exhaustion and emotional compunction. The scene of anguish is, moreover, also one of learning. The English translator intensifies the notion that this experience of suffering is an occasion to think, a moment in Mary's education when she becomes a deliberate student of her own soul. The Latin chooses a single construction to describe Mary's thinking: 'uix aliquando ob quam causam prohibebar uidere uiuificum lignum in cogitatione reduxi' (487–89, just a little later I recalled in my thoughts the reason why I was prevented from seeing the lifegiving cross). In contrast, the Old English text uses three verbs to emphasise Mary's intellectual search for understanding, *wenan*, *smeagan*, and *þencan*. As in the other texts explored in this book, pain is a stimulus to thinking and understanding.

Mary's reward for her meditation in the courtyard is compunction. She imagines herself in the presence of the Virgin Mary, and after begging her to chase away foul thoughts, is rewarded with illumination:

> Ðonne ic soðlice oferflowendlice sorgigende weop, and ic heardlice mine breost cnyssende þonne geseah leoht gehwanon me ymbutan scinende, and me þonne sona sum staþolfæstlic smyltnyss to becom. (637–41)

> Then I truly wept with overflowing sorrow, and I beat my breast harshly. Then I saw a light shining from all sides around me, and then a steadfast tranquillity suddenly came to me.

The gestures she uses to express her contrition echo other moments in the *Life*. Later, in the desert, when tempted by the memory of the lewd songs she used to enjoy, she repeats these movements of sorrow, 'wepende, mine breost mid minum handum cnyssende' (630, weeping, beating my breast with my hands). The Old English translation reinforces the repeated image of Mary beating her chest by rendering the different Latin verbs for striking with the same English word: while the Latin varies diction with 'pectus tundere' (492), 'pectus ... percutiens' (612–13), and 'pectus ... tundebam' (619–20) respectively, the Old English regularly uses *cnyssan*. Since *cnyssan* can be used in Old English figuratively for the violent motions of the mind, the translator also uses it to gloss *pulsare* earlier in the story.⁴⁶ Zosimus, at the peak of his supposed perfection, is 'pulsatus ... a quibusdam cogitationibus' (69–70) or 'gecnyssed fram sumum geþancum' (59), although he happens to be struck by the wrong thoughts. The Old English text thus suggests a connection between Zosimus' and Mary's spiritual progress, unifying their moments of painful self-reflection under one word.

Despite this foreshadowing, when Zosimus 'pulsates' he has yet to learn how to assess himself correctly. In a sense, also, he must learn how to suffer, having wallowed in the false tranquillity of pride. In the course of hearing the story of Mary's conversion and witnessing her miraculous powers, he both understands his own fallibility and suffers in a way that echoes her travails. After seeing her walk on the surface of the Jordan, he acknowledges his imperfection: 'Wuldor sy þe, Drihten God, þu þe me þurh þas þine þeowene æteowdest hu micel ic ... on minre agenre gesceawunge on þam gemete þæra oþra fulfremodnysse' (820–23, Glory be to you, Lord God, who through this your maidservant showed me how much I [am inferior] in my own observation when compared to the perfection of others). Finally, when faced with the daunting prospect of burying Mary's corpse in the hard desert earth, he comes to resemble Mary aching to enter the church in Jerusalem:

> And seo eorðe wæs swiðe heard, and ne mihte he adelfan, forþon he wæs swiðe gewæced ægðer ge mid fæstene ge on þam langan geswince, and he mid sworettungum wæs genyrwed, and mid þære heortan deopnysse geomrode. (915–19)

> And the earth was very hard, and he could not dig, because he was very weakened both with fasting and due to the long toil, and he was oppressed with panting, and mourned from the deepness of his heart.

Exhausted with futile physical labour, sighing and mourning from his heart, Zosimus recalls Mary's suffering in the courtyard. Rather than a key early moment in a saintly *Bildungsroman*, however, physical and emotional distress seem to be part of Zosimus' main lesson, the completion of the education he began when he left his first monastery.

Seen from this perspective, Mary's teaching of Zosimus seems to strike just the right balance between introspection and exemplarity, inner and outer teaching. She describes for him both the intellectual processes leading to her compunction and the gestures with which she performs her shame; he learns to feel what she feels, to weep as she weeps. Moreover, since Mary asks him to keep her story secret only while she lives, her eventual death liberates him to tell his fellow monks about the wonders he saw and heard in the desert. At the end we are told that the monks 'ealle Godes mærða wurðodon' (952–53, all praised God's glories), a conclusion which seems nicely to resolve the problem of secrecy introduced at the *Life*'s beginning. However, describing the *Life*'s pedagogy in this way leaves out the main force driving the relationship between Mary and Zosimus, and indeed, underpinning much education in the *Life*: desire. For while the *Life* presents its readers with a salutary ending – Zosimus recognises his fallibility, he learns to suffer and praise the Lord – the path to this conclusion is a treacherous one. Mary's pedagogy of desire brings up anxieties concerning representation, compulsion, seduction, and temptation, all of which are braided throughout this tense instructional relationship.

While Mary's instruction of Zosimus incorporates pedagogical methods in use at the two monasteries, its characteristic quality is the presence of desire. Mary gains her authority to teach not only from the feats of abnegation she performs after her conversion, but from the *passio* she endured in the midst of her iniquity, a suffering coterminous with lust. Her insatiable passions lead her to find God, and she manipulates Zosimus' longing for her and her story to teach him the power of divine grace. In short, desire, even when directed towards the wrong object, propels the characters towards compunction and illumination. The *Life*'s perspective on spiritual improvement is thus in line with Geoffrey Harpham's observation that 'while asceticism recognizes that desire stands between human life and perfection, it also understands that desire is the only means of achieving perfection, and that the movement towards ideality is necessarily a movement of desire'.[47] My discussion of *Solomon and Saturn I* demonstrated how the poem uses Saturn's curiosity about a prayer he will never possess to spur new enthusiasm for the Pater Noster in the minds of literate Christian readers. The *Life of St Mary of Egypt* structures desire in a similar, though not identical, fashion. It is not a story of yearning for impossible things, for indeed, both main characters ultimately achieve their spiritual goals. Instead, it repeatedly shows Mary and Zosimus hastening towards an object, often without even knowing what it is they have begun to desire, their eagerness increasing as they encounter obstacles on the way, and, finally, reaching satisfaction. Despite the fact that most of its action takes place in the desert, the *Life* is filled with borders and barriers: the door to Zosimus' new monastery, the valley separating Mary and Zosimus at their first meeting, the temple door that repels Mary, the Mediterranean sea, and the Jordan river.[48] In a recurrent visual motif, these features of the *Life*'s landscape act as hurdles, delaying the characters' physical or spiritual gratification. Appropriately enough, Mary, with her sun-scorched skin, recalls the bride in the *Song of Songs*.[49] The *Song*, with its depiction of a bride and bridegroom approaching each other yet kept apart, represents a similar understanding of the way desire is evoked, frustrated, and increased. Patricia Cox Miller has traced Jerome's use of the *Song of Songs* to describe ascetic longing, as it 'constructs erotic love in such a way that its climax is always deferred, never quite reached, yet it holds out union as the end toward which the lovers strive'.[50] Gregory the Great used the bride's search for her bridegroom in the *Song* as an illustration of the way wise men's desire for God is often delayed so that it might grow.[51] Mary's dark skin, with its biblical and patristic resonance, would have been yet another visual index of longing increased by frustration.

Although the most successful mode of teaching represented in the *Life* is based on longing, a pedagogy of desire brings with it complications. First, desire can be morally execrable or laudable depending on whether its object is worldly or divine, and the intellectual subset of desire known as curiosity shares this dual nature. The language used to describe longing in the *Life* reflects this wavering between the soul's ardour and the burning of the flesh. The second problem with desire is that it leads to coercion. The lover, the seeker, the one who wants to know and to possess, is also someone who is potentially willing to force satisfaction from the object of desire. For this reason, teaching by desire is an unstable proposition, incorporating both seduction and the threat of violation.

Although the *Life* begins with an account of Zosimus, chronologically speaking the first education in desire is Mary's own. Despite her aggressive pursuit of sex and other gratifications of the flesh early in her story, she is passive in her passion, powerless to resist its urges. As she begins to make her way toward the Cross, we see her longing increase as its object is withheld, first by her difficulties in obtaining passage to Jerusalem, then by being barred from the church. In the desert she eventually learns to master her temptations and basic bodily needs, but as her encounter with Zosimus demonstrates, she also learns to manipulate desire more astutely when dealing with others. This is not to say that desire becomes a tamed, controllable force, for Mary repeatedly indicates that it is not, but that she provokes it more effectively.

Tellingly, during her youthful sexual escapades Mary has not yet understood how desire functions, nor how best to elicit it. She explains that she did not demand any gifts for the loss of her virginity because she wished to satisfy her burning lust:

> ac ic wæs swiðe onæled mid þære hatheortnysse þæs synlustes, þæt ic gewilnode butan ceape þæt hi me þe mænigfealdlicor to geurnon, to þy þæt ic þe eð mihte gefyllan þa scyldfullan gewilnunga mines forligeres (376–79)

but I was so inflamed with the fervour of sinful lust that I wished they would run to me in greater numbers, without pay, so that I could satisfy the wicked desires of my fornication.

The focus here is on her own lechery, but she also wants to awaken desire in others, to have her potential lovers run towards her the way Zosimus later does. As a young woman, she believes the way to do this is to make herself available to all men, or even to force herself on them when they do not readily oblige, as with her fellow sailors on the boat.[52]

Zosimus goes to the desert because he wishes to find a teacher, and in this sense he already has an object of desire before he ever sees Mary. Seeing Mary, he runs towards her in order to know, 'to oncnawenne' (225), what kind of wild animal or 'wildeor' she might be. We are meant to understand his chase of her in the context of his search for enlightenment, but his longing has a violent undertone. Upon seeing her he immediately wants to 'join' himself with her. His fervour seems appropriate as an expression of monastic longing for the sacred, but the chase vascillates between terrifying and ridiculous:

> Sona swa hi Zosimus geseah, þa witodlice, his ealdan ylde ofergetiligende and þæt geswinc his syðfætes ne understandende, mid hrædestan ryne þenigende arn, forþam þe he gewilnode hine geðeodan þam þe ðær fleah. He witodlice hire wæs ehtende, and heo wæs fleonde. (227–31)

> As soon as Zosimus saw her, then truly, overcoming his old age and ignoring the effort of his journey, he hastened, exerting himself with the fastest running, because he wanted to join himself to the one who was fleeing there. He was really pursuing her, and she was fleeing.

As Scheil has also argued, this is a parodic staging of a potential rape scene.[53] Readers of the *Life* would have been familiar with the many tales of female saints whose virginity was threatened by lustful Roman governors and who bravely resisted. We can think even more concretely of how this passage might have been construed by an Anglo-Saxon reader by reading it within its manuscript context in BL Cotton Julius E.vii, where it fits uneasily into the *Lives of Saints*. Ælfric prefers his female saints to be ignorant of the pleasures of the flesh, though they certainly have enough opportunities to learn. Examples abound: the wicked pagan suitor of Saint Lucy attempts to take her to a brothel; Saint Agatha is sent by her cruel suitor to a prostitute to be perverted; Saint Agnes' suitor has her stripped and led naked to a brothel.[54] Read in this context, the chase scene in the Old English *Life of St Mary of Egypt* not only reminds its audience of the way female saints are usually victimised by their eager suitors, but renders the generic sexual aggression of hagiographies comical by replacing the virile pagan governor with a gasping senile ascetic, and the nubile virgin with a repentant, elderly harlot.

While Zosimus had searched for a 'father', his need for a mentor is transformed into a more complex emotion, combining the urge to learn with yearning for the beloved teacher, and expressed in the erotic vocabulary of monastic devotion. After their first meeting, Zosimus prays that God will show him 'þone gewilnodan andwlitan' (761–62, that desired face) again. Granted another brief encounter a year later, he laments: 'Eala, wære me gelyfed þæt ic moste þinum swaðum fyligan and þines deorwurðan andwlitan gesihðe brucan!' (840–42, Oh, that it would be permitted to me to follow in your footsteps and enjoy the sight of your precious face!). Another year afterwards, he returns to the desert, searching for her once again:

> Þa æfter oferfarenum þæs geares ryne, becom on þæt widgille westen and geornlice efste to þære wuldorlican gesihðe, and þær lange hyderes and þyderes secende for, oþþæt he sum swutol tacn þære gewilnedan gesihðe and wilnunge þære stowe undergeat, and he geornlice mid his eagena scearpnyssum hawigende ge on þa swiðran healfe ge on þa wynstran, swa swa se gleawesta hunta, gif he þær mihte þæt sweteste wildeor gegripan. (867–75)

> After the year's course had passed, he came to the vast desert and zealously hurried to that glorious sight, and there he went, searching for a long time hither and thither, until he perceived some clear sign of the desired sight and of the desire of that place. And with the sharpness of his eyes he eagerly looked right and left, like the most skilful hunter, whether he could seize the sweetest wild animal there.

While at this late point in the narrative Zosimus recognises Mary's ascetic authority, his longing for her is still expressed in terms both erotic and brutalising.[55] Once again, she is more animal than human, and once again, an undercurrent of violence characterises Zosimus' pursuit of her.

If the language of monastic longing for the divine is here used in a way that draws attention to its base, sexual valence, so is Zosimus' curiosity. One of Mary's speeches conflates Zosimus' need to know with his need to see or have her, a reference to the carnal dimension of curiosity, or to what Augustine described as 'concupiscentia oculorum':[56]

> Hwi wæs þe, la abbod Zosimus, swa micel neod me synful wif to geseonne, oððe hwæs wilnast þu fram me to hæbbenne oþþe to witenne, þæt þu ne slawedest swa micel geswinc to gefremmanne for minum þingum? (271–75)

Oh, Abbot Zosimus, why did you have such a need to see me, a sinful woman, or what do you want to have or to know from me, that you did not rest from going to so much trouble on account of me?

Still, despite the aggressive implications of his curiosity, in chasing Mary he also resembles her as she hastened towards baptism in the River Jordan: 'Ða þa ic þone weg wiste, ic wepende be þam siðfæte arn, symle þa axunga þære ascan towriðende, and gemang þam ðæs dæges siðfæt wepende gefylde' (569–72, When I knew the way, I ran along that path weeping, constantly twisting inquiry onto inquiry, and in the course of this I finished the day's journey weeping). Like Zosimus, she runs, weeps, and asks, desperate to know the path to salvation. Her goal in this case is an unambiguously positive one, but the recurring motif of longing, chasing, desiring to see, know, and experience remains profoundly ambivalent. While desire is central to the teaching encounter between Mary and Zosimus, and indeed, part of what makes it so transformative for the latter, the *Life* understands it as a dangerous emotion, uneasily wavering between spiritual and physical objects. The Latin version of Mary's life already depicts teaching as a morally precarious undertaking, and, as I will show, the Old English translation systematically emphasises how hazardous Mary and Zosimus are to one another.

The Danger of Teaching

It is not hard to read the *Life of St Mary of Egypt* along orthodox lines. Mary embodies the voracious sexuality of woman unbridled by Christian doctrine, and her conversion results in the extreme discipline of her soul and body and submission to masculine institutional authority. Her turn to God, as Lynda Coon puts it, 'could teach Christian audiences that redemption is possible even for the most loathsome sinners'.[57] Moreover, as Magennis points out, the *Life*'s 'suggestion of spiritual self-sufficiency' is tempered by Mary's insistence on receiving the Eucharist, a sacrament for which she is dependent on priests.[58] Zosimus, in turn, despite the signs of pride he displays at the start of the story, is zealous in pursuit of spiritual betterment and correctly identifies Mary as the ideal teacher to lead him to it. Yet despite the fact that the *Life* ultimately depicts the successful education of both Mary and Zosimus, the teaching encounter between these two characters demonstrate the ways effective pedagogy can incorporate threatening subtexts and conflicting vectors of power. The meeting of these two ascetics is a complex tango of danger and desire: bodies threaten to be either deceptive apparitions or temptingly tangible, words recall sins and compel their repeating.

The meeting between Zosimus and Mary is fraught with potential danger starting with his first sidelong glimpse of her. His initial reaction to the sight of Mary is fear, 'forþan þe he wende þæt hit wære sumes gastes scinhyw þæt he þær geseah' (209–10, because he thought that it was the illusion of some spirit that he saw there). In both the Latin and Old English versions, Mary is a vision at double remove from physical reality, 'fantasia alicuius spiritus' (215–16, the fantasy of some spirit), highlighting her potentially deceptive nature. Zosimus' momentary fear that Mary may be a ghost or demon suggests more than a mere mirage. The great challenge facing hermits of the desert from St Antony onwards was to withstand the temptations of demons, who might appear as seductive women, ugly hags, or Ethiopian boys.[59] Scheil notes that Mary is reminiscent of the demons who tempt Antony in Athanasius' *Life of St Antony*, especially since her skin, blackened by the sun, is a visual echo of the demon who appears in the shape of an ugly black boy.[60] This kind of demon could be sexually suggestive, as in the *Sayings of the Desert Fathers*, where Abba Heraclides tells of a would-be monk who sins, 'a prey to *accidie*', and is frightened by a black Ethiopian in his bed.[61] The Old English translator recognised and elaborated the menacing implications of Mary's appearance. His choice of *scinhyw* to translate *fantasia*, a 'fancy, mental image, imagination',[62] brings in even more dangerous connotations than the original. According to Bosworth-Toller, *scinhiw* denotes 'a form produced by magic, phantom, spectre', and glosses not only *fantasia*, as here, but also *fantasma, imaginatio*, and *delusio mentis*.[63] The translator's choice conveys the idea that Mary, at first sidelong glance, is not just a false apparition or imagined vision, but one potentially brought about by sorcery.

In an oscillation characteristic of the *Life*, both the narrator and Mary herself subsequently draw attention to her corporeality; in a contradiction equally typical of the *Life*, Mary-as-body is even more threatening than Mary-as-ghost. For if a desert demon might tempt Zosimus with the deceptive appearance of a woman's form, Mary's flesh is present and visible, albeit not as seductive as it once was. Mary's speeches throughout the story maintain Zosimus' interest by alternately concealing and revealing in a rhetorical striptease. Despite her protests, she maintains his interest by being at once available and untouchable, vividly present and always turning out of sight. The way she refers to her own body demonstrates this effect:

> Ða witodlice se *lichama* þe ðær fleah ðyllice stemne forð sende and þus cwæð: 'Ðu abbod Zosimus, miltsa me for Gode, ic þe bidde, forþon ic ne mæg me þe geswutelian and ongeanweardes þe gewenden, forþon ic

eom wifhades mann and eallunga *lichamlicum* wæfelsum bereafod, swa swa
þu sylf gesihst, and þa sceame mines *lichaman* hæbbende unoferwrigene.'
(250–56)

Then truly the body who fled there sent such a voice out and spoke
thus: 'You, abbot Zosimus, have mercy on me for God's sake, I pray you,
because I may not show myself to you and turn towards you, for I am a
woman and bereft of all bodily clothing, as you see yourself, and the shame
of my body is not covered.'

The Old English *lichama*, 'body', echoes the Latin text's triple use of *corpus*, giving a sense of Mary as a body, rather than a person, even when she
is first heard speaking. We can read this as Mary's insistence on her own
frail humanity and lack of demonic power, though the narrator's description of her as a mere *lichama* emitting a voice strikes an uncanny note.
However, Mary also underscores her femininity by referring to her body,
drawing attention to her visible sex – 'swa swa þu sylf gesihst' – even as
she turns to hide it. Mary's is a rhetoric of inverse performatives, directing
Zosimus' gaze to the precise area she wants concealed.

A little later during this first encounter, in a section missing from
BL Cotton Julius E.vii but found in fragmentary form in Gloucester,
Cathedral Library 35, Zosimus sees Mary praying and floating above the
ground. Throwing himself down in holy terror, he begins to wonder if 'hit
gast wære þæt ðær mid hwylcere hiwunga gebæde hi' (338–39, it might
be a spirit that prayed there with a kind of pretense). *Hiwung* can mean
'form, figure' as well as 'pretence, hypocrisy, dissimulation'.[64] While it is
often used for dissimulated belief, it can also describe the deceptive shape
or appearance of a devil, as in the Old English prose *Life of St Guthlac* and
the *Rule of Chrodegang*.[65] Mary reads Zosimus' thoughts, and chastises him
for his suspicion:

To hwy gedrefest þu abbot þine geþohtas to geæswicianne on me swylce ic
hwylc gast syrwiende gebedu fremme? Ac wite þu man þæt ic eom synful
wif, swa þeahhwæðere utan ymbseald mid þam halgan fulluhte, and ic nan
gast ne eom ac æmerge and axe and eall flæsc, and nan gastlice. (340–45)

Why do you trouble your thoughts, abbot, to be offended with me as
though I were some spirit praying craftily? But know, man, that I am a sinful woman, even though protected from without by holy baptism. And I am
no spirit, but dust, and ash, and all flesh, and nothing spiritual.

The tone of Mary's speech here, as in so much of what she says, is rich
and modulated, flickering between offended chastisement, unflinching

humility, and ironic flirtation. Again, read in context, Mary's rhetorically laden insistence on the materiality and sinfulness of her own flesh is meant to assure Zosimus that she is not a demonic apparition. It is also a first moral lesson to her eager student: she is telling Zosimus to look more carefully, to be more discerning, to understand how lowly she is and, perhaps more importantly, to learn from her belief in her own worthlessness. As always, however, Mary's lessons have a double edge: in telling Zosimus that she is not dangerous because she is not a spirit pretending to pray, she reminds him of the presence of her body, once seductive and the source of sin.[66] She may not be a spirit, or *gast*, but she is also not exactly the spiritual mother, or 'gastlice modor' (289) Zosimus has in mind.

The translator's choice of *hiwung* to describe Mary betrays an anxiety regarding representation more generally true for the *Life of St Mary of Egypt*, and links this passage to a moment later in the narrative when Mary really is a deceptive teacher. When describing her sexual adventures on the boat to Jerusalem, Mary will claim that 'nis nan asecgendlic oððe unasecgendlic fracodlicnysse *hiwung* þæs ic ne sih tihtende and lærende' (432–34, there is no speakable or unspeakable form of obscenity that I did not provoke and teach. My italics). The lexical link between these two passages, present in the Old English and not in the Latin, highlights the precariousness of the teaching encounter between Mary and Zosimus, and the danger of trusting a teacher whose previous lessons were, in fact, sinful deceptions. Moreover, the Old English expands on the Latin to underscore the seductive aspects of teaching. While the Latin Mary says she became a teacher to the sailors (445–46, magistra … effecta), the translator extends the idea into two verbs. *Læran* primarily means 'to teach', while *tyhtan* includes this meaning, but is more often used for 'to incite, persuade, provoke' (both God and the devils do it).[67] The translator's choice emphasises Mary's dual role as a teacher who instigates her first pupils to sin, then exhorts her later student to more profound virtue. Early in their first meeting, Zosimus looks for a teacher in Mary, but suspects her of being a ghost who practises *hiwung* in the sense of 'deception'. She argues against that suspicion, but we learn later that she is, in fact, a teacher of *hiwung*, or perversion, and that her speeches can enflame her students to sin.

Mary's coercion of the sailors, conveyed in Latin by *compellere* and in English by *genydan*, is also part of the larger drama of compulsion present in the *Life*. While Mary uses *genydan* to refer to her past sexual predation, she also uses it in two speeches that express her misgivings about confessing these sins to Zosimus in the first place. The first of these is the passage that began this chapter, in which she recoils in horror as she relates how she bartered for the passage to Jerusalem with her body. She repeats plaintively, 'Đu halga wer, miltsa me, þæt þu me ne *genyde* to areccenne mine gescyndnysse' (404–407, You holy man, take pity on me, so that you do not compel me to recount my confusions). While her next line betrays her awareness that this story, so necessary for Zosimus' understanding of her prior sinfulness, threatens to defile both him and the air, she also clearly thinks of herself as forced by Zosimus to recount her shameful deeds. Whereas Zosimus' earlier chase of Mary across the desert could be read a slapstick version of a hagiographic rape scene, this passage marks the moment when his desire to join himself to Mary becomes truly threatening.[68] The use of *compellere*/*genydan* to describe both the way Zosimus forces Mary to tell her story and how Mary forces the sailors to submit to her sexual advances suggests a disturbing parallel between his Christian, ascetic desire for knowledge of her life and her pre-baptismal yearning for sexual adventure.

Mary also uses *compellere* to describe the peril of relating her story to Zosimus. When relating the seventeen years of temptation she endured in the desert after her conversion, she once again expresses her frustration at having to tell her story:[69]

> Cogitationes autem que ad fornicationem iterum *conpellebant* me, quomodo enarrari possum tibi? Abba, ignosce, ignis intus infelix corpus meum nimius succendebat, et omnem me per omnia exurebat, et ad desiderium mixtionis trahebat. (622–26)

> How can I describe to you the thoughts which drove me again to fornication? Abba, have mercy, a fire wholly lit up my unhappy body from within, and consumed me wholly, and drew me to the desire for intercourse.

In the perilous dynamic between Mary and Zosimus, one based on compulsion of sex, speech, and thoughts, this speech is the final, dangerous reverberation. Mary is a sexually voracious woman who forces men to fulfil her lusts and threatens to tempt Zosimus too. She is a troubling teacher, though one who recognises the hazard she embodies, at once bestial and seductive, when she says to him that if she were to begin relating things about herself, 'sona þu flihst fram me on þi gemete swilc man næddran fleo' (353–54, you will soon flee from me in the same way one flees a snake). For his part, Zosimus is threatening due to the violence of his curiosity and intensity of his desire for her as teacher. Not only are they dangerous to each other, but by accepting the role of teacher, Mary becomes dangerous to herself. To fulfil his need for enlightenment, she must revisit her debasement, an encounter with her past necessary for his education:

> Ac me sceamað nu to gereccenne hu ic on þam fruman ærest minne fæmn-had besmat and hu ic unablinnendlice and unafyllendlice þam leahtrum þære synlusta læg underþeoded. Þis is nu witodlice sceortlice to areccenne, ac ic nu swaþeah hrador gecyðe þæt þu mæge oncnawan þone unalyfedan bryne minra leahtra þe ic hæfde on þære lufe þæs geligeres. (365–71)

> But I am ashamed now to recount how, in the beginning, I first defiled my virginity and how I unceasingly and insatiably lay subjected to the fault of desiring to sin. This really should be told quickly now, but I nevertheless say it more readily so that you might understand the illicit burning of my sins that I had in the love of fornication.

Mary only half-willingly accepts that she must describe the full extent of her burning lust: she will speak, but speak quickly, and only because knowledge is at stake, so that Zosimus may understand.

Recounting her past sexual escapades is certainly humiliating to Mary, but can it reasonably be said to be dangerous to her hard-won equilibrium? She did, after all, spend a total of forty-seven years in the wilderness before first encountering Zosimus, and when discussing her battle with temptation she only focuses on the first seventeen, implying that the subsequent three decades were placid. However, while the Latin Mary maintains a relatively clear sequence of events in her description of her desert desires, her Old English counterpart makes a number of telling slips that fuse the time of her temptation to the present moment. As a result, the Old English text presents its readers with a Mary still potentially troubled by her bodily needs. This ongoing temptation heightens the tension of her exchange with Zosimus, since it really does imperil her to teach him. Moreover, she teaches him not with the authority of someone who is perfectly and permanently purified of sin, but as a living example of ongoing emotional struggle in the pursuit of asceticism. In both the Latin and Old English texts, Mary explicitly states that recalling her temptations in the desert could renew them. When Zosimus asks her how she was able to withstand fleshly desire over the space of so many years, Mary replies:

> Heo þa gedrefedu him andswarode, 'Nu þu me axast þa ðincg þe ic swiðe þearle sylf befortige, gif me nu to gemynde becumað ealle þa frecednysse þe ic ahrefnode and þæra unwislicra geþanca þe me oft gedrefedon, þæt ic eft fram þam ylcan geþohtum sum geswinc þrowige.' (608–12)

Then, troubled, she answered him: 'Now you are asking me about those things which I myself fear very much, if all the dangers I endured and the unwise thoughts that often troubled me should come to my memory now, [I fear] that I might suffer some affliction again from those same thoughts.'

While the Latin text is already conscious of the difficulty of discussing temptation without succumbing to it, the Old English version succinctly presses the case even further. This speech is introduced in the Latin text with an unembellished 'et illa dixit' (592). The English Mary is worried about the thoughts that troubled (*gedrefedon*) her earlier, but the description of her as troubled (*gedrefedu*) as she answers Zosimus reveals that his question has already disturbed her composure. Her use of *þrowige*, a direct translation of the Latin *patiar* (596), amplifies the English text's fusion of saintly suffering with erotic desire (403).

The Old English text's heightened attention to temptation is again evident in the passage where Mary worries that revealing her thoughts might drive her again to sex. We have seen how this speech, in both Latin and Old English, helps construct a triangular dynamic of erotic compulsion between Mary, Zosimus, and her own thoughts. Still, the Latin version of the passage at lines 622–26, strictly read, only indicates an aporia: Mary cannot begin to relate the thoughts that previously compelled her to sin. The Old English text reads somewhat differently:

> Ara me nu, abbud. Hu mæg ic ðe gecyðan mine geþances, ða ic me ondræde eft genydan to þam geligre, þæt swyðlice fyr minne ungesæligan lichaman innan ne forbernde? (642–45)

> Forgive me now, abbot. How may I relate my thoughts to you, when I fear to be compelled again to fornication, lest an intense fire burn up my unfortunate body from the inside?

In the Latin version of this passage, Mary describes the intensity of her emotions in the imperfect tense. The Old English introduces the idea of fearing the thoughts themselves, and brings their implied danger into the present.[70] Thus relating them to Zosimus is no longer simply a matter of facing her own shame, but of being compelled once again to sin. The Old English text also complicates the chronology of Mary's desires when describing other desires. When relating how she continued to long for the wine she used to consume to the point of drunkenness, the Latin Mary still keeps her longing clearly in the past, that is, in the first seventeen years in the desert: 'desiderabam uinum delectabile mihi; erat ualde in desiderium [sic]' (603–604, I desired the wine that was delicious to me; I had a great longing for it). The English Mary is rather thirstier, with the addition of both 'nu' and 'eac' indicating a deliberate transposition of her need into the present: 'Ic gewilnode þæs wines … and nu hit is me eac swilce swyðe on gewilnunga' (620–23, I desired the wine … and now it is also very much in my desires).

If these small changes make the Old English Mary seem less sure in her continence despite the three decades that followed her seventeen years of tormented longing, another passage accidentally erases that intervening period altogether. In it, Mary explains to Zosimus how she fought with sexual temptation by praying to the Virgin Mary:

> Semper itaque cordis mei oculos ad illam fideiussorem meam sine cessa-tione erigebam, deprecans eam auxiliari mihi in hac solitudine et penitentie. Habui adiutorium et cooperatricem ipsam quae genuit castitatis auctorem, et sic decem et septem annorum curriculum, periculis multis, ut dixi, eluc-tans, a tunc ergo usque hodie adiutorium meum Dei genitricis mihi adstitit, uirgo per omnia et in omnibus me dirigens. (633–40)

> And so I would always and without ceasing lift the eyes of my heart to her, my guarantor, pleading with her to help me in this desert and peni-tence. I had as support and fellow labourer the woman who gave birth to the model of chastity. And so, struggling over the course of seventeen years with many dangers, as I said, from then until today the support of God's mother helped me, the virgin guiding me in all things, through all things.

The Latin passage is clear on several points. Mary of Egypt twice describes the Virgin as her helper, giving a sense of the assurance she had when praying for guidance and assistance. Second, the period of her tempta-tion is explicitly confined to the first seventeen years. Finally, the phrase 'a tunc ergo usque hodie' defines the period of time since the seventeen years of active temptation, a period in which the Virgin has guided her completely. The Old English translation of this speech differs in a few sug-gestive respects:

> Symle ic witodlice minre heortan eagan to þære minre borhhanda on nydþearfnysse up ahof, and hi biddende þæt heo me gefultumode on þysum westene to rihtre dædbote, þa þe þone ealdor æghwilcre clænnysse acende. And þus ic seofontyne geare rynum on mænigfealdum frecednyssum, swa swa ic ær cwæð, winnende wæs on eallum þingum oþ þisne andweardan dæg, and me on fultume wæs and mine wisan reccende seo halige Godes cennestre. (651–59)

Truly, in my necessity I constantly raised the eyes of my heart to my guarantor, praying to her that she help me in this desert to real penitence, she who gave birth to the source of all chastity. And thus over the course of seventeen years, as I said earlier, I was struggling with many dangers until this present day, and the holy mother of God was a support to me and directed my ways.

Although the context in which the first sentence appears confirms the Virgin's help to Mary, the Old English presents Mary as praying to the Virgin, but unlike the Latin, does not explicitly state that she received that assistance. The more important sense of doubt about Mary's full penitence and cleansing comes later in the passage. The Old English translation has no counterpart to the Latin 'a tunc', and the placement of the Old English 'oþ þisne andweardan dæg' (until this present day) corresponds to Mary's struggles, not to the Virgin's succour. The suggestion in this mistranslation is that the penitent Mary continued to struggle with her temptations even while the Virgin was guiding her, that her sexual desires endured to the very day when she met Zosimus. This change or mistake momentarily erases the thirty years that we know, according to the Latin version, to have passed between this scene and Mary's meeting with Zosimus. In contrast, a few lines later, when describing how she dealt with the lack of food, the Old English Mary does differentiate between the first seventeen years of struggle and the later years when divine power protected her, with the phrase 'þa siþþan oþ þeosne andweardan dæg' (676–77, since then until this present day) closely translating 'a tunc et usque in hac die' (652, from then and until this day). The cumulative effect of the manipulation of and slippage in time in the Old English translation of the *Life* is a sense that Mary's sexual longings did not end after seventeen years in the desert. Instead, they threaten to inhabit the present, especially when teaching Zosimus requires her to revisit them in detail.

The translation strategies of the Old English *Life of St Mary of Egypt* persistently highlight the dangers of teaching with desire. Zosimus' education is driven by his fervent longing for his teacher and her story. Mary rewards him with the narrative of an unusual passion, one in which all the usual hagiographic coordinates – body and soul, lust and chastity, pleasure and suffering, even truth and deception – are turned on their heads. Their encounter, with its give and take of compulsion and fulfilment, plays as much in the fissures of the text as it does on the surface. When Mary claims she has taught every 'speakable or unspeakable form of obscenity'

(433, asecgendlic oððe unasecgendlic fracodlicnysse hiwung), one might ask, in Virginia Burrus' words, 'What reader does not at this point strain to imagine the unspeakable?'[71] Like *Solomon and Saturn I* and *Andreas*, the *Life of St Mary of Egypt* invites its readers to fill in the gaps with their own imaginations, to long with Zosimus for a more naked revelation, a deeper mystery.[72]

Conclusion
The Ends of Teaching

Farewell, thou canst not teach me to forget.

William Shakespeare, *Romeo and Juliet*[1]

This book began with the observation that educated Anglo-Saxons were deeply interested in learning. They wrote textbooks on grammar, metrics, and rhetoric. They commented on Scripture for literate audiences and preached it to the laity. They praised excellent teachers like Aidan and Cuthbert and complained of fallen learning in the wake of Viking invasions. They copied and translated texts from the continent concerned with the basics of Latin composition, the psychological nuances of pastoral care, and the spiritual comforts of philosophy. I have argued, however, that Anglo-Saxon writing also betrays a more intimate concern with pedagogy, a complex engagement with the difficult emotions that are part both of the process of learning and of the relationship between master and disciple. In order to trace these affective energies it is often necessary to read between the lines, to pay attention to what is quietly emphasised or excised, to subtle echoes, to meaningful silences. This is a type of reading some scholars of the Anglo-Saxon period eschew, concerned about the purported excesses of interpretation.[2] Such an attitude would have surprised Bede or Ælfric, for whom exclusively literal interpretation would have been a sign of deficient literacy and wisdom.

In the course of interpreting the subtexts of Anglo-Saxon instructional moments, I have painted a chiaroscuro picture of relationships between teachers and students. These scenes are shaded by fear, pain, confusion, and sexual temptation, and occasionally illuminated by moments of bright recognition or liberation. There is often much at stake in Anglo-Saxon scenes of instruction, far beyond the bare matter to be learned. The process of education is seen as an entryway into something larger: a new identity, faith, or community. This may be why early English depictions of teaching are so often set in liminal zones. In *Andreas*, Andrew meets Christ on the shore of Achaea, is taught by him on the high seas, and recognises the truth when he wakes up on the beach, near the walls of Mermedonia. Mary of Egypt's lessons are spaced along a series of boundaries: the port of Alexandria, the door of the church in Jerusalem, the Jordan River, even the dry riverbed that separates her from Zosimus during their first encounter. Scenes of education play on the thresholds of communities, tracing the divisions between inside and out. The boys of Ælfric Bata's *Colloquies* send one of their own outside to spy on the approaching master, affirming both classroom and mind as spaces of interiorised discipline. Bede's treatment of outsiders in the *Ecclesiastical History* highlights their varying relationships to institutional structures: Cædmon's learning brings him into the folds of Abbess Hild's monastery, while the youth whose speech and body are healed by John of Beverley chooses to remain unconstrained. Learning happens on the edge, and it does so most profoundly at the point of death, that most liminal of experiences. In *Solomon and Saturn I*, Saturn's lesson of the Pater Noster threatens his annihilation. While justifying Alfred's late study of letters and Scripture, Asser imagines the Good Thief beginning his Christian education while hanging on the cross. Zosimus learns Mary's name, and understands the extent of her power, upon finding her corpse in the desert. Today education is often associated with the childhood and beginnings, but Anglo-Saxon texts show the intimate connection between learning and the end of life.

Death is indeed a teacher in medieval writing, and not solely in a figurative sense. St Paul's statement in I Corinthians 13:12, 'videmus nunc per speculum in enigmate, tunc autem facie ad faciem' (we see now through a glass in a dark manner; but then face to face), gestures towards that perfect knowledge only available after death. Paul's remarks are obliquely reflected in the Anglo-Saxon love for riddles and enigmata, especially in educational settings. Enigmas imply a teaching dialogue, and, as Galit Hasan-Rokem and David Schulman note, are 'poised on the boundary between domains, at the edge of life and death, where each issues into the other'.[3] This is why life-or-death challenges are often solved by riddles, as in the Oedipus myth and *Apollonius of Tyre*. Conversely, the passage into death, at least in Anglo-Saxon writing and its late antique sources, is frequently accompanied by mysterious teaching and enigmatic glances into the beyond.

In their reflections on the pedagogic value of mortality, Anglo-Saxon writers were likely influenced by Gregory the Great, who spent much of the fourth book of his *Dialogues* relating miracles surrounding death and describing the state of the soul in the afterlife. In section 27 of Book 4, Peter asks Gregory why the dying are often given to prophecy. Gregory's answer, given here in Werferth's Old English translation, is a key to the rest of his book:

> soðlice þæt mægn sylf þara sawla is þyllic, þæt hwilum hi hit ongytað for heora smeaþancolnesse, hwilum þa ut gangendan sawla of lichaman ongytað þa toweardan þing þurh hwylcehugu onwrigennesse, hwilum eac hit gelimpeð, þæt þonne hit byþ neah þon, þæt hi sculon forlætan þone lichaman, þæt hi beoþ þonne godcundlice inblawene 7 onsændað þæt unlichamlice eage þæs modes to þam heofonlicum deogelnessum.[4]

> Truly that very power of souls is such, that sometimes they perceive it due to their acuteness, sometimes the souls going out of the body perceive future things through some revelation, sometimes it also happens that when [the time] is near in which they must leave the body, they are divinely inspired and send the incorporeal eye of the mind forth to the heavenly mysteries.

The lessons of death are strangely accessible in Gregory's *Dialogues*, filled as the book is with people who return from death to give first-hand accounts of the afterlife. Some are even schooled in a more traditional sense, like the young servant Armentarius who, after dying of the plague, going to heaven, and returning to life, not only foretells which members of the household will die but explains that he has learned to speak all languages. In the two days that remain before he permanently expires, the previously monolingual boy is tested on Greek and Bulgarian and passes with flying colours.[5] But in the passage quoted above, Gregory traces something more subtle, a way of glimpsing mystery while still in this life. Just as our physical eyes can see far along a road we traverse more slowly with our bodies, so can the incorporeal eye run ahead of the soul. As soul prepares to leave body, its spiritual 'eyes' already pierce the secrets of heaven.

Two Anglo-Saxon hagiographies influenced by Gregory's *Dialogues*[6] feature scenes of deathbed teaching and revelation that reflect the church father's understanding of spiritual knowledge. In Bede's prose *Life of St Cuthbert*, Boisil, the prior of Melrose, realises he has only a week to live and offers to teach his pupil Cuthbert in that time. In his *Life of St Guthlac*, Felix has the saint reveal certain divine mysteries to his servant Beccel before expiring. Felix knew Bede's *Life* and drew on it heavily throughout his own work, but these parallel scenes of final teaching show that the two authors had quite different ideas about the possibilities of spiritual learning at the threshold of death.[7]

Guthlac begins dying as medieval readers might have expected of a holy man. He predicts his own demise, rejoices at the prospect of entering God's kingdom, takes the Eucharist, then preaches to Beccel, 'who swears that he had never before or after heard such a great depth of knowledge from anyone's mouth' (154, qui numquam ante neque post tam magnam profunditatem scientiae ab ullius ore audisse testatur). Beccel begs him for a few parting words, and Guthlac gives instructions for announcing his death to his sister and disposing of his body appropriately. Beccel is not satisfied with this standard-issue hagiographic death scene; he wants a glimpse of the divine:

> Obsecro, mi pater, quia infirmitatem tuam intelligo, et moriturum te audio, ut dicas mihi unum, de quo olim te interrogare non ausus diu sollicitabar. Nam ab eo tempore, quo tecum, domine, habitare coeperam, te loquentem vespere et mane audiebam, nescio cum quo. Propterea adiuro te, ne me sollicitum de hac re post obitum tuum dimittas. (156)

> I beg you, my father, for I understand that you are sick and I hear that you will die, to tell me one thing which has bothered me for a long time but I did not dare ask you about. For since that time, lord, that I began to live with you, I have heard you speak in the evening and morning with I know not who. So I urge you not to leave me troubled by this issue after your death.

At this point the real instruction begins. Guthlac tells Beccel that he has been visited in Crowland by an angel who consoled him, revealed to him 'mysteries which no man may relate' (156, misteria, quae non licet homini narrare), helped him in his labours, and showed him absent things as if they were present. Guthlac's access to holy mysteries is not based on his approaching demise; rather, much like Equitius and Zosimus, his ascetic way of life had earned him a divine tutor and guide. It is, however, at the border between life and death that Guthlac can initiate the curious Beccel into his secret, serving as a gateway to the beyond. Through his teacher, Beccel, and by extension, Felix and readers of the *Life*, join in a pedagogical genealogy that reaches from the divine through the mortal. Guthlac's death is a moment of provocative enigmas, but it is also one of recognition, identification, and the forging of less perishable bonds.

Bede's prose *Life of St Cuthbert* features a number of miracles related to the deaths of holy men, but the most moving is Boisil's. Bede is the only source for the story of the dying monk, who offers his protégé a final week of instruction.[8] Cuthbert asks him which book he could read in one week, and Boisil suggests the Gospel of John:

> Est autem mihi codex habens quaterniones septem, quas singulis diebus singulas possumus Domino adiuuante legendo, et quantum opus est inter nos conferendo percurrere. Factumque est ut dixerat. Quam ideo lectionem

tam citissime complere ualebant, quia solam in ea fidei quae per dilectionem operatur simplicitatem, non autem questionum profunda tractabant.[9]

'I have a book with seven gatherings. We can read one every day with the help of God, passing through it and discussing as much as necessary between us.' It was done as he said. They were able to finish the reading so fast because they discussed only the simple things of faith, which works by love, and not deep inquiries.

Boisil's approaching death, along with his sanctity, allow him to see further than other men. He predicts Cuthbert's entire future, including his eventual bishopric, an unpleasant fate for the anchoritic saint. Bede's focus, however, is on the intimate scene of common reading, one that puts aside intellectual inquiry for loving communion and faith. The illuminator tasked with depicting this scene of instruction in BL Yates Thompson 26, a twelfth-century English manuscript featuring Cuthbert's prose *Life* and other works by Bede, chose to highlight the familiarity between the two men: while Boisil lectures, Cuthbert sits next to his bed, face attentive, chin on hand, his fingers resting lightly on his mentor's feet.[10] Although Bede does not specify how they shared the book, it seems likely that Cuthbert read it to Boisil on his deathbed, stopping as needed to discuss points that came up.

Why did Boisil and Cuthbert read the Gospel of John? It is not the shortest Gospel, either in chapters or in amount of text. Mark would have taken less time. It is possible that John was simply the book the historical Boisil happened to have. Even if that were the case, Bede may have recognised the fitting nature of the Gospel of John for this final reading. For one thing, Bede understood John the Evangelist to be the author of Revelation, an appropriate book for a deathbed vision.[11] Moreover, the Gospel of John, unlike the other three canonical Gospels, does not close with Jesus' address to the apostles and their preaching. Rather, it focuses on the rumours of immortality around one man, the 'disciple whom Jesus loved … who also leaned on his breast at supper' (John 21:20, *discipulum quem diligebat Iesus … qui et recubuit in cena super pectus eius*), identified in John 21:24 as the author of the Gospel itself. The disciple whom Jesus loved is mentioned several times in the Book of John, but in none of the other Gospels. At the Last Supper, he leans on Jesus' chest (John 13:23, *recumbens … in sinu Iesu*), stands with Mary at the foot of the Cross (John 19:25–27), and outruns Peter to the empty sepulchre, where he 'saw and believed' (John 20:8, *vidit et credidit*).[12] The Gospel focuses, especially at its close, on the special relationship between Jesus and his beloved disciple. This adherent, identified early on as the apostle John, son of Zebedee, is tasked with bearing true witness to his teacher's deeds for the world. I suspect that Bede and his monastic readers would have understood the appropriateness of the Book of John for Cuthbert and Boisil's week of reading, its image of a disciple leaning on his doomed teacher's chest suitable for the two monks' affectionate final lesson. Teaching, as these men would have known, is a turbulent mingling of suffering and memory and longing and death. It is a chosen genealogy, the forging of a link in the chain of history. But it is also a matter of love.

Notes

Introduction

1 Rabelais, *Gargantua* (Paris: Gallimard, 1969), 59. It would suit you to be wise, to smell, feel, and value these beautiful, well-fattened books, to be agile in the pursuit and bold in the encounter, and afterwards, through careful reading and frequent meditation, to break the bone and suck the nourishing marrow.

2 In this I am influenced by Leo Strauss, himself an interpreter of medieval philosophy. Strauss' hermeneutic is rooted in an engagement with medieval biblical interpretation, more specifically with Maimonides' attempt to explain the secrets of the Bible without laying them bare to the vulgar. Although Strauss considers esoteric writing to be a defensive strategy used by philosophers throughout the ages, the bedrock of his analysis in *Persecution and the Art of Writing* is the abstruse style of the Hebrew Bible, which posed interpretative challenges similar to those of the Christian Bible.

3 Strauss, *Persecution*, 30. The approach has affinities to the 'hermeneutics of suspicion' and 'symptomatic reading', but differs in certain details. Paul Ricoeur coined the term 'hermeneutics of suspicion' to describe the demystifying reading practices of Marx, Freud, and Nietzsche, who used interpretation to uncover false consciousness. Paul Ricoeur, *Freud and Philosophy: An Essay on Interpretation*, 32–36. My own reading is not Freudian or Marxist, and I rarely assume that the dynamics I claim to uncover in texts are the result of unrecognised ideology. The one partial exception to this is my analysis of the Old English *Life of St Mary of Egypt*, which does reveal what I consider telling copying errors alongside deliberate choices in translation. Louis Althusser and Étienne Balibar used symptomatic reading or 'lecture symptomale' in their analysis of Marx, seeking to understand the unstated philosophical underpinnings of *Das Kapital*. Their approach, like Ricoeur's, was influenced by Freud and Marx, and thus works with different assumptions about the function of 'symptoms' than I do. However, their strategy of paying attention to 'les lacunes, les blancs et les défaillances de la rigueur' (the gaps, the blanks, and the failures of rigour) is similar to Strauss'. Louis Althusser and Étienne Balibar, *Lire le Capital*, vol. 1, 183. Rita Felski's lively critiques of the fashion for

suspicious, symptomatic reading in the contemporary literary classroom are valuable reading in this respect. While showing how formulaic these reading practices now are, and how standardised the stance of the critic who uncovers oppressive ideologies is, Felski does not argue against 'deep' interpretation *per se*. Rather, she proposes that interpretation needs to be revitalised, which means 'cultivating a greater receptivity to the multifarious and many-shaded moods of texts'. Rita Felski, 'Digging Down and Standing Back', 21; 'After Suspicion'; 'Context Stinks!'; 'Suspicious Minds'. A different reaction to symptomatic reading can be seen in recent calls for a turn to 'surface reading', which in some of its formulations ironically circle back to resemble New Criticism. See Stephen Best and Sharon Marcus' introduction to their special themed issue in 'Surface Reading: An Introduction', 10.

4 Strauss, *Persecution*, 64.

5 Ibid., 32.

6 Ibid., 36.

7 Ibid., 75.

8 Richard Marsden, 'The Bible in English', 224; John J. Contreni, 'The Patristic Legacy to c. 1000', 508–10, 519–22. On the complex transmission of Scripture in Anglo-Saxon England, see Richard Marsden, *The Text of the Old Testament in Anglo-Saxon England*; 'Wrestling with the Bible: Textual Problems for the Scholar and Student'. Marsden points out that 'complete Bibles were a comparative rarity in the earlier medieval period', ibid., 72. I sometimes refer to 'the Bible' for convenience and variation, not assuming that any particular Anglo-Saxon writer was using a complete text. On the tradition of allegorical interpretation, see Martin Irvine, *The Making of Textual Culture: 'Grammatica' and Literary Theory, 350–1100*, 244–71.

9 On the study of the literal or historical meaning of Scripture, underpinned at Canterbury by the tradition of Antiochene exegesis, see Bernhard Bischoff and Michael Lapidge, eds., *Biblical Commentaries from the Canterbury School of Theodore and Hadrian*, 243–49.

10 Richard Marsden, ed., *The Old English Heptateuch and Ælfric's Libellus de Veteri Testamento et Novo, Volume One: Introduction and Text* (EETS 330).

11 Alexander Pope, 'An Essay on Criticism', in *Poetry and Prose of Alexander Pope*, 44, lines 215–16.

12 Martin Irvine, 'Bede the Grammarian and the Scope of Grammatical Studies in Eighth-Century Northumbria', 25, 17.

13 Julius Zupitza, ed., *Aelfrics Grammatik und Glossar*; C. W. Jones, ed., *Bedae Venerabilis Opera, Pars I, Opera didascalica*. See also Vivien Law, 'The Study of Latin Grammar in Eighth-Century Southumbria'.

14 N. J. Higham, *(Re-)Reading Bede: The Ecclesiastical History in Context*, 72–75.

15 See the influential studies: D. W. Robertson, Jr, 'Historical Criticism'; *A Preface to Chaucer: Studies in Medieval Perspectives*. For examples in the study of Old English, see Bernard F. Huppé, *Doctrine and Poetry: Augustine's Influence on Old English Poetry*; Judith N. Garde, *Old English Poetry in Medieval Christian Perspective: A Doctrinal Approach*. For sceptical reviews of figurative or patristic

interpretation as applied to Old English poetry, see Wilhelm Busse, 'Neo-Exegetical Criticism and Old English Poetry: A Critique of the Typological and Allegorical Appropriation of Medieval Literature'; Alvin A. Lee, 'Symbolism and Allegory'.

16 Kevin R. Dungey, 'Faith in the Darkness: Allegorical Theory and Aldhelm's Obscurity', 17–20; Irvine, *The Making of Textual Culture*, 230–34, 94.

17 Stephen Moore and Yvonne Sherwood claim that 'it was biblical scholarship that originally provided literary scholarship with the model for close reading of the literary text', adding that 'biblical commentary … would provide the model for both literary scholarship (textual criticism, annotated editions, and the like) and literary criticism (explication of the meaning of words, lines, passages, and entire works)'. Moore and Sherwood also note the mutual influence in the twentieth century between biblical scholarship and New Criticism. In *The Invention of the Biblical Scholar: A Critical Manifesto*, 75–77, quotation at 75.

18 Seth Lerer, ' "Dum ludis floribus": Language and Text in the Medieval English Lyric'; Christopher Cannon, *The Grounds of English Literature*; D. Vance Smith, *The Book of the Incipit: Beginnings in the Fourteenth Century*; 'Destroyer of Forms: Chaucer's *Philomela*'; Maura Nolan, *John Lydgate and the Making of Public Culture*; Eleanor Johnson, *Practicing Literary Theory in the Middle Ages: Ethics and the Mixed Form in Chaucer, Gower, Usk, and Hoccleve*.

19 Marjorie Levinson, 'What Is New Formalism?'

20 Richard Strier, 'How Formalism Became a Dirty Word, and Why We Can't Do Without It', 210.

21 Respectively: Cannon, *Grounds*; Johnson, *Practicing Literary Theory*, 4–8. For discussions of New Formalism's varied uses to Middle English studies, see Lerer, 'The Endurance of Formalism in Middle English Studies'; Cannon, 'Form'; Helen Marshall and Peter Buchanan, 'New Formalism and the Forms of Middle English Literary Texts'; D. Vance Smith, 'Medieval *Forma*: The Logic of the Work'.

22 Michael Lapidge, 'Three Latin Poems from Æthelwold's School at Winchester', 96–99; 'Dialogues'. While I refer here to dialogues as a general category, there are important subgenres of dialogues in ancient and medieval literature. Carmen Cardelle de Hartmann distinguishes between didactic dialogues (including catechisms or question-and-answer dialogues), hagiographic dialogues, disputations, philosophical dialogues, contemplative dialogues (like those of Boethius, Augustine, and Isidore), and books of consolation. *Lateinische Dialoge 1200–1400: Literaturhistorische Studie und Repertorium*, 4–10.

23 Hans Hecht, ed., *Bischofs Wærferth von Worcester Übersetzung der Dialoge Gregors des Grossen*; Thomas A. Carnicelli, ed., *King Alfred's Version of St. Augustine's Soliloquies*; *OEB*.

24 Lapidge, 'Three Latin Poems'.

25 Joel C. Relihan, *The Prisoner's Philosophy: Life and Death in Boethius's Consolation*.

26 Seth Lerer, *Boethius and Dialogue: Literary Method in the Consolation of Philosophy*, 5–6.

27 Asser's biography makes a greater claim to historical truth than Old English poems and Latin school dialogues, at least from a modern perspective, but scholars have also recognised the work's literary structure and careful depiction of Alfred as a king who fulfils Carolingian and Gregorian ideals of kingship. Marie Schutt, 'The Literary Form of Asser's *'Vita Alfredi'*; Anton Scharer, 'The Writing of History at King Alfred's Court'; Paul Kershaw, 'Illness, Power and Prayer in Asser's *Life of King Alfred*'; Thomas D. Hill, 'The Crowning of Alfred and the Topos of *Sapientia et Fortitudo* in Asser's *Life of King Alfred*'. While the authenticity of the *Life* has been debated for almost two centuries, the majority of scholarly opinion holds in its favour. Simon Keynes and Michael Lapidge, eds., *Alfred the Great: Asser's Life of King Alfred and other Contemporary Sources*, 48–58. My own reading of the *Life* assumes that it is, indeed, the work of a man who knew King Alfred personally. Moreover, I consider the narrator's odd rhetorical steps and occasional fears of misinterpretation to be evidence that he both tried to establish his own authority as Alfred's teacher and worried about how his claims might be received; these calibrated defensive moves would be unnecessary in a forgery written centuries later.

28 Scharer, 'The Writing of History', 191–93.

29 Mishtooni Bose, 'From Exegesis to Appropriation: The Medieval Solomon', 187–88.

30 William Henry Stevenson and Dorothy Whitelock, eds., *Asser's Life of King Alfred: Together with the Annals of Saint Neots Erroneously Ascribed to Asser*, ch. 74, ll. 52–53.

31 David Pratt also discusses the theory that Alfred's second illness was Crohn's disease, and suggests ultimately that *ficus* indicates the anal lesions which are early indicators of Crohn's. 'The Illnesses of King Alfred the Great', 81. Kershaw describes *ficus* as disease of the skin or eyes in 'Illness, Power and Prayer', 209.

32 Pratt, 'The Illnesses', 63–64.

33 Stevenson and Whitelock, *Asser's Life of King Alfred*, ch. 74, ll. 76–77.

34 Ibid., ch. 25, ll. 27–28.

35 Alfred's body is 'at once regal and saintly because it suffers', writes Jeffrey Jerome Cohen, emphasising that this suffering allowed Alfred to show that he was 'powerful enough to triumph over the limitations of mere flesh'. *Medieval Identity Machines*, xix–xx. Kershaw agrees that Alfred's illnesses, in Asser's narration of them, helped his authority, and he shows how Alfred's resulting humility fitted into a ninth-century Carolingian valuation of penitential practice among rulers. Kershaw, 'Illness', 219–20.

36 On this borrowing see Michael Lapidge, *The Anglo-Saxon Library*, 115–19.

37 See the brief overview of Patrizia Lendinara, 'The World of Anglo-Saxon Learning'.

38 These projects have resulted in a number of essay collections on different aspects of Anglo-Saxon learning, for example: Rolf Hendrik Bremmer and Kees Dekker, eds., *Foundations of Learning: The Transfer of Encyclopaedic Knowledge in the Early Middle Ages*; Patrizia Lendinara, Loredana Lazzari,

and Maria Amalia D'Aronco, eds., *Form and Content of Instruction in Anglo-Saxon England in the Light of Contemporary Manuscript Evidence*; Rolf Hendrik Bremmer and Kees Dekker, eds., *Practice in Learning: The Transfer of Encyclopaedic Knowledge in the Early Middle Ages*; László Sándor Chardonnens and Bryan Carella, eds., *Secular Learning in Anglo-Saxon England: Exploring the Vernacular*.

39 Lendinara, 'The World of Anglo-Saxon Learning', 278.

40 Relevant studies include Edna Rees Williams, 'Ælfric's Grammatical Terminology'; Vivien Law, *The Insular Latin Grammarians*; 'The Study of Latin Grammar in Eighth-Century Southumbria'; 'Grammar in the Early Middle Ages: A Bibliography'; *Wisdom, Authority and Grammar in the Seventh Century: Decoding Virgilius Maro Grammaticus*; Irvine, 'Bede the Grammarian and the Scope of Grammatical Studies in Eighth-Century Northumbria'; *The Making of Textual Culture*; Helmut Gneuss, 'The Study of Language in Anglo-Saxon England'; Martha Bayless, '*Beatus Quid Est* and the Study of Grammar in Late Anglo-Saxon England'; Melinda J. Menzer, 'Ælfric's Grammar: Solving the Problem of the English-Language Text'; 'Ælfric's English *Grammar*'; Gabriele Knappe, 'The Rhetorical Aspect of Grammar Teaching in Anglo-Saxon England'; David W. Porter, *Excerptiones de Prisciano: The Source for Ælfric's Latin–Old English Grammar*.

41 W. H. Stevenson, ed., *Early Scholastic Colloquies*; G. N. Garmonsway, ed., *Ælfric's Colloquy*; Scott Gwara, ed., *Latin Colloquies from Pre-Conquest Britain*; Scott Gwara and David Porter, *Anglo-Saxon Conversations: The Colloquies of Ælfric Bata*.

42 Nancy Porter Stork, *Through a Gloss Darkly: Aldhelm's Riddles in the British Library MS Royal 12.C.xxiii*; Scott Gwara, *Education in Wales and Cornwall in the Ninth and Tenth Centuries: Understanding De raris fabulis*.

43 Patrizia Lendinara, 'The *Colloquy* of Ælfric and the *Colloquy* of Ælfric Bata'; 'Contextualized Lexicography'.

44 On Anglo-Saxon school texts, see Lapidge, *The Anglo-Saxon Library*, 54, 66, 81, 127. On the Psalms in Anglo-Saxon education, see George H. Brown, 'The Psalms as the Foundation of Anglo-Saxon Learning'; Patricia Hollahan, 'The Anglo-Saxon Use of the Psalms: Liturgical Background and Poetic Use', 3–4.

45 Bischoff and Lapidge, *Biblical Commentaries*.

46 Lapidge, *The Anglo-Saxon Library*, 54, 128; *OEB*, vol. 1, 209–12.

47 Sally Crawford, *Childhood in Anglo-Saxon England*, 139–53; Nicholas Orme, *Medieval Schools: From Roman Britain to Renaissance England*, 15–50.

48 *EH*, Cuthbert: bk 4, ch. 27 (25); Aidan: bk 3, ch. 5; Hild: bk 4, ch. 23 (21); John of Beverley: bk 5, ch. 2; Theodore and Hadrian: bk 4, ch. 2; Clare Lees and Gillian Overing, *Double Agents: Women and Clerical Culture in Anglo-Saxon England*, 19–45.

49 For Aldhelm, see Rudolf Ehwald, ed., *Aldhelmi Opera Omnia*, MGH, Auctores Antiquissimi, 479–80, 86–94; Scott Gwara, '*Doubles Entendres* in the Ironic Conclusion to Aldhelm's *Epistola ad Heahfridum*'; Michael Herren, 'The Transmission and Reception of Graeco-Roman Mythology in Anglo-Saxon

England, 670–800', 93. For Boniface see Lees and Overing, *Double Agents*, 41–42, 54; Michael Tangl, ed., *Die Briefe des heiligen Bonifatius und Lullus*, MGH, Epistolae Selectae.

50 D. A. Bullough, 'The Educational Tradition in England from Alfred to Ælfric: Teaching *utriusque linguae*'; Malcolm Godden, 'King Alfred's Preface and the Teaching of Latin in Anglo-Saxon England'; Nicole Guenther Discenza, *The King's English: Strategies of Translation in the Old English Boethius*.

51 Mechthild Gretsch, *The Intellectual Foundations of the English Benedictine Reform*; Christopher A. Jones, 'Ælfric and the Limits of "Benedictine Reform"'; Rebecca Stephenson, *The Politics of Language: Byrhtferth, Ælfric, and the Multilingual Identity of the Benedictine Reform*.

52 Mary Carruthers, *The Book of Memory: A Study of Memory in Medieval Culture*; *The Craft of Thought: Meditation, Rhetoric, and the Making of Images, 400–1200*; Jody Enders, 'Rhetoric, Coercion, and the Memory of Violence'; Mitchell B. Merback, *The Thief, the Cross and the Wheel: Pain and the Spectacle of Punishment in Medieval and Renaissance Europe*; Jody Enders, *The Medieval Theater of Cruelty: Rhetoric, Memory, Violence*; Bruce W. Holsinger, *Music, Body, and Desire in Medieval Culture: Hildegard of Bingen to Chaucer*; Robert Mills, *Suspended Animation: Pain, Pleasure and Punishment in Medieval Culture*.

53 *EH*, bk 3, ch. 5, p. 228.

54 Bede cites Gregory, including the *Pastoral Care*, extensively. Lapidge, *The Anglo-Saxon Library*, 211–12.

55 Gregory I, *Liber regulae pastoralis*, PL 77, bk 3, prologue, Col. 49C; Henry Sweet, ed., *King Alfred's West Saxon Version of Gregory's Pastoral Care*, sec. 23, 173–74. See also Caroline Schreiber, ed., *King Alfred's Old English Translation of Pope Gregory the Great's Regula pastoralis and Its Cultural Context*.

56 GL, pp. 890, 912.

57 Christina M. Heckman, 'Things in Doubt: *Inventio*, Dialectic, and Jewish Secrets in Cynewulf's *Elene*'; Irvine, *The Making of Textual Culture*, 169–89; 'Anglo-Saxon Literary Theory Exemplified in Old English Poems: Interpreting the Cross in *The Dream of the Rood* and *Elene*'.

58 On monastic culture see Jean Leclercq, *The Love of Learning and the Desire for God: A Study of Monastic Culture*.

59 Ibid., 29–33; Lapidge, *The Anglo-Saxon Library*, 127.

60 All of these works are attested in Anglo-Saxon manuscripts, and Gregory's *Dialogues* were also translated by Werferth as part of Alfred's educational program. Hecht, *Bischofs Wærferth*.

61 I borrow the term from Louis Althusser, 'Ideology and Ideological State Apparatuses (Notes towards an Investigation)'.

62 I discuss this theory of teaching in greater detail in Chapter 4.

63 Relihan, *The Prisoner's Philosophy*, 4–5.

64 Irina A. Dumitrescu, 'The Practice of Dissent'.

65 Elaine Tuttle Hansen, *The Solomon Complex: Reading Wisdom in Old English Poetry*; Seth Lerer, *Literacy and Power in Anglo-Saxon Literature*; Irvine, *The*

Making of Textual Culture; Clare A. Lees, *Tradition and Belief: Religious Writing in Late Anglo-Saxon England*; Lees and Overing, *Double Agents*; Katherine O'Brien O'Keeffe, *Stealing Obedience: Narratives of Agency and Identity in Later Anglo-Saxon England.*

66 Carruthers, *The Book of Memory*; *The Craft of Thought*; Rita Copeland, *Rhetoric, Hermeneutics, and Translation in the Middle Ages: Academic Traditions and Vernacular Texts*; *Criticism and Dissent in the Middle Ages*; *Pedagogy, Intellectuals, and Dissent in the Later Middle Ages: Lollardy and Ideas of Learning*; Marjorie Curry Woods, 'Rape and the Pedagogical Rhetoric of Sexual Violence'; 'Weeping for Dido: Epilogue on a Premodern Rhetorical Exercise in the Postmodern Classroom'; *Classroom Commentaries: Teaching the Poetria Nova across Medieval and Renaissance Europe*; Enders, *The Medieval Theater of Cruelty*; Edward Wheatley, *Mastering Aesop: Medieval Education, Chaucer, and His Followers*; Holsinger, *Music, Body, and Desire*; Jill Mann, '"He Knew Nat Catoun": Medieval School-Texts and Middle English Literature'; Peter W. Travis, *Disseminal Chaucer: Rereading the Nun's Priest's Tale.*

1. Letters

1 Walt Whitman, *Complete Poetry and Selected Prose*, 10.
2 Scott DeGregorio, 'Literary Contexts: Cædmon's Hymn as a Center of Bede's World', 58.
3 Nicholas Howe, 'Rome: Capital of Anglo-Saxon England', 149–51.
4 Roger Ray, 'Who Did Bede Think He Was?', 11.
5 DeGregorio, 'Literary Contexts', 52–59.
6 David Cowart, *Trailing Clouds: Immigrant Fictions in Contemporary America*, 108.
7 William D. McCready, *Miracles and the Venerable Bede*, 154–55; Werner Jaager, ed., *Bedas metrische Vita s. Cuthberti*, 57.
8 Quotations from Bede's *History* and their translations are from *EH*. Quotations from Scripture are from Robert Weber, ed., *Biblia sacra iuxta Vulgatam versionem.*
9 I cite mentions of the miracle throughout this chapter but have not found any sustained discussion of it aside from a few pages in McCready, *Miracles and the Venerable Bede*, 154–55.
10 Allen J. Frantzen, *Desire for Origins: New Language, Old English, and Teaching the Tradition*, 139–40.
11 Lerer, *Literacy and Power*, 37–38.
12 Stephen J. Harris, 'Bede and Gregory's Allusive Angles', 272.
13 Uppinder Mehan and David Townsend, '"Nation" and the Gaze of the Other in Eighth-Century Northumbria', 7.
14 Nicholas Howe, *Migration and Mythmaking in Anglo-Saxon England*, 120.
15 James Berger, 'Falling Towers and Postmodern Wild Children: Oliver Sacks, Don DeLillo, and Turns against Language', 347.
16 'Cum autem omnium linguarum scientia difficilis sit cuiquam, nemo tamen tam desidiosus est ut in sua gente positus suae gentis linguam nesciat. Nam

quid aliud putandus est nisi animalium brutorum deterior? Illa enim propriae vocis clamorem exprimunt, iste deterior qui propriae linguae caret notitiam.' W. M. Lindsay, ed., *Isidori Hispalensis episcopi Etymologiarum sive originum libri XX*, bk 9, ch. 1, sec. 10. (Even though the knowledge of all languages is difficult for anyone, still no one is so lazy as not to know the language of his people when placed among them. But how is he to be thought of unless worse than insensible beasts? Indeed, those express cries in their own voices. He who does not know his own language is worse.)

17 Vnitatem linguarum quam superbia Babylonis disperserat humilitas ecclesiae recolligit, spiritaliter autem uarietas linguarum dona uariarum significant gratiarum. M. L. W. Laistner, ed., 'Expositio Actuum Apostolorum', in *Bedae Venerabilis Opera, Pars II, Opera Exegetica*, 16. (The pride of Babylon scattered the unity of languages, which the humility of the church gathers up again; on the other hand, the variety of languages spiritually indicates the gifts of various graces.)

18 Alaric Hall, 'Interlinguistic Communication in Bede's *Historia ecclesiastica gentis Anglorum*', 46; Robert Stanton, 'Linguistic Fragmentation and Redemption before King Alfred', 23.

19 In book 4 of *De doctrina christiana*, Augustine argues that eloquence can be learned by observation and imitation, just as babies learn speech: 'cum ex infantibus loquentes non fiant nisi locutiones discendo loquentium'. R. P. H. Green, ed., *Augustine: De doctrina christiana* (Oxford: Clarendon Press, 1995), 200; bk 4, sec. 12 (… if infants become speakers by learning speech from those who speak). For medieval reading pedagogy, see Irvine, *The Making of Textual Culture*, 277. The relationship to Bede's pedagogical treatises is noted in J. M. Wallace-Hadrill, *Bede's Ecclesiastical History of the English People: A Historical Commentary*, 176.

20 Susan Boynton, 'Training for the Liturgy as a Form of Monastic Education'; Bruce Holsinger, 'The Parable of Caedmon's *Hymn*: Liturgical Invention and Literary Tradition', 157–58; Michelle P. Brown, 'The Role of the Wax Tablet in Medieval Literacy: A Reconsideration in Light of a Recent Find from York'; Calvin B. Kendall, 'Bede and Education', 105.

21 'De orthographia' and 'De arte metrica et De schematibus et tropis', in *Bedae Venerabilis Opera, Pars I, Opera didascalica*, ed. C. W. Jones, 1–57, 60–171.

22 Louis Holtz, ed., *Donat et la tradition de l'enseignement grammatical: Étude et édition critique*.

23 *Et expuens tetigit linguam eius.* Expuens quippe dominus linguam tangit aegroti cum ad confessionem fidei ora cathecizatorum instruit. Sputum namque domini saporem designat sapientiae. D. Hurst, ed., *Bedae Venerabilis Opera, Pars II. Opera exegetica. In Lucae euangelium expositio. In Marci euangelium expositio*, 526. (*And spitting, he touched his tongue.* In fact the Lord spits and touches the tongue of the sick man just as he teaches the mouths of the catechised to confess the faith. For truly the spit denotes the taste of the Lord's wisdom.)

24 Roman Jakobson, *Child Language, Aphasia, and Phonological Universals*, 42.

25 Susan E. Wilson, ed., *The Life and After-Life of St. John of Beverley: The Evolution of the Cult of an Anglo-Saxon Saint*, 172–73.

26 Another miracle, in the *Alia miracula I*, features a man deaf and mute from birth who, on hearing the *Gloria in excelsis* sung in Beverley, not only begins to speak but does so in French and English. In the *Vita Sancti Johannes*, commissioned around 1066, Folcard retells Bede's miracle, following closely the narrative in the *History*. However, he does not name the letters or specify that they are followed by syllables. Ibid., 148. Alcuin also relates the miracle in his poem *Versus de patribus regibus et sanctis Euboricensis ecclesiae*, but his version offers even less detail and presents the speech miracle as taking place instantaneously. Peter Godman, ed., *Alcuin: The Bishops, Kings, and Saints of York*, 89.

27 André Crépin, 'Bede and the Vernacular', 184; Wallace-Hadrill, *Bede's Ecclesiastical History*, 175.

28 Quae causa est praecipientibus ut, etiam cum satis adfixisse eas pueris recto illo quo primum scribi solent contextu videntur, retro agant rursus et varia permutatione turbent, donec litteras qui instituuntur facie norint, non ordine: quapropter optime sicut hominum pariter et habitus et nomina edocebuntur. Quintilian, *The Orator's Education. Books 1–2*, trans. Russell, 76. I have consulted Donald A. Russell's translation.

29 Jakobson, *Child Language*, 13–34.

30 For a discussion of Jakobson's importance in developmental phonology and of some of the field's shortcomings, see Yishai Tobin, *Phonology as Human Behavior: Theoretical Implications and Clinical Applications*, 173–82.

31 Orme, *Medieval Schools*, 55–58.

32 Melinda Menzer has made a similar argument, claiming that Ælfric's *Grammar* can serve as a grammar of English and that Ælfric intended to show that reading English requires interpretative skills honed by grammatical study just as reading Latin does. Menzer, 'Ælfric's English *Grammar*'; 'Ælfric's Grammar'.

33 Nicholas Orme has suggested to me that there may be a connection between the sign of the cross made by John and the 'Christ cross' or 'alphabet cross' that preceded written alphabets in later primers to such an extent that the alphabet, known in the middle ages as 'ABC' or 'abece', came also to be called a 'Christ-cross row' or 'cross row' in the Tudor and Stuart periods. This is difficult to prove in the absence of manuscript evidence of alphabet crosses in the Anglo-Saxon period, but his description of alphabet recitation as prayer suggests a fusion of elementary reading and worship that should colour our reading of Bede's miracle: 'The alphabet cross … was a rubric: an instruction to readers to say a short prayer before they pronounced the letters that followed. The recitation of the letters also became a prayer, and the word "amen" was said at the end of the process, just as it was at the end of a prayer.' Nicholas Orme, *Medieval Children*, 251.

34 Harris, 'Bede', 271–72; Howe, *Migration*, 122.

35 Sharon M. Rowley, 'Reassessing Exegetical Interpretations of Bede's *Historia Ecclesiastica Gentis Anglorum*'; Allen J. Frantzen, 'All Created Things: Material Contexts for Bede's Story of Cædmon', 139.

36 Bertram Colgrave, 'Historical Introduction', in *EH*, xxxiii–xxxiv; DeGregorio, 'Literary Contexts', 75.

37 Jaager, *Bedas metrische Vita s. Cuthberti*, 57.

38 McCready, *Miracles and the Venerable Bede*, 155; Dorothy Whitelock, 'Bede and His Teachers and Friends', 21.

39 Cædmon is discussed as an oral-formulaic poet in Francis P. Magoun, Jr, 'Bede's Story of Cædman: The Case History of an Anglo-Saxon Oral Singer'; Yu. A. Kleiner, 'The Singer and the Interpreter: Caedmon and Bede'. For analyses of Cædmon as a poet of learning, see Bernard F. Huppé, 'Caedmon's *Hymn*'; Donald W. Fritz, 'Caedmon: A Traditional Christian Poet'; N. F. Blake, 'Cædmon's Hymn'.

40 On Cædmon as adapter of Germanic poetics to Christianity, see Kemp Malone, 'Cædmon and English Poetry'; E. G. Stanley, 'New Formulas for Old: *Cædmon's Hymn*'; Constance B. Hieatt, 'Cædmon in Context: Transforming the Formula'. The description of Cædmon's hymn as 'rather tedious' comes from Peter Hunter Blair, 'Whitby as a Centre of Learning in the Seventh Century', 23. See also Daniel Paul O'Donnell, 'Material Differences: The Place of Cædmon's Hymn in the History of Anglo-Saxon Vernacular Poetry', 47. The hymn is considered a back translation by Kevin S. Kiernan, 'Reading Cædmon's "Hymn" with Someone Else's Glosses', 164; G. R. Isaac, 'The Date and Origin of *Cædmon's Hymn*', 210.

41 On the nature of the miracle, see C. L. Wrenn, 'The Poetry of Cædmon', 286–88; Andrew James Johnston, 'Caedmons mehrfache Anderssprachigkeit: Die Urszene der altenglischen Literatur im Spannungsfeld frühmittelalterlicher Sprach- und Kulturgegensätze'. For further bibliography, see Daniel Paul O'Donnell, *Cædmon's Hymn: A Multimedia Study, Archive and Edition*, 197–201; Stanley B. Greenfield and Fred C. Robinson, *A Bibliography of Publications on Old English Literature to the end of 1972*.

42 Blair, 'Whitby', 23–26.

43 Indeed, Bede was ordained deacon at nineteen years of age and priest at thirty by John of Beverley, under the direction of his own teacher and abbot, Ceolfrith (566–67; bk 5, ch. 24), thus participating to a lesser extent in the didactic and spiritual relationships I note above.

44 Nellie Slayton Aurner, 'Bede and Pausanias'; Fritz, 'Christian Poet'; Fr. Klaeber, 'Analogues of the Story of Cædmon'; G. A. Lester, 'The Cædmon Story and Its Analogues'; O'Donnell, *Cædmon's Hymn*, 29–46, 191–202; Louise Pound, 'Caedmon's Dream Song'; G. Shepherd, 'The Prophetic Cædmon'; L. Whitbread, 'An Analogue of the Cædmon Story'.

45 C. Grant Loomis, 'The Miracle Traditions of the Venerable Bede'.

46 Adalbert de Vogüé, ed., *Grégoire le Grand: Dialogues: Livres I–III*, vol. 2, 44; bk 1, ch. 4, par. 8.

47 Virginia Day, 'The Influence of the Catechetical *Narratio* on Old English and Some Other Medieval Literature', 51–55; Faith Wallis, 'Cædmon's Created World and the Monastic Encyclopedia', 87.

48 Compare Scott DeGregorio's claim that the Cædmon narrative is 'the one and only instance in Bede's oeuvre where he goes so far as to depict the use of the vernacular in action'. DeGregorio, 'Literary Contexts', 59.

49 Donald W. Fritz, 'Caedmon: A Monastic Exegete', 361.

50 The orality of Latin is discussed in Martin Irvine, 'Medieval Textuality and the Archaeology of Textual Culture'; Holsinger, 'The Parable of Caedmon's Hymn', 170. The dual Germanic and Latin nature of Old English verse is described in Andy Orchard, 'The Word Made Flesh: Christianity and Oral Culture in Anglo-Saxon Verse'.

51 Daniel Paul O'Donnell, 'Bede's Strategy in Paraphrasing *Cædmon's Hymn*', 423–24.

52 Lerer, *Literacy and Power*, 35–37.

53 The source of this miracle is Gregory's *Dialogues*: Vogüé, *Grégoire le Grand: Dialogues: Livres I–III*, 222–26; bk 2, ch. 31. See Loomis, 'The Miracle Traditions', 409; John Moorhead, 'Some Borrowings in Bede', 712.

54 Lerer, *Literacy and Power*, 33.

55 I am grateful to Christian Leitmeir for this suggestion. The rite generally differed from the biblical model, in which Christ touches the ears and mouth of the man. Ambrose ascribes the difference to the inappropriateness of touching the mouths of female candidates. However, Leidrad of Lyon (d. 817) writes in a letter to Charlemagne of an existing practice of touching the mouth and ears. Bryan D. Spinks, *Early Medieval Rituals and Theologies of Baptism: From the New Testament to the Council of Trent*, 59–60; Josef Schmitz, *Gottesdienst im altchristlichen Mailand: Eine liturgiewissenschaftliche Untersuchung über Initiation und Meßfeier während des Jahres zur Zeit des Bischofs Ambrosius (†397)*, 77–84.

56 Bede, *Homilies on the Gospels. Book Two: Lent to The Dedication of the Church*, 54; D. Hurst, *Bedae Venerabilis Opera, Pars III: Opera homiletica*, 222.

57 Peter Dendle, *Satan Unbound: The Devil in Old English Narrative Literature*; Schmitz, *Gottesdienst im altchristlichen Mailand*, 84; Spinks, *Early Medieval Rituals*, 111.

58 Lawrence T. Martin has noted Bede's 'structural wordplay', a conscious repetition of words in their literal and extended moral meanings. Lawrence T. Martin, 'Bede as a Linguistic Scholar', xxvii.

59 Respectively: Howe, *Migration*, 118–21; Harris, 'Bede'; Allen J. Frantzen, *Before the Closet: Same-Sex Love from Beowulf to Angels in America*, 266–70; 'Bede and Bawdy Bale: Gregory the Great, Angels, and the "Angli"'; Mehan and Townsend, '"Nation" and the Gaze'.

60 Howe, *Migration*, 119.

61 Mehan and Townsend, '"Nation" and the Gaze', 9–10.

62 The anonymous Whitby *Life* and Bede's *History* are often described as drawing independently on oral tradition. Bertram Colgrave, ed., *The Earliest Life of Gregory the Great, by an Anonymous Monk of Whitby*, 53. However, Walter Goffart has argued that Bede made creative use of three major sources for his

history: Gildas' *De excidio Britanniae* (undisputed), Stephen of Ripon's *Life of Wilfrid*, and the Whitby *Life*. In *The Narrators of Barbarian History (A.D. 550–800): Jordanes, Gregory of Tours, Bede, and Paul the Deacon*, 299, 303–307. I subscribe to Goffart's argument because of the close textual correspondences between the Whitby narrative and Bede's history but also because of what I consider conscious narrative decisions by Bede. Most of my discussion of Bede's version and of its correspondence with bk 5, ch. 2, remains relevant even if he is considered to draw only on oral history.

63 Colgrave, *The Earliest Life*, 144; Mehan and Townsend, '"Nation" and the Gaze', 19.
64 Mehan and Townsend, '"Nation" and the Gaze', 19.
65 Colgrave, *The Earliest Life*, 90–91.
66 For the divine associations of white, Latin *candidus*, and Old English *hwite*, see Stephen J. Harris, *Race and Ethnicity in Anglo-Saxon Literature*, 53. See also R. E. Latham, *Revised Medieval Latin Word-List from British and Irish Sources*, 'candidatio'.
67 Harris, *Race and Ethnicity*, 47.
68 Ibid., 49.
69 Ibid., 48–49.
70 Wallace-Hadrill, *Bede's Ecclesiastical History*, 176.
71 Orme, *Medieval Schools*, 25–26; Crawford, *Childhood in Anglo-Saxon England*, 148.
72 Lerer, *Literacy and Power*, 47.
73 M. L. W. Laistner, ed., *Bedae Venerabilis Opera, Pars II: Opera Exegetica*, CCSL 121, 24. For a discussion of the way Bede's historical work was influenced by his early study of Acts, see A. H. Merrills, *History and Geography in Late Antiquity*, 240–42.
74 Laistner, *Bedae Venerabilis Opera, Pars II: Opera Exegetica*, 16.
75 Ibid., 16–17.

2. Prayer

1 Christopher Marlowe, *The Complete Plays*, 339.
2 Katherine O'Brien O'Keeffe, *Visible Song: Transitional Literacy in Old English Verse*, 50.
3 Marie Nelson sees the poem as a literary dramatisation of an oral form, namely, the charm. Marie Nelson, 'King Solomon's Magic: The Power of a Written Text'.
4 Slavoj Žižek, 'The Truth Arises from Misrecognition', 201.
5 I use the edition in Daniel Anlezark, ed., *The Old English Dialogues of Solomon and Saturn*.
6 Mary J. Carruthers, 'Invention, Mnemonics, and Stylistic Ornament in *Psychomachia* and *Pearl*', 205; John P. Hermann, 'The Pater Noster Battle Sequence in *Solomon and Saturn* and the *Psychomachia* of Prudentius', 206–10.
7 Ker 32, GL 39.

8 Ker 70, GL 110. There are four Old English dialogues with Solomon and Saturn as interlocutors. The *Prose Solomon and Saturn* contains a series of questions and answers on mostly biblical trivia. James E. Cross and Thomas D. Hill, eds., *The Prose Solomon and Saturn and Adrian and Ritheus*. The other three dialogues appear in CCCC 422. The poems were previously edited in John Mitchell Kemble, ed., *The Dialogue of Salomon and Saturnus*; Arthur Vincenti, *Drei altenglische Dialoge von Salomon und Saturn: Eine litterarge-schichtliche, sprachliche und Quellen-Untersuchung*; Robert J. Menner, ed., *The Poetical Dialogues of Solomon and Saturn*, and most recently in Anlezark, *Old English Dialogues*. Kemble and Menner print the prose dialogue; it is also cursorily edited in Gilda Cilluffo, 'Il Salomone e Saturno in Prosa del ms. CCCC 422'. Thomas Hill also prints text and translation of the prose dialogue in Thomas D. Hill, 'The Devil's Forms and the Pater Noster's Powers: "The Prose Solomon and Saturn *Pater Noster* Dialogue" and the Motif of the Transformation Combat', 166–67. I cite CCCC 422 throughout, unless the line or passage only occurs in CCCC 41 or is corrupt in CCCC 422.

9 Respectively: Menner, *Poetical Dialogues*, 6; John Earle, *Anglo-Saxon Literature*, 210; E. Gordon Duff, ed., *The Dialogue or Communing between the Wise King Solomon and Marcolphus*, xiv.

10 Anlezark, *Old English Dialogues*; Charles D. Wright, *The Irish Tradition in Old English Literature*; Patrick P. O'Neill, 'On the Date, Provenance and Relationship of the "Solomon and Saturn" Dialogues'; Antonina Harbus, 'The Situation of Wisdom in *Solomon and Saturn II*'; O'Brien O'Keeffe, *Visible Song*.

11 *EH*, 228; bk 3, ch. 5. The language of taste, especially the sweetness of honey, recalls the synaesthetic writing of monastic spirituality, and its relationship to teaching is particularly vivid in Bede. Leclercq, *Love of Learning*, 66, 73.

12 Bede, *On the Song of Songs and Selected Writings*, trans. Holder, 108.

13 Ibid., 125.

14 Ibid., 127. habet mel et lac sub lingua cum recte nouit discernere quae incipientibus quae sint dicenda proficientibus quae item eis qui in scientia sunt eius et caritate perfecti. 'In Cantica Canticorum libri vi', in Bede, *Bedae Venerabilis Opera, Pars II, Opera Exegetica, 2B*, ed. D. Hurst, bk 3, ch. 4, l. 660.

15 'Die heiligen Worte dieser beiden Formeln durften nicht aufgeschrieben werden; nur auf die Tafeln des Herzens sollte sie der Täufling schreiben; in seinem Gedächtnis sollten sie als unverlierbarer, köstlicher Schatz ruhen.' Josef Andreas Jungmann, *Gewordene Liturgie*, 168.

16 Michael Kunzler, *Die Liturgie der Kirche*, 386.

17 Jungmann, *Gewordene Liturgie*, 139–40.

18 Roy Hammerling, 'The *Pater Noster* in Its Patristic and Medieval Context: The Baptismal-Catechetic Interpretation of the Lord's Prayer', 7.

19 Charles Plummer, ed., *Venerabilis Bedae opera historica*, vol. 1, 408–409.

20 For their translations and homilies on the Lord's Prayer, see Peter Clemoes, ed., *Ælfric's Catholic Homilies: The First Series*, 325–34. Dorothy Bethurum, ed., *The Homilies of Wulfstan*, 166–68.

21 Cited in *The Homilies of Wulfstan*, 157.

22 Orme, *Medieval Schools*, 58 and passim; Patricia Crain, *The Story of A: A Poetics of Alphabetization in America from The New England Primer to The Scarlet Letter*, 19, 23; E. Jennifer Monaghan, *Learning to Read and Write in Colonial America*; Eamon Duffy, *The Stripping of the Altars: Traditional Religion in England 1400–1580*, 80–85.

23 This is BL Harley 208, a ninth-century continental manuscript that found its way to England in the tenth or eleventh centuries. Ker 229, GL 417. Reference from Orme, *Medieval Children*, 247.

24 See, for example, Brown, 'Psalms', 3.

25 Donald G. Scragg, *The Vercelli Homilies and Related Texts*, 97, l. 178. The connection is made in Wright, *Irish Tradition*, 263.

26 Responses include translations and expositions of the Lord's Prayer. See, for example, the Anglo-Norman Pater Noster edited in Tony Hunt, 'An Anglo-Norman Pater Noster'. This offers the Latin lines, followed by Anglo-Norman translation followed by a brief exposition. For later English versions, see Florent Gérard Antoine Marie Aarts, ed., *The Pater Noster of Richard Ermyte: A Late Middle English Exposition of the Lord's Prayer*. Ella Keats Whiting, ed., *The Poems of John Audelay*. For parodic treatments of the prayer, see Jean Subrenat, 'Quatre patrenostres parodiques', 515–47; Bengt Löfstedt, 'Sekundäre Bedeutungen von "Pater Noster"', 212–14; Jan M. Ziolkowski, 'The Erotic Paternoster', 31–34; 'The Erotic Pater Noster, Redux', 329–32; Martha Bayless, *Parody in the Middle Ages: The Latin Tradition*, 114–15. See also the rhymed Pater Noster in Paul Lehmann, *Die Parodie im Mittelalter*, 195–97.

27 'Here begynneth a lytell geste how the plowman lerned his pater noster'.

28 'The proude wyues pater noster that wolde go gaye, and vndyd her husbonde and went her waye.'

29 Subrenat, 'Quatre patrenostres parodiques'; Ziolkowski, 'The Erotic Paternoster'; 'The Erotic Pater Noster, Redux'; Löfstedt, 'Sekundäre Bedeutungen von "Pater Noster"'.

30 George Lawless, *Augustine of Hippo and his Monastic Rule*, 84, ll. 70–71.

31 Wright, *Irish Tradition*, 243 n. 114.

32 Charlton T. Lewis and Charles Short, eds., *A Latin Dictionary*, 'sollers'.

33 Menner, *Poetical Dialogues*, 34.

34 John C. Pope, ed., *Homilies of Ælfric: A Supplementary Collection*, vol. 2, 682. On Anglo-Saxon euhemerism see Robert J. Menner, 'Two Notes on Mediaeval Euhemerism', 246–48. as well as Wulfstan's homily on false gods in Bethurum, *The Homilies of Wulfstan*, 221–24.

35 Albrecht Diem, 'Encounters between Monks and Demons in Latin Texts of Late Antiquity and the Early Middle Ages', 51–67, at 54–55.

36 Bose, 'From Exegesis to Appropriation', 187–210, at 187–88.

37 O'Brien O'Keeffe, *Visible Song*, 50.

38 Ibid., 49. BT takes 'gebrydded' as the past form of *ge-bryddan*, which it defines as 'to frighten, terrify', and refers to *broddetan*, defined as 'to tremble, quake, to pant for fear'. BT, 'ge-bryddan', 'broddetan'. Menner believes the wording

too strong for the context; he prefers 'shaken' or 'overawed', and approvingly cites Grein's suggestion that 'gebrydded' is a scribal error for 'gebryrded' (incited, inspired), an emendation adopted by Krapp and Dobbie. Menner, *Poetical Dialogues*, 106. The *DOE* interprets the word as a form of *bryrdan*, 'to guide, direct' or 'to inspire, stimulate'.

39 O'Brien O'Keeffe, *Visible Song*, 55.

40 Cross and Hill, *Prose Solomon and Saturn*, 39.

41 Ibid., 154–55. For a modern edition of the *Collectanea*, see Martha Bayless and Michael Lapidge, eds., *Collectanea Pseudo-Bedae*, 142 n. 75.

42 *Sollicitudo* is used by Thomas of Aquinas, *religiosa curiositate* by Peter of Celle. Carruthers, *The Craft of Thought*, 99, 195.

43 Michael Petschenig, ed., *Iohannis Cassiani Conlationes XXIIII*, CSEL 17, 306–307; bk 10, sec. 13.

44 Leclercq, *Love of Learning*, 73–75.

45 O'Neill, 'Date, Provenance and Relationship', 157.

46 Anlezark, *Old English Dialogues*, 32.

47 *OEB*, 334; B Text, ch. 35, ll. 133–34; Stanton, 'Linguistic Fragmentation and Redemption before King Alfred', 24–25.

48 Martin Skutella, ed., *S. Aureli Augustini confessionum libri xiii*, 251; bk 10, ch. 35, sec. 55, ll. 2–6. On this passage of Augustine see P. G. Walsh, 'The Rights and Wrongs of Curiosity (Plutarch to Augustine)', 82–84.

49 Peter J. Lucas, ed., *Exodus*.

50 Anlezark notes that 'the interlocutors are borrowing and developing each other's ideas and metaphors', but does not draw the same reading from this. Anlezark, *Old English Dialogues*, 103.

51 Stanley B. Greenfield, 'The Formulaic Expression of the Theme of "Exile" in Anglo-Saxon Poetry', 354, 357.

52 Merrel Dare Clubb, ed., *Christ and Satan: An Old English Poem*.

53 BT, 'ungesib'.

54 Leslie Lockett, *Anglo-Saxon Psychologies in the Vernacular and Latin Traditions*, 57. Lockett discusses the *Solomon and Saturn* poems at ibid., 64, 425. Old English poetry often understands the chest as a source of eloquence, song, and speech more generally. Eric Jager, 'Speech and the Chest in Old English Poetry: Orality or Pectorality?'

55 BT defines *fyrwet* simply as 'curiosity'. *DOE* offers three definitions under *fyr-witt*: 'curiosity, inquisitiveness', 'sexual desire, lust', and as a gloss for *ardor*, '(spiritual) passion, intensity'.

56 Rosemary Woolf, ed., *Juliana*.

57 *DOE*, 'fyr-witt'.

58 Ker 107, GL 244.

59 Inge B. Milfull, *The Hymns of the Anglo-Saxon Church: A Study and Edition of the 'Durham Hymnal'*, 28, 40–41.

60 Ibid., 130.

61 Thomas Hill glosses *stigað*, however, as 'descend' or 'fall on', and explains the passage from ll. 43–48 as an Old English version of an apotropaic motif in Old

Norse literature in which the prayers of holy people cause burning drops to fall on demons. Thomas D. Hill, 'Tormenting the Devil with Boiling Drops: An Apotropaic Motif in the Old English "Solomon and Saturn I" and Old Norse-Icelandic Literature'.

62 Menner suggests it is a heathen relic, perhaps used for sacrifice. Menner, *Poetical Dialogues*, 110.

63 Leclercq, *Love of Learning*, 73–77.

64 Hollahan, 'The Anglo-Saxon Use of the Psalms', 137–39.

65 The allegorical introductions to the psalms in the Paris Psalter, for example, frequently offer a moral interpretation of the prayers, inviting the singer to identify with their content. Patrick P. O'Neill, ed., *King Alfred's Old English Prose Translation of the First Fifty Psalms*.

66 Leclercq, *Love of Learning*.

67 Scott DeGregorio, 'Affective Spirituality: Theory and Practice in Bede and Alfred the Great', 132. Citation from Bede, 'In Cantica Canticorum libri vi', *Bedae Venerabilis Opera, Pars II, Opera Exegetica, 2B*, 247; bk 2, ch. iv, sec. 3, ll. 159–60.

68 *Qualis est dilectus tuus ex dilecto o pulcherrima mulierum qualis est dilectus tuus ex dilecto quia sic adiurasti nos?* Quod est aperte fratrem fratri fidelem fideli dicere, Obsecro quia caritate redemptoris te feruere comperio mihi quoque de eo uerba facias me salutari exhortatione confirmes quatenus et meo in corde caritas eadem auditis eius beneficiis ac donis augescat. Ibid., 283; bk 3, ch. 5, sec. 9, ll. 467–72.

69 Milfull, *Hymns*, 130.

70 Jonathan Wilcox compares this passage to three biblical passages that use the motif of eating books for 'acquisition of divine knowledge': Revelation 10:9–10, Jeremiah 15:16, and Ezechiel 3:1–3. 'Eating Books: The Consumption of Learning in the Old English Poetic *Solomon and Saturn*', 115–18; Kathryn Powell, 'Orientalist Fantasy in the Poetic Dialogues of *Solomon and Saturn*', 117–43.

71 See, for example, Henri-Irénée Marrou, *Histoire de l'éducation dans l'antiquité. 1. Le monde grec*, 228–31; *Histoire de l'éducation dans l'antiquité. 2. Le monde romain*, 69. For an interesting parallel, see the description of the very similar methods used to teach Hebrew letters to medieval Jewish children in Judith Olszowy-Schlanger, 'Learning to Read and Write in Medieval Egypt: Children's Exercise Books from the Cairo Geniza', 47–69.

72 Carruthers, 'Invention', 201–13, at 209–10.

73 Travis, *Disseminal Chaucer*, 53.

74 BT, 'began', 'ingemynd'; *DOE*, 'be-gan'.

75 Carruthers, 'Invention'; Carruthers, *The Book of Memory*.

76 An interesting text in this respect is the *Catechesis Celtica*, a Hiberno-Latin text which contains three expositions on the Pater Noster, and includes what Wright calls 'a verbal transformation combat' in which the devil's speeches are counteracted with lines from the Pater Noster: 'Diabolus enim dixit: Nescio Deum! Nos humiliter dicere iubemur: *Paternoster qui es in celis*. Diabolus

dixit: *Ero similes altissimo.* Nos dicimus: *Adueniat regnum tuum.* Diabolus dixit: *Super astra Dei solium meum exultabo.* Nos dicimus: *Fiat uoluntas tua sicut in cello et in terra.'* (For the devil said, 'I do not know God!' We are bidden to say humbly: 'Our Father who art in heaven.' The devil said: 'I will be like the most High.' We say: 'Thy kingdom come.' The devil said: 'I will exalt my throne above the stars of God.' We say: 'Thy will be done on earth, as it is in heaven.') Here, the tendency of the Pater Noster to be taken apart and commented upon results in a dialogue, and one in which the argument is carried about by a series of appositions: the individual lines are not so much answers to each other as they are translations of the same idea into different registers, or, in this case, moral worlds. Dialogue quoted and translated in Wright, *Irish Tradition*, 237.

77 Don C. Skemer, *Binding Words: Textual Amulets in the Middle Ages*, 90–91. The SATOR formula has a particular connection to the Pater Noster: its words, 'sator arepo tenet opera rotas', comprise a palindrome and can be arranged into a word square that reads the same in all directions, but the letters can also be laid out in a cross of two *paternosters*, with two extra A's and O's. See Raymond J. S. Grant, *Cambridge, Corpus Christi College 41: The Loricas and the Missal*, 20.

78 Hill, 'Tormenting the Devil', 157.

79 R. I. Page notes their 'almost complete absence … from Anglo-Saxon manuscript charms which survive in large numbers', and notes their use as 'reference marks' in manuscripts. R. I. Page, *An Introduction to English Runes*, 112, 98.

80 Carruthers, *The Book of Memory*, 109.

81 Marrou, *Histoire de l'éducation. 1. Le monde grec*, 228.

82 Carruthers, *The Book of Memory*, 137.

83 Carruthers, 'Invention', 109; Hermann, 'The Pater Noster Battle Sequence in *Solomon and Saturn* and the *Psychomachia* of Prudentius'.

84 Elaine Scarry, *Dreaming by the Book*.

85 Enders, *The Medieval Theater of Cruelty*, 150.

86 Anlezark, *Old English Dialogues*, 108.

87 Cogitationibus seu diuersis umoribus excitatis abducere mentem nostram a supplicationis intentione festinans et per hoc eam tepefacere a coepto feruore contendens. John Cassian, in *Iohannis Cassiani De institutis coenobiorum et De octo principalium vitiorum remediis libri xii; De incarnatione Domini contra Nestorium libri vii*, ed. Michael Petschenig, 26; bk 2, chs. 10–11, ll. 5–23. Frederick Jonassen also interprets the letters as part of monastic reading practice and predilection for puzzles and games. 'The Pater Noster Letters in the Poetic *Solomon and Saturn'*.

88 Carruthers, *The Craft of Thought*, 189–90.

89 Joseph Roach explains that 'this faculty, which flourishes in that mental space where imagination and memory converge, is a way of thinking through movements – at once remembered and reinvented – the otherwise unthinkable'. *Cities of the Dead: Circum-Atlantic Performance*, 27.

90 Hecht, *Bischofs Wærferth*, 112, ll. 12–14.

91 Law, *The Insular Latin Grammarians*, 43; *Wisdom, Authority and Grammar*.

92 Ob tres causas fona finduntur. Prima est, ut sagacitatem discentium nostrorum in inquirendis atque in inueniendis his quae obscura sunt adprobemus; secunda est propter decorem aedificationemque eloquaentiae; tertia ne mistica quaeque et quae solis gnaris pandi debent, passim ab infimis ac stultis facile reperiantur, ne secundum antiquum prouerbium sues gemmas calcent. Bengt Löfstedt, ed., *Virgilius Maro Grammaticus Opera Omnia*, 213; Epitome 10, ll. 4–11; Lucie Doležalová, 'On Mistake and Meaning: *Scinderationes fonorum* in Medieval *artes memoriae*, Mnemonic Verses, and Manuscripts', 128.

93 Doležalová, 'On Mistake and Meaning'.

94 Sed multis et multiplicibus obscuritatibus et ambiguitatibus decipiuntur qui temere legunt, aliud pro alio sentientes. Quibusdam autem locis quid vel falso suspicentur non inveniunt: ita obscure dicta quaedam densissimam caliginem obducunt. Quod totum provisum esse divinitus non dubito, ad edomandam labore superbiam et intellectum a fastidio renovandum, cui facile investigata plerumque vilescunt. Edition and translation from Green, *Augustine: De doctrina christiana*, 60–61.

95 Qui enim prorsus non inveniunt quod quaerunt, fame laborant; qui autem non quaerunt, quia in promptu habent, fastidio saepe marcescunt. In utroque autem languor cavendus est. Ibid., 62–63.

3. Violence

1 Alfred de Musset, *Poésies nouvelles 1836–1852*, 126.

2 Fred C. Robinson, '*Medieval, the Middle Ages*', 753–54.

3 A. F. Leach, *The Schools of Medieval England*, 89.

4 Pierre Riché, *Éducation et culture dans l'occident barbare. VIe–VIIIe siècles*, 500–502.

5 Walter J. Ong, 'Latin Language Study as a Renaissance Puberty Rite', 124. Philippe Ariès offers a slightly different account: he claims that references to whipping of pupils are rare up until the fourteenth century, but increase in frequency and severity afterwards. Philippe Ariès, *Centuries of Childhood: A Social History of Family Life*, 258.

6 Enders, 'Rhetoric, Coercion', 26. See also Bruce W. Holsinger, 'Musical Violence and the Pedagogical Body: The Prioress's Tale and the Ideologies of "Song"', in *Music, Body, and Desire*; Woods, 'Rape and the Pedagogical Rhetoric'; Enders, *The Medieval Theater of Cruelty*.

7 Ben Parsons, 'The Way of the Rod: The Functions of Beating in Late Medieval Pedagogy', 10–11. Bede's speech miracle is, in his view of history, evidence for how monastic teaching 'could cross from coercion to mortification', since John of Beverley forcefully grabs the mute youth by the chin to heal him. Ibid., 11. Parsons misses the baptismal connotation of this gesture.

8 The edition used is *ÆBC*. All translations are my own, though I have also consulted Porter's translation of the *Colloquies*.

9 Scott Gwara, 'Ælfric Bata's Manuscripts', 240.

10 David W. Porter, 'The Latin Syllabus in Anglo-Saxon Monastic Schools'.

11 Nicholas Brooks suggests that Bata may have served as master at the monastic community at Christ Church, but notes that the *Colloquies* are written 'for a community ruled by an abbot, not by an archbishop or dean'. Nicholas Brooks, *The Early History of the Church of Canterbury: Christ Church from 597 to 1066*, 266.

12 Ker 362, GL 686.

13 Michael Lapidge, 'The Hermeneutic Style in Tenth-Century Anglo-Latin Literature', 98–99.

14 *ÆBC*, 7.

15 Porter, 'Latin Syllabus', 464.

16 Ibid., 469.

17 The standard edition of Ælfric's *Colloquy* is that of Garmonsway, who bases his text on the version found in BL Cotton Tiberius A.iii; Garmonsway prioritises the Old English glosses, rendering the originally primary Latin text in a smaller type. Stevenson edits the text from Oxford, St John's College 154, but expands it with additions from Cotton Tiberius A.iii, in *Early Scholastic Colloquies*, 75–102. Joyce Hill edits a version of the *Colloquy* now divided between Antwerp, Plantin-Moretus Museum M. 16.2, and BL Add. 32246. Joyce Hill, 'Ælfric's *Colloquy*: The Antwerp/London Version'. *De raris fabulis* is edited by Stevenson (1–11), and by Gwara (*Hermeneumata* 123–35), and translated by Gwara in Gwara, *Education*, 47–79. The *Retractata* is edited by Stevenson (21–26) and Gwara in *Latin Colloquies*. I cite the Gwara edition. The standard edition of the *Hermeneumata Pseudodositheana* is that of Georgius Goetz.

18 David W. Porter, 'Ælfric's *Colloquy* and Ælfric Bata'. For a detailed comparative study of Ælfric's *Colloquy* and Bata's *Colloquies*, as well as of Ælfric's *Grammar* and *Glossary*, see Lendinara, 'The *Colloquy* of Ælfric'.

19 Garmonsway, *Ælfric's Colloquy*, 14; Joyce Hill, 'Learning Latin in Anglo-Saxon England: Traditions, Texts and Techniques', 17–18.

20 Gwara, *Education*, 37–38.

21 David W. Porter, 'Anglo-Saxon Colloquies: Ælfric, Ælfric Bata and *De Raris Fabulis Retractata*'; Gwara, *Education*, 8–13.

22 A. C. Dionisotti, 'Greek Grammars and Dictionaries in Carolingian Europe', 26–31.

23 Gwara, *Latin Colloquies*, 15; 'Ælfric Bata's Manuscripts', 247–55.

24 Alex J. Novikoff, *The Medieval Culture of Disputation: Pedagogy, Practice, and Performance*, 26–28.

25 Stevenson, *Early Scholastic Colloquies*, vii.

26 William Stubbs, ed., *Memorials of Saint Dunstan, Archbishop of Canterbury*, 136, 227.

27 *ÆBC*, 15.

28 Christopher A. Jones, 'The Irregular Life in Ælfric Bata's *Colloquies*', 248–51.

29 Boynton, 'Training for the Liturgy', 15–16; *ÆBC*, 8–12.

30 G. N. Garmonsway, 'The Development of the Colloquy', 260.

31 Michael Lapidge, 'The Study of Latin Texts in Late Anglo-Saxon England [1] The Evidence of Latin Glosses', 100–1.

32 Irina A. Dumitrescu, 'The Grammar of Pain in Ælfric Bata's *Colloquies*'.

33 Ayers Bagley, 'Grammar as Teacher: A Study in the Iconics of Education'; Rudolf Wittkower, ' "Grammatica": From Martianus Capella to Hogarth'.

34 See, for example, Ralph Hanna III, 'School and Scorn: Gender in *Piers Plowman*', 220.

35 Irvine, *The Making of Textual Culture*.

36 Ælfric's *Colloquy* exists in three different versions, all in Latin; the Old English glosses on one of the texts were reconstructed into a colloquy by Henry Sweet which has since become a mainstay of Old English education. Garmonsway edits the Old English 'text', including, by way of footnote, a Latin text of the *Colloquy*, in Garmonsway, *Ælfric's Colloquy*. Joyce Hill has done essential work to disambiguate the various versions and editions of the *Colloquy* in Hill, 'Ælfric's *Colloquy*: The Antwerp/London Version'; 'Learning Latin in Anglo-Saxon England: Traditions, Texts and Techniques'; 'Winchester Pedagogy and the *Colloquy* of Ælfric'.

37 Zupitza, *Aelfrics Grammatik*. Ælfric's main source for the grammar is the grammatical compilation *Excerptiones de Prisciano*, though he also used Donatus' *Ars minor* and *Ars maior*. Jeannine M. Bender-Davis, 'Ælfric's Techniques of Translation and Adaptation as Seen in the Composition of his Old English "Latin Grammar" ', 6–7; Porter, *Excerptiones de Prisciano: The Source for Ælfric's Latin–Old English Grammar*, 31–33.

38 On Ælfric's *Grammar* as a grammar of English as well as of Latin, see Menzer, 'Ælfric's English *Grammar*', 106–24. and 'Ælfric's Grammar', 637–52.

39 Zupitza, *Aelfrics Grammatik*, 9.

40 Note that the only illustrations given by BT for *word* as 'verb' are from Ælfric's *Grammar*.

41 Ibid., 'weorc'.

42 Ibid., 'þrowing'.

43 Mary Carruthers, 'Reading with Attitude, Remembering the Book'; *The Book of Memory*; 'Invention'.

44 Lindsay, *Isidori Hispalensis Etymologiarum*, bk 1, ch. 9, sec. 7.

45 Jones, 'The Irregular Life', 245.

46 Colin Spencer, *British Food: An Extraordinary Thousand Years of History*, 24–25, at 24.

47 Jones, 'The Irregular Life', 248.

48 non solum fratres sed etiam abbates adolescentes uel puerulos non brachiis amplexando uel labris leuiter deosculando, sed caritatiuo animi affectu sine uerbis adulatoriis reuerenter cum magna cautela diligant. Thomas Symons and Sigrid Spath, 'Regularis concordia anglicae nationis', in *Consuetudinum saeculi X/XI/XII monumenta non-Cluniacensia*, 76.

49 Jones, 'The Irregular Life', 251.

50 One version of the *Regularis concordia* survives in BL Cotton Tiberius A.iii, a manuscript connected to Ælfric Bata. Bata's name appears on the original

first page of the work (folio 117), first as 'Eluricus Bate' at the top of the page and in the second item on the table of contents, 'Regula elurici bate glosata anglice' (The rule of Ælfric Bata glossed in English). Ker has suggested that 'it was thought at Christ Church in s. xii that he was the author of the Regularis concordia'. Ker, 241. Bata may also have made small changes to the version of Ælfric's *Colloquy* contained in the same manuscript. Porter, 'Ælfric's Colloquy', 643.

51 Gerd Zimmermann, *Ordensleben und Lebensstandard: Die Cura Corporis in den Ordensvorschriften des abendländischen Hochmittelalters*, 409.

52 According to Gwara the expression 'don't stand between me and the light' originates in an apocryphal conversation between Diogenes of Sinope and Alexander the Great, though in this case is distorted and misunderstood. Scott Gwara, 'Diogenes the Cynic in the Scholastic Dialogues Called *De raris fabulis*', 3–6.

53 On the enduring use of Latin *culus* for 'anus', see J. N. Adams, '*Culus, Clunes* and their Synonyms in Latin', 231–35; *The Latin Sexual Vocabulary*, 110–12.

54 Mayke de Jong, *In Samuel's Image: Child Oblation in the Early Medieval West*, 148.

55 Zimmermann, *Ordensleben*, 121, 411.

56 Nec ad obsequium priuatum quempiam illorum nec saltim sub spiritualis rei obtentu deducere praesumant, sed uti regula praecipit sub sui custodis uigilantia iugiter maneat. Nec ipse custos cum singulo aliquo puerulo sine tertio qui testis assistat migrandi licentiam habeat. Symons and Spath, 'Regularis concordia', 76–77.

57 *ÆBC*, 14.

58 Jones, 'The Irregular Life', 248.

59 For examples, see Martin Rule, ed., *Eadmeri historia novorum in Anglia, et opuscula duo de vita sancti Anselmi et quibusdam miraculis ejus*, 339–41; Stubbs, *Memorials*, 136–38.

60 Mayke de Jong, 'Growing up in a Carolingian monastery: Magister Hildemar and his Oblates', 106–108.

61 M. Bradford Bedingfield, *The Dramatic Liturgy of Anglo-Saxon England*; Joerg O. Fichte, 'The *Visitatio Sepulchri* as Actualization of Dramatic Impulses in the Ninth and Tenth Centuries', 226.

62 John C. Pope, 'Dramatic Voices in *The Wanderer* and *The Seafarer*', 170–71; Allen J. Frantzen, 'Drama and Dialogue in Old English Poetry: The Scene of Cynewulf's *Juliana*', 106.

63 Carol Symes, 'The Appearance of Early Vernacular Plays: Forms, Functions, and the Future of Medieval Theater', 783.

64 Ibid., 826–28.

65 Joyce Coleman, *Public Reading and the Reading Public in Late Medieval England and France*; Evelyn Birge Vitz, *Orality and Performance in Early French Romance*; Evelyn Birge Vitz, Nancy Freeman Regalado, and Marilyn Lawrence, eds., *Performing Medieval Narrative*.

66 Boynton, 'Training for the Liturgy'; Holsinger, 'The Parable of Caedmon's Hymn'.

67 Seth Lerer, *Children's Literature: A Reader's History, from Aesop to Harry Potter*, 64. Katherine O'Brien O'Keeffe argues that Ælfric's *Colloquy*, 'by its nature as a text to be memorized and then performed in interaction with others … is at once a schoolroom exercise in language learning and a means for building and installing identity in the oblates who perform it after committing it to memory'. O'Brien O'Keeffe, *Stealing Obedience*, 106. I am grateful to O'Brien O'Keeffe for allowing me to read an earlier manuscript version of her chapter on the *Colloquy*.

68 Erving Goffman, *The Presentation of Self in Everyday Life*, 81–82.

69 Frantzen, 'Drama and Dialogue', 113; George Klawitter, 'Dramatic Elements in Early Monastic Induction Ceremonies', 215–16.

70 Woods, 'Rape and the Pedagogical Rhetoric', 160–61; Frantzen, *Before*, 161.

71 John MacAloon argues that cultural performances follow a routine, script, or 'program of activity', adding that 'there is no performance without pre-formance'. John J. MacAloon, 'Introduction: Cultural Performances, Culture Theory', 9. I use the term 'pre-formance' to refer to an activity which is both performance and a loose script in the making.

72 Richard Schechner, *Between Theater and Anthropology*, 6.

73 Janice Carlisle, 'Spectacle as Government: Dickens and the Working-Class Audience', 168.

74 Joe Winston, 'Between the Aesthetic and the Ethical: Analysing the Tension at the Heart of Theatre in Education', 317.

75 Helga Noice and Tony Noice, 'What Studies of Actors and Acting Can Tell Us about Memory and Cognitive Functioning', 14–15.

76 Helga Noice et al., 'Improving Memory in Older Adults by Instructing Them in Professional Actors' Learning Strategies', 317, 323.

77 Christina L. Scott, Richard Jackson Harris, and Alicia R. Rothe, 'Embodied Cognition through Improvisation Improves Memory for a Dramatic Monologue', 301–303.

78 Porter, 'Latin Syllabus', 469.

79 Dorthe Kirkegaard Thomsen and Dorthe Berntsen, 'The Long-Term Impact of Emotionally Stressful Events on Memory Characteristics and Life Story', 585.

80 Ibid., 584.

81 Jun Liu, 'Process Drama in Second- and Foreign-Language Classrooms', 54.

82 Brian Edmiston, 'Drama as Ethical Education', 68.

83 Liu, 'Process Drama', 57, 62; Sarah L. Dodson, 'FAQs: Learning Languages through Drama', 133.

84 Patricia S. Dickson, 'Acting French: Drama Techniques in the Second Language Classroom', 300, 310.

85 Jonathan Levy, 'Theatre and Moral Education', 67–68.

86 Joe Winston, 'Theorising Drama as Moral Education', 464, 470.

87 Joe Winston, *Drama, Narrative and Moral Education: Exploring Traditional Tales in the Primary Years*, 66; Edmiston, 'Drama as Ethical Education', 64, 67; Mallika Henry, 'Drama's Ways of Learning', 56.

88 Michel Foucault, *Surveiller et punir: naissance de la prison*, 204.

89 Brown, 'Psalms'.

90 The modern term for this process is language socialisation, which, according to Jane Zuengler and KimMarie Cole, is 'the practice by which children or novices to a community are socialized both to the language forms and, through language, to adopt the values, behaviors, and practices of that community'. Jane Zuengler and KimMarie Cole, 'Language Socialization and Second Language Learning', 301. Along similar lines, Earl Anderson has argued that Ælfric's *Colloquy* inculcates oblates into humility, obedience, and the Benedictine monastic ideal. Earl R. Anderson, 'Social Idealism in Ælfric's *Colloquy*'.

91 Lahaye-Geusen, *Das Opfer der Kinder*, 367–72.

92 Wilbur Samuel Howell, trans., *The Rhetoric of Alcuin and Charlemagne*.

93 Alan Morinis, 'The Ritual Experience: Pain and the Transformation of Consciousness in Ordeals of Initiation'.

94 The function of pedagogical pain extends, then, beyond discipline or correction. Walter Ong, making a similar argument about the role of Latin in Renaissance education, discusses humanists 'who had "gone through" the *rites de passage* and who look back on such experiences, with their aura of lawlessness, as trials which others should perhaps go through not so much for learning's sake as simply to prove their prowess as members of the "gang" and to achieve a sense of belonging'. Ong, 'Latin Language Study', 136.

95 Weber, *Biblia sacra iuxta Vulgatam versionem*.

96 David B. Capes, 'Imitatio Christi and the Gospel Genre', 11.

4. Recollection

1 A. T. Quiller-Couch, ed., *The Oxford Book of English Verse 1250–1900*, 611.

2 For overviews of the relevant texts, see Kenneth R. Brooks, ed., *Andreas and the Fates of the Apostles*, xv–xviii; Robert Boenig, *The Acts of Andrew in the Country of the Cannibals: Translations from the Greek, Latin, and Old English*, i–xxxix.

3 Constantin Tischendorf edited the *Praxeis* in Constantin Tischendorf, ed., *Acta apostolorum apocrypha*, 132–66. Maximilien Bonnet published a version of the *Praxeis* intercalated with the text of the Bonnet Fragment in Richard Adelbert Lipsius and Maximilien Bonnet, eds., *Acta apostolorum apocrypha*, *Praxeis*: 65–116, Bonnet Fragment: 85–88. The *Praxeis* and Bonnet Fragment were reprinted (separately) by Franz Blatt in his edition of the *Casanatensis* and the *Vaticanus*. Franz Blatt, ed., *Die lateinischen Bearbeitungen der Acta Andreae et Matthiae apud anthropophagos*.

4 CCCC 198 is Ker 48, GL 64. The Blickling Homilies are Ker 382, GL 905. For editions, see R. Morris, ed., *The Blickling Homilies*, 228–49; James W. Bright and James R. Hulbert, eds., *Bright's Anglo-Saxon Reader*, 113–28.

5 Ker 394, GL 941. The similarity between *Andreas* and the poems of Cynewulf, along with the lack of distinction between *Andreas* and *Fates of the Apostles*, led scholars at the end of the nineteenth century and the beginning of the twentieth

to debate whether *Andreas* was in fact a Cynewulfian composition. The poet is now seen to have been rather a student or imitator of Cynewulf. For an overview of the early discussion, primarily intended to counter Cynewulfian authorship of *Andreas*, see Claes Schaar, *Critical Studies in the Cynewulf Group*, 98–104. See also the dissertation by Ellen Clune Buttenwieser, *Studien über die Verfasserschaft des Andreas*. In their forthcoming edition of *Andreas*, Richard North and Michael Bintley propose that *Andreas* was written under Alfredian patronage between c. 888 and 893, and that St Edith of Wilton later copied out *Andreas* and *Fates* as a gift to Dunstan, who had them recopied into the Vercelli Book. I am grateful to Richard North for allowing me to use his edition in manuscript. Quotations are from Brooks' edition.

6 Jonathan Wilcox, 'Eating People Is Wrong: Funny Style in *Andreas* and its Analogues', 208–10; Andrew P. Scheil, *The Footsteps of Israel: Understanding Jews in Anglo-Saxon England*, 234.

7 Roberta Frank, 'North-Sea Soundings in Andreas', 1.

8 See for example G. Sarrazin's arguments for Cynewulfian authorship of *Beowulf*. Gregor Sarrazin, 'Beowulf und Kynewulf'.

9 Compare *Beo.* 38–40a, 'Ne hyrde ic cymlicor ceol gegyrwan/ hildewæpnum ond heaðowædum,/ billum ond byrnum' and *And.* 360b–62, 'æfre ic ne hyrde/ þon cymlicor ceol gehladenne/ heahgestreonum'. Brooks, *Andreas*, xxiv.

10 R. D. Fulk, Robert E. Bjork, and John D. Niles, eds., *Klaeber's Beowulf*.

11 George Philip Krapp, ed., *The Vercelli Book*, 108; Schaar, *Critical Studies*, 277–78. Krapp offers a lengthy list of parallels between *Andreas* and the Cynewulfian poems in his early edition: George Philip Krapp, ed., *Andreas and The Fates of the Apostles: Two Anglo-Saxon Narrative Poems*, lvi–lvii. Schaar discusses the nature of *Andreas*' borrowings from *Beowulf*, the poetry of Cynewulf, and other Old English poems, generally arguing that the use of the phrases in *Andreas* is ill-fitting compared to the source. *Critical Studies*, 261–97. For a detailed argument that the passage in *Andreas* is neither a borrowing nor grammatically exceptional, see Hans Schabram, 'Andreas und Beowulf: Parallelstellen als Zeugnis für literarische Abhängigkeit', 208–14.

12 Satyendra Kumar Das, *Cynewulf and the Cynewulf Canon*, 230–31.

13 Leonard J. Peters, 'The Relationship of the Old English *Andreas* to *Beowulf*'.

14 Anita R. Riedinger, 'The Formulaic Relationship between *Beowulf* and *Andreas*'.

15 Note Powell's caveat regarding 'verbatim repetition' – it 'allows for small differences such as number, gender, case, tense or mood, different affixes and variation in minor, unstressed words such as conjunctions, articles and prepositions'. Alison M. Powell, 'Verbal Parallels in *Andreas* and its Relationship to *Beowulf* and Cynewulf', 44. See also Andy Orchard, 'Both Style and Substance: The Case for Cynewulf'.

16 Powell, 'Verbal Parallels', especially 104, 167, 232.

17 Ibid., 235.

18 David Hamilton, 'The Diet and Digestion of Allegory in *Andreas*'; '*Andreas* and *Beowulf*: Placing the Hero'; Anita Riedinger, '*Andreas* and the Formula in Transition'; Lisa J. Kiser, '*Andreas* and the *Lifes Weg*: Convention and

Innovation in Old English Metaphor'; Paul Cavill, '*Beowulf* and *Andreas*: Two Maxims'.

19 Thomas D. Hill, 'Figural Narrative in *Andreas*: The Conversion of the Meremedonians'; Joseph Trahern, 'Joshua and Tobias in the Old English *Andreas*'; Penn R. Szittya, 'The Living Stone and the Patriarchs: Typological Imagery in *Andreas*, Lines 706–810'; John Casteen, '*Andreas*: Mermedonian Cannibalism and Figural Narration'; Constance B. Hieatt, 'The Harrowing of Mermedonia: Typological Patterns in the Old English "Andreas"'; Marie Michelle Walsh, 'The Baptismal Flood in the Old English "Andreas": Liturgical and Typological Depths'; Robert E. Boenig, '*Andreas*, the Eucharist, and Vercelli'; James W. Earl, 'The Typological Structure of *Andreas*'; Frederick M. Biggs, 'The Passion of Andreas: *Andreas* 1398–1491'; Robert Boenig, *Saint and Hero: Andreas and Medieval Doctrine*.

20 As Daniel Calder bracingly puts it, the typological equivalences critics find in *Andreas* are not only to be found in its source and in most Old English hagiography, but 'in all eternity'. 'Figurative Language and its Contexts in *Andreas*: A Study in Medieval Expressionism', 118.

21 Hamilton, 'Diet and Digestion', 154–57; Ivan Herbison, 'Generic Adaptation in *Andreas*', 207; Edward B. Irving Jr, 'A Reading of *Andreas*: The Poem as Poem', 233.

22 Amity Reading, 'Baptism, Conversion, and Selfhood in the Old English *Andreas*'.

23 Ibid., 8.

24 Scheil, *The Footsteps of Israel*, 235.

25 Scheil notes Andrew's blindness too: 'Of course, the poet plays here on the irony of the situation, for it is the "clear-minded" Andrew who sits in blissful ignorance as he chats with his Savior.' Ibid., 234–35.

26 On the importance of the Jews' blindness in the poem, see Irving Jr, 'A Reading of Andreas', 226–27.

27 The *Praxeis*, in Robert Boenig's translation: 'You did not sin, but I did these things to you because you said, "I will not be able to go into the city of the cannibals in three days", but I will show you that I am able to do all things and appear to each person just as I wish.' Boenig, *The Acts of Andrew*, 12. Christ is more generous in *Casanatensis*: 'Totum tibi dimictam, totum tibi parcam, totum indulgeam, quoniam fideliter agebas, fideliter loquebas, fidelissime permanebas.' (I will settle everything for you, I will spare you everything, I will indulge you everything, because you acted faithfully, you spoke faithfully, you endured most faithfully.) Blatt, *Die lateinischen Bearbeitungen*, 67.

28 Biggs, 'The Passion of Andreas', 415–17.

29 Tertullian, *Ad martyres liber*, *PL* 1, Ch. iv, cols. 624C–26A.

30 H. J. Thomson, ed., *Prudentius*, vol. ii, Loeb Classical Library (Cambridge, MA: Harvard University Press, 1953), 176; *EH*, 30; bk 1, ch. 7.

31 Biggs, 'The Passion of Andreas', 417–20.

32 For contemporary discussions, see C. E. B. Cranfield, *The Gospel According to Mark: An Introduction and Commentary*, 458–59; D. H. Milling, 'History and Prophecy in the Marcan Passion Narrative', 50; Harvey D. Lange, 'The

Relationship between Psalm 22 and the Passion Narrative'; Esther M. Menn, 'No Ordinary Lament: Relecture and the Identity of the Distressed in Psalm 22', 331; Harold W. Attridge, 'Giving Voice to Jesus: Use of the Psalms in the New Testament', 102; Stephen P. Ahearne-Kroll, 'Challenging the Divine: LXX Psalm 21 in the Passion Narrative of the Gospel of Mark', 140–44. For early Christian uses of the Psalms, see 'Psalms in the New Testament'; Brian Daley, 'Finding the Right Key: The Aims and Strategies of Early Christian Interpretation of the Psalms'.

33 Jerome, *Commentariorum in evangelium Matthaei ad Eusebium libri quator*, cols. 212A–B.

34 'Commentarioli in Psalmos', in *S. Hieronymi Presbyteri Opera, Pars I. Opera Exegetica*, ed. G. Morin, 198.

35 D. E. Dekkers and J. Fraipont, eds., *Sancti Aurelii Augustini Enarrationes in psalmos i–l*, CCSL (Turnhout: Brepols, 1956), 123.

36 M. Adriaen, ed., *Magni Aurelii Cassiodori Expositio Psalmorum i–lxx*, CCSL 97, 190.

37 Bede, *In Marci evangelium expositio*, PL 92, cols. 290C–91A.

38 Dominic Scott, *Recollection and Experience: Plato's Theory of Learning and its Successors*, 15.

39 Brian Stock, *Augustine's Inner Dialogue: The Philosophical Soliloquy in Late Antiquity*, 13–14.

40 The manuscript, BL Royal 8.C.iii, was produced at St Augustine's, Canterbury, and contains a number of texts on baptism. GL 475. Aldhelm mentions Augustine's book, 'quem de magistro praetitulavit' (which he called 'On the teacher') in 'De metris et enigmatibus ac pedum regulis'. Ehwald, *Aldhelmi Opera Omnia*, 81. Reference from Lapidge, *The Anglo-Saxon Library*, 179.

41 Augustine's *Soliloquies* are found in two extant manuscripts, and Boethius' *Consolation* in seventeen, according to Gneuss. For the Old English *Soliloquies*, see Carnicelli, *King Alfred's Version of St. Augustine's Soliloquies*. There is little evidence of interest in *The Consolation of Philosophy* in Europe until the late eighth century, when Alcuin used it for his dialogue *De vera philosophia*. It became popular among the Carolingians, whose commentaries also influenced English reception and translation of the *Consolation*. The earliest evidence for interest in the *Consolation* in the British Isles dates to the ninth century, and includes the Old English translation of Boethius and a single Latin manuscript, heavily glossed. In the tenth century, the *Consolation* became a standard text in England. See D. K. Bolton, 'The Study of the Consolation of Philosophy in Anglo-Saxon England'; Margaret T. Gibson, 'Boethius in the Carolingian Schools'; Lapidge, *The Anglo-Saxon Library*, 127–28; Malcolm Godden, 'King Alfred and the *Boethius* Industry'; OEB, 4–5; Joseph Wittig, 'The Old English Boethius, the Latin Commentaries, and Bede'; Rosalind C. Love, 'The Latin Commentaries on Boethius's *De consolatione philosophiae* from the 9th to the 11th Centuries'; Paul E. Szarmach, 'Boethius's Influence in Anglo-Saxon England: The Vernacular and the *De consolatione philosophiae*'.

42 Edmund T. Silk, 'Boethius's *Consolatio Philosophiae* as a Sequel to Augustine's *Dialogues* and *Soliloquia*'.

43 Discenza, *The King's English: Strategies of Translation in the Old English Boethius*; Carnicelli, *King Alfred's Version*, 29–40; *OEB*, 135–36.

44 Harald Fuchs and Hanspeter Müller, eds., *Aurelius Augustinus: Selbstgespräche. Von der Unsterblichkeit der Seele*, 150; bk 2, sec. 35, ll. 4–5; Roland Teske, 'Augustine's Philosophy of Memory', 148–50.

45 Quotations of the Latin *Consolation* are from Claudio Moreschini, ed., *Anicius Manlius Severinus Boethius: De consolatione philosophiae. Opuscula theologica*, 2nd ed. I cite line numbers for both verse and prose.

46 Translations of the *Consolation* are from Boethius, *The Consolation of Philosophy*, trans. Richard Green. Occasionally, I have adjusted the translation to reflect the original.

47 Citations and translations of both prose and verse versions of the Old English Boethius are from *OEB*. They date the two versions of Boethius 'between about 885 and the middle of the tenth century', and argue against Alfredian authorship. Ibid., 1: 8, 44–46, 140–51. For surveys of Boethius in the middle ages, see Gibson, 'Boethius in the Carolingian Schools'; Pierre Courcelle, *La consolation de philosophie dans la tradition littéraire: antécédents et postérité de Boèce*.

48 Cross and Hill, *Prose Solomon and Saturn*. An edition of the *Disputatio* is found in Lloyd William Daly and Walther Suchier, *Altercatio Hadriani Augusti et Epicteti Philosophi*, 137–43.

49 Alcuin, *The Rhetoric of Alcuin and Charlemagne*, 128–29.

50 On the influence of Boethius on Old English poetry, see William Witherle Lawrence, 'The Song of Deor'; Murray F. Markland, 'Boethius, Alfred, and Deor'; W. F. Bolton, 'Boethius, Alfred, and *Deor* Again'; Kevin S. Kiernan, '*Deor*: The Consolations of an Anglo-Saxon Boethius'; W. F. Bolton, 'Boethius and a Topos in *Beowulf*'; A. D. Hogan, '*The Wanderer* – A Boethian Poem?'; Szarmach, 'Boethius's Influence in Anglo-Saxon England: The Vernacular and the *De consolatione philosophiae*', 243–53. See also the sceptical approaches of Alan H. Roper, 'Boethius and the Three Fates of *Beowulf*'; Richard North, 'Boethius and the Mercenary in *The Wanderer*'; Paul S. Langeslag, 'Boethian Similitude in *Deor* and *The Wanderer*'.

51 Powell, 'Verbal Parallels', 176–77.

52 Earl R. Anderson, *Cynewulf: Structure, Style, and Theme in His Poetry*, 17; P. O. E. Gradon, ed., *Cynewulf's Elene*, 22–23; R. D. Fulk, 'Cynewulf: Canon, Dialect, and Date'. Patrick Conner argues that Cynewulf wrote in the tenth century in 'On Dating Cynewulf'. Citations of *Elene* are from Gradon's edition, with slight modernisations and changes in punctuation.

53 The reading of *Elene* as a poem about learning is widely acknowledged. Ellen Wright argues that *Elene* is about the difficulty of attaining spiritual wisdom in 'Cynewulf's *Elene* and the "Singal Sacu"'. Jackson Campbell discusses the multiple revelations in *Elene*, which build up a 'pattern of ignorance, revelation, conversion, baptism, and salvation' in 'Cynewulf's Multiple Revelations',

232. Catharine Regan sees in the empress Helen's encounters with the Jews 'a dramatization of the relationship between the teaching Church and the individual soul' in 'Evangelicism as the Informing Principle of Cynewulf's *Elene*', 259. Christina Heckman reads *Elene* through dialectic, arguing that the invention or finding of the Cross parallels the process of finding arguments, or *inventio*. 'Things in Doubt'. For cognitive processes in *Elene*, see Norma J. Engberg, '*Mod-Mægen* Balance in *Elene, The Battle of Maldon* and *The Wanderer*'; Antonina Harbus, *Cognitive Approaches to Old English Poetry*, 125–26.

54 For discussions of the Cross as sign requiring reading and interpretation, see Varda Fish, 'Theme and Pattern in Cynewulf's *Elene*'; Irvine, 'Anglo-Saxon Literary Theory'.

55 Alfred Holder, ed., *Inventio sanctae crvcis: actorum Cyriaci pars I. latine et graece ymnvs antiqvs de sancta crvce testimonia inventae sanctae crvcis*, 1–2.

56 Ibid., 7, ll. 200–203.

57 The Judas character is often read as a figure for Jewish blindness and hard-heartedness. Fish, 'Theme and Pattern', 11–17; E. Gordon Whatley, 'Bread and Stone: Cynewulf's "Elene" 611–618'; Scheil, *The Footsteps of Israel*, 222–28.

58 On the typological importance of Stephen, see James Doubleday, 'The Speech of Stephen and the Tone of *Elene*'.

59 Dolores Frese notes the verbal echoes with which the narrator connects himself both to Constantine and to Judas. Dolores Warwick Frese, 'The Art of Cynewulf's Runic Signatures', 335.

60 A number of critics interpret the epilogue as integral to the poem and a completion of its themes. John Gardner, 'Cynewulf's *Elene*: Sources and Structure'; Fish, 'Theme and Pattern'; Campbell, 'Cynewulf's Multiple Revelations'.

61 Antonina Harbus, 'Text as Revelation: Constantine's Dream in *Elene*', 650.

62 Irvine suggests that Cynewulf's second discovery of the Cross is through his own writing. Irvine, 'Anglo-Saxon Literary Theory', 43.

63 Cynthia Zollinger sees *Elene*, especially in the epilogue, as a poem about the search for knowledge in the past, though with a focus on historical traditions rather than personal memory. Cynthia Wittman Zollinger, 'Cynewulf's *Elene* and the Patterns of the Past'.

64 Manish Sharma argues that the movement towards illumination and liberation in *Elene* is paralleled by a similar move back towards 'confinement, darkness, and secrecy', noting the reburial of the Cross. 'The Reburial of the Cross in the Old English *Elene*', 281. Such a reading brings *Elene* into accord with a Boethian understanding of learning, a dynamic process of illumination and forgetting, though I do not argue for specific Boethian influence here.

65 This pedagogy on the high seas may also draw on the classical motif of the open sea as a metaphor for heightened spiritual, poetic, or intellectual efforts. For its use by Anglo-Saxons, see Marijane Osborn, 'Venturing upon Deep Waters in *The Seafarer*', 1–6; Irina A. Dumitrescu, '"Pas de Philologie": On Playful Appropriation and the Anglo-Saxon Scholar', 194–96.

66 The miracle in which Jesus calms the storm is found at Mark 4:35–41, Luke 8:22–25 and Matthew 8:23–27.

67 Kenneth Brooks interprets 'reordberend' as an accusative plural, in which case the translation would be, 'how he taught men under the sky'. However, it could also be nominative singular, and applied to Christ.

68 Boenig, *The Acts of Andrew*, 7.

69 Blatt, *Die lateinischen Bearbeitungen*, 53–55.

70 Wilcox, 'Eating People Is Wrong', 208–11; Ruth Waterhouse, 'Self-Reflexivity and "Wraetlic word" in *Bleak House* and *Andreas*', 218–23.

71 In the *Praxeis*, the relevant passage is: 'And when dawn arrived, Andrew awoke and looked about and found himself sitting upon the ground, and he saw his disciples sitting on the ground and woke them'. Boenig, *The Acts of Andrew*, 13. This is the *Casanatensis* version: 'Cum autem beatus andreas expergefactus esset, aspiciens in omni parte putantes se adhuc esse in mare, et vanuit, cumque vidisset discipulos suos in terram habentes et a sompno tenentes, circumduxit oculos suos, et vidit portam civitatis ipsius mermedonie, cepit celerius mirari valde, et in impetu statim excitabit eos dicens.' Blatt, *Die lateinischen Bearbeitungen*, 63–65. The longer version of the Old English homily reads: 'Þa se mergen geworden wæs, þa se haliga Andreas licgende wæs beforan Marmadonia ceastre, and his discipulos þær slæpende wæron mid him, and he hie aweahte'. Bright and Hulbert, *Bright's Anglo-Saxon Reader*, 118.

72 Bruce Dickins and Alan S. C. Ross, eds., *The Dream of the Rood*.

73 Boenig, *The Acts of Andrew*, 7.

74 Blatt, *Die lateinischen Bearbeitungen*, 51.

75 Brooks, *Andreas*, 116–17.

76 Blatt, *Die lateinischen Bearbeitungen*, 141; Lipsius and Bonnet, *Acta apostolorum apocrypha*, 222, 228; Els Rose, *Ritual Memory: The Apocryphal Acts and Liturgical Commemoration in the Early Medieval West (c. 500–1215)*, 167–70.

77 Kiser, 'Andreas and the Lifes Weg'. Kiser does not cite Boethius as a source. For the *uia* in Boethius, see Lerer, *Boethius and Dialogue*, 8, 106–108, 70–74, and passim.

78 On the *Metres*, see Allan A. Metcalf, *Poetic Diction in the Old English Meters of Boethius*; Karmen Lenz, *Ræd and Frofer: Christian Poetics in the Old English Froferboc Meters*, especially 76–88; Paul E. Szarmach, 'Thirty-one Meters'.

79 A conservative approach to arguing for influence between Old English poems would require us to look for unique parallels between two poems. Since some form of the phrase 'findan on ferðe' appears in four Old English poems, it would not qualify as proof of influence in that sense. I argue, however, that the parallel is still significant due to the specific meaning with which the formula is used. In *Elene*, in *Andreas* (which almost certainly borrowed the phrase from *Elene*), and in *Metre 22*, 'findan on ferðe' is used for digging up knowledge or a story from one's own memory. In *Soul and Body I*, the one poem in which the formula is not reproduced exactly, the phrase also has a different meaning: it describes valuation, not searching.

80 Hamilton, 'Diet and Digestion', 149; Irving Jr, 'A Reading of Andreas', 234; Wilcox, 'Eating People Is Wrong', 201.

81 Denis Ferhatović, '*Spolia*-Inflected Poetics of the Old English *Andreas*', 202.

82 Breen understands *Andreas* as a form of mental pilgrimage. Nathan A. Breen, '"What a long, strange trip it's been": Narration, Movement and Revelation in the Old English *Andreas*'.

83 BT, 'fruma', 'ord', 'ordfruma'; *DOE*, 'fruma'.

84 Boenig, *The Acts of Andrew*, 9; Blatt, *Die lateinischen Bearbeitungen*, 59. The Old English homily excises much of the voyage, including this scene.

85 Boenig, *The Acts of Andrew*, 4; Blatt, *Die lateinischen Bearbeitungen*, 41; Bright and Hulbert, *Bright's Anglo-Saxon Reader*, 116.

86 Boenig, *Saint and Hero*, 63–64.

87 Ibid., 64.

88 Ibid., 66.

89 'Sylfætan' is a hapax. BT, 'self-æta'.

90 Hostetter introduced the term 'cannibal poetics' in his conference paper, Aaron Hostetter, 'A Tasty Turn of Phrase: Cannibal Poetics in Andreas'.

91 Shannon Godlove notes that John Chrysostom described Christ drinking his own blood at the Last Supper, thus making him a kind of auto-cannibal, in 'Bodies as Borders: Cannibalism and Conversion in the Old English *Andreas*', 151.

92 Dale Kinney, '*Spolia: Damnatio* and r*enovatio memoriae*', 119.

93 Ferhatović, 'Spolia-Inflected Poetics', 213–14. Here quoting Michael Chabon, 'Fan Fictions: On Sherlock Holmes', 57.

94 Lori Ann Garner, 'The Old English *Andreas* and the Mermedonian Cityscape', 57. *Tigel*, as both Brooks and Garner note, also appears in *The Ruin* to describe ancient buildings.

95 Brooks, *Andreas*, 106–107. *And.* 1235a parallels *Beo.* 1679a 'enta ærgeweorc', and *And.* 1236a parallels *Beo.* 320a 'stræt wæs stanfah'.

96 Ferhatović, 'Spolia-Inflected Poetics', 212; Boenig, *The Acts of Andrew*, 10.

97 Ferhatović, 'Spolia-Inflected Poetics', 214.

98 In the *Praxeis* version of Andrew's address to the pillar, the corresponding passage reads, 'And you will not say, "I am a stone, and I am not worthy to praise the Lord"; for the Lord moulded us from earth, but you are clear of dirt; because of this, from you was given the tablets of the Law.' Boenig, *The Acts of Andrew*, 20. In the *Casanatensis* version and in the Old English homily, Andrew does not mention the commandments.

99 Powell, 'Verbal Parallels', 131–55.

100 Other than the passages I refer to here, Powell also compares *And.* 1487–95 to *Beo.* 229, 527–30, 926, 1783, and 2003. Ibid., 140.

101 Riddles are in the Krapp and Dobbie numbering. George Philip Krapp and Elliott Van Kirk Dobbie, eds., *The Exeter Book*, ASPR 3.

102 Caroline Walker Bynum, 'Wonder', 15–16. *Andreas* most closely resembles what Bynum calls 'the literature of entertainment', texts describing 'monsters or hybrids, distant races, marvelous lands' as well as catastrophic events. Ibid., 12.

103 Dennis Quinn, '*Me audiendi … stupentem:* The Restoration of Wonder in Boethius's *Consolation*', 449–50.

104 Patricia Dailey, 'Riddles, Wonder and Responsiveness in Anglo-Saxon Literature', 468.

105 BT, 'wrætlic'.

106 Joshua Davies, 'The Literary Languages of Old English: Words, Styles, Voices', 272.

107 Krapp and Dobbie, eds., *The Exeter Book*, 227–29.

108 Roy Liuzza, *Old English Poetry: An Anthology*, 43.

109 Burton Raffel, *Poems and Prose from the Old English*, 19.

110 Davies, 'Literary Languages', 273.

111 *Beo.* 1650a, 891a.

112 Quinn, 'Me audiendi … stupentem', 448.

5. Desire

1 Alexander Pope, *Poetry and Prose of Alexander Pope*, 109, ll. 85–86.

2 Magennis' edition and line numbers. The text was previously edited and translated by Skeat, and Leslie Donovan has also published a translation. Walter W. Skeat, ed., *Aelfric's Lives of Saints*, vol. 2, 2–53; Leslie A. Donovan, *Women Saints' Lives in Old English Prose*, 97–120.

3 BT, 'geweman'.

4 J. F. Niermeyer, *Mediae Latinitatis Lexicon Minus*, 'passio'. An Anglo-Saxon glossator of Boethius twice renders *passio* as *felnes*, a feeling or emotion. Herbert Dean Meritt, 'Old English Glosses, Mostly Dry Point', 444.

5 BT, 'þrowing'.

6 The Supplement to BT adds 'passion, strong feeling' to the definition of *þrowung*, but its only example is this line from the *Life of St Mary of Egypt*. T. Northcote Toller, *An Anglo-Saxon Dictionary Supplement*.

7 In this slippage, the Old English translator echoes Gregory the Great's understanding of the relationship between suffering and concupiscence: Et quia per oculorum uisum carnem secuti sumus, de ipsa carne, quam praeceptis Dei praeposuimus, flagellamur. In ipsa quippe cotidie gemitum, in ipsa cruciatum, in ipsa interitum patimur, ut hoc nobis mira dispositione dominus in poenam uerteret, per quod fecimus culpam; nec aliunde esset interim censura supplicii, nisi unde fuerat causa peccati, ut eius carnis amaritudine homo erudiretur ad uitam, cuius oblectatione superbiae peruenit ad mortem. Gregory I, *Moralia in Iob libri xxiii–xxxv*, ed. M. Adriaen ed., 1193; bk 24, ch. 4, sec. 7, ll. 7–14. (And because we have followed the flesh through the sight of the eyes, we are scourged by that same flesh, which we set before the commands of God. In that very flesh we suffer laments, torture, and destruction daily, so that, by a wonderful arrangement, the lord might turn that with which we committed the sin into a punishment for us; so that there should not be a different source for torturous censure than the cause of the sin; so that man, who arrives at death by the flesh's delight in pride, might be educated to life through the bitterness of that flesh.)

8 This is in line with Lynda Coon's observation: 'While the holy man ventures into the world or the wilderness to battle heroically against evil, the holy woman turns inward to heal the fissures of a corrupted self.' Lynda L. Coon, *Sacred Fictions: Holy Women and Hagiography in Late Antiquity*, xviii.

9 Oþre martyras on heora lichaman þrowodon martyrdom for cristes geleafan: ac seo eadige maria næs na lichamlice gemartyrod. ac hire sawul wæs swiðe geangsumod mid micelre þrowunge. þa ða heo stod dreorig forn angean cristes rode & hire leofe cild geseah mid isenum næglum on heardum treowe gefæstnod: Nu is heo mare þonne martyr for þan ðe heo þrowade þone martyrdom on hire sawle þe oþre martyras þrowodon on heora lichaman. Heo lufode crist ofer ealle oþre menn. & for þy wæs eac hire sarnys be him toforan oþra manna. & heo dyde his deað hire agenne deað for þan ðe his þrowung swa swa swurd þurhferde hire sawle. Ælfric, 'XXX. XVVIII kalendas septembris assumptio Sancte Marie Virginis', in *Ælfric's Catholic Homilies: The First Series*, ed. Peter Clemoes, 433–34, ll. 135–56. (Other martyrs suffered martyrdom on account of Christ's faith in their bodies. But the blessed Mary was not physically martyred. But her soul was powerfully anguished with great suffering when she stood sad in front of Christ's cross and saw her dear child bound to a hard tree with iron nails. She is thus a greater martyr because she suffered that martyrdom in her soul that other martyrs suffer in their bodies. She loved Christ above all other men, and because of that her sorrow regarding him was also beyond that of other men. And she made his death her own death because his suffering pierced her soul like a sword.) Compare the similar passage at 'IX. IIII nonas februarii in purificatione Sanctae Mariae', in *Ælfric's Catholic Homilies: The First Series*, ed. Peter Clemoes, 254, ll. 169–80.

10 Paul Szarmach suggests that Mary can be seen as a martyr, citing Sulpicius Severus' description of Martin of Tours' martyrdom in ascetic practice. Paul E. Szarmach, 'More Genre Trouble: The Life of Mary of Egypt', 163–64.

11 Szarmach also notes the moral danger posed by Mary's need to relate her life story. Ibid., 154–55.

12 All of these concepts are knotted together in the Old English version by the verb *genydan*, to compel. BT, 'ge-nydan'.

13 *OEME*, 23–25.

14 The language of exemplarity in the medieval period can often imply both model behaviour and textual copying. This duality is already present in Latin, in which *exemplar* could mean 'transcript, copy' or a 'pattern, model' in the behavioural sense, while *exemplum* had these senses as well as 'a warning example' and a 'way, manner'. Lewis and Short, *A Latin Dictionary*, 'exemplar', 'exemplum'. Old English *bysen* was primarily used for behavioural and moral exemplarity and for illustrative stories, but is also attested for textual copying. *DOE*, 'bysen'. Middle English *saumplarie* was, likewise, used for a written exemplar and spiritual example. *Middle English Dictionary Online*, 'saumplarie'.

15 Jane Stevenson, 'The Holy Sinner: The Life of Mary of Egypt', 20–21.

16 *OEME*, 10–11, 30; 'On the Sources of Non-Ælfrician Lives in the Old English *Lives of Saints*, with Reference to the Cotton-Corpus Legendary'. The Life of Mary of Egypt was also very popular in the later middle ages, with multiple versions in English, Spanish, French, and Norse, as well as translations into Italian, German, Dutch, Irish, Welsh, and Portuguese. *OEME*, 12. For an edition of the various versions in French, see Peter F. Dembowski, ed., *La vie de sainte Marie l'Égyptienne*. For the German tradition, see Konrad Kunze's study of the legend's afterlife in German-speaking lands and his edition of a number of the relevant texts. Konrad Kunze, *Studien zur Legende der heiligen Maria Aegyptiaca im deutschen Sprachgebiet*; *Die Legende der heiligen Maria Aegyptiaca: Ein Beispiel hagiographischer Überlieferung in 16 unveröffentlichten deutschen, niederländischen und lateinischen Fassungen*.

17 *OEME*, 12–13.

18 Peter Jackson and Michael Lapidge, 'The Contents of the Cotton-Corpus Legendary', 32–34. For a critical edition of the Latin *Life* based on tenth- and eleventh-century English manuscripts, along with a translation into English, see Stevenson, 'Vita Sanctae Mariae Egiptiacae'.

19 GL 344 and 754.5 respectively.

20 *OEME*, 30–35, 139.

21 Ibid., 140–209.

22 Ker 162, GL 339.

23 Hugh Magennis, 'Contrasting Features in the Non-Ælfrician Lives in the Old English *Lives of Saints*', 333. For a detailed discussion of the *Life*'s manuscript context, see Szarmach, 'More Genre Trouble', 142–45.

24 Magennis, 'Contrasting Features', 319, 336.

25 Ker 177 and 17, GL 355 and 262 respectively. Only two short passages are present for comparison in all three manuscripts: lines 554–72 and 958–60 in the Magennis edition. *OEME*, 14–15.

26 'Contrasting Features', 336. He has more recently revised his opinion on the style of the work. The translation is now 'a notably formal kind of Old English narrative prose', thought by Magennis to be deliberately shaped to attain 'a register appropriate to the spiritually inspiring subject matter of the story and reflective of its dignity and seriousness'. *OEME*, 44–45.

27 Ruth Mazo Karras notes about later medieval English lives of Mary of Egypt that in versions where she did not charge for sex, her sin was considered 'aggravated by her refusal to accept payment'. Ruth Mazo Karras, *Common Women: Prostitution and Sexuality in Medieval England*, 124.

28 Magennis suggests a comic reading of Zosimus and Mary's geriatric chase scene and of their drawn out, overly polite ritual of asking for a blessing. He adds, however, that the Old English translator does nothing to exacerbate the humour already present in the Latin and Greek versions. 'A Funny Thing Happened on the Way to Heaven: Humorous Incongruity in Old English Saints' Lives'. Andy Orchard traces how the Old English translator uses echo words to render similarly recurring words and phrases in the Latin source. 'Rhetoric and Style in the Old English Life of Mary of Egypt'; 'Hot Lust in

a Cold Climate: Comparison and Contrast in the Old Norse Versions of the Life of Mary of Egypt'. Catherine Brown Tkacz asks how much knowledge of Byzantine theology made it into the Old English version, and to what extent this material would have been understood, in 'Byzantine Theology in the Old English *De transitu Mariae Ægyptiace*'.

29 Clare Lees and Gillian Overing read *Mary of Egypt* allegorically, arguing that the Old English version of the story foregrounds 'the relation of seeing to knowing, the visual to the visionary'. *Double Agents*, 132. See also Lees' essay presenting the same argument, Clare A. Lees, 'Vision and Place in the Old English Life of Mary of Egypt'. Their claim that the *Life* must be read from an allegorical perspective draws on Erich Auerbach's famous essay 'Figura', in which he briefly alludes to Mary of Egypt as a figure for the people of Israel, and on Lynda Coon's contention that the first half of Mary of Egypt's *vita* 'replicates Eve's expulsion from paradise', and that the saint is subsequently transformed into the 'inviolable Virgin Mary'. Erich Auerbach, 'Figura', 61; Coon, *Sacred Fictions*, xiii–xiv. David William Foster also reads the tale allegorically, arguing that Mary is 'very much a new Adam', once again demonstrating the pliancy of the figural approach. David William Foster, 'De Maria Egyptiaca and the Medieval Figural Tradition', 41. Robin Norris argues that the anonymous author of the life wishes to present Mary as a confessor, that is a saint who dies from natural causes rather than through martyrdom, in '*Vitas Matrum*: Mary of Egypt as Female Confessor'. Paul Szarmach argues that the text challenges its readers' generic 'horizon of expectations' in 'More Genre Trouble', 164.

30 Onnaca Heron argues for 'Zosimus' emasculated status' and 'Mary's role as immasculated woman' but her examples in support of the claim that Mary is a 'manly woman' do not demonstrate Mary's manliness as much as they do the general indeterminacy of Mary's character, gender, and body. 'The Lioness in the Text: Mary of Egypt as Immasculated Female Saint', 25–27.

31 Colin Chase, 'Source Study as a Trick with Mirrors: Annihilation of Meaning in the Old English "Mary of Egypt"', 31.

32 Andrew P. Scheil, 'Bodies and Boundaries in the Old English *Life of St. Mary of Egypt*', 137–56.

33 Lees and Overing, *Double Agents*, 141–42.

34 Diane Watt and Clare A. Lees, 'Age and Desire in the Old English *Life of St Mary of Egypt*: A Queerer Time and Place?', 59.

35 Patricia Cox Miller, 'Is There a Harlot in This Text? Hagiography and the Grotesque', 423.

36 For translations of their *vitae* and a brief discussion, see Benedicta Ward, ed., *Harlots of the Desert: A Study of Repentance in Early Monastic Sources*. See also: Ruth Mazo Karras, 'Holy Harlots: Prostitute Saints in Medieval Legend'. On the exemplary usefulness of converted sinners like Mary Magdalene and Mary of Egypt in later medieval England, see Catherine Sanok, *Her Life Historical: Exemplarity and Female Saints' Lives in Late Medieval England*, 126–32.

37 Virginia Burrus, *The Sex Lives of Saints: An Erotics of Ancient Hagiography*, 131. In her discussion of 'erotic chastity', Ruth Mazo Karras argues that medieval people would have clearly delineated between carnal and spiritual love, even when vividly erotic language was used to describe the latter. *Sexuality in Medieval Europe: Doing unto Others*, 67–75. I hold that erotic language used for spiritual ends would lose much of its power if it did not carry carnal associations.

38 Peter Brown, 'The Saint as Exemplar in Late Antiquity', 1.

39 Chapters 3 and 4 show how Anglo-Saxon texts also problematise the idea of exemplary teaching.

40 C. Stephen Jaeger, *The Envy of Angels: Cathedral Schools and Social Ideals in Medieval Europe, 950–1200*, 77–78.

41 Colin Chase points out the addition of *bysen* later in line 61, when the narrative describes how Zosimus worries that he had nothing left to learn. Chase correctly notes that the Latin did not include any version of the word *exemplum*, stating as it does only that Zosimus considered himself 'alterius non indigens in nullo doctrina' (71, not needing any other man's teaching). His conclusion is that 'the addition of *bysen* in the Old English context, where no *exemplum* existed in its predecessors, has given a slightly different sense to spiritual discipleship in the Old English Mary story than it had in the earlier versions. The master is an "exemplar" of spiritual doctrine according to whom, one may suppose, the disciple might correct himself.' It is more accurate, however, to say that the Old English translator strengthens rather than introduces the theme of exemplary teaching; the Latin word does appear in the previous section, where *eius exemplis atque doctrinis* (51, to his examples and teachings) is rendered *to his bysne and to his larum*. Despite this adjustment, the point stands that the Old English translator recognised the depiction of Zosimus as an exemplary, charismatic teacher in the classical form. Chase, 'Source Study', 29.

42 On the use of the *Verba Seniorum* in late Anglo-Saxon England, see O'Brien O'Keeffe, *Stealing Obedience*, 43–46. Biggs et al. cite more than a hundred complete manuscripts of the *Verba Seniorum* from the seventh century to the fifteenth, but stress the difficulty of determining direct use in any given case, especially given the use of intermediate sources in the early Anglo-Saxon period. *Sources of Anglo-Saxon Literary Culture: A Trial Version*, 162–63, 'Vitae patrum'.

43 Illas priores culpas et peccata propter humilitatem sustinui, ut peccatorem me esse crederetis. Novimus enim quod si custodiatur humilitatis virtus, magna salus est animae. *Verba seniorum, PL* 73, col. 751D.

44 Skeat, *Aelfric's Lives of Saints*, 29.

45 Neither BT nor the Supplement give a meaning of 'attempt' for *prowian*.

46 BT, 'cnyssan'; *DOE*, 'cnyssan'.

47 Geoffrey Galt Harpham, *The Ascetic Imperative in Culture and Criticism*, 45.

48 Scheil, 'Bodies and Boundaries'.

49 Coon, *Sacred Fictions*, xiii, 93. Virginia Burrus refines the reference, suggesting that Mary in fact recalls 'Jerome's description of himself as transformed by the

burning sun of the desert into the black beauty celebrated in Song of Songs'. Burrus cites an unpublished essay by Paul B. Harvey for this point. Burrus, *The Sex Lives of Saints*, 148–49.

50 Patricia Cox Miller, 'The Blazing Body: Ascetic Desire in Jerome's Letter to Eustochium', 29.

51 Gregory I, *Moralia in Iob libri i–x*, 222–23; bk 5, ch. 4, sec. 6, ll. 27–34. See also Leclercq, *Love of Learning*, 85.

52 The Old English manuscripts vary on whether Mary raped her fellow passengers or not. BL Cotton Julius E.vii, on which Magennis bases his edition, reads: 'and hu ic to syngigenne genydde ægðer ge þa earman willendan and þa earman syllendan' (430–32, and how I forced to sin both the poor willing ones and the poor ones who gave). BL Cotton Otho B.x reads *nellendan*, suggesting a rather more violent approach (and closer to the Latin and Greek versions). *OEME*, 125; 'Contrasting Features', 332–33.

53 Scheil, 'Bodies and Boundaries', 144.

54 On the relevance of scenes describing sexual endangerment of female saints, see Clare A. Lees, 'Engendering Religious Desire: Sex, Knowledge, and Christian Identity in Anglo-Saxon England', 32.

55 The hunting simile recalls a corresponding trope in Ovid's *Ars amatoria*, where the lover is also described as *venator*. Eleanor Winsor Leach, 'Georgic Imagery in the *Ars amatoria*'. Hunting is frequently used as an erotic metaphor in later medieval literature. In Northrop Frye's words, 'the hunt is normally an image of the masculine erotic, a movement of pursuit and linear thrust, in which there are sexual overtones to the object being hunted'. Northrop Frye, *The Secular Scripture: A Study of the Structure of Romance*, 104. See also Marcelle Thiébaux, *The Stag of Love: The Chase in Medieval Literature*.

56 See the discussion in Chapter 2.

57 Coon, *Sacred Fictions*, 94.

58 *OEME*, 8–9.

59 Diem, 'Encounters', 54–55.

60 Scheil, 'Bodies and Boundaries', 141–42. For the passage in the *Life of St Antony* see Carolinne White, ed., *Early Christian Lives*, 12. Coon believes that Zosimus' first sight of Mary is intended to allude to Jesus' desert encounter with the devil. However, there are no close textual parallels between the description of Mary and Zosimus' meeting and the passage at Matthew 4:1–3 that would prove this is the hagiographer's intention. Coon, *Sacred Fictions*, 86.

61 Benedicta Ward, ed., *The Sayings of the Desert Fathers: The Alphabetical Collection*, 72.

62 Latham, *Revised Medieval Latin Word-List*, 'phantas/ia'.

63 Related words in Old English give a sense of the added associations *scinhiw* attaches to Zosimus' first sight of Mary. A *scinere* is 'one who produces deceptive appearances, a magician', and a *scinlæca* is also 'a magician, necromancer, sorcerer'. *Scingelac* is 'a magical practice', *scingedwola* 'a delusion produced by magic, delusive appearance, phantom', and *scinlac* ranges from 'sorcery', 'a delusion produced by magic', and a 'superstition', to 'a delusive appearance, a spectre, apparition, phantom'.

64 BT, 'hiwung'.

65 In the vernacular prose *Life of St Guthlac* demons appear in a variety of animal shapes, and 'woldon mid heora hiwunge þæs halgan weres mod awendan' (wanted to turn the holy man's mind with their shapes). Paul Gonser, ed., *Das angelsächsische Prosa-Leben des hl. Guthlac*, 139; ch. 8, l. 10. Section 85 of the *Rule of Chrodegang* warns priests against the 'scynlican hiwinga deofla prættes' (phantasmal figures of the devils' trickery). Arthur S. Napier, ed., *The Old English Version of the Enlarged Rule of Chrodegang together with the Latin Original*, 98.

66 Compare David Brakke's point that 'in monastic literature the real women that instruct male monks by shaming them with their virtue inhabit the same world as the real women who tempt male monks by seducing them with their sexuality, often as the instruments of demons ... In some stories these two identities combine.' David Brakke, 'The Lady Appears: Materializations of "Woman" in Early Monastic Literature', 392.

67 BT, 'læran', 'tyhtan'.

68 For a brief discussion of Zosimus' relentless desire for Mary's confession, based on the Greek text of the *Life*, see Virginia Burrus, *Saving Shame: Martyrs, Saints, and Other Abject Subjects*, 143–45.

69 I cite the Latin text here because the Old English translation will be discussed later, but the Old English translation also uses a form of *genydan* for *compellere*.

70 This is how Skeat translates the passage, though Magennis translates 'ondræde' as 'I feared', arguing that 'the verb should be taken as in the preterite indicative, thus conforming to the rule that *þa*, "when", occurs only with the preterite indicative'. Magennis' evidence for this comes from Bruce Mitchell's work on mood and tense. However, Mitchell cites this passage in the *Life of St Mary of Egypt* as an exception to his rule. See Skeat, *Aelfric's Lives of Saints*, 39. *OEME*, p. 127, note to l. 643; Bruce Mitchell, 'Some Problems of Mood and Tense in Old English', 46–47. Elsewhere, Mitchell notes this as one of three 'difficult examples': *Old English Syntax*, Volume 2: *Subordination, Independent Elements, and Element Order*, 310, §2564.

71 Burrus, *The Sex Lives of Saints*, 151.

72 For a similar argument about the rhetoric of desire in Augustine's *Confessions*, see Virginia Burrus, Mark D. Jordan, and Karmen MacKendrick, *Seducing Augustine: Bodies, Desires, Confessions*, 3–4; Margaret R. Miles, *Desire and Delight: A New Reading of Augustine's Confessions*.

Conclusion

1 William Shakespeare, *Romeo and Juliet*, 1.1.228.

2 Note, for example, Allen Frantzen's fulminations about scholars of Old English who 'continue to multiply possibilities rather than assess probabilities' in their interpretations of *Beowulf*. 'Afterword: *Beowulf* and Everything Else', 245.

3 Galit Hasan-Rokem and David Shulman, eds., *Untying the Knot: On Riddles and Other Enigmatic Modes*, 3.

4 Hecht, *Bischofs Wærferth*, 296–97; bk 4, sec. 27.

5 Ibid., 300–301; bk 4, sec. 27.
6 Bertram Colgrave, ed., *Two Lives of Saint Cuthbert*, 16; *Felix's Life of Saint Guthlac*, 16–17.
7 For the purposes of my argument I am comparing Guthlac's death to Boisil's, but it is worth noting that Felix includes textual echoes of Cuthbert's death scene in this passage.
8 For both the prose and verse lives of Cuthbert, Bede used the *Anonymous Life of St Cuthbert*, likely composed at Lindisfarne, as well as the testimony of Herefrith, an abbot of the same monastery. Colgrave, *Two Lives of Saint Cuthbert*, 11–16. For the verse *Life*, see Jaager, *Bedas metrische Vita s. Cuthberti*.
9 Colgrave, *Two Lives of Saint Cuthbert*, 182; ch. 8.
10 The image is on f. 21r of the manuscript, and on the cover of this book.
11 Bede, *Commentary on Revelation*, trans. Faith Wallis, 108 n. 5.
12 Francis J. Moloney, *The Gospel of John*, 6–7.

Bibliography

Reference Works

Adams, J. N. *The Latin Sexual Vocabulary*. London: Gerald Duckworth & Co. Ltd., 1982.

Biggs, Frederick M., Thomas D. Hill, Paul E. Szarmach, with Karen Hammond, eds. *Sources of Anglo-Saxon Literary Culture: A Trial Version*. Center for Medieval and Early Renaissance Studies, State University of New York at Binghamton, 1990.

Bosworth, Joseph, and T. Northcote Toller. *An Anglo-Saxon Dictionary*. London: Oxford University Press, 1898.

Cameron, Angus, Ashley Crandell Amos, Antonette diPaolo Healey et al., *Dictionary of Old English: A to H online*. Toronto: Dictionary of Old English Project, 2016.

Gneuss, Helmut, and Michael Lapidge. *Anglo-Saxon Manuscripts: A Bibliographical Handlist of Manuscripts and Manuscript Fragments Writtten or Owned in England up to 1100*. University of Toronto Press, 2014.

Greenfield, Stanley B., and Fred C. Robinson. *A Bibliography of Publications on Old English Literature to the end of 1972*. University of Toronto Press, 1980.

Ker, N. R. *Catalogue of Manuscripts Containing Anglo-Saxon*. Oxford: Clarendon Press, 1957.

Lapidge, Michael. *The Anglo-Saxon Library*. Oxford University Press, 2006.

Latham, R. E. *Revised Medieval Latin Word-List from British and Irish Sources*. London: British Academy, 1965.

Lewis, Charlton T., and Charles Short, eds. *A Latin Dictionary*. Oxford: Clarendon Press, 1879.

Middle English Dictionary Online. Ann Arbor: University of Michigan Press, 2001. http://quod.lib.umich.edu/m/med/.

Mitchell, Bruce. *Old English Syntax*. Volume 2: *Subordination, Independent Elements, and Element Order*. 2 vols. Oxford: Clarendon Press, 1985.

Niermeyer, J. F. *Mediae Latinitatis Lexicon Minus*. Leiden: E. J. Brill, 1984.

Toller, T. Northcote. *An Anglo-Saxon Dictionary Supplement*. Oxford University Press, 1921.

Primary Sources

Aarts, Florent Gérard Antoine Marie, ed. *The Pater Noster of Richard Ermyte: A Late Middle English Exposition of the Lord's Prayer*. Nijmegen: Gebr. Janssen, 1967.

Adriaen, M., ed. *Magni Aurelii Cassiodori Expositio Psalmorum i–lxx*, CCSL 97, 1958.

Anlezark, Daniel, ed. *The Old English Dialogues of Solomon and Saturn*. Cambridge: D. S. Brewer, 2009.

Bayless, Martha, and Michael Lapidge, eds. *Collectanea Pseudo-Bedae, Scriptores Latini Hiberniae*. Dublin: Dublin Institute for Advanced Studies, 1998.

Bede. *Commentary on Revelation*, trans. Faith Wallis. Liverpool University Press, 2013.

   Homilies on the Gospels. Book Two: Lent to The Dedication of the Church, trans. Lawrence T. Martin and David Hurst. Kalamazoo, MI: Cistercian Publications, 1991.

   In Marci evangelium expositio. PL 92. Cols. 131D–302C.

   On the Song of Songs and Selected Writings, trans. Arthur Holder. The Classics of Western Spirituality. New York and Mahwah, NJ: Paulist Press, 2011.

Bethurum, Dorothy, ed. *The Homilies of Wulfstan*. Oxford: Clarendon Press, 1957.

Bischoff, Bernhard, and Michael Lapidge, eds. *Biblical Commentaries from the Canterbury School of Theodore and Hadrian*. Cambridge University Press, 1994.

Blatt, Franz, ed. *Die lateinischen Bearbeitungen der Acta Andreae et Matthiae apud anthropophagos*. Gießen: Alfred Töpelmann, 1930.

Boenig, Robert. *The Acts of Andrew in the Country of the Cannibals: Translations from the Greek, Latin, and Old English*. Garland Library of Medieval Literature. New York and London: Garland Publishing, 1991.

Boethius. *The Consolation of Philosophy*, trans. Richard Green. Indianapolis, IN: Bobbs-Merrill, 1962.

Bright, James W., and James R. Hulbert, eds. *Bright's Anglo-Saxon Reader*. New York: Holt, Reinhart and Winston, 1963.

Brooks, Kenneth R., ed. *Andreas and the Fates of the Apostles*. Oxford: Clarendon Press, 1961.

Carnicelli, Thomas A., ed. *King Alfred's Version of St. Augustine's Soliloquies*. Cambridge, MA: Harvard University Press, 1969.

Cassian, John. 'De institutis coenobiorum.' In *Iohannis Cassiani De institutis coenobiorum et De octo principalium vitiorum remediis libri xii; De incarnatione Domini contra Nestorium libri vii*, ed. Michael Petschenig. CSEL 17. Vienna: F. Tempsky, 1888. 1–231.

Cilluffo, Gilda. 'Il Salomone e Saturno in Prosa del ms. CCCC 422.' *Quaderni di Filologia Germanica* 2 (1981).

Clemoes, Peter, ed. *Ælfric's Catholic Homilies: The First Series*. EETS SS 17. London: Oxford University Press, 1997.

Clubb, Merrel Dare, ed. *Christ and Satan: An Old English Poem*. New Haven, CT: Yale University Press, 1925.

Colgrave, Bertram, and R. A. B. Mynors, eds. *Bede's Ecclesiastical History of the English People.* Oxford: Clarendon Press, 1969.

Colgrave, Bertram, ed. *The Earliest Life of Gregory the Great, by an Anonymous Monk of Whitby.* Lawrence, KS: University of Kansas Press, 1968.

Felix's Life of Saint Guthlac. Cambridge University Press, 1956.

Two Lives of Saint Cuthbert. Cambridge University Press, 1940.

Cross, James E., and Thomas D. Hill, eds. *The Prose Solomon and Saturn and Adrian and Ritheus.* University of Toronto Press, 1982.

Daly, Lloyd William, and Walther Suchier. *Altercatio Hadriani Augusti et Epicteti Philosophi.* Urbana, IL: University of Illinois Press, 1939.

Dekkers, D. E., and J. Fraipont, eds. *Sancti Aurelii Augustini Enarrationes in Psalmos i–l,* CCSL 38. Turnhout: Brepols, 1956.

Dembowski, Peter F., ed. *La vie de sainte Marie l'Égyptienne.* Geneva: Libraire Droz, 1977.

Dickins, Bruce, and Alan S. C. Ross, eds. *The Dream of the Rood.* Methuen's Old English Library. London: Methuen, 1963.

Donovan, Leslie A. *Women Saints' Lives in Old English Prose.* Cambridge: D. S. Brewer, 1999.

Duff, E. Gordon, ed. *The Dialogue or Communing between the Wise King Solomon and Marcolphus.* London: Lawrence and Bullen, 1892.

Ehwald, Rudolf, ed. *Aldhelmi Opera Omnia.* MGH, Auctores Antiquissimi, 15. Berlin, 1919.

Fuchs, Harald, and Hanspeter Müller, eds. *Aurelius Augustinus: Selbstgespräche. Von der Unsterblichkeit der Seele.* Düsseldorf: Artemis & Winkler, 2002.

Fulk, R. D., Robert E. Bjork, and John D. Niles, eds. *Klaeber's Beowulf.* 4th ed. University of Toronto Press, 2014.

Garmonsway, G. N., ed. *Ælfric's Colloquy.* 2nd ed. Methuen's Old English Library. London: Methuen, 1947.

Godden, Malcolm, and Susan Irvine, eds. *The Old English Boethius.* 2 vols. Oxford University Press, 2009.

Godman, Peter, ed. *Alcuin: The Bishops, Kings, and Saints of York.* Oxford: Clarendon Press, 1982.

Goetz, Georgius, ed. *Hermeneumata Pseudodositheana, Corpus Glossariorum Latinorum.* Amsterdam: Adolf M. Hakkert, 1965.

Gonser, Paul, ed. *Das angelsächsische Prosa-Leben des hl. Guthlac.* Heidelberg: Carl Winter, 1909.

Gradon, P. O. E., ed. *Cynewulf's Elene.* Methuen's Old English Library. London: Methuen, 1958.

Gregory I. *Liber regulae pastoralis. PL* 77. Cols. 13A–128A.

Moralia in Iob libri i–x, ed. M. Adriaen. CCSL 143, 1979.

Moralia in Iob libri xxiii–xxxv, ed. M. Adriaen. CCSL 143B, 1985.

Green, R. P. H., ed. *Augustine: De doctrina christiana.* Oxford: Clarendon Press, 1995.

Gwara, Scott, ed. *Latin Colloquies from Pre-Conquest Britain.* Toronto: Pontifical Institute of Mediaeval Studies, 1996.

Gwara, Scott, and David Porter, eds. *Anglo-Saxon Conversations: The Colloquies of Ælfric Bata*. Woodbridge: Boydell Press, 1997.

Hecht, Hans, ed. *Bischofs Wærferth von Worcester Übersetzung der Dialoge Gregors des Grossen*. Darmstadt: Wissenschaftliche Buchgesellschaft, 1965.

'Here begynneth a lytell geste how the plowman lerned his pater noster.' London: Wynkyn de Worde, 1510.

Holder, Alfred, ed. *Inventio sanctae crvcis: actorum Cyriaci pars I. latine et graece ymnvs antiqvs de sancta crvce testimonia inventae sanctae crvcis*. Leipzig: Teubner, 1889.

Holtz, Louis, ed. *Donat et la tradition de l'enseignement grammatical: Étude et édition critique*. Paris: Centre National de la Recherche Scientifique, 1981.

Howell, Wilbur Samuel, trans. *The Rhetoric of Alcuin and Charlemagne*. New York: Russell and Russell, 1965.

Hurst, D., ed. *Bedae Venerabilis Opera, Pars II. Opera exegetica. In Lucae euangelium expositio. In Marci euangelium expositio*. CCSL 120, 1960.

Bedae Venerabilis Opera, Pars II, Opera exegetica, 2B. CCSL 121B, 1983.

Bedae Venerabilis Opera, Pars III. Opera homiletica. CCSL 122, 1955.

Jaager, Werner, ed. *Bedas metrische Vita s. Cuthberti*. Leipzig: Mayer & Müller, 1935.

Jones, C. W., ed. *Bedae Venerabilis Opera, Pars I, Opera didascalica*, CCSL 123A. Turnhout: Brepols, 1975.

Jerome. *Commentariorum in evangelium Matthaei ad Eusebium libri quator*. PL 26. Cols. 15–218D.

Kemble, John Mitchell, ed. *The Dialogue of Salomon and Saturnus*. London: Ælfric Society, 1857. Reprint, New York: AMS Press, 1974.

Krapp, George Philip, ed. *Andreas and The Fates of the Apostles: Two Anglo-Saxon Narrative Poems*. Boston, MA: Ginn & Company, 1906.

The Vercelli Book, ASPR 2. New York: Columbia University Press, 1932.

Krapp, George Philip, and Elliott Van Kirk Dobbie, eds. *The Exeter Book*, ASPR 3. New York: Columbia University Press, 1936.

Kunze, Konrad, ed. *Die Legende der heiligen Maria Aegyptiaca: Ein Beispiel hagiographischer Überlieferung in 16 unveröffentlichten deutschen, niederländidschen und lateinischen Fassungen*. Berlin: Erich Schmidt Verlag, 1978.

Laistner, M. L. W., ed. *Bedae Venerabilis Opera, Pars II, Opera Exegetica*, Volume 4, CCSL 121, 1975.

Lapidge, Michael. 'Three Latin Poems from Æthelwold's School at Winchester.' *ASE* 1 (1972): 85–137.

Lawless, George. *Augustine of Hippo and his Monastic Rule*. Oxford: Clarendon Press, 1987.

Lindsay, W. M., ed. *Isidori Hispalensis episcopi Etymologiarum sive originum libri XX*. 2 vols. Oxford University Press, 1911.

Lipsius, Richard Adelbert, and Maximilien Bonnet, eds. *Acta apostolorum apocrypha*, Volume 1. Leipzig: Hermann Mendelssohn, 1898.

Liuzza, Roy. *Old English Poetry: An Anthology*. Peterborough, ON: Broadview, 2014.

Löfstedt, Bengt, ed. *Virgilius Maro Grammaticus Opera Omnia*. Munich and Leipzig: K. G. Saur, 2003.

Lucas, Peter J., ed. *Exodus*. University of Exeter Press, 1994.

Magennis, Hugh, ed. *The Old English Life of St Mary of Egypt*. University of Exeter Press, 2002.

Marlowe, Christopher. *The Complete Plays*. Harmondsworth, Middlesex: Penguin, 1969.

Marsden, Richard, ed. *The Old English Heptateuch and Ælfric's Libellus de Veteri Testamento et Novo*, Volume 1: *Introduction and Text, EETS 330*. Oxford University Press, 2008.

Menner, Robert J., ed. *The Poetical Dialogues of Solomon and Saturn*. London: Oxford University Press, 1941.

Milfull, Inge B. *The Hymns of the Anglo-Saxon Church: A Study and Edition of the 'Durham Hymnal'*. Cambridge University Press, 1996.

Moreschini, Claudio, ed. *Anicius Manlius Severinus Boethius: De consolatione philosophiae. Opuscula theologica*. 2nd ed. Munich: K. G. Saur, 2005.

Morin, G., ed. *S. Hieronymi Presbyteri Opera, Pars I. Opera Exegetica*. CCSL 72, 1959.

Morris, R., ed. *The Blickling Homilies*. EETS 58, 63, 73. London: Oxford University Press, 1967.

Musset, Alfred de. *Poésies nouvelles 1836–1852*. Paris: Bibliothèque-Charpentier, 1908.

Napier, Arthur S., ed. *The Old English Version of the Enlarged Rule of Chrodegang together with the Latin Original …*, EETS, OS 150. London: Kegan Paul, Trench, Trübner & Co., and Humphrey Milford, Oxford University Press, 1916.

North, Richard, and Michael Bintley, eds. *Andreas: An Edition*. Liverpool University Press, 2015.

O'Neill, Patrick P., ed. *King Alfred's Old English Prose Translation of the First Fifty Psalms*. Cambridge, MA: Medieval Academy of America, 2001.

Petschenig, Michael, ed. *Iohannis Cassiani Conlationes XXIIII*, ed. Michael Petschenig. CSEL 13, part 2. Vienna: C. Gerold's Sons, 1886.

Plummer, Charles, ed. *Venerabilis Bedae opera historica*. 2 vols. Volume 1. Oxford: Clarendon Press, 1896.

Pope, Alexander. *Poetry and Prose of Alexander Pope*, ed. Aubrey Williams. Boston: Houghton Mifflin, 1969.

Pope, John C., ed. *Homilies of Ælfric: A Supplementary Collection*. Volume 2, EETS OS 260. London: Oxford University Press, 1967.

Porter, David W., ed. *Excerptiones de Prisciano: The Source for Ælfric's Latin–Old English Grammar*. Cambridge: D. S. Brewer, 2002.

Porter, Nancy Stork, ed. *Enigmata*. In *Through a Gloss Darkly: Aldhelm's Riddles in the British Library MS Royal 12.C.xxiii*. Toronto: Pontifical Institute of Mediaeval Studies, 1990.

'The proude wyues pater noster that wolde go gaye, and vndyd her husbonde and went her waye.' London: In Paules Churche yearde at the sygne of the Swane by Iohn Kynge, 1560.

Quiller-Couch, A. T., ed. *The Oxford Book of English Verse 1250–1900*. Oxford: Clarendon Press, 1906.

Quintilian. *The Orator's Education. Books 1–2*. Trans. Donald A. Russell. Loeb Classical Library. Cambridge, MA: Harvard University Press, 2001.

Rabelais. *Gargantua*. Paris: Gallimard, 1969.

Raffel, Burton. *Poems and Prose from the Old English*. New Haven, CT: Yale University Press, 1998.

Rule, Martin, ed. *Eadmeri historia novorum in Anglia, et opuscula duo de vita sancti Anselmi et quibusdam miraculis ejus*. London: Her Majesty's Stationery Office, 1884.

Schreiber, Caroline, ed. *King Alfred's Old English Translation of Pope Gregory the Great's Regula pastoralis and its Cultural Context*. Frankfurt am Main: Peter Lang, 2002.

Scragg, Donald G., ed. *The Vercelli Homilies and Related Texts*. EETS OS 300. Oxford University Press, 1992.

Shakespeare, William. *Romeo and Juliet*, ed. G. Blakemore Evans. Updated ed. The New Cambridge Shakespeare. Cambridge University Press, 2003.

Skeat, Walter W., ed. *Aelfric's Lives of Saints*. Volume 2, EETS OS 94. London: Keegan Paul, 1900.

Skutella, Martin, ed. *S. Aureli Augustini confessionum libri xiii*. Berlin: Walter de Gruyter, 2009.

Stevenson, William Henry, ed. *Early Scholastic Colloquies*. Oxford: Clarendon Press, 1929.

Stevenson, William Henry, and Dorothy Whitelock, eds. *Asser's Life of King Alfred: Together with the Annals of Saint Neots Erroneously Ascribed to Asser*. Oxford University Press, 1998.

Stubbs, William, ed. *Memorials of Saint Dunstan, Archbishop of Canterbury*. London: Her Majesty's Stationery Office, 1874. Reprint, Wiesbaden: Kraus Reprint Ltd, 1965.

Subrenat, Jean. 'Quatre patrenostres parodiques.' In *La Prière au moyen-age (littérature et civilisation)*. Senefiance, 515–47. Aix-en-Provence: CUER MA, Université de Provence, 1981.

Sweet, Henry, ed. *King Alfred's West Saxon Version of Gregory's Pastoral Care*, EETS OS 45. London: K. Paul, 1871. Reprint, 1909.

Symons, Thomas, and Sigrid Spath, eds. *Regularis concordia anglicae nationis. In Consuetudinum saeculi X/XI/XII monumenta non-Cluniacensia*, ed. Kassius Hallinger, 61–147. Corpus Consuetudinum Monasticarum. Siegburg, 1984.

Tangl, Michael, ed. *Die Briefe des heiligen Bonifatius und Lullus, MGH, Epistolae Selectae*. Berlin: Weidmannsche Buchhandlung, 1916.

Tertullian. *Ad martyres liber*. PL 1. Cols. 619–628A.

Thomason, H. J., ed. *Prudentius*. Volume 2, Loeb Classical Library. Cambridge, MA: Harvard University Press, 1953.

Tischendorf, Constantin, ed. *Acta apostolorum apocrypha*. Leipzig: Avenarius and Mendelssohn, 1851.

Verba seniorum. PL 73. Cols. 740–810C.

Vogüé, Adalbert de, ed. *Grégoire le Grand: Dialogues. Livres I–III,* Volume 2. Sources Chrétiennes 260. Paris: Éditions du Cerf, 1979.

Ward, Benedicta, ed. *Harlots of the Desert: A Study of Repentance in Early Monastic Sources*. Kalamazoo, MI: Cistercian Publications, 1987.

The Sayings of the Desert Fathers: The Alphabetical Collection. Kalamazoo, MI: Cistercian Publications, 1975.

Weber, Robert, ed. *Biblia sacra iuxta Vulgatam versionem*. Stuttgart: Deutsche Bibelgesellschaft, 1994.

White, Carolinne, ed. *Early Christian Lives*. London: Penguin Books, 1998.

Whiting, Ella Keats, ed. *The Poems of John Audelay*. EETS OS 184. Oxford: Humphrey Milford, Oxford University Press, 1931.

Whitman, Walt. *Complete Poetry and Selected Prose*, ed. James E. Miller, Jr. Boston, MA: Houghton Mifflin, 1959.

Woolf, Rosemary, ed. *Juliana*. Methuen's Old English Library. New York: Appleton-Century-Crofts, 1966.

Zupitza, Julius, ed. *Aelfrics Grammatik und Glossar*. Berlin: Max Niehans Verlag, 1966. Reprint, 1880 edition, with preface by Helmut Gneuss.

Secondary Sources

Adams, J. N. '*Culus, Clunes* and their Synonyms in Latin.' *Glotta* 59.3/4 (1981): 231–64.

Ahearne-Kroll, Stephen P. 'Challenging the Divine: LXX Psalm 21 in the Passion Narrative of the Gospel of Mark.' In *The Trial and Death of Jesus: Essays on the Passion Narrative in Mark*, eds. Geert van Oyen and Tom Shepherd, 119–48. Leuven: Peeters, 2006.

'Psalms in the New Testament.' In *The Oxford Handbook of the Psalms*, ed. William P. Brown, 269–80. Oxford University Press, 2014.

Althusser, Louis. 'Ideology and Ideological State Apparatuses (Notes towards an Investigation).' Trans. Ben Brewster. In *Lenin and Philosophy, and Other Essays*, 85–126. New York: Monthly Review Press, 2001.

Althusser, Louis, and Étienne Balibar. *Lire le Capital*. 2 vols. Volume 1. Paris: François Maspero, 1973.

Anderson, Earl R. *Cynewulf: Structure, Style, and Theme in His Poetry*. Rutherford: Fairleigh Dickinson University Press, 1983.

'Social Idealism in Ælfric's *Colloquy*.' *ASE* 3 (1974): 153–62.

Ariès, Philippe. *Centuries of Childhood: A Social History of Family Life*, trans. Robert Baldick. New York: Vintage, 1960.

Attridge, Harold W. 'Giving Voice to Jesus: Use of the Psalms in the New Testament.' In *Psalms in Community: Jewish and Christian Textual, Liturgical, and Artistic Traditions*, eds. Harold W. Attridge and Margot Elsbeth Fassler, 101–12. Leiden: Brill, 2003.

Auerbach, Erich. 'Figura.' In *Scenes from the Drama of European Literature: Six Essays*, 11–76. New York: Meridian Books, 1959.

Aurner, Nellie Slayton. 'Bede and Pausanias.' *MLN* 41.8 (1926): 535–36.

Bagley, Ayers. 'Grammar as Teacher: A Study in the Iconics of Education.' *Studies in Medieval and Renaissance Teaching* 1.1 (Spring 1990): 17–48.

Bayless, Martha. '*Beatus Quid Est* and the Study of Grammar in Late Anglo-Saxon England.' In *History of Linguistic Thought*, ed. Law (q.v.), 67–110.
  Parody in the Middle Ages: The Latin Tradition. Ann Arbor, MI: University of Michigan Press, 1996.
Bedingfield, M. Bradford. *The Dramatic Liturgy of Anglo-Saxon England*. Woodbridge, Suffolk: Boydell Press, 2002.
Bender-Davis, Jeannine M. 'Ælfric's Techniques of Translation and Adaptation as Seen in the Composition of his Old English "Latin Grammar".' Unpublished doctoral thesis, Pennsylvania State University (1985).
Berger, James. 'Falling Towers and Postmodern Wild Children: Oliver Sacks, Don DeLillo, and Turns against Language.' *PMLA* 120.2 (2005): 341–61.
Best, Stephen, and Sharon Marcus. 'Surface Reading: An Introduction.' *Representations* 108.1 (2009): 1–21.
Biggs, Frederick M. 'The Passion of Andreas: *Andreas* 1398–1491.' *Studies in Philology* 85.4 (1988): 413–27.
Bjork, Robert E., ed. *The Cynewulf Reader*. New York and London: Routledge, 2001.
Blair, Peter Hunter. 'Whitby as a Centre of Learning in the Seventh Century.' In *Learning and Literature in Anglo-Saxon England: Studies Presented to Peter Clemoes on the Occasion of his Sixty-fifth Birthday*, eds. Michael Lapidge and Helmut Gneuss, 2–32. Cambridge University Press, 1985.
Blake, N. F. 'Cædmon's Hymn.' *N&Q* 207 (1962): 243–46.
Boenig, Robert. '*Andreas*, the Eucharist, and Vercelli.' *JEGP* 79.3 (1980): 313–31.
  Saint and Hero: Andreas and Medieval Doctrine. Lewisburg, PA: Bucknell University Press, 1991.
Bolton, D. K. 'The Study of the Consolation of Philosophy in Anglo-Saxon England.' *Archives d'histoire doctrinale et littéraire du moyen age* 52 (1978): 3–78.
Bolton, W. F. 'Boethius, Alfred, and *Deor* Again.' *MP* 69.3 (1972): 222–27.
  'Boethius and a Topos in *Beowulf*.' In *Saints, Scholars, and Heroes: Studies in Medieval Culture in Honour of Charles W. Jones*, eds. Margot H. King and Wesley M. Stephens, 15–43. Collegeville, MN: Hill Monastic Manuscript Library, Saint John's Abbey and University, 1979.
Bonner, Gerald, ed. *Famulus Christi: Essays in Commemoration of the Thirteenth Centenary of the Birth of the Venerable Bede*. London: SPCK, 1976.
Bose, Mishtooni. 'From Exegesis to Appropriation: The Medieval Solomon.' *Medium Aevum* 65.2 (1996): 187–210.
Boynton, Susan. 'Training for the Liturgy as a Form of Monastic Education.' In *Medieval Monastic Education*, eds. George Ferzoco and Carolyn Muessig, 7–20. London and New York: Leicester University Press, 2000.
Brakke, David. 'The Lady Appears: Materializations of "Woman" in Early Monastic Literature.' *JMEMS* 33.3 (Fall 2003): 387–402.
Breen, Nathan A. '"What a long, strange trip it's been": Narration, Movement and Revelation in the Old English *Andreas*.' *Essays in Medieval Studies* 25 (2008): 71–79.
Bremmer, Rolf Hendrik, and Kees Dekker, eds. *Foundations of Learning: The Transfer of Encyclopaedic Knowledge in the Early Middle Ages*. Paris, Leuven, and Dudley, MA: Peeters, 2007.

Practice in Learning: The Transfer of Encyclopaedic Knowledge in the Early Middle Ages. Paris, Leuven, and Dudley, MA: Peeters, 2010.

Brooks, Nicholas. *The Early History of the Church of Canterbury: Christ Church from 597 to 1066*. Leicester University Press, 1984.

Brown, George H. 'The Psalms as the Foundation of Anglo-Saxon Learning.' In *The Place of the Psalms in the Intellectual Culture of the Middle Ages*, ed. Nancy Van Deusen, 1–23. Albany, NY: State University of New York Press, 1999.

Brown, Michelle P. 'The Role of the Wax Tablet in Medieval Literacy: A Reconsideration in Light of a Recent Find from York.' *British Library Journal* 20 (1994): 1–16.

Brown, Peter. 'The Saint as Exemplar in Late Antiquity.' *Representations* 2 (1983): 1–25.

Bullough, D. A. 'The Educational Tradition in England from Alfred to Ælfric: Teaching *utriusque linguae.*' In *Carolingian Renewal: Sources and Heritage*, 297–334. Manchester University Press, 1991.

Burrus, Virginia. *Saving Shame: Martyrs, Saints, and Other Abject Subjects*. Philadelphia, PA: University of Pennsylvania Press, 2008.

The Sex Lives of Saints: An Erotics of Ancient Hagiography. Philadelphia, PA: University of Pennsylvania Press, 2004.

Burrus, Virginia, Mark D. Jordan, and Karmen MacKendrick. *Seducing Augustine: Bodies, Desires, Confessions*. New York: Fordham University Press, 2010.

Busse, Wilhelm. 'Neo-Exegetical Criticism and Old English Poetry: A Critique of the Typological and Allegorical Appropriation of Medieval Literature.' *REAL. The Yearbook of Research in English and American Literature* 2 (1984): 1–54.

Buttenwieser, Ellen Clune. *Studien über die Verfasserschaft des Andreas*. Heidelberg: E. Geisendörfer, 1898.

Bynum, Caroline Walker. 'Wonder.' *American Historical Review* 102.1 (1997): 1–26.

Calder, Daniel G. 'Figurative Language and its Contexts in *Andreas*: A Study in Medieval Expressionism.' In *Modes of Interpretation in Old English Literature: Essays in Honour of Stanley B. Greenfield*, eds. Phyllis Rugg Brown, Georgia Ronan Crampton and Fred C. Robinson, 115–36. University of Toronto Press, 1986.

Campbell, Jackson J. 'Cynewulf's Multiple Revelations.' In *The Cynewulf Reader*, ed. Bjork (q.v.), 229–50.

Cannon, Christopher. 'Form.' In *Oxford Twenty-First Century Approaches to Literature: Middle English*, ed. Paul Strohm, 177–90. Oxford University Press, 2007.

The Grounds of English Literature. Oxford University Press, 2004.

Capes, David B. 'Imitatio Christi and the Gospel Genre.' *Bulletin for Biblical Research* 13.1 (2003): 1–19.

Carlisle, Janice. 'Spectacle as Government: Dickens and the Working-Class Audience.' In *The Performance of Power: Theatrical Discourse and Politics*, eds. Sue-Ellen Case and Janelle Reinelt, 163–80. Iowa City, IA: University of Iowa Press, 1991.

Carruthers, Mary. *The Book of Memory: A Study of Memory in Medieval Culture.* Cambridge University Press, 1990.

The Craft of Thought: Meditation, Rhetoric, and the Making of Images, 400–1200. Cambridge University Press, 1998.

'Invention, Mnemonics, and Stylistic Ornament in *Psychomachia* and *Pearl.*' In *The Endless Knot: Essays on Old and Middle English in Honor of Marie Borroff*, eds. M. Teresa Tavormina and R. F. Yeager, 201–13. Cambridge: D. S. Brewer, 1995.

'Reading with Attitude, Remembering the Book.' In *The Book and the Body*, eds. Dolores Warwick Frese and Katherine O'Brien O'Keeffe, 1–33. University of Notre Dame, 1997.

Casteen, John. '*Andreas*: Mermedonian Cannibalism and Figural Narration.' *NM* 75.1 (1974): 74–78.

Cavill, Paul. '*Beowulf* and *Andreas*: Two Maxims.' *Neophilologus* 77 (1993): 479–87.

Chabon, Michael. 'Fan Fictions: On Sherlock Holmes.' In *Maps and Legends: Reading and Writing along the Borderlands*, 35–57. San Francisco, CA: McSweeney's Books, 2008.

Chardonnens, László Sándor, and Bryan Carella, eds. *Secular Learning in Anglo-Saxon England: Exploring the Vernacular.* Amsterdam: Rodopi, 2012.

Chase, Colin. 'Source Study as a Trick with Mirrors: Annihilation of Meaning in the Old English "Mary of Egypt".' In *Sources of Anglo-Saxon Culture*, eds. Paul E. Szarmach with Virginia Darrow Oggins, 23–33. Kalamazoo, MI: Medieval Institute Publications, 1986.

Cohen, Jeffrey Jerome. *Medieval Identity Machines.* Minneapolis, MN: University of Minnesota Press, 2003.

Coleman, Joyce. *Public Reading and the Reading Public in Late Medieval England and France.* Cambridge University Press, 1996.

Conner, Patrick W. 'On Dating Cynewulf.' In *The Cynewulf Reader*, ed. Bjork (q.v.), 23–56.

Contreni, John J. 'The Patristic Legacy to c. 1000.' In *The New Cambridge History of the Bible*, eds. Marsden and Matter (q.v.), 505–35.

Coon, Lynda L. *Sacred Fictions: Holy Women and Hagiography in Late Antiquity.* Philadelphia, PA: University of Pennsylvania Press, 1997.

Copeland, Rita, ed. *Criticism and Dissent in the Middle Ages.* Cambridge University Press, 1996.

Pedagogy, Intellectuals, and Dissent in the Later Middle Ages: Lollardy and Ideas of Learning. Cambridge University Press, 2001.

Rhetoric, Hermeneutics, and Translation in the Middle Ages: Academic Traditions and Vernacular Texts. Cambridge University Press, 1991.

Courcelle, Pierre. *La consolation de philosophie dans la tradition littéraire: Antécédents et postérité de Boèce.* Paris: Études Augustiniennes, 1967.

Cowart, David. *Trailing Clouds: Immigrant Fictions in Contemporary America.* Ithaca, NY: Cornell University Press, 2006.

Crain, Patricia. *The Story of A: A Poetics of Alphabetization in America from The New England Primer to The Scarlet Letter.* Stanford University Press, 2000.

Cranfield, C. E. B. *The Gospel According to Mark: An Introduction and Commentary*. Cambridge University Press, 1959.

Crawford, Sally. *Childhood in Anglo-Saxon England*. Stroud: Sutton Publishing, 1999.

Crépin, André. 'Bede and the Vernacular.' In *Famulus Christi*, ed. Bonner (q.v.), 170–92.

Dailey, Patricia. 'Riddles, Wonder and Responsiveness in Anglo-Saxon Literature.' In *The Cambridge History*, ed. Lees (q.v.), 451–72.

Daley, Brian. 'Finding the Right Key: The Aims and Strategies of Early Christian Interpretation of the Psalms.' In *Psalms in Community: Jewish and Christian Textual, Liturgical, and Artistic Traditions*, eds. Harold W. Attridge and Margot Elsbeth Fassler, 189–205. Leiden: Brill, 2003.

Das, Satyendra Kumar. *Cynewulf and the Cynewulf Canon*. Calcutta University Press, 1942.

Davies, Joshua. 'The Literary Languages of Old English: Words, Styles, Voices.' In *The Cambridge History*, ed. Lees (q.v.), 257–77.

Day, Virginia. 'The Influence of the Catechetical *Narratio* on Old English and Some Other Medieval Literature.' *ASE* 3 (1974): 51–61.

DeGregorio, Scott. 'Affective Spirituality: Theory and Practice in Bede and Alfred the Great.' *Essays in Medieval Studies* 22 (2005): 129–39.

'Literary Contexts: Cædmon's Hymn as a Center of Bede's World.' In *Cædmon's Hymn*, eds. Frantzen and Hines (q.v.), 51–79.

Dendle, Peter. *Satan Unbound: The Devil in Old English Narrative Literature*. University of Toronto Press, 2001.

Dickson, Patricia S. 'Acting French: Drama Techniques in the Second Language Classroom.' *French Review* 63.2 (1989): 300–11.

Diem, Albrecht. 'Encounters between Monks and Demons in Latin Texts of Late Antiquity and the Early Middle Ages.' In *Miracles and the Miraculous in Medieval Germanic and Latin Literature*, eds. K. E. Olsen, A. Harbus, and T. Hofstra, 51–67. Leuven: Peeters, 2004.

Dionisotti, A. C. 'Greek Grammars and Dictionaries in Carolingian Europe.' In *The Sacred Nectar of the Greeks: The Study of Greek in the West in the Early Middle Ages*, ed. Michael W. Herren, 1–56. University of London King's College, 1988.

Discenza, Nicole Guenther. *The King's English: Strategies of Translation in the Old English Boethius*. Albany, NY: State University of New York Press, 2005.

Dodson, Sarah L. 'FAQs: Learning Languages through Drama.' *Texas Papers in Foreign Language Education* 5.1 (2000): 129–41.

Doležalová, Lucie. 'On Mistake and Meaning: *Scinderationes fonorum* in Medieval *artes memoriae*, Mnemonic Verses, and Manuscripts.' *Language and History* 52.1 (2009): 26–40.

Doubleday, James. 'The Speech of Stephen and the Tone of *Elene*.' In *Anglo-Saxon Poetry*, eds. Nicholson and Frese (q.v.), 116–23.

Duffy, Eamon. *The Stripping of the Altars: Traditional Religion in England 1400–1580*. 2nd ed. New Haven, CT: Yale University Press, 2005.

Dumitrescu, Irina A. 'Bede's Liberation Philology: Releasing the English Tongue.' *PMLA* 128.1 (2013): 40–56.

'The Grammar of Pain in Ælfric Bata's *Colloquies*.' *Forum for Modern Language Studies* 45.3 (2009): 239–53.

'"Pas de Philologie": On Playful Appropriation and the Anglo-Saxon Scholar.' In *Des nains ou de géants? Emprunter et créer au Moyen Âge*, eds. Claude Andrault-Schmitt, Edina Bozoky, and Stephen Morrison, 181–200. Turnhout: Brepols, 2015.

'The Practice of Dissent.' *postmedieval FORUM* 3 (2012). http://postmedieval-forum.com/forums/forum-iii-dissent/the-practice-of-dissent-irina-dumitrescu/.

'Violence, Performance and Pedagogy in Ælfric Bata's *Colloquies*.' *Exemplaria* 23.1 (2011): 67–91.

Dungey, Kevin R. 'Faith in the Darkness: Allegorical Theory and Aldhelm's Obscurity.' In *Allegoresis: The Craft of Allegory in Medieval Literature*, ed. J. Stephen Russell, 3–26. New York: Garland, 1988.

Earl, James W. 'The Typological Structure of *Andreas*.' In *Old English Literature in Context*, ed. John D. Niles, 66–89. Cambridge: D. S. Brewer, 1980.

Earle, John. *Anglo-Saxon Literature*. London: Society for Promoting Christian Knowledge, 1884.

Edmiston, Brian. 'Drama as Ethical Education.' *Research in Drama Education* 5.1 (2000): 63–84.

Enders, Jody. *The Medieval Theater of Cruelty: Rhetoric, Memory, Violence*. Ithaca, NY: Cornell University Press, 1999.

'Rhetoric, Coercion, and the Memory of Violence.' In *Criticism and Dissent*, ed. Copeland (q.v.), 24–55.

Engberg, Norma J. '*Mod-Mægen* Balance in *Elene*, *The Battle of Maldon* and *The Wanderer*.' *NM* 85.2 (1984): 212–26.

Felski, Rita. 'After Suspicion.' *Profession* (2009): 28–35.

'Context Stinks!'. *New Literary History* 42 (2011): 573–91.

'Digging Down and Standing Back.' *English Language Notes* 51.2 (2013): 7–23.

'Suspicious Minds.' *Poetics Today* 32.2 (2011): 215–34.

Ferhatović, Denis. '*Spolia*-Inflected Poetics of the Old English *Andreas*.' *Studies in Philology* 110.2 (2013): 199–219.

Fichte, Joerg O. 'The *Visitatio Sepulchri* as Actualization of Dramatic Impulses in the Ninth and Tenth Centuries.' *NM* 77.2 (1976): 211–26.

Fish, Varda. 'Theme and Pattern in Cynewulf's *Elene*.' *NM* 76.1 (1975): 1–25.

Foster, David William. 'De Maria Egyptiaca and the Medieval Figural Tradition.' *Italica* 44.2 (1967): 135–43.

Foucault, Michel. *Surveiller et punir: Naissance de la prison*. Paris: Gallimard, 1975.

Frank, Roberta. 'North-Sea Soundings in Andreas.' In *Early Medieval English Texts and Interpretations: Studies Presented to Donald G. Scragg*, eds. Elaine Treharne and Susan Rosser, 1–11. Tempe, AZ: ACMRS, 2002.

Frantzen, Allen J. 'Afterword: *Beowulf* and Everything Else.' In *The Dating of Beowulf: A Reassessment*, ed. Leonard Neidorf, 235–47. Cambridge: D. S. Brewer, 2014.

'All Created Things: Material Contexts for Bede's Story of Cædmon.' In *Cædmon's Hymn and Material Culture in the World of Bede*, eds. Allen J. Frantzen and John Hines, 111–49. Morgantown, WV: West Virginia University Press, 2007.

'Bede and Bawdy Bale: Gregory the Great, Angels, and the "Angli".' In *Anglo-Saxonism and the Construction of Social Identity*, ed. Allen J. Frantzen, 17–59. Gainesville, FL: University Press of Florida, 1997.

Before the Closet: Same-Sex Love from Beowulf to Angels in America. University of Chicago Press, 1998.

Desire for Origins: New Language, Old English, and Teaching the Tradition. New Brunswick, NJ: Rutgers University Press, 1990.

'Drama and Dialogue in Old English Poetry: The Scene of Cynewulf's *Juliana*.' *Theatre Survey* 48.1 (2007): 99–119.

Frese, Dolores Warwick. 'The Art of Cynewulf's Runic Signatures.' In *The Cynewulf Reader*, ed. Bjork (q.v.), 323–46.

Fritz, Donald W. 'Caedmon: A Monastic Exegete.' *American Benedictine Review* 25.3 (1974): 351–63.

'Caedmon: A Traditional Christian Poet.' *Mediaeval Studies* 31 (1969): 334–37.

Frye, Northrop. *The Secular Scripture: A Study of the Structure of Romance.* Cambridge, MA: Harvard University Press, 1976.

Fulk, R. D. 'Cynewulf: Canon, Dialect, and Date.' In *The Cynewulf Reader*, ed. Bjork (q.v.), 3–21.

Garde, Judith N. *Old English Poetry in Medieval Christian Perspective: A Doctrinal Approach.* Cambridge: D. S. Brewer, 1991.

Gardner, John. 'Cynewulf's *Elene*: Sources and Structure.' *Neophilologus* 54.1 (1970): 65–75.

Garmonsway, G. N. 'The Development of the Colloquy.' In *The Anglo-Saxons: Studies in Some Aspects of Their History and Culture Presented to Bruce Dickins*, ed. Peter Clemoes, 248–61. London: Bowes & Bowes, 1959.

Garner, Lori Ann. 'The Old English *Andreas* and the Mermedonian Cityscape.' *Essays in Medieval Studies* 24 (2007): 53–63.

Gibson, Margaret T. 'Boethius in the Carolingian Schools.' *Transactions of the Royal Historical Society*, Fifth Series, 32 (1982): 43–56.

Gneuss, Helmut. 'The Study of Language in Anglo-Saxon England.' *Bulletin of the John Rylands University Library of Manchester* 72.1 (1990): 3–32.

Godden, Malcolm. 'King Alfred and the *Boethius* Industry.' In *Making Sense: Constructing Meaning in Early English*, eds. Antonette diPaolo Healey and Kevin Kiernan, 116–38. Toronto: Pontifical Institute of Mediaeval Studies, 2007.

'King Alfred's Preface and the Teaching of Latin in Anglo-Saxon England.' *English Historical Review* 117.472 (2002): 596–604.

Godlove, Shannon N. 'Bodies as Borders: Cannibalism and Conversion in the Old English *Andreas*.' *Studies in Philology* 106.2 (2009): 137–60.

Goffart, Walter. *The Narrators of Barbarian History (A.D. 550–800): Jordanes, Gregory of Tours, Bede, and Paul the Deacon.* Princeton University Press, 1988.

Goffman, Erving. *The Presentation of Self in Everyday Life*. New York: Doubleday, 1959.

Grant, Raymond J. S. *Cambridge, Corpus Christi College 41: The Loricas and the Missal*. Amsterdam: Rodopi, 1978.

Greenfield, Stanley B. 'The Formulaic Expression of the Theme of "Exile" in Anglo-Saxon Poetry.' In *Essential Articles for the Study of Old English Poetry*, eds. Jess B. Bessinger and Stanley J. Kahrl, 352–62. Hamden, CT: Archon Books, 1968.

Gretsch, Mechthild. *The Intellectual Foundations of the English Benedictine Reform*. Cambridge University Press, 1999.

Gwara, Scott. 'Ælfric Bata's Manuscripts.' *Revue d'histoire des textes* 27 (1997): 239–55.

'Diogenes the Cynic in the Scholastic Dialogues Called *De raris fabulis*.' *American N&Q* 17.1 (2004): 3–6.

'*Doubles Entendres* in the Ironic Conclusion to Aldhelm's *Epistola ad Heahfridum*.' *Archivum Latinitatis Medii Aevi* 53 (1995): 141–52.

Education in Wales and Cornwall in the Ninth and Tenth Centuries: Understanding De raris fabulis. Kathleen Hughes Memorial Lectures on Mediaeval Welsh History. Cambridge: Department of Anglo-Saxon, Norse & Celtic, University of Cambridge, 2004.

Hall, Alaric. 'Interlinguistic Communication in Bede's *Historia ecclesiastica gentis Anglorum*.' In *Interfaces between Language and Culture in Medieval England: A Festschrift for Matti Kilpiö*, eds. Alaric Hall, Olga Timofeeva, Ágnes Kiricsi, and Bethany Fox, 37–80. Leiden: Brill, 2010.

Hamilton, David. '*Andreas* and *Beowulf*: Placing the Hero.' In *Anglo-Saxon Poetry*, eds. Nicholson and Frese (q.v.), 81–98.

'The Diet and Digestion of Allegory in *Andreas*.' *ASE* 1 (1972): 147–58.

Hammerling, Roy. 'The *Pater Noster* in Its Patristic and Medieval Context: The Baptismal-Catechetic Interpretation of the Lord's Prayer.' *Proceedings of the Patristic, Mediaeval and Renaissance Conference* 18 (1993–94): 1–24.

Hanna III, Ralph. 'School and Scorn: Gender in *Piers Plowman*.' *New Medieval Literatures* 1 (1999): 213–27.

Hansen, Elaine Tuttle. *The Solomon Complex: Reading Wisdom in Old English Poetry*. University of Toronto Press, 1988.

Harbus, Antonina. *Cognitive Approaches to Old English Poetry*. Cambridge: D. S. Brewer, 2012.

'The Situation of Wisdom in *Solomon and Saturn II*.' *Studia Neophilologica* 75 (2003): 97–103.

'Text as Revelation: Constantine's Dream in *Elene*.' *Neophilologus* 78 (1994): 645–53.

Harpham, Geoffrey Galt. *The Ascetic Imperative in Culture and Criticism*. University of Chicago Press, 1987.

Harris, Stephen J. 'Bede and Gregory's Allusive Angles.' *Criticism* 44.3 (2002): 271–89.

Race and Ethnicity in Anglo-Saxon Literature. New York: Routledge, 2003.

Hartmann, Carmen Cardelle de. *Lateinische Dialoge 1200–1400: Literaturhistorische Studie und Repertorium*. Leiden: Brill, 2007.

Hasan-Rokem, Galit, and David Shulman, eds. *Untying the Knot: On Riddles and Other Enigmatic Modes*. Oxford University Press, 1996.

Heckman, Christina M. 'Things in Doubt: *Inventio*, Dialectic, and Jewish Secrets in Cynewulf's *Elene*.' *JEGP* 108.4 (2009): 449–80.

Henry, Mallika. 'Drama's Ways of Learning.' *Research in Drama Education* 5.1 (2000): 45–62.

Herbison, Ivan. 'Generic Adaptation in *Andreas*.' In *Essays on Anglo-Saxon and Related Themes in Memory of Lynne Grundy*, eds. Jane Roberts and Janet Nelson, 181–211. London: Centre for Late Antique and Medieval Studies, 2000.

Hermann, John P. 'The Pater Noster Battle Sequence in *Solomon and Saturn* and the *Psychomachia* of Prudentius.' *NM* 77.2 (1976): 206–10.

Heron, Onnaca. 'The Lioness in the Text: Mary of Egypt as Immasculated Female Saint.' *Quidditas* 21 (2000): 23–44.

Herren, Michael. 'The Transmission and Reception of Graeco-Roman Mythology in Anglo-Saxon England, 670–800.' *ASE* 27 (1998): 87–103.

Hieatt, Constance B. 'Cædmon in Context: Transforming the Formula.' *JEGP* 84.4 (1985): 485–97.

'The Harrowing of Mermedonia: Typological Patterns in the Old English "Andreas".' *NM* 77.1 (1976): 49–62.

Higham, N. J. *(Re-)Reading Bede: The Ecclesiastical History in Context*. London and New York: Routledge, 2006.

Hill, Joyce. 'Ælfric's *Colloquy*: The Antwerp/London Version.' In *Latin Learning and English Lore*, eds. O'Brien O'Keeffe and Orchard (q.v.), 331–48.

'Learning Latin in Anglo-Saxon England: Traditions, Texts and Techniques.' In *Learning and Literacy in Medieval England and Abroad*, ed. Sarah Rees Jones, 7–29. Turnhout: Brepols, 2003.

'Winchester Pedagogy and the *Colloquy* of Ælfric.' *Leeds Studies in English N.S.* 29 (1998): 137–52.

Hill, Thomas D. 'The Crowning of Alfred and the Topos of *Sapientia et Fortitudo* in Asser's *Life of King Alfred*.' *Neophilologus* 86 (2002): 471–76.

'The Devil's Forms and the Pater Noster's Powers: "The Prose Solomon and Saturn *Pater Noster* Dialogue" and the Motif of the Transformation Combat.' *Studies in Philology* 85.2 (Spring 1988): 164–76.

'Figural Narrative in *Andreas*: The Conversion of the Meremedonians.' *NM* 70.2 (1969): 261–73.

'Tormenting the Devil with Boiling Drops: An Apotropaic Motif in the Old English "Solomon and Saturn I" and Old Norse-Icelandic Literature.' *JEGP* 92.2 (1993): 157–66.

Hofstra, T., L. A. J. R. Houwen, and A. A. MacDonald, eds. *Pagans and Christians: The Interplay between Christian Latin and Traditional Germanic Cultures in Early Medieval Europe*. Groningen: Egbert Forsten, 1995.

Hogan, A. D. '*The Wanderer* – A Boethian Poem?' *RES* 38.149 (1987): 40–46.

Hollahan, Patricia. 'The Anglo-Saxon Use of the Psalms: Liturgical Background and Poetic Use.' Unpublished doctoral thesis, University of Illinois at Urbana-Champaign (1977).

Holsinger, Bruce. *Music, Body, and Desire in Medieval Culture: Hildegard of Bingen to Chaucer*. Stanford University Press, 2001.

'The Parable of Caedmon's *Hymn*: Liturgical Invention and Literary Tradition.' *JEGP* 106.2 (2007): 149–75.

Hostetter, Aaron. 'A Tasty Turn of Phrase: Cannibal Poetics in Andreas.' Unpublished conference paper presented at 'Pleasure in Anglo-Saxon England', Yale University, 2008. Available online at: http://anglosaxonpoetry.blogspot.de/2008/02/update-to-translation-assc-conference.html.

Howe, Nicholas. *Migration and Mythmaking in Anglo-Saxon England*. New Haven, CT: Yale University Press, 1989.

'Rome: Capital of Anglo-Saxon England.' *JMEMS* 34.1 (2004): 147–72.

Hunt, Tony. 'An Anglo-Norman Pater Noster.' *N&Q* 42.1 (March 1995): 16–18.

Huppé, Bernard F. 'Caedmon's *Hymn*.' In *Old English Literature: Twenty-Two Analytical Essays*, eds. Martin Stevens and Jerome Mandel, 117–38. Lincoln, NE: University of Nebraska Press, 1968.

Doctrine and Poetry: Augustine's Influence on Old English Poetry. State University of New York, 1959.

Irvine, Martin. 'Anglo-Saxon Literary Theory Exemplified in Old English Poems: Interpreting the Cross in *The Dream of the Rood* and *Elene*.' In *Old English Shorter Poems: Basic Readings*, ed. Katherine O'Brien O'Keeffe, 31–63. New York: Garland, 1994.

'Bede the Grammarian and the Scope of Grammatical Studies in Eighth-Century Northumbria.' *ASE* 15 (1986): 15–44.

The Making of Textual Culture. 'Grammatica' and Literary Theory, 350–1100. Cambridge University Press, 1994.

'Medieval Textuality and the Archaeology of Textual Culture.' In *Speaking Two Languages: Traditional Disciplines and Contemporary Theory in Medieval Studies*, ed. Allen J. Frantzen, 181–210. Albany, NY: State University of New York Press, 1991.

Irving Jr., Edward B. 'A Reading of *Andreas*: The Poem as Poem.' *ASE* 12 (1983): 215–37.

Isaac, G. R. 'The Date and Origin of *Cædmon's Hymn*.' *NM* 98.3 (1997): 217–28.

Jackson, Peter, and Michael Lapidge. 'The Contents of the Cotton-Corpus Legendary.' In *Holy Men and Holy Women: Old English Prose Saints' Lives and Their Contexts*, ed. Paul E. Szarmach, 131–46. Albany, NY: State University of New York Press, 1996.

Jaeger, C. Stephen. *The Envy of Angels: Cathedral Schools and Social Ideals in Medieval Europe, 950–1200*. Philadelphia, PA: University of Pennsylvania Press, 1994.

Jager, Eric. 'Speech and the Chest in Old English Poetry: Orality or Pectorality?' *Speculum* 65.4 (1990): 845–59.

Jakobson, Roman. *Child Language, Aphasia, and Phonological Universals*. Trans. Allan R. Keiler. The Hague and Paris: Mouton, 1968.

Johnson, Eleanor. *Practicing Literary Theory in the Middle Ages: Ethics and the Mixed Form in Chaucer, Gower, Usk, and Hoccleve*. University of Chicago Press, 2013.

Johnston, Andrew James. 'Caedmons mehrfache Anderssprachigkeit: Die Urszene der altenglischen Literatur im Spannungsfeld frühmittelalterlicher Sprach- und Kulturgegensätze.' In *Exophonie: Anders-Sprachigkeit (in) der Literatur*, eds. Susan Arndt, Dirk Naguschewski, and Robert Stockhammer, 66–86. Berlin: Kulturverlag Kadmos, 2007.

Jonassen, Frederick B. 'The Pater Noster Letters in the Poetic *Solomon and Saturn*.' *Modern Language Review* 83.1 (1988): 1–9.

Jones, Christopher A. 'Ælfric and the Limits of "Benedictine Reform".' In *A Companion to Ælfric*, eds. Hugh Magennis and Mary Swan, 67–108. Leiden: Brill Academic Publishers, 2009.

'The Irregular Life in Ælfric Bata's *Colloquies*.' *Leeds Studies in English* N.S. 37 (2006): 241–60.

Jong, Mayke de. 'Growing up in a Carolingian monastery: Magister Hildemar and his Oblates.' *Journal of Medieval History* 9 (1983): 99–128.

In Samuel's Image: Child Oblation in the Early Medieval West. Leiden: E. J. Brill, 1996.

Jungmann, Josef Andreas. *Gewordene Liturgie*. Leipzig: Felizian Rauch Innsbruck, 1941.

Karkov, Catherine E., and George Hardin Brown, eds. *Anglo-Saxon Styles*. Albany, NY: State University of New York Press, 2003.

Karras, Ruth Mazo. *Common Women: Prostitution and Sexuality in Medieval England*. Oxford University Press, 1996.

'Holy Harlots: Prostitute Saints in Medieval Legend.' *Journal of the History of Sexuality* 1.1 (July 1990): 3–32.

Sexuality in Medieval Europe: Doing unto Others. 3rd ed. London: Routledge, 2017.

Kaylor, Noel Harold, Jr., and Philip Edward Phillips, eds. *A Companion to Boethius in the Middle Ages*. Leiden: Brill, 2012.

Kendall, Calvin B. 'Bede and Education.' In *The Cambridge Companion to Bede*, ed. Scott DeGregorio, 99–112. Cambridge University Press, 2010.

Kershaw, Paul. 'Illness, Power and Prayer in Asser's *Life of King Alfred*.' *Early Medieval Europe* 10.2 (2001): 201–24.

Keynes, Simon, and Michael Lapidge, eds. *Alfred the Great: Asser's Life of King Alfred and Other Contemporary Sources*. Harmondsworth, Middlesex: Penguin Books, 1983.

Kiernan, Kevin S. '*Deor*: The Consolations of an Anglo-Saxon Boethius.' *NM* 79.4 (1978): 333–40.

'Reading Cædmon's "Hymn" with Someone Else's Glosses.' *Representations* 32 (1990): 157–74.

Kinney, Dale. '*Spolia: Damnatio* and r*enovatio memoriae*.' *Memories of the American Academy in Rome* 42 (1997): 117–48.

Kiser, Lisa J. '*Andreas* and the *Lifes Weg*: Convention and Innovation in Old English Metaphor.' *NM* 85.1 (1984): 65–75.

Klaeber, Fr. 'Analogues of the Story of Cædmon.' *MLN* 42.6 (1927): 390.

Klawitter, George. 'Dramatic Elements in Early Monastic Induction Ceremonies.' *Comparative Drama* 15.3 (Fall 1981): 213–30.

Kleiner, Yu. A. 'The Singer and the Interpreter: Caedmon and Bede.' *Germanic Notes* 19 (1988): 2–6.

Knappe, Gabriele. 'The Rhetorical Aspect of Grammar Teaching in Anglo-Saxon England.' *Rhetorica* 17.1 (Winter 1999): 1–35.

Kunze, Konrad. *Studien zur Legende der heiligen Maria Aegyptiaca im deutschen Sprachgebiet*. Berlin: Erich Schmidt Verlag, 1969.

Kunzler, Michael. *Die Liturgie der Kirche*. Paderborn: Bonifatius, 1995.

Lahaye-Geusen, Maria. *Das Opfer der Kinder: Ein Beitrag zur Liturgie- und Sozialgeschichte des Mönchtums im Hohen Mittelalter*. Altenberge: Oros Verlag, 1991.

Lange, Harvey D. 'The Relationship between Psalm 22 and the Passion Narrative.' *Concordia Theological Monthly* 43.9 (1972): 610–21.

Langeslag, Paul S. 'Boethian Similitude in *Deor* and *The Wanderer*.' *NM* 109.2 (2008): 205–22.

Lapidge, Michael. 'Dialogues.' In *The Wiley-Blackwell Encyclopedia of Anglo-Saxon England*, eds. Michael Lapidge, John Blair, Simon Keynes, and Donald Scragg, 144–45. Chichester: Wiley-Blackwell, 2014.

'The Hermeneutic Style in Tenth-Century Anglo-Latin Literature.' *ASE* 4 (1975): 67–111.

'The Study of Latin Texts in late Anglo-Saxon England [1] The Evidence of Latin Glosses.' In *Latin and the Vernacular Languages in Early Medieval Britain*, ed. Nicholas Brooks, 99–140. Leicester University Press, 1982.

Law, Vivien. 'Grammar in the Early Middle Ages: A Bibliography.' In *History of Linguistic Thought*, ed. Law (q.v.), 25–47.

The Insular Latin Grammarians. Woodbridge, Suffolk: Boydell Press, 1982.

'The Study of Latin Grammar in Eighth-Century Southumbria.' *ASE* 12 (1983): 43–71.

Wisdom, Authority and Grammar in the Seventh Century: Decoding Virgilius Maro Grammaticus. Cambridge University Press, 1995.

Law, Vivien, ed. *History of Linguistic Thought in the Early Middle Ages*. Amsterdam: John Benjamins, 1993.

Lawrence, William Witherle. 'The Song of Deor.' *MP* 9.1 (1911): 23–45.

Leach, A. F. *The Schools of Medieval England*. New York: Macmillan, 1915.

Leach, Eleanor Winsor. 'Georgic Imagery in the *Ars amatoria*.' *Transactions and Proceedings of the American Philological Association* 95 (1964): 142–54.

Leclercq, Jean. *The Love of Learning and the Desire for God: A Study of Monastic Culture*. Trans. Catherine Misrahi. 3rd ed. New York: Fordham University Press, 1982.

Lee, Alvin A. 'Symbolism and Allegory.' In *A Beowulf Handbook*, eds. Robert E. Bjork and John D. Niles, 233–54. University of Exeter Press, 1996.

Lees, Clare A. 'Engendering Religious Desire: Sex, Knowledge, and Christian Identity in Anglo-Saxon England.' *JMEMS* 27.1 (1997): 17–46.

Tradition and Belief: Religious Writing in Late Anglo-Saxon England. Minneapolis, MN: University of Minnesota Press, 1999.

'Vision and Place in the Old English Life of Mary of Egypt.' In *The Old English Life of Mary of Egypt*, ed. Scragg (q.v.), 57–78.

ed. *The Cambridge History of Early Medieval English Literature*. Cambridge University Press, 2013.

Lees, Clare, and Gillian Overing. *Double Agents: Women and Clerical Culture in Anglo-Saxon England*. Philadelphia, PA: University of Pennsylvania Press, 2001.

Lehmann, Paul. *Die Parodie im Mittelalter*. 2nd ed. Stuttgart: Anton Hiersemann, 1963.

Lendinara, Patrizia. 'The *Colloquy* of Ælfric and the *Colloquy* of Ælfric Bata.' In *Anglo-Saxon Glosses and Glossaries*, 207–87. Aldershot: Ashgate Variorum, 1999.

'Contextualized Lexicography.' In *Latin Learning and English Lore*, eds. O'Brien O'Keeffe and Orchard (q.v.), 108–31.

'The World of Anglo-Saxon Learning.' In *The Cambridge Companion to Old English Literature*, eds. Malcolm Godden and Michael Lapidge, 264–81. Cambridge University Press, 1991.

Lendinara, Patrizia, Loredana Lazzari, and Maria Amalia D'Aronco, eds. *Form and Content of Instruction in Anglo-Saxon England in the Light of Contemporary Manuscript Evidence*. Turnhout: Brepols, 2007.

Lenz, Karmen. *Ræd and Frofer: Christian Poetics in the Old English Froferboc Meters*. Amsterdam: Rodopi, 2012.

Lerer, Seth. *Boethius and Dialogue: Literary Method in the Consolation of Philosophy*. Princeton University Press, 1985.

Children's Literature: A Reader's History, from Aesop to Harry Potter. University of Chicago Press, 2008.

'"Dum ludis floribus": Language and Text in the Medieval English Lyric.' *Philological Quarterly* 87.3/4 (2008): 237–55.

'The Endurance of Formalism in Middle English Studies.' *Literature Compass* 1.1 (2003): 1–15.

Literacy and Power in Anglo-Saxon Literature. Lincoln, NE: University of Nebraska Press, 1991.

Lester, G. A. 'The Cædmon Story and its Analogues.' *Neophilologus* 58.2 (1974): 225–37.

Levinson, Marjorie. 'What Is New Formalism?' *PMLA* 122.2 (2007): 558–69.

Levy, Jonathan. 'Theatre and Moral Education.' *Journal of Aesthetic Education* 31.3 (1997): 65–75.

Liu, Jun. 'Process Drama in Second- and Foreign-Language Classrooms.' In *Body and Language: Intercultural Learning through Drama*, ed. Gerd Bräuer, 51–70. Westport, CT and London: Ablex Publishing, 2002.

Lockett, Leslie. *Anglo-Saxon Psychologies in the Vernacular and Latin Traditions*. University of Toronto Press, 2011.

Löfstedt, Bengt. 'Sekundäre Bedeutungen von "Pater Noster".' *NM* 59.2 (1988): 212–14.

Loomis, C. Grant. 'The Miracle Traditions of the Venerable Bede.' *Speculum* 21.4 (1946): 404–18.

Love, Rosalind C. 'The Latin Commentaries on Boethius's *De consolatione philosophiae* from the 9th to the 11th Centuries.' In *A Companion to Boethius*, eds. Kaylor and Phillips (q.v.), 75–133.

MacAloon, John J. 'Introduction: Cultural Performances, Culture Theory.' In *Rite, Drama, Festival, Spectacle: Rehearsals toward a Theory of Cultural Performance*, ed. John J. MacAloon, 1–15. Philadelphia, PA: Institute for the Study of Human Issues, 1984.

Magennis, Hugh. 'Contrasting Features in the Non-Ælfrician Lives in the Old English *Lives of Saints.*' *Anglia* 104 (1986): 316–48.

'A Funny Thing Happened on the Way to Heaven: Humorous Incongruity in Old English Saints' Lives.' In *Humour in Anglo-Saxon Literature*, ed. Jonathan Wilcox, 137–57. Cambridge: D. S. Brewer, 2000.

'On the Sources of Non-Ælfrician Lives in the Old English *Lives of Saints*, with Reference to the Cotton-Corpus Legendary.' *N&Q* N.S. 32 (1985): 292–99.

Magoun, Jr., Francis P. 'Bede's Story of Cædman: The Case History of an Anglo-Saxon Oral Singer.' *Speculum* 30.1 (1955): 49–63.

Malone, Kemp. 'Cædmon and English Poetry.' *MLN* 76.3 (1961): 193–95.

Mann, Jill. '"He Knew Nat Catoun": Medieval School-Texts and Middle English Literature.' In *The Text in the Community: Essays on Medieval Works, Manuscripts, Authors, and Readers*, eds. Jill Mann and Maura Nolan, 41–74. University of Notre Dame Press, 2006.

Markland, Murray F. 'Boethius, Alfred, and Deor.' *MP* 66.1 (1968): 1–4.

Marrou, Henri-Irénée. *Histoire de l'éducation dans l'antiquité*, Volume 1:*Le monde grec*. Paris: Éditions du Seuil, 1948.

Histoire de l'éducation dans l'antiquité, Volume 2: *Le monde romain*. Paris: Éditions du Seuil, 1948.

Marsden, Richard. 'The Bible in English.' In *The New Cambridge History of the Bible*, eds. Marsden and Matter (q.v.), 217–38.

The Text of the Old Testament in Anglo-Saxon England. Cambridge University Press, 1995.

'Wrestling with the Bible: Textual Problems for the Scholar and Student.' In *The Christian Tradition in Anglo-Saxon England: Approaches to Current Scholarship and Teaching*, ed. Paul Cavill, 69–90. Cambridge: D. S. Brewer, 2004.

Marsden, Richard, and E. Ann Matter, eds. *The New Cambridge History of the Bible, Volume 2: From 600 to 1450*. Cambridge University Press, 2012.

Marshall, Helen, and Peter Buchanan. 'New Formalism and the Forms of Middle English Literary Texts.' *Literature Compass* 8.4 (2011): 164–72.

Martin, Lawrence T. 'Bede as a Linguistic Scholar.' *American Benedictine Review* 35.2 (1984): 204–17.

McCready, William D. *Miracles and the Venerable Bede*. Toronto: Pontifical Institute of Mediaeval Studies, 1994.

Mehan, Uppinder, and David Townsend. '"Nation" and the Gaze of the Other in Eighth-Century Northumbria.' *Comparative Literature* 53.1 (2001): 1–26.

Menn, Esther M. 'No Ordinary Lament: Relecture and the Identity of the Distressed in Psalm 22.' *Harvard Theological Review* 93.4 (2000): 301–41.

Menner, Robert J. 'Two Notes on Mediaeval Euhemerism.' *Speculum* 3.2 (1928): 246–48.

Menzer, Melinda J. 'Ælfric's English *Grammar*.' *JEGP* 103.1 (2004): 106–24.
   'Ælfric's Grammar: Solving the Problem of the English-Language Text.' *Neophilologus* 83 (1999): 637–52.

Merback, Mitchell B. *The Thief, the Cross and the Wheel: Pain and the Spectacle of Punishment in Medieval and Renaissance Europe*. University of Chicago Press, 1998.

Meritt, Herbert Dean. 'Old English Glosses, Mostly Dry Point.' *JEGP* 60.3 (1961): 441–50.

Merrills, A. H. *History and Geography in Late Antiquity*. Cambridge University Press, 2005.

Metcalf, Allan A. *Poetic Diction in the Old English Meters of Boethius*. The Hague: Mouton, 1973.

Miles, Margaret R. *Desire and Delight: A New Reading of Augustine's Confessions*. Eugene, OR: Wipf and Stock, 1991.

Miller, Patricia Cox. 'The Blazing Body: Ascetic Desire in Jerome's Letter to Eustochium.' *Journal of Early Christian Studies* 1.1 (1993): 21–45.
   'Is There a Harlot in This Text? Hagiography and the Grotesque.' *JMEMS* 33.3 (Fall 2003): 419–35.

Milling, D. H. 'History and Prophecy in the Marcan Passion Narrative.' *Indian Journal of Theology* 16.1–2 (1967): 42–53.

Mills, Robert. *Suspended Animation: Pain, Pleasure and Punishment in Medieval Culture*. London: Reaktion Books, 2005.

Mitchell, Bruce. 'Some Problems of Mood and Tense in Old English.' *Neophilologus* 49.1 (1965): 44–57.

Moloney, Francis J. *The Gospel of John*. Collegeville, MN: Liturgical Press, 1998.

Monaghan, E. Jennifer. *Learning to Read and Write in Colonial America*. Amherst, MA: University of Massachusetts Press, 2005.

Moore, Stephen D., and Yvonne Sherwood. *The Invention of the Biblical Scholar: A Critical Manifesto*. Minneapolis, MN: Fortress Press, 2011.

Moorhead, John. 'Some Borrowings in Bede.' *Latomus* 66.3 (2007): 710–17.

Morinis, Alan. 'The Ritual Experience: Pain and the Transformation of Consciousness in Ordeals of Initiation.' *Ethos* 13.2 (Summer 1985): 150–74.

Nelson, Marie. 'King Solomon's Magic: The Power of a Written Text.' *Oral Tradition* 5.1 (1990): 20–36.

Nicholson, Lewis E., and Dolores Warwick Frese, eds. *Anglo-Saxon Poetry: Essays in Appreciation. For John C. McGalliard*. University of Notre Dame Press, 1975.

Noice, Helga, and Tony Noice. 'What Studies of Actors and Acting Can Tell Us about Memory and Cognitive Functioning.' *Current Directions in Psychological Science* 15.1 (2006): 14–18.

Noice, Helga, Tony Noice, Pasqualina Perrig-Chiello, and Walter Perrig. 'Improving Memory in Older Adults by Instructing Them in Professional Actors' Learning Strategies.' *Applied Cognitive Psychology* 13 (1999): 315–28.

Nolan, Maura. *John Lydgate and the Making of Public Culture.* Cambridge University Press, 2005.

Norris, Robin. '*Vitas Matrum*: Mary of Egypt as Female Confessor.' In *The Old English Life of Mary of Egypt*, ed. Scragg (q.v.), 79–109.

North, Richard. 'Boethius and the Mercenary in *The Wanderer*.' In *Pagans and Christians*, eds. Hofstra, Houwen, and MacDonald (q.v.), 71–98.

Novikoff, Alex J. *The Medieval Culture of Disputation: Pedagogy, Practice, and Performance.* Philadelphia, PA: University of Pennsylvania Press, 2013.

O'Brien O'Keeffe, Katherine. *Stealing Obedience: Narratives of Agency and Identity in Later Anglo-Saxon England.* University of Toronto Press, 2012.

   Visible Song: Transitional Literacy in Old English Verse. Cambridge University Press, 1990.

O'Brien O'Keeffe, Katherine, and Andy Orchard. *Latin Learning and English Lore: Studies in Anglo-Saxon Literature for Michael Lapidge.* 2 vols. University of Toronto Press, 2005.

O'Donnell, Daniel Paul. 'Bede's Strategy in Paraphrasing *Cædmon's Hymn*.' *JEGP* 103.4 (2004): 417–32.

   Cædmon's Hymn: A Multimedia Study, Archive and Edition. Cambridge: D. S. Brewer, 2005.

   'Material Differences: The Place of Cædmon's Hymn in the History of Anglo-Saxon Vernacular Poetry.' In *Cædmon's Hymn*, eds. Frantzen and Hines (q.v.), 15–50.

Olszowy-Schlanger, Judith. 'Learning to Read and Write in Medieval Egypt: Children's Exercise Books from the Cairo Geniza.' *Journal of Semitic Studies* 48.1 (2003): 47–69.

O'Neill, Patrick P. 'On the Date, Provenance and Relationship of the "Solomon and Saturn" Dialogues.' *ASE* 26 (1997): 139–68.

Ong, Walter J. 'Latin Language Study as a Renaissance Puberty Rite.' In *Rhetoric, Romance, and Technology: Studies in the Interaction of Expression and Culture*, 113–41. Ithaca, NY: Cornell University Press, 1971.

Orchard, Andy. 'Both Style and Substance: The Case for Cynewulf.' In *Anglo-Saxon Styles*, eds. Karkov and Brown (q.v.), 271–305.

   'Hot Lust in a Cold Climate: Comparison and Contrast in the Old Norse Versions of the Life of Mary of Egypt.' In *The Legend of Mary of Egypt*, eds. Poppe and Ross (q.v.), 175–204.

   'Rhetoric and Style in the Old English Life of Mary of Egypt.' In *The Old English Life of Mary of Egypt*, ed. Scragg (q.v.), 31–55.

   'The Word Made Flesh: Christianity and Oral Culture in Anglo-Saxon Verse.' *Oral Tradition* 24.2 (2009): 293–318.

Orme, Nicholas. *Medieval Children.* New Haven, CT: Yale University Press, 2001.

Medieval Schools: From Roman Britain to Renaissance England. New Haven, CT: Yale University Press, 2006.

Osborn, Marijane. 'Venturing upon Deep Waters in *The Seafarer*.' *NM* 79.1 (1978): 1–6.

Page, R. I. *An Introduction to English Runes*. 2nd ed. Woodbridge, Suffolk: Boydell Press, 2006.

Parsons, Ben. 'The Way of the Rod: The Functions of Beating in Late Medieval Pedagogy.' *MP* 113 (2015): 1–26.

Peters, Leonard J. 'The Relationship of the Old English *Andreas* to *Beowulf*.' *PMLA* 66.5 (1951): 844–63.

Pope, John C. 'Dramatic Voices in *The Wanderer* and *The Seafarer*.' In *Franciplegius: Medieval and Linguistic Studies in Honor of Francis Peabody Magoun, Jr.*, eds. Jr. Jess B. Bessinger and Robert P. Creed, 164–93. New York University Press, 1965.

Poppe, Erich, and Bianca Ross, eds. *The Legend of Mary of Egypt in Medieval Insular Hagiography*. Dublin: Four Courts Press, 1996.

Porter, David W. 'Ælfric's *Colloquy* and Ælfric Bata.' *Neophilologus* 80 (1996): 639–60.

'Anglo-Saxon Colloquies: Ælfric, Ælfric Bata and *De Raris Fabulis Retractata*.' *Neophilologus* 81 (1997): 467–80.

'The Latin Syllabus in Anglo-Saxon Monastic Schools.' *Neophilologus* 78 (1994): 463–82.

Pound, Louise. 'Caedmon's Dream Song.' In *Studies in Philology: A Miscellany in Honor of Frederick Klaeber*, eds. Kemp Malone and Martin B. Ruud, 232–39. Minneapolis, MN: University of Minnesota Press, 1929.

Powell, Alison M. 'Verbal Parallels in *Andreas* and its Relationship to *Beowulf* and Cynewulf.' Unpublished doctoral thesis, University of Cambridge (2002).

Powell, Kathryn. 'Orientalist Fantasy in the Poetic Dialogues of *Solomon and Saturn*.' *ASE* 34 (2005): 117–43.

Pratt, David. 'The Illnesses of King Alfred the Great.' *ASE* 30 (2001): 39–90.

Quinn, Dennis. '*Me audiendi … stupentem:* The Restoration of Wonder in Boethius's *Consolation*.' *University of Toronto Quarterly* 57.4 (1988): 447–70.

Ray, Roger. 'Who Did Bede Think He Was?' In *Innovation and Tradition in the Writings of the Venerable Bede*, ed. Scott DeGregorio, 11–35. Morgantown, WV: West Virginia University Press, 2006.

Reading, Amity. 'Baptism, Conversion, and Selfhood in the Old English *Andreas*.' *Studies in Philology* 112.1 (2015): 1–23.

Regan, Catharine A. 'Evangelicism as the Informing Principle of Cynewulf's *Elene*.' In *The Cynewulf Reader*, ed. Bjork (q.v.), 251–80.

Relihan, Joel C. *The Prisoner's Philosophy: Life and Death in Boethius's Consolation*. University of Notre Dame Press, 2007.

Riché, Pierre. *Éducation et culture dans l'occident barbare: VIe–VIIIe siècles*. 3rd ed. Paris: Éditions du Seuil, 1962.

Ricoeur, Paul. *Freud and Philosophy: An Essay on Interpretation.* Trans. Denis Savage. New Haven, CT: Yale University Press, 1970.

Riedinger, Anita R. '*Andreas* and the Formula in Transition.' In *Hermeneutics and Medieval Culture*, eds. Patrick J. Gallacher and Helen Damico, 183–91. Albany, NY: State University of New York Press, 1989.

'The Formulaic Relationship between *Beowulf* and *Andreas*.' In *Heroic Poetry in the Anglo-Saxon Period: Studies in Honor of Jess B. Bessinger, Jr.*, eds. Helen Damico and John Leyerle, 283–312. Kalamazoo, MI: Medieval Institute Publications, Western Michigan University, 1993.

Roach, Joseph. *Cities of the Dead: Circum-Atlantic Performance.* New York: Columbia University Press, 1996.

Robertson, D. W., Jr. 'Historical Criticism.' In *English Institute Essays 1950*, ed. Alan S. Downer, 3–31. New York: AMS Press, 1965.

A *Preface to Chaucer: Studies in Medieval Perspectives.* Princeton University Press, 1962.

Robinson, Fred C. '*Medieval, the Middle Ages*.' *Speculum* 59.4 (1984): 745–56.

Roper, Alan H. 'Boethius and the Three Fates of *Beowulf*.' *Philological Quarterly* 41.2 (1962): 386–400.

Rose, Els. *Ritual Memory: The Apocryphal Acts and Liturgical Commemoration in the Early Medieval West (c. 500–1215).* Leiden: Brill, 2009.

Rowley, Sharon M. 'Reassessing Exegetical Interpretations of Bede's *Historia Ecclesiastica Gentis Anglorum*.' *Literature & Theology* 17.3 (2003): 227–43.

Sanok, Catherine. *Her Life Historical: Exemplarity and Female Saints' Lives in Late Medieval England.* Philadelphia, PA: University of Pennsylvania Press, 2007.

Sarrazin, Gregor. 'Beowulf und Kynewulf.' *Anglia* 9 (1886): 515–50.

Scarry, Elaine. *Dreaming by the Book.* New York: Farrar, Straus and Giroux, 1999.

Schaar, Claes. *Critical Studies in the Cynewulf Group.* Lund: C. W. K. Gleerup, 1949.

Schabram, Hans. 'Andreas und Beowulf. Parallelstellen als Zeugnis für literarische Abhängigkeit.' *Nachrichten der Giessener Hochschulgesellschaft* 34 (1965): 201–18.

Scharer, Anton. 'The Writing of History at King Alfred's Court.' *Early Medieval Europe* 5.2 (1996): 177–206.

Schechner, Richard. *Between Theater and Anthropology.* Philadelphia, PA: University of Pennsylvania Press, 1985.

Scheil, Andrew P. 'Bodies and Boundaries in the Old English *Life of St. Mary of Egypt*.' *Neophilologus* 84 (2000): 137–56.

The *Footsteps of Israel: Understanding Jews in Anglo-Saxon England.* Ann Arbor, MI: University of Michigan Press, 2004.

Schmitz, Josef. *Gottesdienst im altchristlichen Mailand: Eine liturgiewissenschaftliche Untersuchung über Initiation und Meßfeier während des Jahres zur Zeit des Bischofs Ambrosius (†397).* Köln-Bonn: Peter Hanstein Verlag, 1975.

Schutt, Marie. 'The Literary Form of Asser's "*Vita Alfredi*".' *English Historical Review* 72.283 (1957): 209–20.

Scott, Christina L., Richard Jackson Harris, and Alicia R. Rothe. 'Embodied Cognition through Improvisation Improves Memory for a Dramatic Monologue.' *Discourse Processes* 31.3 (2001): 293–305.

Scott, Dominic. *Recollection and Experience: Plato's Theory of Learning and its Successors*. Cambridge University Press, 1995.

Scragg, Donald, ed. *The Old English Life of Mary of Egypt*. Old English Newsletter *Subsidia* 33. Kalamazoo, MI: Medieval Institute, Western Michigan University, 2005.

Sharma, Manish. 'The Reburial of the Cross in the Old English *Elene*.' In *New Readings in the Vercelli Book*, eds. Samantha Zacher and Andy Orchard, 280–97. University of Toronto Press, 2009.

Shepherd, G. 'The Prophetic Cædmon.' *RES* N.S. 5.18 (1954): 113–22.

Silk, Edmund T. 'Boethius's *Consolatio Philosophiae* as a Sequel to Augustine's *Dialogues* and *Soliloquia*.' *Harvard Theological Review* 32.1 (1939): 19–39.

Skemer, Don C. *Binding Words: Textual Amulets in the Middle Ages*. University Park, PA: Pennsylvania State University Press, 2006.

Smith, D. Vance. *The Book of the Incipit: Beginnings in the Fourteenth Century*. Minneapolis, MN: University of Minnesota Press, 2001.

'Destroyer of Forms: Chaucer's *Philomela*.' In *Readings in Medieval Textuality: Essays in Honour of A. C. Spearing*, eds. Cristina Maria Cervone and D. Vance Smith, 135–55. Cambridge: D. S. Brewer, 2016.

'Medieval *Forma*: The Logic of the Work.' In *Reading for Form*, eds. Susan J. Wolfson and Marshall Brown, 66–79. Seattle, WA: University of Washington Press, 2015.

Spencer, Colin. *British Food: An Extraordinary Thousand Years of History*. New York: Columbia University Press, 2003.

Spinks, Bryan D. *Early Medieval Rituals and Theologies of Baptism: From the New Testament to the Council of Trent*. Aldershot: Ashgate, 2006.

Stanley, E. G. 'New Formulas for Old: *Cædmon's Hymn*.' In *Pagans and Christians*, eds. Hofstra, Houwen and MacDonald (q.v.), 131–48.

Stanton, Robert. 'Linguistic Fragmentation and Redemption before King Alfred.' *Yearbook of English Studies* 36.1 (2006): 12–26.

Stephenson, Rebecca. *The Politics of Language: Byrhtferth, Ælfric, and the Multilingual Identity of the Benedictine Reform*. University of Toronto Press, 2015.

Stevenson, Jane. 'The Holy Sinner: The Life of Mary of Egypt.' In *The Legend of Mary of Egypt*, eds. Poppe and Ross (q.v.), 19–50.

'Vita Sanctae Mariae Egiptiacae.' In *The Legend of Mary of Egypt*, eds. Poppe and Ross (q.v.), 51–98.

Stock, Brian. *Augustine's Inner Dialogue: The Philosophical Soliloquy in Late Antiquity*. Cambridge University Press, 2010.

Strauss, Leo. *Persecution and the Art of Writing*. University of Chicago Press, 1988.

Strier, Richard. 'How Formalism Became a Dirty Word, and Why We Can't Do Without It.' In *Renaissance Literature and Its Formal Engagements*, ed. Mark David Rasmussen, 207–15. New York: Palgrave, 2002.

Symes, Carol. 'The Appearance of Early Vernacular Plays: Forms, Functions, and the Future of Medieval Theater.' *Speculum* 77.3 (2002): 778–831.

Szarmach, Paul E. 'Boethius's Influence in Anglo-Saxon England: The Vernacular and the *De consolatione philosophiae*.' In *A Companion to Boethius*, eds. Kaylor and Phillips (q.v.), 221–54.

'More Genre Trouble: The Life of Mary of Egypt.' In *Writing Women Saints in Anglo-Saxon England*, ed. Paul E. Szarmach, 140–64. University of Toronto Press, 2013.

'Thirty-One Meters.' In *… un tuo serto di fiori in man recando: Scritti in onore di Maria Amalia D'Aronco*, ed. Patrizia Lendinara, 409–25. Udine: Editrice Universtaria Udinese, 2008.

Szittya, Penn R. 'The Living Stone and the Patriarchs: Typological Imagery in *Andreas*, Lines 706–810.' *JEGP* 72.2 (1973): 167–74.

Teske, Roland. 'Augustine's Philosophy of Memory.' In *The Cambridge Companion to Augustine*, eds. Eleonore Stump and Norman Kretzmann, 148–58. Cambridge University Press, 2001.

Thiébaux, Marcelle. *The Stag of Love: The Chase in Medieval Literature*. Ithaca, NY: Cornell University Press, 1974.

Thomsen, Dorthe Kirkegaard, and Dorthe Berntsen. 'The Long-Term Impact of Emotionally Stressful Events on Memory Characteristics and Life Story.' *Applied Cognitive Psychology* 23 (2009): 579–98.

Tkacz, Catherine Brown. 'Byzantine Theology in the Old English *De transitu Mariae Ægyptiace*.' In *The Old English Life of Mary of Egypt*, ed. Scragg (q.v.), 9–29.

Tobin, Yishai. *Phonology as Human Behavior: Theoretical Implications and Clinical Applications*. Durham, NC: Duke University Press, 1997.

Trahern, Joseph. 'Joshua and Tobias in the Old English *Andreas*.' *Studia Neophilologica* 42.2 (1970): 330–32.

Travis, Peter W. *Disseminal Chaucer: Rereading the Nun's Priest's Tale*. University of Notre Dame, 2010.

Vincenti, Arthur. *Drei altenglische Dialoge von Salomon und Saturn: Eine litterargeschichtliche, sprachliche und Quellen-Untersuchung*. Lippert: Naumburg, 1904.

Vitz, Evelyn Birge. *Orality and Performance in Early French Romance*. Cambridge: D. S. Brewer, 1999.

Vitz, Evelyn Birge, Nancy Freeman Regalado, and Marilyn Lawrence, eds. *Performing Medieval Narrative*. Cambridge: D. S. Brewer, 2005.

Wallace-Hadrill, J. M. *Bede's Ecclesiastical History of the English People: A Historical Commentary*. Oxford University Press, 1988.

Wallis, Faith. 'Cædmon's Created World and the Monastic Encyclopedia.' In *Cædmon's Hymn*, eds. Frantzen and Hines (q.v.), 80–110.

Walsh, Marie Michelle. 'The Baptismal Flood in the Old English "Andreas": Liturgical and Typological Depths.' *Traditio* 33 (1977): 137–58.

Walsh, P. G. 'The Rights and Wrongs of Curiosity (Plutarch to Augustine).' *Greece & Rome* 35.1 (1988): 73–85.

Waterhouse, Ruth. 'Self-Reflexivity and "Wraetlic Word" in *Bleak House* and *Andreas*.' *Journal of Narrative Technique* 18.3 (1988): 211–25.

Watt, Diane, and Clare A. Lees. 'Age and Desire in the Old English *Life of St Mary of Egypt*: A Queerer Time and Place?' In *Middle-Aged Women in the Middle Ages*, ed. Sue Niebrzydowski, 53–67. Cambridge: D. S. Brewer, 2011.

Whatley, E. Gordon. 'Bread and Stone: Cynewulf's "Elene" 611–618.' *NM* 76.4 (1975): 550–60.

Wheatley, Edward. *Mastering Aesop: Medieval Education, Chaucer, and His Followers*. Gainesville, FL: University Press of Florida, 2000.

Whitbread, L. 'An Analogue of the Cædmon Story.' *RES* 15.59 (1939): 333–35.

Whitelock, Dorothy. 'Bede and His Teachers and Friends.' In *Famulus Christi*, ed. Bonner (q.v.), 19–39.

Wilcox, Jonathan. 'Eating Books: The Consumption of Learning in the Old English Poetic *Solomon and Saturn*.' *American N&Q* 4.3 (July 1991): 115–18.

'Eating People is Wrong: Funny Style in *Andreas* and its Analogues.' In *Anglo-Saxon Styles*, eds. Karkov and Brown (q.v.), 201–22.

Williams, Edna Rees. 'Ælfric's Grammatical Terminology.' *PMLA* 73.5 (1958): 453–62.

Wilson, Susan E., ed. *The Life and After-Life of St. John of Beverley: The Evolution of the Cult of an Anglo-Saxon Saint*. Aldershot: Ashgate, 2006.

Winston, Joe. 'Between the Aesthetic and the Ethical: Analysing the Tension at the Heart of Theatre in Education.' *Journal of Moral Education* 34.3 (September 2005): 309–23.

Drama, Narrative and Moral Education: Exploring Traditional Tales in the Primary Years. London: Falmer Press, 1998.

'Theorising Drama as Moral Education.' *Journal of Moral Education* 28.4 (1999): 459–71.

Wittig, Joseph. 'The Old English Boethius, the Latin Commentaries, and Bede.' In *The Study of Medieval Manuscripts of England: Festschrift in Honor of Richard W. Pfaff*, eds. George Hardin Brown and Linda Ehrsam Voigts, 225–52. Tempe: ACMRS, 2010.

Wittkower, Rudolf. ' "Grammatica": From Martianus Capella to Hogarth.' *Journal of the Warburg Institute* 2.1 (1938): 82–84.

Woods, Marjorie Curry. *Classroom Commentaries: Teaching the Poetria Nova across Medieval and Renaissance Europe*. Columbus, OH: Ohio State University Press, 2010.

'Rape and the Pedagogical Rhetoric of Sexual Violence.' *Criticism and Dissent*, ed. Copeland (q.v.), 56–86.

'Weeping for Dido: Epilogue on a Premodern Rhetorical Exercise in the Postmodern Classroom.' In *Latin Grammar and Rhetoric: From Classical Theory to Medieval Practice*, ed. Carol Dana Lanham, 284–94. London and New York: Continuum, 2002.

Wrenn, C. L. 'The Poetry of Cædmon.' *Proceedings of the British Academy* 32 (1946): 277–95.

Wright, Charles D. *The Irish Tradition in Old English Literature*. Cambridge University Press, 1993.

Wright, Ellen F. 'Cynewulf's *Elene* and the "Singal Sacu".' *NM* 76.4 (1975): 538–49.

Zimmermann, Gerd. *Ordensleben und Lebensstandard: Die Cura Corporis in den Ordensvorschriften des abendländischen Hochmittelalters.* Münster Westfallen: Aschendorffsche Verlagsbuchhandlung, 1973.

Ziolkowski, Jan M. 'The Erotic Paternoster.' *NM* 88.1 (1987): 31–34.

'The Erotic Pater Noster, Redux.' *NM* 97.3 (1996): 329–32.

Žižek, Slavoj. 'The Truth Arises from Misrecognition.' In *Lacan and the Subject of Language*, eds. Ellie Ragland-Sullivan and Mark Bracher, 188–212. New York and London: Routledge, 1991.

Zollinger, Cynthia Wittman. 'Cynewulf's *Elene* and the Patterns of the Past.' *JEGP* 103.2 (2004): 180–96.

Zuengler, Jane, and KimMarie Cole. 'Language Socialization and Second Language Learning.' In *Handbook of Research in Second Language Teaching and Learning*, ed. Eli Hinkel, 301–16. Mahwah, NJ: Lawrence Erlbaum Associates, Publishers, 2005.

Index

Cambridge Studies in Medieval Literature

Titles in Series

CPSIA information can be obtained
at www.ICGtesting.com
Printed in the USA
LVHW080105210219
608202LV00011B/179/P